DEVELOPING SPORT COACHES

Evolving from the concept of coach education, which is generally accepted to be the more formal, didactic mode of transmitting information to coaches and prospective coaches, coach development is a relatively new field of research and practice. *Developing Sport Coaches* is a new text that supports the holistic long-term development of sport coaches as well as help aid existing sport coaches to understand their development.

Research in coach learning and coach education has raised important questions about the effectiveness, relevance and value placed on traditional coach education by sport coaches in relation to their practice. The dissatisfaction expressed by many coaches, at all stages of coaching practice, has led to the inception of coach development. This text enables coach development to be studied in higher education institutions as well as enabling organisations to embed coach developers within their organisations.

Written for the sport coaching and expanding coach development market, this book will be used by higher education institutions students as both a core and additional text to advance research and knowledge in this area. At the same time, this book is also a useful reading for practising sport coaches, coach developers and organisations who are currently examining their structures and processes to move their coaching provision from a formal coach education delivery to a more bespoke offering.

Christine Nash (PhD) is the Head of Institute for Sport, Physical Education and Health Sciences (ISPEHS) in the Moray House School of Education and Sport at the University of Edinburgh, UK.

DEVELOPING SPORT COACHES

Edited by Christine Nash

NEW YORK AND LONDON

Designed cover image: SeventyFour / Getty Images

First published 2023
by Routledge
605 Third Avenue New York, NY 10158

and by Routledge
4 Park Square, Milton Park, Abingdon, Oxon, OX14 4RN

Routledge is an imprint of the Taylor & Francis Group, an informa business

© 2023 selection and editorial matter, Christine Nash; individual chapters, the contributors

The right of Christine Nash to be identified as the author of the editorial material, and of the authors for their individual chapters, has been asserted in accordance with sections 77 and 78 of the Copyright, Designs and Patents Act 1988.

All rights reserved No part of this book may be reprinted or reproduced or utilised in any form or by any electronic, mechanical, or other means, now known or hereafter invented, including photocopying and recording, or in any information storage or retrieval system, without permission in writing from the publishers.

Trademark notice: Product or corporate names may be trademarks or registered trademarks, and are used only for identification and explanation without intent to infringe.

ISBN: 978-1-032-16992-7 (hbk)
ISBN: 978-1-032-16988-0 (pbk)
ISBN: 978-1-003-25130-9 (ebk)

DOI: 10.4324/9781003251309

Typeset in Bembo
by KnowledgeWorks Global Ltd.

CONTENTS

List of Figures   *viii*
List of Tables   *ix*
Contributors   *x*

SECTION I
Coach Development: The Current Picture   1

1 Setting the Context   3
  Penny Crisfield and John Bales

2 Career Development of Elite Coach Developers   19
  Christine Nash

3 International Perspectives on Coach Development:
  A Global Snapshot   36
  *Melissa Thompson, Michel Milistetd, Shigeki Sarodo,
  Pelle Kvalsund and Hikabwa Chipande*

4 Coach Education and Development: The What and How to   53
  Kristen Dieffenbach and Stiliani "Ani" Chroni

5 Transitions into Coach Development: You Coached
  So You Can Develop   68
  Kristen Dieffenbach and Stiliani "Ani" Chroni

SECTION II
Approaches to Developing Coaches — 85

6 Knowledge Auditing for Coaches: Where Are the Gaps? — 87
Miguel Crespo and Rafael Martínez-Gallego

7 Apprenticeship and Coaches' Development: The Potential of Recognizing the Workplace as Learning Organizations — 104
Michel Milistetd, William das Neves Salles and Heitor de Andrade Rodrigues

8 The Importance of Critical Thinking in Coaching: Separating the Wheat from the Chaff — 119
Loel Collins and Chris Eastabrook

9 Sensemaking for the Coach Developer — 133
Jamie Taylor and Christine Nash

10 Accelerating Expertise: Principles for Coach Developers — 151
Christine Nash

SECTION III
Systems Approach to Coach Development — 167

11 Volunteer-Led Sport (And Coach) Development: A Case Study of Pickleball in Scotland — 169
Pippa Chapman, Nanette Mutrie and Sharon MacKechnie

12 The Coach Developer as a System Builder: Maintaining a High-Performing Sport System — 183
Cameron Kiosoglous

13 Diversifying Coach Development — 197
Diane M. Culver, Siobhan Rourke and Tim Konoval

14 Cultural Competence and Intercultural Effectiveness in Coaching and Coach Development — 215
Andrea J. Woodburn, Vladislav A. Bespomoshchnov and Mika Saarinen

15 Evaluating Coach Education and Development Programmes 236
Hans Vangrunderbeek and Liam McCarthy

SECTION IV
Where Next for Coach Development? 251

16 Coach Developers as Agents of Change 253
Christine Nash

Index 265

FIGURES

1.1	Role of a Coach Developer.	5
1.2	Changes in coach education.	7
1.3	Trends in coach development.	9
1.4	Five elements of professional practice.	14
1.5	Coach Developer and trainer of Coach Developer pathways.	16
3.1	Structure of coach education in Brazil (see Milistetd et al., 2016).	40
4.1	Coach knowledge areas (see ICCE, 2013, p. 30).	54
4.2	International Sport Coaching Framework (see ICCE, 2013, p. 31).	57
4.3	Sciences supporting best practices in sport coaching.	58
5.1	Coach developer roles.	70
5.2	Sciences supporting best practices in sport coaching.	75
9.1	Data Frame model (see Klein et al., 2006b, p. 89).	139
11.1	Pickleball paddle.	170
11.2	Pickleball ball.	171
11.3	Pickleball court.	171
11.4	Ambassadors in training.	179
12.1	Representation of the SPLISS pillars.	189
12.2	Representation of the US high-performance sport model.	190
14.1	Three levels of uniqueness in human mental programming (see Hofstede, 1994, p. 6).	218
14.2	Theoretical model of relations among ten motivational types of value (see Schwartz, 2012).	220
14.3	A general framework for cross-cultural competence in army leaders (see Abbe et al., 2007, p. 2).	221
15.1	Monitoring and evaluating input, throughput and output through FICOMS.	241
15.2	Adaptive theory (see Layder, 1998).	246

TABLES

1.1	Attributes of Coach Developers	10
1.2	Criteria for coach-centred design	12
6.1	Summary of the strategies coach developers can use to implement KA	100
7.1	Dimensions of learning organizations (adapted from Garvin et al., 2008)	110
8.1	The components and importance of EIC	122
8.2	Not all sources are created equal adapted from Eaton (2018)	125
10.1	Coach development vignettes	158
15.1	Approaches to coach education programme	238
15.2	A summary of the changes made to the FA Level 3 (UEFA B) in coaching football project, which is the subject of evaluation in this case study	244

CONTRIBUTORS

John Bales is President of the International Council for Coaching Excellence (ICCE), the international organisation with the mission of enhancing the quality of coaching at every level of sport. He was co-director of the Nippon Sport Science University Coach Developer Academy (NCDA) from 2014 to 2021 and CEO of the Coaching Association of Canada from 1997 to 2013. John has an MBA from INSEAD (Institut Européen d'Administration des Affaires, Fontainebleau, France) and was a national and Olympic coach in sprint canoe for Canada.

Vladislav A. Bespomoshchnov is a Learning and Development Coordinator at the Sports Institute of Finland and a Lecturer in Degree Programme in Sports Coaching and Management at the Haaga-Helia University of Applied Sciences, Vierumäki, Finland. His fields of interest and research include coach and athlete development, skill acquisition, concussion prevention and the socio-historic context surrounding sports. His background is in ice hockey coaching, and strength and conditioning.

Pippa Chapman (PhD) is a Lecturer in Sport Management and Sport Development at the University of Edinburgh where she leads the undergraduate Sport Management degree and lectures on courses across undergraduate and postgraduate programmes. Pippa research primarily focuses on various aspects of sport policy and governance. She has a background working in the sport industry, beginning as a local authority and club volunteer coach, through to working in international sport development with UK Sport and holding research roles at Women in Sport and England Netball.

Hikabwa Chipande is Head of the African Union Sport Council Secretariat, a Specialised Technical Office of the African Union responsible for sports. Over his career, Chipande has worked with inter-governmental sports organisations and NGOs involved in sports development and sports for development. Prior to joining the African Union, he was lecturing sports studies at the University of Zambia in Lusaka. He has a PhD from Michigan State University in the USA and an MSc and BSc in Sports from the Norwegian School of Sport Science in Oslo.

Stiliani "Ani" Chroni is a native of Greece currently residing in Norway. She holds a PhD in sport psychology and is a certified coach developer. She's a full professor in sport psychology, pedagogy and sports coaching and leads her university's Sport and Social Sciences research group. Her scholar focus has been on women's welfare matters (women athletes' sexual exploitation, cultural silence) and athlete/coach mental game nuances (athlete-to-coach transition, elite coach stress, self-talk, hardiness, competitiveness, coping). Her research is fused by real-world knowledge and practice gaps and has informed national and international bodies' practices and policy documents as well as her teaching.

Loel Collins (DProf in Elite Performance) is a Lecturer in Sports Coaching in the University of Edinburgh, Institute of Sport, Physical Education and Health Sciences. His research and practical interests lie in coaching action and adventure sports, coach development and education. He holds multiple high-level coaching qualifications, principally in kayaking and canoeing and has enjoyed a 35-five year career coaching and in coach development prior to joining the university. His recent work investigates the specifics of coaching adventure sports and the development of coach judgement and decision-making in dynamic environments.

Miguel Crespo is the Head of Participation and Education of the Development Department, at the International Tennis Federation (ITF). He conducts courses, writes resources, organises conferences and coordinates research applied to tennis. A former captain of Spanish National Teams and Director of the Spanish Tennis Federation Coaching School, Miguel holds three PhDs in Psychology, Law and Business Administration. He is Treasurer of the International Council for Coaching Excellence (ICCE). Miguel has written academic and coaching books, as well as numerous articles on different sports sciences applied to tennis and has participated as a speaker in national and international courses and conferences.

Penny Crisfield leads the work on coach developers for the International Council for Coaching Excellence (ICCE), as well as having her own training company, Apollinaire. She has worked in coach education with most sports federations in the UK as well as in many countries overseas. She has a first-class BEd and an MSc in sport psychology and was a former national lacrosse coach and player. She was inducted into the Coaching Hall of Fame in 2005, winning the Dyson Award for coach education.

Diane M. Culver is a full professor at the School of Human Kinetics at the University of Ottawa in sport pedagogy and psychology. She was a senior coaching consultant for the Coaching Association of Canada before entering academia in July 2007. Her research interests are coaching and coach development, social learning theory and women in sport leadership. Her previous working experience includes coaching for the Canadian National and New Zealand Olympic Ski Teams. She consults with athletes and coaches and often uses social learning spaces to build learning capability in various sport networks and communities of practice.

Kristen Dieffenbach is the director of the Center for Applied Coaching and Sport Sciences at West Virginia University and a professor in the School of Sport Sciences. She is the executive director of the United States Center for Coaching Excellence, a Fellow in the Association of Applied Sport Psychology and a graduate of the Nippon Sport Science University (NSSU) Coach Developer Academy. She has been a professional endurance sport coach and a sport psychology and coaching educational consultant for over 20 years working with developmental through Olympic level athletes, coaches and organisations. Her research interests focus on coach developer training, coaching and professionalism and supporting athlete to coach transitions.

Chris Eastabrook (PhD) is the Executive Director of Bryntysilio Outdoor Education Centre in Llangollen Wales having previously worked in mainstream and higher education, and as a coach and coach developer. Chris is a pracademic focusing on both the educative role of coaches and the use of coaching within educative learning objectives, specifically in adventure and outdoor settings. The Adventure Education Development Hub that Chris leads is particularly interested in investigating challenges faced by coaches and educators for practical, applied solutions for practitioners. This includes academic research, grey literature, Continuing Professional Development courses and training programmes.

Cameron Kiosoglous is an Assistant Clinical Professor and Sport Coaching Leadership Program Director at Drexel University. For the last five Olympic cycles, he has supported high-performance athletes and coaches and is currently the Director of National Team Sport Science with US Rowing. He also serves as President with the United States Center for Coaching Excellence (USCCE). He has consulted with a variety of organisations in coaching development.

Tim Konoval is a Lecturer in the Faculty of Kinesiology, Sport and Recreation at the University of Alberta. He teaches undergraduate and graduate courses in sport sciences, sport management and adapted physical activity. His research interests lie at the intersection sport, inclusion, technology, coaching and coach development. In particular, he uses critical social lens to explore the inclusion of all individuals in sport. He is currently consulting with the Coaching Association of Canada and the Canadian Paralympic Committee to help make coach education programmes more accessible and inclusive.

Pelle Kvalsund works as a Coach Developer and Advisor for the Norwegian Olympic and Paralympic Committee and Confederation of Sport. As a trained coach, physical education teacher and coach educator, he primarily views himself as a hungry learner constantly chasing improvement, a mindset that has allowed him to gain different understanding and perspectives on coaching and coach development, through his work in a number of countries and cultures for over two decades.

Sharon MacKechnie is a Teaching Fellow in Physical Education at the University of Edinburgh. She has taught physical education in Scottish primary and secondary schools, was a University Teacher at the University of Glasgow, and she has written a number of national primary and secondary school resources for learning through the contexts of badminton and pickleball. She has also had a career in sport event management, having worked at European, Commonwealth and Olympic Games. Before joining the University of Edinburgh, Sharon was employed by Badminton Scotland as the Major Events Operations Manager, specifically for the 2017 Badminton World Championships.

Rafael Martínez-Gallego holds a PhD in Sports Science and a master's degree in Research in Sports Sciences. He is currently professor of a Sports Science Degree at the University of Valencia, and also in various other masters and postgraduate courses. He is an ITF-certified international tutor and he has been a tutor for the Royal Spanish Tennis Federation and other regional federations. He was the head coach of El Puig Tennis Club (Valencia, Spain) for more than 15 years. Rafa has participated in numerous conferences and courses, training coaches from more than 50 countries and has published a significant number of articles in scientific journals.

Liam McCarthy (PhD) is a Senior Lecturer in Sport Coaching at the Carnegie School of Sport, Leeds Beckett University. Liam has worked extensively for, and with, national governing bodies (NGBs), higher education institutions (HEIs) and international sport organisations to support the professional development of coaches and coach developers. His research largely focuses on coach learning and assessment. He is a graduate of the International Council for Coaching Excellence (ICCE) Nippon Sport Science University Coach Developer Academy (NCDA) in Tokyo.

Michel Milistetd (PhD) is an Associate Professor at the Federal University of Santa Catarina (UFSC), Brazil, Head of the Sports Pedagogy Research Center, Coach Developer certified by the International Council for Coaching Excellence

(ICCE) and consultant in sports federations and sports clubs to design coach and athlete development programmes. His main research focus is coach development, coaching and positive youth development.

Nanette Mutrie retired as Chair of Physical Activity for Health at the University of Edinburgh in 2022. She is now Professor Emerita and will continue to be associated with Edinburgh's Physical Activity for Health Research Centre. Her research relates to helping people 'move more'. She has over 300 peer reviewed publications and the 4th edition of the textbook she co-authors 'The Psychology of Physical Activity for Health' was published by Routledge in 2021. Nanette received an MBE from the Queen in 2015 for services to Physical Activity for Health in Scotland. Nanette is Coaching and Training officer with Pickleball Scotland https //www.pickleballscotland.org and loves her regular games. Her other activities involve dog walking, walking the golf course and commuting by bike whenever possible.

Heitor de Andrade Rodrigues (PhD) is an Associate Professor at the Federal University of Goiás (UFG), Brazil and a coach developer certified by the International Council for Coaching Excellence (ICCE). He is a researcher in the field of Sports Coaching, with experience in the investigation of coach education, coach development and the coach profession in Brazil.

Siobhan Rourke is a PhD student at the University of Ottawa. Her work focuses specifically on coach development and gender equity in sport. She is interested in creating more comprehensive coach education opportunities for coaches of adolescent girls' sport to aid in reducing girls' dropout from sport. Her other research interests include the use of social learning spaces in parasport coach education and better understanding the barriers for young girls' engagement in sport. She is also affiliated with the Canadian Sport Psychology Association as a professional member through her work with athletes and coaches as a Mental Performance Consultant.

Mika Saarinen is a Senior Lecturer in the Degree Programme in Sports Coaching and Management at Haaga-Helia University of Applied Science, Vierumäki, Finland. His areas of teaching are sports coaching, skill acquisition and sports performance analysis. He has worked as the director of the International Ice Hockey Centre of Excellence (IIHCE), when he was also responsible for the Finnish Ice Hockey Association's (FIHA) highest coach development programme. He has long-term high-performance coaching experience in ice hockey, working as a coach in the Finnish League (Liiga), Continental Hockey League (KHL) and the Finnish national team.

William das Neves Salles (PhD) is an Elementary and High School Physical Education teacher, with experience in the areas of learner-centred teaching and sport pedagogy. He is a volunteer researcher of the Sports Pedagogy Research Center at Federal University of Santa Catarina (UFSC), Brazil.

Shigeki Sarodo is an Associate Professor in the Faculty of Sport Science at Nippon Sports Science University (NSSU) in Japan and also serves as a Research Fellow at the NSSU Coach Developer Academy (NCDA). His current research focuses on the application of Ancient Greek Philosophy to coaching studies. Beyond his research, he has been working for the Japan Basketball Association as a member of the coach development committee and the Japan Sport Association as a coach trainer.

Jamie Taylor is a Senior Coach Developer at Grey Matters, an Assistant Professor at Dublin City University, a lecturer in Sports Coaching at the University of Edinburgh and coach at Wasps Rugby. His background is as an experienced coach and coach developer. Previous roles include coaching at Leicester Tigers, Loughborough University and pathway coaching lead at the English Institute of Sport. As a coach developer, he consults across variety of organisations and has worked with over 100 coaches in a developmental capacity. This has included working with coaches at the elite and academy level in football, rugby union, rugby league, tennis and a variety of Olympic sports.

Melissa Thompson is a Professor in the School of Kinesiology and Nutrition at the University of Southern Mississippi. Her research agenda focuses on coach development, specifically the development of coaching ethics and the impact of the internship process. She is credentialed as a Certified Mental Performance Consultant and Fellow through the Association of Applied Sport Psychology and as a Certified Strength and Conditioning Specialist. Melissa was an inaugural board member for the United States Center for Coaching Excellence and has continued involvement as the chair of the research committee.

Hans Vangrunderbeek (PhD) is coach education manager at the Flemish School for Coach Education (Sport Vlaanderen), which is responsible for developing, organising and recognising coach education in Flanders. In his doctoral work, he focussed on the scientific development of physical education and sports in Belgium. In 2011, he obtained a grant for a research stay at Harvard University in Cambridge. He published more than 40 papers within the fields of sports (coaching, history, ethics) and gave lectures at several international congresses. Hans is an alumni of the Nippon Sport Science University Coach Developer Academy. He is currently involved in an International Council for Excellence (ICCE) global working group, exploring monitoring and evaluation of coach education programmes.

Andrea J. Woodburn (PhD) is Associate Professor in the Département d'éducation physique at Université Laval, Canada. Her research interests include coach learning and professional development, and barriers to inclusion in competitive sport. She has worked extensively in Canada's National Coaching Certification Program as a trainer, coach developer and a curriculum developer. Recently, she worked as a trainer in the Nippon Sport Science University Coach Developer Academy (NCDA), in partnership with the International Council for Coaching Excellence (ICCE), and currently serves on several ICCE committees related to coach education and development.

SECTION I
Coach Development
The Current Picture

This section consists of five chapters and sets the context for coach development from a number of perspectives. Context can consist of the background, environment, framework or current practices in a domain, in this case developing sport coaches. Setting the context in this case focuses attention on the key similarities or differences and seeks to provide explanation.

There are exemplars given by key organisations involved in developing sport coaches, case studies provided by Coach Developers in different areas of practice and snapshots provided of countries who are at different stages of coach development. These examples are not being provided as the only way of achieving coach development but to show the range of practices that are available for interested individuals or organisations to examine and consider whether aspects would work in their context. Anecdotal evidence suggests that adopting systems with little tweaking does not work in the long terms; however, principles can be adapted and reshaped to fit many situations.

1
SETTING THE CONTEXT

Penny Crisfield and John Bales

Introduction

In this introductory section, we look at how coaching has and is changing, the need for quality coach education and the changing role of Coach Developers.

Coaching has changed and evolved significantly in the last ten years. Coaching today is highly dynamic and increasingly demanding, for coaches are no longer viewed simply as teachers of the sport but as developers of people. Good coaches coach the person rather than sport and so contribute to their participants' development socially and emotionally, as well as physically and technically. There are millions of volunteer, part-time and full-time coaches around the world who guide and support children, adolescents, adults and whole communities to fulfil their sporting and social objectives as well as individual's holistic development. Coaches work with increasingly diverse populations. There is a growing demand on coaches from their athletes, their parents, administrators and fans. Even voluntary coaches are expected to fulfil a variety of roles such as educator, guide, sport psychologist, fitness trainer, social convenor and business manager. In addition, coaches of high-performance athletes are expected to be highly successful competitively but also contribute to athletes' overall development.

Coaching has changed and continues to change; it is much more demanding and so the need for quality coaches becomes paramount in order to fulfil their extended roles and responsibilities. This in turn places additional demands on those charged with educating and developing coaches. The term 'coach developer' was advocated in the first International Coach Developer Framework (ICDF) published in 2014 where it was defined as those 'trained to develop, support and challenge coaches to go on honing and improving their knowledge and skills to provide positive and effective sport experiences for all participants' (ICDF, 2014, p. 8).

This ICDF document was intended to provide a structure to help those responsible for coach education and development in their countries and organisations to review the way they supported and developed their coaches. It encouraged a shift towards a learner-centred approach and the adoption of a facilitative rather than instructional methodology. It also promoted a broader view of coach development which moved beyond knowledge transmission, often confined to technical and tactical information, to also embrace informal and non-formal learning opportunities. 'Coach developers aren't only subject matter experts, aren't only concerned with delivering courses; they have a key role to play in different learning situations and bring significant expertise in the process of learning' (ICDF, 2014, p. 10). Since the publication of the ICDF in 2014, there has been exponential growth in the Coach Developer workforce globally; the term Coach Developer is now commonly used, and there is a growing appreciation of the importance of their broader role in meeting the diverse and individual needs of the coach in pursuit of becoming an even better coach.

In the last ten years, a great deal has also changed in our understanding of how coaches learn and how best to support them in practice; in how much the context and culture in which they operate influences the way Coach Developers need to work. This has arisen not only from the growing expertise of Coach Developer practitioners in the field and from enhanced Coach Developer training and networking but also to the significant growth in research. Building on the core messages from the original framework, the second edition recognises the multiple ways Coach Developers support coaches to create lasting behavioural change in their coaching practice. It emphasises the need for Coach Developers to become experts in learning and defines the role as 'all-encompassing and it is not a one size fits all' (ICCE, in press). It goes on to describe their educational, developmental and support roles in helping coaches to learn in a group or one-to-one; in the field and/or in the classroom. It explains how effective Coach Developers operate in a way that increases coaches' self-awareness and encourages them to take responsibility for their own ongoing development to become even better coaches. A more detailed description is provided in Figure 1.1.

The second edition stresses the importance of providing support for coaches in the field where they operate (informal learning opportunities) and not only relying on coach education workshops, clinics and conferences (formal and non-formal learning opportunities). All this reflects the wide variety of roles Coach Developers must play from informal mentoring relationships to facilitating coach learning in formal coach education programmes. It reflects the need to be mindful of different contexts: the difference between working with those coaches working at a participation level and those preparing elite athletes; equally differences between supporting less and more experienced coaches. It embraces the contributions of programmes offered by sport federations, coaching organisations as well as higher education institutions. The Coach Developer is becoming a critical element of sophisticated coaching development programmes across the globe.

> A Coach Developer is someone who:
> - has significant experience as a coach (or expert working with coaches such as sports nutrition, strength and conditioning) and the relevant knowledge (eg sport technical) to teach at the particular level at which they wish to operate
> - helps coaches develop their knowledge, skills and behaviours in order to become an even more effective coach
> - has received some form of initial training or equivalent (eg an apprenticeship) about how best to do this
> - is working formally (eg on coach education programmes) or informally (eg one-to-one in a club) with coaches
> - develops an attitude of lifelong learning among the coaches with whom he or she works (ICCE, in press).

FIGURE 1.1 Role of a Coach Developer.

Outline of Coach Education and Development

It is clear from both the perspective of the researcher and the practitioner that the way sports coaches develop their practice and become more expert has evolved significantly in the past decade. It has become increasingly evident that coaches learn in a variety of ways through engagement in a wide range of opportunities, that it is a continuous journey and not a linear process (Turner, Nelson and Potrac, 2012). Ultimately the objective of any coach development programme is to enhance coaching practice by reinforcing effective coaching behaviours and changing ineffective ones. This requires a more comprehensive approach, not simply the transference of knowledge from a content expert to a coach.

In this section, we offer some clarification of terms and a summary of the general trends from the past, present and looking towards best practice in the future.

Terminology

Terminology can be both a help and a hindrance in the complex world of developing coaching expertise. Some make the distinction between coach education and coach development where:

- *Coach education* refers to learning through a more formal and structured curriculum often leading to some form of approved qualification that signifies a level of competency and capability.
- *Coach development* refers to an inclusive blend of learning opportunities, for example, the informal and non-formal learning opportunities gained for example through on-the-job learning (e.g., through apprenticeships), peer to peer interaction, mentoring and reflective practice.

Others differentiate between *mediated and unmediated learning* opportunities and some build on Moon's model (2004) and refer to:

- *Formal* when the learning takes place as part of an education system, follows a curriculum, usually result in a qualification and where learners engage in it intentionally (e.g., coach education programmes run by sports federations, coaching degree programmes run by universities).
- *Non-formal* learning takes place within some organisational framework but without a formal curriculum or accreditation process. It is once again intentional and often addressed the mastery of a particular skill or area of knowledge (e.g., coaching clinic, conference, master class, mentoring).
- *Informal* learning takes place outside educational systems and arises unintentionally, with no particular learning purpose in mind; it is an involuntary and inescapable part of daily life (e.g., through conversation with another coach, communities of practice, reading an article, watching a video).

Looking Back and Looking Forward

Traditional coach education programmes have typically provided formal structured learning situations (e.g., classroom-based workshops). Historically the focus has been on knowledge transmission often confined to information about the technical and tactical aspects of the sport and perhaps some performance-related knowledge from sport science (e.g., strength training, energy systems, biomechanics, mental skills). Over the last 20 years education, and coach education, has undergone considerable change (see Figure 1.2). The role of those we now call Coach, is shifting significantly from *knowledge transfer* where the content is the focus towards more *coach-centred facilitation*. The latter recognises the unique nature, needs, experience and motives of the learner coach as well as the context in which they coach. For example:

- who they coach (e.g., children, participatory adults, talent pathway athletes, competitive elite athletes),
- where they coach (e.g., club, community facility, training venue) and
- how frequently they coach (e.g., one session per week vs full-time involvement).

One of the criticisms levelled at many coach education programmes is the lack of authenticity and so the difficulty coaches have in applying their new learning to their own coaching context. Currently there is a reliance on facilitated coaching workshops but often with little or no follow-up support for coaches when they return to their club. Coaches are expected to take on board and apply significant amounts of new knowledge, to adopt different approaches and use some brand new skills that are not yet well honed, all without any ongoing support in the field. The International Council for Coaching Excellence (ICCE) is now

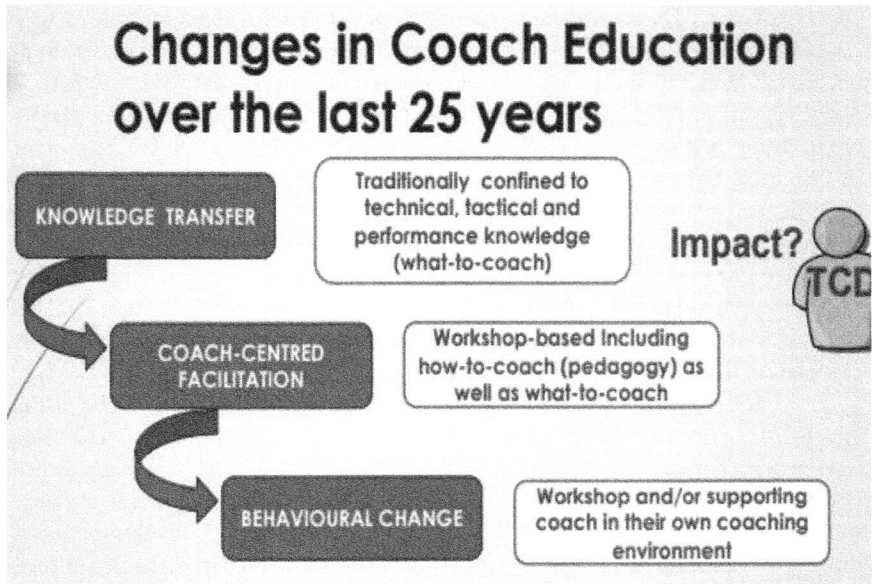

FIGURE 1.2 Changes in coach education.

strongly advocating the need for *coach support on-the-job*, in the field, both as a follow-on from a formal coach education workshop to facilitate application and to offer a range of informal as well as formal learning opportunities to enable and encourage coaches to go on reflecting and learning as their experience grows (ICCE, 2022). If the role of the Coach Developer is to help coaches improve their coaching performance and enhance the quality of coaching in their organisation, the job is only partially done by imparting the knowledge and skills prescribed on a course. The job is not complete until coaches can apply the new knowledge and skills in their coaching practice. This often requires the support of someone else, a more experienced coach or better still a skilled Coach Developer working with the coach, ideally over a period of time.

In addition to a more learner-centred facilitative approach, the 'curriculum' on formal coach education programmes typically has also expanded to consider not only what they coach (i.e., the sport), but also:

- who they coach (the level, experience and motives of the athlete),
- how they coach (coaching/teaching pedagogy, skill development, principles and practice; how-to-coach skills such as how to reflect, how to provide feedback, how to observe, how to demonstrate) and
- why they coach the way they do (coaching philosophy and values).

Traditionally, it has been the role of more experienced coaches to provide the training for less experienced coaches. There is now a growing recognition that effective Coach Developers are not just experienced coaches; they need to be carefully *selected and trained* to do the job effectively. The very best coaches do not necessarily make the best Coach Developers; in the same way the best athletes do not always makes the best coaches. Coach Developers need a deep understanding of coaching (most indeed are active or former coaches with successful experience in coaching although some may be experts in specific fields such as strength training or sport psychology) and ideally some experience of teaching adults. They also need to become experts in learning and able to model best practice. They need to portray a hunger for learning and personal development, a growth mindset and enhanced critical reflective skills and, above all, a desire to help coaches (rather than athletes) to get better. The motivation to coach coaches is completely different from the motivation to coach athletes.

Coach Developer training is now more generally recognised to be different from course or programme orientation, which focuses on the exact content with guidance on its specific delivery. Coach Developer training is about upskilling to be able to optimise coach learning through a deeper understanding of how coaches learn, combined with the development of a range of skills and strategies to implement the most coach-centred approach possible. Coach Developers embarking on this training should already have the necessary content knowledge, context and coaching experience (or equivalent for disicpline experts). The difference can be likened to a cook, who follows a specific recipe to make a predetermined dish often created by someone else, and a chef, who understands how different foods can be combined and flavoured with different herbs and spices to create their own unqiue dish. Coach Developer training should be about educating 'chefs' who already have the knowledge about different foods and flavours and so can create and adapt recipes to meet the unique needs and tastes of their clientelle, a form of adaptive expertise. Potential Coach Developers should already have the content knowledge to be able to deliver the types of learning for which they have been recruited. More about specific programmes for Coach Developer training are covered in Chapter 3 plus some case studies from different systems in Chapters 11 and 12.

There are also changes in *how and where the coach education programmes are offered*. Typically, in the past coach education programmes have been provided by individual sports organisations (e.g., for a single sport such as a badminton or swimming federations) or a national coaching organisation (e.g., often a multi-sport organisation such as the Coaching Association of Canada). There is now a growing trend for universities to offer coaching degrees and the ICCE has consulted with Higher Education Institutions (HEIs) to draw up International Sport Coaching Degree Standards which provide an internationally accepted reference point for those HEIs wishing to contribute to the development of the coaching workforce worldwide.

Figure 1.3 attempts to summarise the general trends from the past, present and looking towards best practice in the future.

ASPECT	PAST	PRESENT	FUTURE
HOW ARE COACHES EDUCATED AND DEVELOPED?	Reliance on formal face-to-face coach education workshops	Increase in blended learning (on-line plus face-to-face) and growing recognition of need to provide coach support in the field as well as formal coach education programmes	Broad range of remote and face-to-face formal, informal and non-formal learning opportunities that support coaches in the field
HOW ARE FORMAL PROGRAMMES DELIVERED AND BY WHOM?	Instructional transmission of knowledge provided by more experienced coaches and subject experts	More learning facilitation provided more often by Coach Developers with some training (sometimes more programme orientation)	Coach-centred formal facilitated learning and long-term behavioural change provided by Coach Developers trained as experts in learning
WHAT IS THE CURRICULUM OF FORMAL COACH EDUCATION PROGRAMMES?	Limited to technical and tactical knowledge of the sport and some sport science	Plus coaching pedagogy, how-to-coach skills, reflective practice, coaching values and related to specific populations (eg children)	Blended learning with mix of on-line and face-to-face (coach-centred with an emphasis on problem-solving and decision-making and an increased focus on interpersonal and intrapersonal knowledge and skills.
WHO LEADS FORMAL COACH EDUCATION WORKSHOPS?	More experienced coaches and subject experts	Mostly trained Coach Developers	Trained Coach Developers with the skill to facilitate the input of subject and coaching experts
WHO PROVIDES COACH LEARNING OPPORTUNITIES?	National and international sports federations, coaching organisations	Plus higher education institutions (eg through coaching degrees)	Integrated provision that recognises, values and complements the contribution of each
HOW ARE COACHES ASSESSED?	Knowledge tests	Summative assessment of coaches' competence (knowledge, experience through portfolio and practical often through simulated peer-coaching)	Formative assessment for and as learning, designed and fully integrated into learning programmes
WHAT TRAINING IS PROVIDED FOR COACH DEVELOPERS?	None	Increased use of facilitation training, some reliance only on programme orientation, limited training in supporting coaches' practice	Comprehensive training about learning, learner-centred facilitation and supporting coaches in their practice.

FIGURE 1.3 Trends in coach development.

What Makes a Coach Developer Effective?

It might be argued that your Coach Developer workforce is the most important one for it is responsible for the quality of your coaching workforce which in turn impacts on the quality of the sport experience for all: children's sport programmes, recreational, health and club participants, as well as performance athletes. In this section, we look in more detail at how to select, train, support and evaluate your Coach Developer workforce to ensure it is effective and describe some Coach Developer standards that may be a useful guide.

It has already been stressed that great coaches do not automatically make great Coach Developers so how do we select and train them to be able to carry out the diverse and important role of developing and supporting coaches' learning, encouraging coaches to become more reflective and self-aware as well as continuing to take more responsibility for their own ongoing development and growing expertise?

Needs Analysis and Selection

It is not only important to select the right people but also to select the right number of potential Coach Developers. Too many Coach Developers may spread the support for them too thinly and limit their opportunties to work with coaches, making it very difficult for them to develop the necessary expertise to become highly effective. Therefore, a needs analysis is best carried out initially to identify the demand and the exisitng support network for new Coach Developers (this is covered more fully in Chapter 6).

It is helpful then to draw up a contextualised job description and person specification for potential Coach Developers. This will influence those who apply

TABLE 1.1 Attributes of Coach Developers

Mindset and attitudes	• An openness to learning
	• A passion for and a belief in the power of coaching
	• A desire to help coaches become the best they can be
	• A willingness to engage in critical self-reflection coupled with a hunger for ongoing personal growth and development
Experience	• Significant and successful coaching experience in one or more coaching contexts **or**
	• Substantial experience working with athletes and coaches in a supporting discipline (e.g., strength and conditioning, mental skills)
Skills	• Excellent facilitation skills*
* these may be further developed through CD training	• Good questioning, listening, reviewing and feedback skills*
	• Sound planning, monitoring and evaluation skills
	• Well-honed self-reflective skills, self-awareness and high emotional intelligence
Knowledge	• Professional knowledge (learning, teaching, assessment)*
* these may be further developed through CD training	• Up-to-date content knowledge in the area/s in which they will teach (sport's technical and tactical, coaching pedagogy, sport science discipline, sports medicine, talent development, coaching children, disability sport)
	• Interpersonal knowledge (e.g., relationships, social context)
	• Intra-personal skills (e.g., lifelong learning)

as well as improve the quality of applicants. Table 1.1 shows some of the necessary qualities and skills of a Coach Developer, that could be incorporated into any advertisement. The job description needs not only to describe the role and resonsibilities, expectations, experience and qualities required but also to ensure they *already have* the necessary knowledge and skills to work with the coaches in your system.

Training

It has already been argued that Coach Developer training needs to focus on helping them to become 'experts in learning' rather than provide an opportunity for upskilling or updating coaching tactical and technical knowledge or providing sport science input. If the key role of a Coach Developer is to help coaches to learn, they need to understand and respect how diffferent people learn. This is not an easy task as coaching is a complex activity and so too is learning and behavioural change. Trying to establish how coaches learn best is fraught with difficulties and reinforces the fact that the path to learning how to coach is idiosyncratic; coaches progress in different ways and use different methods. There is plenty of research and anecdotal evidence to support the idea that coaches develop their skills and knowledge in a range of ways and through different learning situations (Chapter 2 considers some research evidence, along with some key case studies). Coach Developers need to focus on the amount of learning that has taken place and the coaches' ability to transfer and apply it in their own coaching context. Coach Developers, like coaches, may be highly motivating and engaging entertainers, they may involve their coaches in the learning process through activities and discussion but if no learning, reflection and application takes place, they cannot be deemed effective. The focus for Coach Developers is not therefore only on the process but also on the *outcome*, whether or not learning is taking place and whether there is ultimately a change in the coaching practice of the learner coaches.

Therefore, the content of Coach Developer training needs to focus on understanding the variety of ways in which coaches learn, the learning principles that underpin their practice, the facilitation skills required and the challenges involved in adopting a coach-centred approach. Course content is not front and centre as it traditionally has been placed but the focus is on the skills required for learning and development (content might be a separate orientation workshop for a specific programme). In a *coach-centred approach* Coach Developers should focus on:

- the uniqueness of each individual learner coach,
- building on the coaches' prior knowledge, skills and experiences,
- creating positive learning environments and relationships where all views are respected and valued and
- engaging coaches in the process of learning and encouraging them to take responsibility for their own learning.

The challenges involved in adopting a truly coach-centred approach cannot be underestimated for they require the following:

- A paradigm shift for some organisations, requiring a redesign of their existing curriculum.
- A significant investment in the training and support of Coach Developers. This needs to ensure Coach Developers are skilled in coping with greater variability and uncertainty, have the ability to adapt according to the needs and predispositions of the coaches, are skilful in managing problem-based learning and confident and willing to relinquish some control so that the learner coaches take more responsibility for course design, delivery and assessment while still identifying key learning objectives.
- Understanding of the maturity, self-motivation and prior experience of the learner coaches enables the Coach Developer to encourage the learner coach to take more responsibility for their own learning, be capable of more independent work, be open to new ideas, able to process and apply knowledge, able to reason and make judgements, and work cooperatively with others. The requirement for greater self-direction may be more effective with highly experienced coaches; those with limited prior coaching experience may require more direction and guidance.

- The adoption of a coach-centred approach is likely to be more labour intensive and costly than simple information transmission or the facilitative approach that currently dominates the sector.

Paquette and Trudel (2018) published empirical and theoretical recommendations to enable coach education providers to support learner-centred coach education in terms of programme design, facilitation and coach engagement. Table 1.2 highlights a summary of their findings for each of these areas – one of the first research informed papers to offer guidance for best practice in the field of Coach Development.

TABLE 1.2 Criteria for coach-centred design

Programme design	*Facilitation*	*Coach engagement*
1. **Become a learner-centred leader** (e.g., need for strong leadership to overcome the challenges that occur with learner-centred teaching and a deep understanding of constructivist learning assumptions)	5. **Recruit facilitators, not instructors** (i.e., more careful selection to ensure Coach Developer share the values and approach embedded in learner-centred teaching)	8. **Help coaches to recognise their view of learning and to understand learner-centred teaching** (i.e., the need to overcome the anticipated resistance to this approach by providing 'learning to learn' introductory modules)
2. **Use a variety of learning strategies to achieve specified learning outcomes** (end of course outcomes and outcomes related to application in their coaching context; strategies to include action-research, problem-based case scenarios, self-reflection, group activities and discussions, practical training, role play)	6. **Provide learner-centred facilitator training** (i.e., the need to provide learner-centred facilitation training)	9. **Prioritise making content meaningful for coaches.** (i.e., the importance of Coach Developers knowing the background of each coach and overtly helping them to reflect and apply material to their own context)
3. **Deliberately develop learning skills** (i.e., helping coaches to learn how to learn to enable them to apply the literature critically and become lifelong learners)	7. **Regularly assess facilitator performance** need to check to ensure consistent learner-centred facilitation and to provide ongoing training and tools to aid self-assessment reflection)	10. **Empower coaches with increased autonomy and learning options** (i.e., increase intrinsic motivation by encouraging coaches to make decisions about content and approach)
4. **Unite assessment with learning** (i.e., understanding the complex interplay between content, assessment and learning and need to use a range of assessment strategies including peer and self-assessment, debriefing and formative feedback)		

Programme Monitoring and Evaluation

Programme monitoring and evaluation are crucial and too frequently forgotten or ignored (this is addressed in more detail in Chapter 15). This should be undertaken by the organisation both regularly and systematically and could include:

- monitoring the delivery of the coaching education programme to identify disparities and ensure feedback from both Coach Developers (delivering the programme) and coaches (who have completed the programme) is both incorporated into future planning,
- needs assessment related to the numbers of coaches and Coach Developers needed in the sport or region and
- evaluating the impact of Coach Developers in formal and non-formal training events.

Accreditation and licensing or registration schemes can be used to monitor currency, regular active involvement, continual professional development and professional standards and compliance with codes of conduct for coaches and Coach Developers.

Standards

The second edition of the ICDF has drawn up Coach Developer standards to provide a set of quality expectations to which Coach Developers should aspire (ICCE, 2022). These are offered as a guideline for any organisation (e.g., national or international sport federations, coaching organisations or higher education institutions) providing training and support for Coach Developers or indeed for individual Coach Developers seeking to self-assess and develop their expertise. The standards focus on promoting coach learning and providing leadership for coaching systems by identifying the knowledge, skills and qualities that Coach Developers require to fulfil their two major roles:

- group facilitation, typically a more formal and structured learning opportunity and
- supporting coaches in the field, often one-to-one, more informal and less structured.

Both roles are essential to enhance coach learning, and the standards have been based on five elements (see Figure 1.4) which contribute to their professional practice:

- *Learning and Behavioural Change*, which provides the foundation on which all work with coaches should be based.
- *Group Facilitation*, which identifies the unique knowledge, skills and qualities required to facilitate and accelerate the learning of a group of coaches in a relatively formal and structured environment.

FIGURE 1.4 Five elements of professional practice.

- *Coach Support in the Field*, which covers the very broad range of ways in which Coach Developers might support and guide the learning of individual coaches in less formal situations.
- *Coach Education Leadership* describes the way Coach Developers contribute to the coaching system at a local, regional or national level.
- *Personal and Professional Skill and Development*, which includes the way Coach Developers act as a role model to coaches, operate as self-reflective practitioners, engage in ongoing professional development and adapt the way they work to the unique environment of the coach/organisation.

Coach Developer Pathway

While a long-term coach development (LTCD) pathway for coaches has become a feature of many organisations involved in coach education and development, a career pathway for Coach Developers is less well established. There is no doubt that the Coach Developer workforce globally and nationally is expanding and so the need for a model for optimal career progression may be useful. This may be particularly helpful as guide to the way organisations recruit, train, support and deploy their Coach Developers.

Like coaches, Coach Developers are likely to come from a variety of starting points (see Chapter 2 for a further discussion):

- Some coaches informally start supporting less experienced coaches in their club or organisation.
- Other coaches with appropriate motivation, sufficient experience and a genuine desire to develop other coaches may choose to take on this role after stepping back from active coaching.

- Some may be recruited more formally by their organisations to train and support less experienced coaches as an adjunct to their normal coaching responsibilities.
- Similarly, specialists in the coaching sciences may supplement their work with athletes and teams to deliver coaching courses.
- More recently, there are increasing opportunities for Coach Developers to work full-time in this role or for this to be a significant amount of their job responsibilities, in positions like Academy Head of Coaching, Club Technical Director or Regional Coach Developer for a federation.

Regardless of the entry point for a Coach Developer, the acquisition of the knowledge and skills to advance from a novice to an expert in this field requires considerable training and experience.

Any pathway for Coach Developers, however, needs to be flexible for different cultures, countries and organisations require different coaching systems, varying levels of sophistication and unique requirements of their Coach Developer workforce (please see Chapters 11, 12 and 14 for further detail). For this reason, the ICCE in the second edition of the ICDF is now recommending a more accessible and flexible Coach Developer pathway that aligns more closely to those of other professions while still enabling organisations to develop systems and pathways that work for them (ICCE, 2022).

The proposed ICCE model embraces those volunteers just starting out on their Coach Developer Pathway and operating infrequently, as well as those working perhaps more formally and regularly or even exclusively and professionally as a Coach Developer. For this reason, different levels are advocated (see Figure 1.5).

- *Coach Developer* describes those working formally (e.g., assisting on coach education programmes) or informally (e.g., one-to-one in a club) to help coaches improve their coaching skills and knowledge. Often these Coach Developers are starting out on their Coach Developer journey or operating in this role infrequently (e.g., as a subject specific expert). They have received some form of introductory Coach Developer training (or equivalent) but have not yet been certified. They generally operate in a supporting rather than leading role (see case study examples).
- *Senior Coach Developer* describes those who have undergone facilitation and/or one-to-one support training and certification (or gained that competence in a different way such as through some form of apprenticeship). They have gained experience in the field where they have applied and developed their skills and demonstrated the underpinning competences at this level. They operate regularly in both a formal and/or informal context. Often they take a lead role but typically operate in a vocational and part-time capacity.
- *Chartered Coach Developer* describes those who have progressed in the field to the expert level and are usually working in a full-time professional capacity. They have exceptional practical skills in facilitating, analysing, synthesising

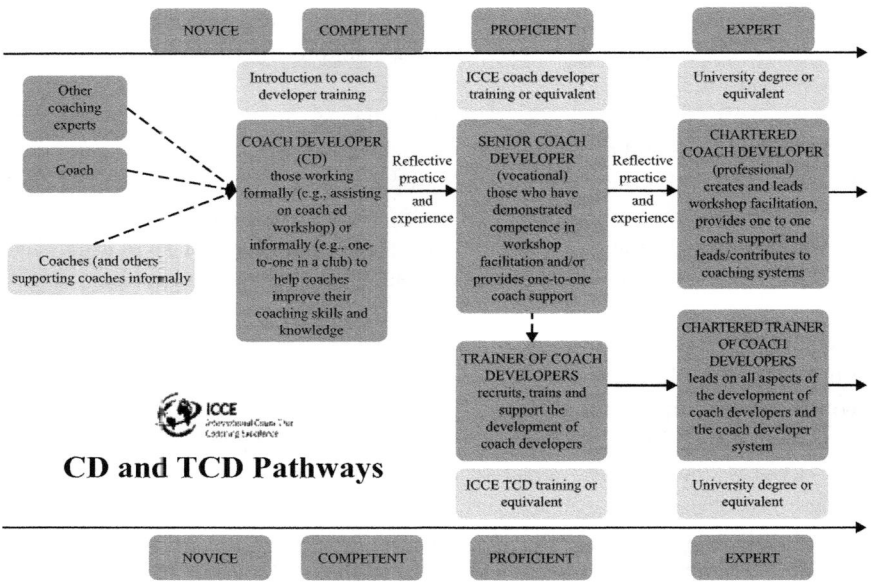

FIGURE 1.5 Coach Developer and trainer of Coach Developer pathways.

and evaluating coach learning and, in addition, have undertaken academic study of learning (or equivalent). They have specialist knowledge and expertise operating with different populations, stages, environments and specialisms, becoming an expert in one or more aspects of their work with coaches. They contribute either directly or indirectly to their organisation's coaching system and to the professionalisation of Coach Developers and coaches.
- *Trainers of Coach Developers* are those with a wealth of knowledge, skills, experience and expertise as a Coach Developer across multiple populations, stages, environments and specialisms. In this trainer role, they use their skills in a different context to recruit, train and support Coach Developers (rather than coaches) to develop their skills, knowledge and behaviours. They will also have knowledge and expertise in and of systems development, innovative practices and strategy development. Often Trainers of Coach Developers operate across sport or in multi-sport settings and so must be able to transfer their skills, draw meaningful examples and create valid activities for Coach Developers from different sports.

Global Reach of Coach Development: Making a Difference Worldwide

Although the role of Coach Developer is new, the publication of the ICDF in 2014 resulted in many organisations reviewing the more traditional, knowledge-transfer approach they had been using in their coach education programmes (e.g., SASCOC in South Africa). They began to adopt the approach advocated here of preparing experts in learning to not only convey new knowledge but also use facilitative, learner-centred methods and focus on applying the learning by supporting coaches in the field.

A significant boost to the adoption of Coach Developers as key leaders of an advanced coach development system was the launch of the Nippon Sport Science University Coach Developer Academy (NCDA) in partnership with ICCE in February 2015 (further detail is covered in Chapter 4). The NCDA was a Tokyo Olympic and Paralympic legacy programme, initiated by the government of Japan under the banner 'Sport for Tomorrow'. It had the vision 'to build a coaching culture for providing positive sport experiences for people in Japan, Asia and the world', with three specific aims:

- to train international Coach Developers,
- to build an international network of Coach Developers and
- to conduct related research (NCDA 2021).

The NCDA attracted leaders in coach education and development from around the world to attend a blended programme made up of two one-week residential courses in Tokyo, with online e-modules and interaction before and after the face-to-face experiences. The recruitment and selection protocol acknowledged that coach education may include sport-specific courses run by national and international federations, generic sport science and coaching leadership courses, as well as university degree programmes. For this reason, the selected participants in the NCDA reflected a balance of Coach Developers working in these three contexts.

As a result, the aim of building an international network of Coach Developers has been achieved. To date, 110 Coach Developers from 42 countries have participated in the NCDA and are contributing to the quality of coaching in their federations, coaching organisations and universities. With the ICDF as an initial statement of core principles and in many cases with the support of NCDA graduates, a number of federations and countries have enhanced and transformed existing tutor, coach educator or course conductor programmes (e.g., Canada, New Zealand, Finland, Singapore), while others have initiated the creation of a Coach Developer workforce (e.g., Japan, Poland, USA, Zambia, Norway). NDCA Graduates have also formed an informal global network that regularly share their research, ideas and practice. Several have contributed to the writing of the second edition of the ICDF (2022).

In Summary

Coach Development has come a long way over the last 20 years and, like coaching, is continuing to evolve and change as we draw on best practice in the field and learn from more applied research. The field is young, and there are many countries and sports that do not use Coach Developers yet. This chapter has provided an overview to add context and highlight some of the ongoing issues and good practice that is currently taking place around the globe. We hope that this is helpful to establish a basis for the following sections and chapters that examine some of these elements in more detail.

References

International Council for Coaching Excellence. (2014). *International Coach Developer Framework*. Version 1.1. ICCE.

International Council for Coaching Excellence. (in press). *International Coach Developer Framework*. Version 1.2. ICCE.

Moon, J.A. (2004) A Handbook of Reflective and Experiential Learning: Theory and Practice. Hove: Psychology Press.

NCDA (2021) *Learning to Be a Coach Developer*. Nippon Sports Science University.

Paquette, K. & Trudel, P. (2018) Learner-Centered Coach Education: Practical Recommendations for Coach Development Administrators. *International Sport Coaching Journal*, 5: 169–175.

Turner, D. Nelson, L. & Potrac, P. (2012) The Journey Is the Destination: Reconsidering the Expert Sports Coach. *Quest*, 64:4 313–325.

2
CAREER DEVELOPMENT OF ELITE COACH DEVELOPERS

Christine Nash

As has been mentioned in Chapter 1, coach development is a relatively new discipline, people have been involved in related activities for many years; long before these activities were recognised as coach development. As a result, there are several different interpretations of what coach development means. The Australian Sports Commission (n.d.) (https://www.sportaus.gov.au/coaches_ and_officials/sport_specific_training/coach_developer_resources) defines the role of the coach developer as 'a combination of training the trainer and mentoring, with a focus on supporting the coach on the job.' In the United Kingdom, the Chartered Institute for Management of Sport and Physical Activity (CIMSPA, 2022, p. 4) states 'Coach developers are expert support practitioners who plan for, implement, and sustain strategies and interventions in support of skilled performance in sport coaching.' The USCCE (2022) considers 'Coach development is a deliberately inclusive term to embrace all aspects of learning that coaches use and subsequently operationalize into their practice, importantly, it encompasses coach education.' Although there is some agreement in the various interpretations, there is no universally accepted definition of the coach developer or coach development. This lack of consensus often frustrates attempts to define the role, responsibilities and skills required to be considered a coach developer.

Coach development is a relatively recent innovation in the field of sport coaching. As a result, there has been little empirical research and few reports of the skills and knowledge associated with practitioners in this developing field. Coach developers generally differ from coach educators in terms of scope and scale (McQuade & Nash, 2015). Effective coaches are recognised as those who adapt their behaviour to meet the demands of their coaching environment, whereas coach developers must meet the diverse needs of coaches.

Sport organisations have established criteria to follow when recruiting elite athletes into coaching and are clearer on how to support retiring elite athletes transitioning to coaching careers (Chroni et al., 2021). To date, little evidence has been gathered to describe how coach developers are recruited into their roles, or indeed, how they transitioned into or through the coach development environment. A preliminary study, using an interview approach adapted from a previous study, examined the evolution of elite coach developers (n = 10) through various stages in their careers (Nash & Sproule, 2009). Findings suggested these coach developers followed an idiosyncratic pathway during their 'career.' They also considered their skills were transferable and transcended any specific sport. As a result, there was a perception that some sporting organisations did not value their skills and had a preference for more traditional technical/tactical approaches (Nash, 2019).

The following three case studies demonstrate the different entry points into coaching, coach development, the learning pathways followed by each coach developer and what each considers to be their most important takeaway. It was a deliberate choice to highlight coach developers from different countries, at different levels within the performance pathway and with different remits. Each case study focuses on a different environment in which coach developers can operate – sporting organisation, educational context, and private company. *Note:* Each coach developer provided this information verbally and was asked to verify the resulting case studies to ensure they agreed with the representations.

The first case study examines the route into coach development taken by a member of a national organisation.

CASE STUDY 1

Michelle De Highden
Current Position: AIS High Performance Coach Development Senior Lead (Australian Institute of Sport)

Background in sport

My whole family growing up was involved in sport, and I was the middle child of five children. Obviously, you do whatever sport your family does. I did dancing, I did hockey, I did some netball and did a lot of running but always wanted to do gymnastics, but we lived on a farm. There was no gymnastics club and we lived out of town. When I was 16, we moved to Brisbane from a farm in New South Wales and I started gymnastics then. I started coaching and judging in the same year, so I think I'd always been involved in sport. That's probably an Australian culture thing and part of that, you know my family influence as well.

Gymnastics

I was probably a bit of an anomaly because I had done years and years of dancing. It was probably an easy type of transition, and I was relatively strong from doing lots of other sports. The university I went to had a gymnastics club where you could go and train yourself. There was no coach, so I continued through my university years and then I transferred to the University of Massachusetts in my third year. Then I trained on the gym team there, so yeah, it definitely wasn't a normal pathway for sure.

Coaching

As a family we knew we were going to move again, and we moved to a town three hours inland in Central Queensland and there was no coach. There was a gym club that was in this little hall with minimal equipment, and someone needed to coach. I roped my mum into it and I brought my brother into it and my little sister ended up doing it as well. So, we all ended up running the gym club for a couple of years and then when I left and went to Uni, mum took over and my brother took over after that. I coached consistently from 1981 when I started right through to 2012 and another short stint in 2017 to 2018.

How I got into coach development

In 2012 I was running a high-performance gymnastics club out of a private girls' school in Melbourne and we had about 12–15 athletes who were targeted towards 2012 and 2016 Olympics and I guess as a mother of three, I was struggling to cope. I got to the point where I was like I can't manage. I can't coach and I can't do everything so when I asked for more support they said, 'Oh I don't think we can do that.' So, my role was made redundant. After that I ended up going into full time coach development. I'd always done coach development, whether it was within the club program I was working with, or whether it was when I was on state and national committees for 15 years. I have always been passionate about developing coaches.

Key milestones

- When I went to university, I had an option at the University of Queensland as it was one of the first courses that had the Human Movement Degree. So, after first year you had to make a decision 'do you want to do the teaching degree or do you want to do just sport science component?' I never wanted to teach, but I knew by doing the teaching component it would help me be a better coach.
- My coaching courses – I did my first coaching course in my first year of gymnastics. In Australia we had three levels of coaching, so I did my Level 1. Then I completed Level 2 in the next couple of years and then

maybe about five or six years later I did the Level 3 accreditation. So, I completed all the accreditation program early.
- To be honest, it probably took me a long while to be able to find where I fit, and I say that purely because I was very focused being a mother of three. Running a program and coaching 35 hours a week is probably not conducive to a lot of critical reflection so there were probably periods in there where if I look back now, I would have been a much better coach had I had a critical friend or taken time to be able to think. But every time I looked to do personal development for myself, it was like 'OK if I am not in the gym, I'm meant to be with my family. If I am not with my kids, then I meant to be at work.' So that cycle of reflection probably is not something that I did well.
- I was coaching at the National team level and I had placed athletes on Commonwealth Games and World Championship teams. I was also fulfilling the role of the head coach and the high-performance program manager. Internally within the high-performance club, I had always done a lot of development with the coaches. For example, I developed a mentor program and established some different things that we needed (to do) internally. So, then I started working with (national team) coaches in their daily training environment and at national training camps. I looked to design a framework to support the national team coaches in a more systematic way. I designed a program that could develop National Team and Developing coaches, Mentors and then Athletes Transitioning into high-performance coaching.

Difference between coach education and coach development

I guess the easiest way to explain coach education is it is adopted as an accreditation framework (in Australia). I see it as the baseline of learning, so the accreditation provides a basic learning structure. In the sport of gymnastics, obviously there's key safety components and baseline things that you need to know and you need to be able to deliver for coaches. Whereas in the coach development space, particularly in the high performance, obviously it is very unique. The context is highly competitive, dynamic and intense and provides enormous challenges for developing coaches. Identifying areas of learning and providing support around that means a great deal of that does end up being experiential or blended learning that supports the needs of the individual coach.

Key philosophy

- Building reflective critical thinkers and driving and supporting the curiosity to ask the question why.

- Knowing the high-performance context and the bespoke requirements of every single coach and every single sport is different so you need to understand the context and you need to build relationships with people in order to know how you can support them best.
- The focus of the coach tends to always be on the athlete. To flip the lens on themselves and reflect upon their own actions and how they impact (on athletes and others) can be a challenging thing to do because of ego and culture.

Sporting organisations generally have a remit to develop coaches and coaching in a specific sport or geographical area. Although there are a variety of ways to accomplish these objectives, the most common approach is to set up systems and processes to meet organisational coach development goals. Traditionally, this often involved formal coach education programmes, mainly consisting of large-scale workshops and practical sessions. More recently, many sporting organisations have embraced the more inclusive term of coach development (see Chapter 1) encompassing all forms of coach learning. In this first case study, the Australian Sports Commission, a branch of the Australian Government, stressed the importance they place on coach development by not only creating the position Michelle holds but also the support structures that are in place to implement coach development.

Other countries are also realising the importance of effective coach learning and development strategies. For example, in Finnish sport organisations and systems, especially those involved in high-performance sports, coach development was chosen as one of the focus areas, providing different education paths for coaches, a national network for coaches plus the opportunity for research into coaches' needs and learning experiences (Hämäläinen & Blomqvist, 2016). The United States Center for Coaching Excellence (USCCE) has been running coach developer programmes over the last seven years. The programmes target multiple sports and multiple levels, focusing on facilitation skills for the coach developer, as well as supporting coaches in practice (USCCE, n.d.). Further information on these global coach development programmes is provided in Chapter 3.

The Scottish Football Association (SFA, n.d.) supports coach development but regards this more as a necessary form of professional development, calling the programme Continuous Coach Development (CCD). This programme is aimed at entry-level coaches, ensuring their knowledge and skills remain current and allowing them to deliver quality coaching to their players.

Case study 1 examined the role of the coach developer within sporting organisations, which, depending on the focus of the organisation, may be quite constrained. The second case study considers the developmental process of a coach developer working within the private sector.

CASE STUDY 2

Jamie Taylor
Current Position: Senior Coach Developer, Grey Matters UK

Background in sport

My background is as a failed athlete. Right from the age of 13/14 as rugby player I was digging out articles, reading books, trying to understand how to improve my personal performance. For me, for a variety of different reasons, some of them physical, some of the mental, I was held back by pretty chronic fear of failure. Although I played to a decent level, I never really progressed to the level of performance that I would have wanted to as an early teenager.

Coaching

I went to a very enabling sporty school. Because I was so keen, one of the teachers asked 'Would you fancy coming coaching?' From that point, the school actually moved my free period around so that I could have two games afternoons a week spent coaching younger pupils at the school, which was an amazing experience for me at the time. The school also paid for me to do some early coaching qualifications and employed me as a part time coach when I left. I still didn't think there was a career in it, but I carried that on through university when I was a I was a player and community coach at Championship Rugby club. I went and travelled around Birmingham coaching at different schools, and some age group representative groups. Then as I'm leaving University, my old Director of Rugby called and said 'fancy becoming a teacher?' and I never looked back. I moved from a private school in Birmingham to another private school that bit more of a rugby focus, all while coaching at Leicester Tigers in their academy pathway. I progressed through the Academy to become Academy head coach, I then spent a few seasons coaching at Loughborough University and am now coaching at Wasps academy.

How I got into coach development

I had begun working with some coaches as part of my role at Leicester and, looking back, it was like playing pin the tail on the donkey, because I had never done any coach development. A lot of trial and error and the only real qualification I had was starting a PhD, so I must know what I was talking about. I was then asked to do some coach mentoring for the Premier League across a few academies. As that work increased, I began to build a skill set, began to do more reading, more professional development while I was still full-time coaching. This work was significantly influenced by my PhD supervisor and as my skillset grew, I began to see the potential in doing more of the work. I then moved into the role of head of coaching and curriculum at the English Institute of Sport, working across Olympic and Paralympic Sports, where my full-time role became coach development, and my coaching became a part time role. Then, a few years ago, a good friend and mentor of mine invited me to come work with him as a senior coach developer and I've been working at Grey Matters ever since.

Key milestones

- My first degree had a significant impact, I'd say that as a historian it trains you to think of the world in a particular way taking into account a lots of different complex and interacting factors. There was a particular module I did at university in military strategy which fascinated me. I looked at it and saw the parallels to coaching and performance more broadly.
- Until I started my PhD, nearly all the useful pedagogical education I had come from actual practice and reflection. Whilst I picked up some useful procedural 'tips' in coach education, it didn't really get to the heart of what I needed. Teacher education was similar, but thankfully, for the most part I perceived it to be too fluffy to be useful. There were all sorts in there, learning styles, NLP … which is a real shame, I could have done with a lot more cognitive psychology.
- The practical experience I got as an early career teacher was fantastic. I was teaching Physical Education (PE) or coaching for probably 6 hours a day for four years. I loved it, was deeply engaged in it. I was getting a very high number of hours on task, but probably without the declarative knowledge to really maximise what I took from that experience.

Key philosophy

- I use a Professional Judgement and Decision Making (PJDM) approach to coach development. I'm working with a coach to understand what a desirable outcome is or formulating intention for impact for the work. Working backwards, then from that intention combining and using the most appropriate methods for that coach in that context towards that that aim.
- As with any educational activity it is my job to meet the wants and needs of the learner. Therefore, there's a very difficult tightrope to walk. I have to go in and work based on what the coach wants and I and ideally work with their needs as well. But it's my job to support them, to improve their practice. Sometimes a coach can't see what they can't see so it's my job to walk that very difficult tightrope.
- I am a pracademic and whilst I am doing the job, I am also aiming to innovate and research as well. I hold positions at Dublin City University and Edinburgh University. That work helps me to refine ideas and test them.

- I'm also trying to equip coaches to do the work by themselves and not become reliant on me. Ultimately trying to move towards more adaptive expertise than routine expertise.

Most important takeaway

As a profession, I really think that we are on a tipping point, more and more people are investing in improving their practice via academic routes. There is therefore an opportunity to do more genuinely applied research that is aimed at practitioners and there is also the opportunity to drive rigour and standards in coaching.

We've poured so much time and money into improving athletes, performance systems and sport, sporting bureaucrats, and very often the people at the end of this who don't get the level of investment they need are coaches. I would love to see that change.

The preserve of independent/self-employed coach developers has been prevalent in the United Kingdom (UK) since the inception of the United Kingdom Coaching Certificate (UKCC). Many sporting organisations (football, golf, equestrian and so on) have traditionally employed external coach development consultants to administer and progress their coaches and programmes. This approach is not exclusive to the UK and has been implemented in several countries, such as USA, Canada, Singapore and Germany. Refer to McQuade and Nash (2015) for further information on the role of the coach developer within the UK.

There are several programmes using external providers to develop coaches but does this make these providers coach developers, especially as their role may be mentor, assessor or course developer? For example, the Women's Sports Leadership Academy (WSLA) offers opportunities for women from any country to develop their skills and make an impact through mentoring (WSLA, n.d.). However, the development opportunities offered to coaches through this initiative are confined to a mentoring, rather than a sport specific role.

It can be difficult for independent coach developers to share their thoughts with their employer. As short-term consultants, they are in a difficult position: Coach development based upon a needs analysis (see Chapter 6) versus the expectation that some coaches/organisations do not want to hear that they are not performing optimally. Ultimately, a review of systems and processes can provide the impetus for change in established organisations (see Chapter 12), but, importantly, new organisations can gain information regarding the key criteria they should consider when developing their systems (see Chapter 11).

The third case study considers the career pathway of a coach developer working within higher education, an often overlooked and misunderstood environment for developing coaches.

CASE STUDY 3

Andrea Woodburn
Current position: Associate Professor, Université Laval

Background in sport

Youth alpine ski coaching at the club and provincial levels, played competitive football (soccer from 12 years university) and senior club football thereafter.

Coaching

I started coaching as a volunteer at the hill where I grew up skiing because they were short coaches and continued coaching on and off for the next 15 years; always in youth sport, because that's been the type of coaching I love to do. At one point I had started a PhD in Exercise Physiology and was coaching and loving it on the weekends. I was spending most of my break time in the lab doing my practice planning. And so my PhD Director wisely said to me at one point, and it was the greatest thing, 'What are you doing here? Your love right now is doing what you're doing in coaching.' So, I left and went out West to coach and continue as a coach developer in the National Coaching Certification Program (NCCP) out there. Then, I ended up moving back East to work at a race club in Nova Scotia full time. While there, I enrolled in the newly opened National Coaching Institute in Halifax. This led to a job that opened up at the Coaching Association of Canada in Ottawa. The combination of coaching and studying was pretty much responsible for me moving around the country a few times!

How got into coach development

I first got into coach development during my undergraduate degree at Acadia University. A professor who became an important mentor to me invited me to join him in delivering NCCP workshops, gradually helping me take on more involvement in that programme. That initial involvement grew over the subsequent years and eventually led to coach development becoming a bit part of my career path. Thinking about this journey serves as a reminder to me of how important one person can be in the life of someone else.

Key milestones

- In Canada, I think the beginning of the shift towards a competency-based approach in the NCCP marked a milestone – a shift in design from what coaches need to know to what they need to be able to do with what they know.

- More broadly, there has been an increased involvement of the university sector in coach education and development as well – both through programmes in coaching and also through collaborative research between sport organisations and academic staff and students. I think this is a positive step in coach education and development and in the professionalisation of coaching.
- The conversation about supporting coaches in the field seems to be becoming more prominent these days. I think there will always be a place (and rightly so) for formal coach education, but I am excited to see this growing interest in supporting coaches around their problems of practice and more working with them in the field. In a way, it represents a shift to seeing coach education and development as a series of courses or workshops and more as supporting the coach in their journey as a lifelong learner.
- Also, through different International Council for Coaching Excellence (ICCE) driven or supported initiatives, I think we are living the beginnings of a global community of coach developers – that is a big win as we will get better together through sharing what we are doing.

Difference between coach education and coach development

It depends on the context in which they terms are used. Perhaps a way to think about distinguishing them is that coach education would refer to the more formal programming that involves structure, curricula and accreditation in some form. Coach development would refer more broadly to any engagement a coach may have in learning towards bettering their coaching and extends beyond and between formal coach education.

Key philosophy

My philosophy regarding coach education and development would be to centre whatever we do on the needs of the coach and allow the coach as much agency as possible in their learning. I don't understand all the complexities of our system in Canada, but I do feel we could improve the cooperation between various stakeholders towards bettering the experiences for coaches regarding their education and development. Sometimes, coaches end up having to do redundant workshops or paying twice for access to accreditation because the different parts of the system can't yet *talk* well to one other. And giving coaches more voice and choice in their learning pathways would go a long way towards making them feel like they are valued.

Most important takeaway

We are living in exciting times in coach education and development! The conversations around coaching seem to have increased exponentially in the past few years. Since the beginning of the pandemic, folks in the coach

> education and development community have been very generous in sharing their expertise and time through webinars, podcasts and the like. This means that there is so much accessible, quality content available to any curious coach with online access, and that coaches have more direct access to expertise on issues that are timely and important to them. I think the pandemic time has also stimulated some positive thinking regarding blended learning strategies and what we chose to do with coaches when we do come together in person. We need to pay much closer attention to how we chose to spend the time when coaches come together in person and treat that time like the precious resource it is.

The university sector, especially in North America, is better known for coaches working with athletes and teams rather than the quality of their coach education provision (see Vallée & Bloom, 2005; Martin et al., 2019). More recently higher education institutions have embraced coach education and coach development at undergraduate and postgraduate levels in many countries. Trudel and colleagues (2020) conducted a review of coaching programmes within universities, noting this is a recent area of research within the context of coach development. The article ends with a warning that the mission statement and research agendas of universities may not always meet the needs of coach development (what/who/when?). Conversely, many universities do have the expertise in learning activities that is so important to effective coach development.

Much of the research into universities as sites for coach development focus on aspects of learning. For example, there is an emphasis on the importance of reflection or reflective practice. Dixon and colleagues (2021) highlighted the advantages of collaborative reflection with groups of student coaches and the impact on coaching effectiveness as a result. Griffiths and Cropley (2018) showed the benefits were threefold; career development was considered important, inter- and intra-personal skills were significantly improved, there was a greater understanding of the industry perspective.

Development of Coach Developers

These three case studies highlight the lack of a clear pathway to becoming a coach developer. The time taken for each individual to reach the level at which they are currently operating varies greatly. These three coach developers, all operating in different contexts, have had distinct but unique routes to their current roles. The studies also revealed there are some individuals advertising themselves as coach developers and working within this environment without certification or credentials.

Having said that, each of the coach developers in the case studies shares some common attributes and also some differences, perhaps related to their coaching context. Importantly, these coach developers have been educated to postgraduate level and display the ability to reflect on their education and experiences; crucially, they all view learning as a lifelong commitment. This is supported by their currency in coaching and coach development research but also their dedication to making a difference – ensuring a change in coaching behaviours. Each of these coach developers also considers that sport, and by extension coach development, is reaching a critical stage of growth and maturity within certain systems (see Chapters 11 and 12). Each acknowledges financial support is imperative but questions whether this is organised and distributed in the most effective manner.

Given that each of these coach developers has NOT specialised in their sport, they are demonstrating that elite coach developers can work across sports. This poses the question as to whether coach development is sport-specific; the case studies would suggest it is not but it does require an understanding of the sporting context and the pressures that coaches are subjected to. Chapter 1 highlighted the need for coach developers to be knowledgeable about the learning process. Despite the different entry points into coach development, all these coach developers were well versed and experienced in teaching and learning scenarios.

Interestingly, these coach developers all embrace a lifelong learning approach; the importance of reflection and building on experience seem to be key. Despite the different contexts in which they operate, all three did not follow a traditional path as a high performance athlete in their sport, although each had competed at some level. They also started coaching early (teens or early 20s) and as a result entered coach development relatively young, either formally or informally. It must be made clear the three case studies included within this chapter are examples from differing domains. There are many different entry points into, and pathways through, coach development; it is an individual process so each case study is an example and should not be regarded as the only way or indeed the optimal way.

It would be remiss to write this chapter on coach development pathways without including the views of practicing coaches. Included below is an extract from a conversation with a frustrated coach, relaying his perceptions of coach developers.

> A highly experienced coach from a team sport within the UK when asked about his coach development experiences replied, 'can I vent?' He continued to explain that over the years he had attended a number of coach development activities but really struggled with the approach of some coach developers. He pointed out that he had to work his way through the system of accreditation in his sport, investing time and money to gain recognition. His argument was that he could not call himself a coach, or be paid for his services, unless he had these qualifications but 'anybody can call themselves a coach developer, with no qualifications, experience or knowledge in the area. This makes a real difference in the take-homes – whether they are useful and actually work in practice.'

> He continued 'I work in performance sport, where we have to make some tough decisions and quickly. It really is highly competitive, and I'll do whatever it takes to be successful – if I don't, I lose my job! I am so fed up with coach developers who have never experienced the pressure of a high-performance environment coming out with anodyne phrases and thoughts about what I could do to better understand my team.'
>
> This coach was keen to learn and wanted to develop his skills so his frustration was not about the ongoing learning requirements mandated by his sport but more around the quality experience offered by some coach developers. While many had a background in his sport and others had experience in learning, as advocated in this book, this coach felt that he was not developing to any great extent as a result of their interventions. He considered 'some of these people are relics of a system that has gone, but they haven't, others are able to say the same thing in a multitude of different ways. Coaching and coaches have moved on with many of my colleagues having higher degrees, I'm undertaking a PhD, so why are we stuck with Coach Developers with no qualifications at all.'

Based on some of the issues raised by this coach, an empirical study, reported below, was devised. The results highlight the views of practicing coaches on their coach development experiences, across a variety of sports.

Coaches Perceptions of Coach Developers

As mentioned earlier, coach development is a long and complex process (for example, Nash & Sproule, 2009; Stoszkowski & Collins, 2016), which can be pursued in individual and ad-hoc ways (e.g. Nash, Sproule & Horton, 2011; Da Silva et al., 2022). Several critiques have demonstrated the low impact of formal provision (see Nash & Sproule, 2012; Stodter & Cushion, 2019). The needs and aspirations of coaches have traditionally been neglected in the design of formal courses, further illustrating coach development should incorporate all forms of coach learning. The needs analysis process, or knowledge auditing (see Chapter 6), is crucial to identify strengths and weaknesses. As coach developers appreciate, it is essential for the development pathway to understand what learners do not know. However, many practicing sport coaches did not always share that view.

Further discussion with sport coaches (167) in a wide variety of sports uncovered the following:

- **Provision was delivered by rote:** These coaches felt that there was a formula for delivery that was followed by the coach developers; for example, spend 15 minutes on the introduction. The courses also followed a predetermined content using a presentation style format. Many coaches felt these are qualification-centred rather than coach-centred.

- **No real interaction planned:** As the courses were delivered according to a formula, the coaches thought the opportunities to interact with the coach developer and the other course participants were limited and carefully managed. This linked to the rote or scripted delivery mentioned above; questions appeared staged, with straightforward answers provided.
- **Most learning happened by accident:** Coaches were convinced any meaningful learning that occurred was not an explicit result of this learning process. Any learning was attributed to the informal chats at coffee breaks or lunch where coaches could interact in meaningful discussion about their problems of practice.
- **Too much focus on 'drills & skills':** There was a strong perception coach developers were skilled in the mechanics of the sport and were able to offer a repertoire of practices for different ages and abilities. These coaches felt the coach developers were able to discuss the 'what' of coaching rather than offer guidance on the 'how.' This reinforced the technical nature of some of the course delivery rather than emphasising the pedagogical skills and coaching process knowledge necessary for delivering high-quality coaching sessions.
- **No transparency in assessment:** The coaches considered the criteria for successful completion of the qualification were not established early in the course. There was also the suggestion some coaches would pass the assessment no matter what their performance because of their previous playing ability.

Many of these coaches were referring to their formal experiences of coach learning and when challenged to consider ad hoc learning opportunities or a more individualised approach, many were unable to do so. This suggests the traditional definition of coach education, consisting of formal sport-related workshops, is still accepted as the norm for many practising coaches. This seems at odds with the perceptions of the coach developers in the three case studies, who feel that coach development is more widely recognised as any form of coach learning.

Coach developers (10) were given the opportunity to comment on the views of the coaches highlighted above. They felt coach development is still a relatively recent innovation in the field of sport coaching and that may explain the focus of the coaches on the formal, organised and often sport-led aspects of coach learning. These coach developers felt they generally differed from coach educators in terms of scope and scale of interaction, but interestingly did not feel the larger-scale delivery options fell into their remit. Furthermore, they considered effective coaches to be those who adapt their behaviour to meet the demands of their particular coaching environment, whereas coach developers must meet the needs of diverse coaches.

These coach developers felt there were many difficulties with the existing coach education process, especially with the content they were expected to cover. Many of these difficulties reflected the technical nature of course content, as few courses concentrated on the 'how' of coaching rather than the 'what' (or why?) of coaching. The coach developers felt they were on a 'continuous treadmill' with a vast amount of content to cover in a short space of time. This can be an issue if the focus from the organisation is on technical content rather than the process of learning and development. There were also difficulties in how some courses were marketed and subscribed to, as some brought together coaches with vastly different levels of experience and expertise. This caused problems for coach developers, in terms of learning potential, as they felt group work and discussions were challenging.

Many of these issues were attributed to the well-documented research surrounding larger scale formal delivery, not reflecting the changing nature of coach learning. These coach developers also considered their skills were transferable and transcended any specific sport. As a result, there was a perception some sporting organisations did not value their skills and preferred more traditional technical/tactical approaches. Many coach developers felt the role of assessor was thrust upon them with little training or understanding of the criteria for success. There was an apparent contradiction between their understanding of the role of coach developer and their function as coach assessor.

There appears to be little correlation between the expectations of coaches and coach developers. If coaches are to attain higher levels of effectiveness, there must be effective dialogue between coaching organisations, coaches and coach developers.

In Summary

Coach development as a career has been practised for many years by a select number of people. There are many positives, but also some caveats, with the current situation. Individuals enter the coach development 'pathway' with an abundance of enthusiasm and an interest in making a difference. However, the unstructured nature of the coaching landscape can have a negative effect on motivation, often contributing to mixed messages to the coach developer and the coach.

The industry needs an accepted definition of a coach developer, which organisations and individuals need to understand and support. This is not to say individuals must follow a prescribed route into coach development. The three case studies illustrated how each person followed an idiosyncratic route, dictated by personal circumstances, opportunities and interest/motivation. Should we, as coach developers, be calling for some regulation or professionalisation of this important aspect of coach development? Do we need to be prescriptive about who can call themselves a coach developer?

Many organisations across the globe have recognised the importance of the coach developer within their sports systems, whether mature or newly formed. The role and function of the coach developer can contribute very positively to the success of sport at all levels. The three case studies highlight coach developers working within three different contexts and all of them are passionate about developing coaches. Can we say that about everyone designated a coach developer?

A key message from all three coach developers highlighted here is they still have a hunger to learn and a passion for developing others. Is this more important than a background in a particular sport? I would suggest these three coach developers have used their considerable experiences in sport, education and life to become self-reliant. In other words, they are able to diagnose any difficulties they may face and come up with solutions to resolve the issues. These solutions may require external input but importantly, these coach developers can identify and act on their experiences – almost becoming autonomous or more able to be independent problem solvers. Is this capacity for self-sufficiency what we should be expecting from our coaches and coach developers?

References

The Australian Sports Commission (n.d.). What is a coach developer and what do they do? https://www.sportaus.gov.au/coaches_and_officials/sport_specific_training/coach_developer_resources. Accessed 27/7/2022.

Chartered Institute for Management of Sport and Physical Activity (2022). CIMSPA Professional Standard: Coach Developer. The Chartered Institute for the Management of Sport and Physical Activity.

Chroni, S., Diefenbach, K., & Pettersen, S. (2021). An exploration of recruitment of elite athletes to coaching within federations. *International Sport Coaching Journal*, 8(3), 315–327.

Da Silva, E.J., Mallett, C.J., Sánchez-Oliva, D., Dias, A., & Palmeira, A. (2022). A coach development program: A guided online reflective practice intervention study. *Journal of Sports Sciences*, 40(9), 1042–1054

Dixon, M., Lee, C., & Corrigan, C. (2021). 'We were all looking at them quite critically': Collaborative reflection on a university-based coach education program. *Reflective Practice*, 22(2). 203–218.

Griffiths, P.J., & Cropley, B. (2018). The flipped university: Exploring student progression in football coaching and development. *Education & Training (London)*, 60(5), 375–388.

Hämäläinen, K., & Blomqvist, M. (2016). A new era in sport organizations and coach development in Finland. *International Sport Coaching Journal*, 3(3), 332–343.

Martin, E.M., Moorcroft, S.J., & Johnson, T.G. (2019). Backwards design and program level approaches to coach development in higher education. *International Sport Coaching Journal*, 6(3), 329–338.

McQuade, S., & Nash, C. (2015). The role of the coach developer in supporting and guiding coach learning. *International Sport Coaching Journal*, 2, 339–346.

Nash, C. (2019). *Career pathways of elite coach developers*. Invited Masterclass at 12th ICCE Global Coach Conference, Tokyo, October 2019.

Nash, C., & Sproule, J. (2009). Career development of expert coaches. *International Journal of Sports Science & Coaching*, 4(1), 121–138.

Nash, C., & Sproule, J. (2012). Coaches perceptions of coach education experiences. *International Journal of Sport Psychology*, 43, 33–52.

Nash, C., Sproule, J., & Horton, P. (2011) Excellence in coaching: The art and skill of elite practitioners. *Research Quarterly in Exercise & Sport*, 82(2), 229–238.

Scottish Football Association (n.d.). Your coaching development. Accessed 25th June 2022 https://www.scottishfa.co.uk/football-development/coaching/development/continuous-coach-development-ccd/.

Stodter, A., & Cushion, C.J. (2019). Evidencing the impact of coaches' learning: Changes in coaching knowledge and practice over time. *Journal of Sports Sciences*, 37(18), 2086–2093.

Stoszkowski, J., & Collins, D. (2016). Sources, topics and use of knowledge by coaches. *Journal of Sports Sciences*, 34(9), 794–802.

Trudel, P., Milestetd, M., & Culver, D.M. (2020). What the empirical studies on sport coach education programs in higher education have to reveal: A review. *International Sport Coaching Journal*, 7(1), 61–73.

United States Center for Coaching Excellence (n.d.). Coach developer academy program. https://uscoachexcellence.org/cd-academy/.

United States Council for Coaching Excellence (2022). What is coach development? https://uscoachexcellence.org/support-the-profession-of-sport-coaching/. Accessed 10th May 2022.

Vallée, C.N., & Bloom, G.A. (2005). Building a successful university program: Key and common elements of expert coaches. *Journal of Applied Sport Psychology*, 17(3), 179–196.

Women in Sports Leadership (WSLA) (n.d.). https://www.wsla.co.uk/2022. Accessed 25th June 2022.

3
INTERNATIONAL PERSPECTIVES ON COACH DEVELOPMENT

A Global Snapshot

Melissa Thompson, Michel Milistetd, Shigeki Sarodo, Pelle Kvalsund and Hikabwa Chipande

Coach development is a complex and individualized process, influenced by personal and contextual factors. In this chapter we provide several case studies illustrating international systems of coach development, which provide a global snapshot of the influence of context and culture. We then explore the factors that impact one's developmental journey as a coach to provide a broad conceptualization of the coach development pathway. The aim is to situate coach development as a process that has structure but is flexible, is formal and informal, has commonality but is individualized, and is lifelong and life wide. Finally, this chapter concludes with a discussion on what the next evolution in coach development may include.

Through the collaboration between the Nippon Sport Science University Coach Developer Academy (NSSU CDA) and the International Council for Coaching Excellence (ICCE), the global landscape of coach development has become more interconnected. For this reason, we begin with a review of the coach development system in Japan.

Coach Development in Japan

The coach development system in Japan has a long history (Nihon Taiiku Kyoukai, 2016). Coaching qualifications are currently administered by the Japan Sport Association (JSPO) which was renamed from Japan Sports Association (*Nihon Taiiku Kyoukai*, from 1948 to 2018) and Japan Amateur Athletic Association (*Dainippon Taiiku Kyoukai*, established in 1911), the first president of which was the founder of judo, Jigoro Kano.

Organized coach development in Japan is considered to have officially begun in 1965, when the Japan Sports Association began developing sports trainers. At that time, the name trainer was used rather than coach, as this coaching program was based on the West German sports leadership qualifications. Later, in 1971, the development of sports instructors began. In 1977, coach development as an official program, or the Japan Sports Association Official Sports Coaching System, began and continues to the present day. The following review provides an overview of the system (Nihon Taiiku Kyoukai, 2016):

- Clarification of the types and roles of coaches for diversified sports activities.
- A consistent system allowing coaches to obtain certification in a step-by-step process.
- A registration system was adopted as a common system among national federations (NFs), prefectural sports associations, and the Japan Sports Association.
- Japan Sports Association promoted organizational collaboration among coaches by sport and by region.
- The sport trainers and sport instructors' development program that had been in place up to that point was incorporated into this Official Sports Coaching System.

The Official Sports Coaching System adopted a curriculum organized into generic (or common) subjects for all coaches and specialized (or specific) subjects for individual sports. For the total of 80 hours in the curriculum, the sessions for generic subjects (40 hours for training science, sports medicine and science, and sports humanities) were conducted by Japan Sports Association, and the sessions for specialized subjects (40 hours) were conducted by each NF. As a result, the coaching coach qualification courses in Japan have been managed primarily by Japan Sports Association with the cooperation of the NFs, and this system is still in place today. However, as of 2022, the Japan Football Association and the Japan Basketball Association are holding courses that include both generic subjects and specialized subjects and they operate their own courses and manage their own coaching qualifications. Since beginning, the JSPO Official Sports Coaching System has been revised three times (1988, 2005, and 2019). The 2019 revision includes changes such as the renaming of the sport-specific coaching qualifications and the creation of a "start coach" class, the most important of which were the changes in the curriculum and in the format of the generic subject coaching course (Japan Sport Association, 2022). Until then, experts in their respective fields (mainly university faculty) had lectured on sports medicine, sports psychology, training science, sports culture, and other subjects along with common textbooks in the on-site coaching course. However, with the 2019 revision, a greater proportion of the content was focused on the so-called interpersonal and intrapersonal knowledge (referenced by Coté & Gilbert in 2009), mainly in the field of coaching, to develop more practical skills and wisdom for coaches. In addition, the course format changed significantly, from a lecture format to an active learning format, with the coach developer facilitating various activities in groups. The course also allowed coaches to reflect on their own past experiences in sports, think about better coaching practices, and engage them through interactions with other coaches.

In Japan, school education has traditionally focused on knowledge acquisition, and the field of coach development has also adopted a lecture-style approach to learning knowledge. However, the tragic suicide in 2011 of the captain of a high school boys basketball team due to corporal punishment by his coach (Hongo, 2013) and other harassment issues has brought about a social re-evaluation of coaching and coach development in Japan. Numerous surveys and studies confirmed such violent coaching was still common in Japan (Miller, 2013; Shiga, 2013), and a certain number of coaches believed it was necessary in some cases (Kira & Yamashita, 2013). Under these circumstances, a lack of coaching and communication skills among coaches has been identified as one of the reasons contributing to the prevalence of corporal punishment and harsh behavior. In 2013, the Coaching Consortium in Japan established by the Japanese Ministry of Education, Culture, Sports, Science and Technology (MEXT) published the Seven Recommendations for becoming a Good Coach (Japan Sports Association, 2013), and in 2016 the Japan Sports Association released a Model Core Curriculum for Coach Development with the aim of improving coach development (Japan Sports Association, 2016). This Model Core Curriculum includes the following areas: coaching philosophy, intrapersonal and interpersonal knowledge, and generic and sport-specific knowledge. The good coaches are required to learn the qualities and abilities that a good coach should possess in a more practical course. In such coaches' learning, it is clearly not enough to just acquire theoretical knowledge. Coaches need to learn in a practical way that will ultimately lead to a change in their own thinking and behavior. It is also essential that coaches have a good coaching philosophy. The JSPO has made significant changes to the format and content of its courses and has introduced coach developers to support coaches' active learning.

The introduction of coach developers to the coach development system in 2019 did not appear suddenly and without context. In 2014, Nippon Sport Science University (NSSU) established the "NSSU Coach Developer Academy," and as a result, the Nippon Coach Developer Academy (NCDA) trained 110 international coach developers from 42 countries from 2014 to 2021, with five participants from Japan. The mission of NCDA was to foster international coach developers and form an international network of coach developers. Masamitsu Ito, professor at NSSU, who plays a central role in the operation of NCDA's Coach Developer Program, also completed the program as one of its first participants. As a result, the proliferation of coach developers in Japan and around the globe resulted in a highly interconnected network.

The. NCDA was established as an international sports academy as one of the pillar programs of Sports For Tomorrow (SFT), an international sports contribution program founded by the Japanese Government. According to its official statement, SFT "aims to share the values of sport and promote the Olympic and Paralympic Movement to people of all generations around the world including developing countries, for a better future for the world, from 2014 toward the Tokyo 2020 Olympic and Paralympic Games." Its sports academy project was commissioned by the MEXT (later by the Japan Sports Agency in 2015–2021) to operate the NCDA as part of the International Sports Academy project in collaboration with the ICCE. In this commissioned project, NCDA organized three main coach development programs:

1. NSSU-ICCE Coach Developer Programme (basic course)
2. Advanced Program
3. Essential Program (introductory course)

The NSSU-ICCE Coach Developer Program brought together participants from three types of organizations: IFs and NFs, multi-sports agencies, and universities, who worked as coach developers in a variety of contexts. The participants deepened their learning around coach development and also learned facilitation skills that are essential for coach developers, as well as support skills for coaches in the field. Coach developers participated in a week-long on-campus residential program over two sessions (in summer and winter) and also practiced their learning locally between the two sessions. Many of the participants continue to be involved in coach development in their home countries after completing the program and returning home. Notable examples include Singapore (CoachSG, Sport Singapore), Zambia (ZAM Coach360), the US (United States Center for Coaching Excellence), and Brazil (Brazilian Olympic Committee). In addition, the Special Olympics is currently establishing a coach development system and was able to send a representative to the NCDA.

The NCDA has, no doubt, had a global impact, but such learning at NCDA is also being used in Japan. Currently in Japan, Masamitsu Ito is leading the training of coach developers at the JSPO as a trainer. The Japan Basketball Association also introduced coach developers to the coaching system in 2019, and coach developers currently serve as facilitators at D- and C-level coaching certification courses. At these courses, participants do not learn specialized knowledge in a lecture format, but through discussions and exchanges among themselves and with coach developers, learning in a way that contributes to their practical application. In the future, coach developers will be trained to be in charge of the higher-level coaching certification courses. As mentioned before, coach developers in Japan at present are mainly positioned as course conductors for the sessions. However, the role of coach developers will be expected to expand in the future to meet the needs of each sports organization.

Coach Development in Brazil

Coaching in Brazil has been a profession since 1998. There is no voluntary coaching in the country, and anyone who wants to work as a coach must hold the university degree in Physical Education (Brazil, 1998). Despite legislation

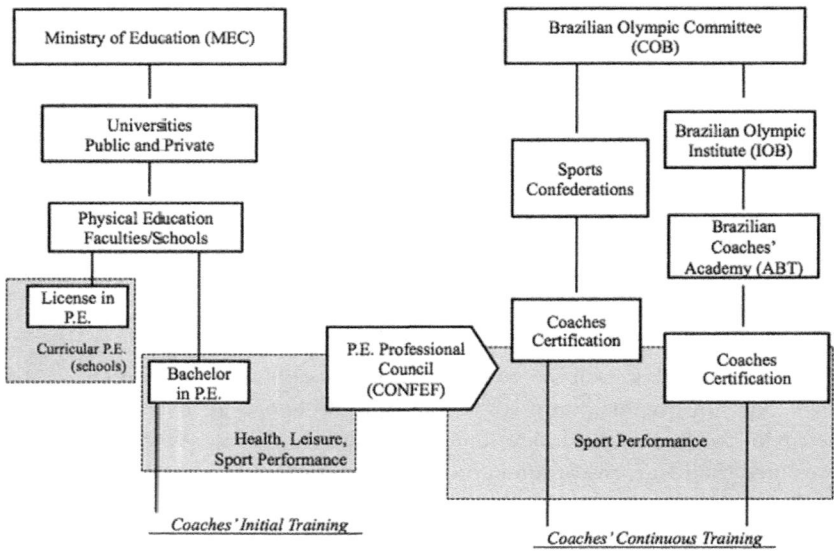

FIGURE 3.1 Structure of coach education in Brazil (see Milistetd et al., 2016).

ensuring preparation at a higher education level, this certification requirement does not guarantee the quality of learning for sports coaches. Since the first publications of the description of coach education in Brazil (Milistetd et al., 2014, 2016), the research agenda has demonstrated the strengths and limitations of coach development in the country. Based on the findings, researchers offer suggestions to the organizations responsible for the initial and continuing training of coaches (Figure 3.1), specifically universities, national sports federations, and the Brazilian Olympic Committee (for example, Galatti et al., 2019; Ciampolini et al., 2021).

Initial Training

The national guidelines for Physical Education programs in Brazil were revised in 2018 (Brazil, 2018). The guidelines define the training in four years with 3,200 hours of preparation based on basic and applied knowledge focused to the areas of promotion of physical activities, sports coaching, physical education in schools, activities toward culture, and leisure. As it is a broad program, only 1/5 of the total workload is concentrated to specific areas of sport (Milistetd et al., 2014) such as courses related to coaching (for example, sport psychology, sport pedagogy) and specific sports courses (for example, theory and methodology of swimming, theory and methodology of volleyball). The program is composed of theoretical and practical classes and different experiential learning strategies.

The experiential learning strategies are about 20% of curriculum workload, performed through curricular pedagogical practices (CPP), internships, and curricular extension projects (CEP). In coaching contexts, CPP represents the opportunity for students to play the coach's role. As example of CPP, the students can teach sports for colleagues during classes. Internships have a minimum of 320 hours in which students will learn outside the university. One example may be assisting coaches with supervisor support. The most recent change in the national guidelines was the increment of CEP activities. CEPs require that students participate in community service projects during their four-year undergraduate preparation. In coaching contexts one of the main CEP activities is being a coach or assistant coach in sports services, acting with varsity teams, grassroots projects, and others. The purpose of CEP activities is to increase the experiential learning opportunities in a more controlled environment, such as under supervision with formal university supervisors.

Despite a packed curriculum based on different learning opportunities across four years of preparation, recent research has suggested improvements to enhance the student-coaches' learning, including:

- Theoretical classes becoming more learner centered (Galatti et al., 2019)
- CPP activities focusing on the development of different coaching competences (Salles, 2019)
- Increasing supervisors' responsibilities in internships (Trudel et al., 2020)
- Increasing use of varsity teams as a legitimate training environment for coaches as CEPs (Milistetd et al., 2018)

Continuous Training

Despite promoting the necessary changes to qualify the preparation of coaches in Physical Education programs in Brazil, there is still a general focus on the preparation of coaches (Brazil, 2018) with few specificities for different sports. Given this reality, continuous training in Brazil plays a central role in certifying coaches to work specifically in environments of participation and sports performance. Currently, some national sports federations offer coach education programs and the Brazilian Olympic Committee has supported the development of new programs.

Milistetd et al. (2016) published a description of coach education offered by NFs. From 30 national sport federations only 12 regularly offered some level of certification. In general, the analysis showed a misalignment among the coach education programs from different sports. The number of levels to achieve certification varies from one to five. The programs' workloads vary according to the federation, ranging from 16-hour courses to up to 560-hour courses. In addition, the content of the programs is mainly based on technical, tactical, and physical aspects of sports, focusing on the development of professional knowledge with little emphasis on interpersonal and intrapersonal knowledge (ICCE, 2013). Lastly, the curricula focus on the development of coaching knowledge instead of coaching competences.

Although the structure represents a traditional view of continuing education for coaches in Brazil, some NFs have shown a more modern training structure. For instance, the Brazilian Rugby Confederation adopts guidelines for coach education from World Rugby. As a result, the curriculum is organized in coaching competences in different levels of domains and coaching contexts. Moreover, the coach developers must be certified in specific programs and be able to implement learner-centered teaching strategies (Ciampolini et al., 2021).

To encourage national sports federations to offer programs of higher quality and based on international perspectives of coach education (ICCE, 2013, 2014), the Brazilian Olympic Committee launched in 2022 (BOC, 2022) the National Guidelines for athletes and coaches' development. In the coaches' section, this document presents principles and tools for the establishment of coach education programs and certification. In addition, the guidelines also present possibilities for adopting coach development initiatives toward specific groups (such as high-performance coaches, women coaches, and so on), transition pathways from high-performance athletes to become coaches, strategies for benchmarking, travel-based learning, and knowledge transfer in sports organizations.

Coaching has been recognized as a profession in Brazil for more than two decades. However, research has shown legal support does not guarantee the quality of the training for coaches. Considering learning as an individual and complex process, the integration of the different organizations responsible for coach education is necessary, as is continuous evaluation of the programs and the learning impact on coach behavior. To this end, the current efforts from the Brazilian Olympic Committee to enhance the quantity and quality of continuing education for coaches are a promising way to create an integrated system of coaches' development in the near future.

Coach Development in the US

The US has a long history of documenting the responsibilities of sport coaches. The first version of the National Standards for Sport Coaches was published in 1995 with revised versions published in 2006 and 2017 (Gano-Overway et al., 2020). In each version, the broad and complex nature of coaching is documented, allowing the standards to serve as a guide for coach development. Although these standards have existed for some time, sport coaching in the US remains a largely unregulated profession. A host of variables influence the minimum requirements or training for acting as a coach, including performance level (that is, grass roots, interscholastic, high performance, and so on), sport, organizational requirements, and more. The variability in requirements for coaching is reflective of the decentralized sport system, providing both benefits and detriments to the overall system and to coaches. A decentralized approach allows for more targeted sport science information and a player-to-coach pathway along with increased flexibility based on prior knowledge and experience. However, this limits the consistency and accountability across the broad coaching landscape and makes it difficult for coaches to transition from one sport to another (specifically at volunteer and grassroots levels).

Perhaps the best approach to summarizing the coach development system in the US is to focus on the national governing bodies (NGBs) and their systems, as many of them support coach development from grassroots through high performance. There are roughly 50 NGBs in the US, each of which function independently with varying levels of financial support from the United States Olympic & Paralympic Committee (USOPC) and their own system of coach and athlete development. Many NGBs incorporate a series of certifications or licenses offering entry level through advanced content knowledge and some NGBs incorporate mentored observations and/or accumulation of coaching hours to progress. For the most part, these systems are content and knowledge-based rather than skill based. However, as noted, the sport system in the US is complex because of the thousands of organizations that run youth sports (Dieffenbach & Villalon, 2021). Further, the interscholastic sport system (that is, high school and college sport) is disconnected from the NGB system. Therefore, requirements to coach in each of these organizations vary, and in some cases, there are no requirements at all. In addition, many sports have stand-alone coaches' associations that serve to provide professional development for coaches (for example, National Fastpitch Coaches Association). The disconnected nature of the sport system is one of the greatest challenges to progressing coach development in the US.

In 2016, the United States Center for Coaching Excellence was launched to serve as an organization that could provide support for coach developers and sport organizations as they worked to refine and/or reform their coach development systems. Shortly after its launch, the USCCE partnered with the ICCE to be the US host for the coach developer academy (connected to the NSSU NCDA program). As a result, there is an ongoing shift in the structure and design of coach development pathways in many organizations to include more practical application of coaching skills, systems of ongoing development, and interactive approaches to learning. While several coach developers have discussed the potential for cross-sport collaborations and multi-sport training materials, we have yet to see collaboration occuring within NGBs on general coaching materials or reciprocity of entry-level coach training.

Coach Development in Zambia

To describe and value a coach development systems efficiency, it is important to consider the culture and context of its operation. An understanding of the history of coach development is important, as is an appreciation of how this history came about, as it typically represents only selected sides of the story. However, to better understand history and its context, and how this has affected the current culture, it is critical to know and understand the people involved. How does the system feel for the players, the coaches, the coach developers and trainers, the sport association leaders, and how do politics have an influence?

Backbone

Despite the growing demands on coach services and expectations, little attention has been given to the development of the women and men tasked with developing Zambian athletes The majority of coaches in Zambia are untrained, or basically trained volunteers from communities undertaking coaching tasks beyond their regular work. Despite limited formal coach training, these coaches do an incredible job by organizing training and activities for younger generations, using their experiences as players to coach as effectively as they can. In addition, there are some coaches trained by non-governmental organizations, private sport academies, teachers, and personnel from the Zambia Police and Zambian Armed Forces organizations. Together with a few professional coaches, mainly from football, these coaches are providing a remarkable service to Zambian sport. The foundation of coaches in Zambia is no different to many other places in the world. It is rooted in passion for the sport, their experiences as athletes, and from what they learnt by observing their own and other coaches. These experiences typically represent valuable learning. Paired with some support from coach developers and formal coach learning opportunities, they are able to maximize their abilities and impact. Efforts are being made to adopt the physical education teachers' training at higher learning institutions to offer coaching certificates in selected sports. In addition, universities and colleges are working toward opening up and providing new exciting coach education pathways in youth sport coaching through short, accredited courses, creating an opportunity for people who base their coaching on practical experience to link to a more formal and recognized path.

Policies and Direction

The Sport Education and Accreditation System (SEAS) was initiated as a regional program by African Union Sport Council Region 5 (formerly known as SCSA Zone VI) around 2011, with the purpose of developing a national accreditation system and database of coaches; and to develop a sports education and training system that would address the needs and entitlements of athletes, coaches, and other sports practitioners in southern Africa. The SEAS program developed a draft framework for coach education and development, but was never fully implemented.

Following the International Council of Coaching Excellence (ICCE) Global Conference in Durban, South Africa, in 2013, AUSC Region 5 hosted a meeting of stakeholders in sport in Lusaka (October 2015) to re-emphasize and push the agenda and development of coaching in the southern African region. This resulted in the "LUSAKA DECLARATIONS of 2015." The Lusaka Declarations committed support and intensified efforts toward implementation of AUSC Region 5, Confederation of Southern African National Olympic Committees (COSANOC), Regional Sport Confederations and National Sport Federations' strategies, plans, and programs aimed at building mutually beneficial relations and supporting sustainable growth and development of coaches. Signatories also agreed to accelerate establishment of strategies to develop and standardize the preparation of regional podium performance programs for athletes. This is something that impacts the coach development efforts in the Member States. One of the central elements of the declaration highlighted the development of local coaches to avoid over reliance on expensive expatriate coaching expertise. This was proposed together with continuous investment in capacity development and advancement of proficient and performing local coaches, based on a clear coach education framework, pathways, and programs.

Zambia National Coaching Framework

Coaching and coach development in Zambia has typically been outward looking, something that has challenged the development of a strong national identity in sport. Coach training has traditionally been run by external sport specific experts sent from international federations. Even Zambia's National Football team, which has started developing a national football coach education framework from the lowest levels, has a long stream of national team football coaches from many countries with different football identities and coaching practices. Since 2000, coaches of the Zambia national team have come from the Netherlands, Denmark, France, Italy, Belgium, and Serbia and now Mr. Aljoša Asanović from Croatia (2021–) with Zambian coaches serving in between. In total 18 people from 8 different countries have served as head-coach for the Chipolopolos in the past 22 years, resulting in confusion, short-term thinking, and lack of national football identity.

This coaching strategy of the Zambian football association has meant a number of Zambian coaches get to work with experienced coaches from abroad. However, the most systematic work in this direction is from the National Olympic Committee of Zambia, which has offered technical coach support for years and is generously aided by the International Olympic Committee's Olympic Solidarity funds. This approach to developing coaches has greatly improved over the years, but it still has some cultural and contextual limitations.

Despite the low number of trained coaches, it is believed that Zambia has sent over a dozen coaches out of the country over the past 20 years for extended periods of time to receive extensive coach training in specific sports: some for track and field coaching to the US, others for team Handball to Hungary, or other countries where sport is organized differently, and coaching has different challenges and opportunities.

One big challenge in Zambia is the close link between coaching and sport politics. It seems leaders of National Sports Associations often selected coaches based on their personal connections and relations rather than on merit and defined coaching needs. Subsequent changes in leadership and a perceived affiliation to old leaders may be a factor in preventing these expert coaches to work, share, and systematically use their skills.

The National Olympic Committee of Zambia developed a comprehensive database of trained coaches and resource personnel to get a clear overview, and to revive and use these coaches better. Following the Lusaka Declarations of 2015, Zambia, through the Ministry of Youth Sport and Art, The National Sport Council and The National Olympic Committee produced a final draft of a National Sport Coaching Framework through a highly inclusive process facilitated by the Ministry of Youth Sport and Art. A sample of stakeholders included in the process are, in addition to the above three mentioned, selected National Sport Associations, the National Paralympic Committee, and the University of Zambia.

ZamCoach360

In line with the Lusaka Declaration of 2015, all countries in the southern African region have been asked to facilitate the establishment of National Coaches Associations (or coaching bodies) with a clear mandate, services, and membership structures to support national coach development efforts. Zambia put together a loose national coaching body called ZamCoach360, operating on a draft mandate from 2018.

The purpose of ZamCoach360 is to work with and for the National Associations of Zambia to provide support and guidance in coach education and development, and to work for the recognition of all coaches through leveraging of different opportunities. Initiated by the Ministry of Youth, Sport and Art, this body is closely connected to the National Olympic Committee of Zambia (NOCZ), National Sports Council of Zambia, and National Paralympic Committee of Zambia. In addition, they are developing strong links with the University of Zambia, something that benefits and strengthens both quality and accreditation value of coach education and the development of coach developers.

Achievement of ZamCoach360

As the first country in Africa, ZamCoach360 has been able to organize, finance, and run three full cohorts of ICCE Coach Developer* trainings (2018–19–21). This has been possible through the financial support of the National Olympic Committee of Zambia in partnership with the Norwegian Olympic and Paralympic Committee and Confederation of Sport. In part due to the success of these trainings, IOC's Olympic Solidarity has agreed with ICCE to financially support future coach developer trainings, not only in Zambia, but other countries and regions as well; a great achievement accredited to the vision and drive of Zambian sport leaders. In 2021 coach developers started to deliver Coaches Corners, short webinars or physical meetings addressing generic issues and dilemmas that impact coaches at various levels from grassroots to high performance.

In Conclusion

Zambian coach development has undergone some major changes. There seems to be government support, in addition to a better collaboration between the NGBs concerning coach development. Also, the University of Zambia is playing a more central role by providing new and more academic pathways for coaches, allowing them to integrate with higher education, resulting perhaps in better CV's and job opportunities. This all complements national sport associations' efforts and, together with the governing bodies supplement and support, strengthens the opportunities for coaches to grow in different directions.

Conceptualizing the Coach Development Pathway

When considering the snapshots from the four countries provided here, several commonalities exist providing insights into the current state of coach development around the globe. Each of these case studies describes complex structures that embed flexibility to support coach-centered development in a variety of formal and informal settings. While there is some consistency in the developmental systems, they are also highly individualized to accommodate individual coach needs in systems that encourage continued professional development both within and outside of sport.

Flexible Structure

Although the idea of flexibility within structure may seem counterintuitive, it is a hallmark of the findings from research examining the coach development journey (Wright et al., 2007; Duarte & Culver, 2014; Ciampolini et al., 2019) and is represented in the cases presented here. Many coach development systems around the globe are structured to integrate content and practice milestones at increasing levels of difficulty over a period of time. However, few of these systems impose hard deadlines and rigid requirements forcing coaches out of the system. Rather, the systems offer flexibility in the process to allow for individual differences in learning needs, financial and time resources, and career goals. The challenge, therefore, is to create systems with multiple entry points and a variety of methods for assessing knowledge and competency that are balanced with quality assurance.

Learning Environments

As referenced in the descriptions of international systems provided and consistent with literature, many coach development systems are evolving a blend of formal, informal, and non-formal learning (Nelson et al., 2006; Mallett et al., 2009; Walker et al., 2018). Lara-Bercial and Mallett (2016) describe the importance of blended learning environments in their review of the developmental pathways of serial winning coaches, noting the preferred learning opportunities of coaches spanned several approaches. While basic sport science information is incorporated in many coach development systems, a recognition of the value and importance of applied practice is emerging. Many systems are incorporating a set number of coaching hours or internships as part of the long-term development system. Creators of advanced systems recognize the value of mentoring and reflection on professional development and are incorporating those strategies in the non-formal and informal settings to maximize and expedite learning (McQuade & Nash, 2015). The challenge with incorporating multiple learning contexts is the learning that occurs within each context will be highly individualized and results as a function of the depth and breadth of coach knowledge, reflection, and experience. In other words, it's difficult to predict which types of learning experiences in which environments will produce lasting change for the coach, exacerbating the difficulty in coach developer systems design. Therefore, while it poses challenge to the systems designer, the inclusion of formal, non-formal, and informal learning environments in coach development systems is essential.

Individualized Coach Development

Research examining developmental pathways of coaches confirms that career trajectories are highly individualized but include some similarities (Nash & Sproule, 2009; Lara-Bercial & Mallett, 2016; Paquette & Trudel, 2018). Undoubtedly, sport participation impacts coaching trajectory for most coaches (Blackett et al., 2020), but the timing and way in which it impacts career development is very individualized (Rynne, 2014). Further, the coaching context plays a pivotal role in coach development. As noted by Turner et al. (2012), the development of expertise in sport coaching is not a finite process, but rather one that is ongoing and impacted by contextual elements. Rather than simply considering coach development as a linear process, understanding the complex process of development that happens over time in multiple contexts is highly individualized. Turner and colleagues (2012) drive this point home with reference to understanding the development of expert math teachers, where Martinovic (2009) noted "Expertise is not a characteristic of a person; rather, it is the product of the interaction between the person and the environment" (p. 168). However, Turner and colleagues argue that, while many coaches experience some similar elements of their developmental process, they also experience challenges and "knowledge loss" when changing contexts. Each of the four cases presented here references the individuality of the coach development processes in their respective countries. Without a doubt, the variability in the coach development process adds a complexity to the system, particularly as coaches progress beyond novice levels. Interestingly, all the cases presented here referenced the important role of the coach developer. The emergence of this role and clarity around the responsibilities have increased in the last five years, resulting in the launch of a revised version of the International Coach Developer Framework this year (ICDF, 2022). The expansion of the role to include more mentoring in support is likely a reflection of the individualized nature of the coach development pathway.

Ongoing Coach Development

None of the coach development systems described here rely on a one-time coach training to meet the needs of coaches. Rather, the systems are designed for long-term coach development that reflects the ongoing learning that coaches experience across the lifespan, both within and outside of sport (Nash & Sproule, 2009; Werthner & Trudel, 2009). Duarte and Culver (2014) were able to demonstrate this concept using life-story methodology in their study of the career development of a developmental adaptive sailing coach. A primary conclusion from this study was the coach learned through a series of formal, informal, and non-formal learning situations that spanned several years and positions, and she attributed portions of her knowledge base to non-sport contexts. Crespo et al. (2006) provide an analysis of what this long-term process looks like in connection to a specific NGB system, the different coaching roles coaches possess, and the accumulation of knowledge over time. They concluded coach development systems had to be highly individualized and should adopt a long-term approach (30+ years) to expertise development. Reflecting on the four cases described here, it's evident more coach development programs are adopting a long-term approach. While the extended nature of coach development poses a challenge to systems designers, it is crucial to the developmental process for the coach.

The Next Evolution of Coach Development Systems

The cases presented in this chapter present a snapshot of the current state of coach development around the globe. However, significant system evolution is taking place. Historically, coach development programs included a heavy emphasis on the traditional lecture format with gaining "knowledge" as the primary objective. In the latest evolution, we can see an emphasis on learning through doing and reflection. We also see the value of directed reflection and other personalized support (Milistetd et al., 2018) provided by a workforce of coach developers. This shift from pedagogical approaches to andragogical approaches to coach development has significantly impacted the systems as these approaches require greater access to information and to other coaches; in other words, more complex systems require more resources. It's quite possible that future systems, specifically when considering the needs of expert coaches, involve more heutagogical approaches to coach development where coaches' capacity to identify their own needs and demonstrate autonomy in the learning process is the objective of the system. In this advanced approach, the coach would maintain autonomy of the learning process, including pace, content, and approach. Coach developers, on the other hand, would connect the coach to resources when requested, supporting the metacognition of the coach and supporting the coach in thinking about the implementation of new knowledge to practice. To make this transition, another shift in the approach to coach development at the systems level must occur. The recent shift in systems to focus on learning through doing and providing coach support through coach developers, along with the internationally connected workforce of coach developers, has laid the groundwork for this next evolution.

References

Blackett, A.D., Evans, A.B., & Pigott, D. (2020). Negotiating a coach identity: A theoretical critique of elite athletes' transitions into post-athletic high-performance coaching roles. *Sport, Education, and Society, 26*, 663–675.

Brazil (1998). Law 9696. Physical Education Professional regulation. Diário oficial da União (Official journal of State). Retrieved March 22, 2022, from http://www.planalto.gov.br/ccivil_03/leis/l9394.htm.

Brazil (2018). National guidelines for undergraduate programs in physical education. Resolution CNE/CES no. 6 December 18, 2018. Brasília: Ministério da Educação. Retrieved March 22, 2022, from http://portal.mec.gov.br/docman/dezembro-2018-pdf/104241-rces006-18/file.

Brazilian Olympic Committee (2022). Molding the future of Olympism and sport: The Olympic Agenda 2020+5. https://www.cob.org.br/en/galleries/news/lenny-abbey-presented-the-plans-of-the-international-olympic-committee-for-the-future/.

Ciampolini, V., Camiré, M., Salles, W., Nascimento, J. V., & Milistetd, M. (2021). Researcher, coach developer, and coaches' perspectives on learner-centered teaching in a rugby coach education program. *International Sport Coaching Journal*. https://doi.org/10.1123/iscj.2020-0100.

Ciampolini, V., Milistetd, M., & Rynne, S. (2019). Research review on coaches' perceptions regarding the teaching strategies experiences in coach education programs. *International Journal of Sport Science & Coaching, 14*, 216–228.

Côté. J. & Gilbert, W. (2009). An integrative definition of coaching effectiveness and expertise. *International Journal of Sport Science and Coaching, 4*, 307–323.

Crespo, M., McInerney, P., & Reid, M. (2006). Long-term tennis coach development. *ITF Coaching & Sports Science Review, 40*, 1–4.

Dieffenbach, K. & Villalon, C. (2021). *National Sport Census*. WVU Center for Applied Coaching and Sport Science and United States Center for Coaching Excellence.

Duarte, T. & Culver, D. (2014). Becoming a coach in developmental adaptive sailing: A lifelong learning perspective. *Journal of Applied Sport Psychology, 26*, 441–456.

Galatti, L., dos Santos, Y. Y. S., & Korsakas, P. (2019). A coach developers' narrative on scaffolding a learner-centred coaching course in Brazil. *International Sport Coaching Journal, 6*(3), 339–348. https://doi.org/10.1123/iscj.2018-0084

Gano-Overway, L., Thompson, M., & Van Mullem, P. (2020). *National Standards for Sport Coaches: Quality Coaches, Quality Sports*. Jones and Bartlett.

Hongo, J. (2013). "Probe details coach's abuses against boy who killed himself." *The Japan Times*. https://www.japantimes.co.jp/news/2013/02/16/national/social-issues/probe-details-coachs-abuses-against-boy-who-killed-himself/.

International Council for Coaching Excellence (2013). *International Sport Coaching Framework*. Version.1.2. Human Kinetics.

International Council for Coaching Excellence (2014). *International Coach Developer Framework*. Version 1.1. ICCE.

International Council for Coaching Excellence (2022). *International Coach Developer Framework*. Version 1.2. ICCE.

Japan Sports Association (2013). 日本体育協会「『グッドコーチに向けた「7つの提言」』について」 (JSPO on "Seven Recommendations for becoming a Good Coach"). https://www.japan-sports.or.jp/news/tabid92.html?itemid=3051 (in Japanese) (accessed 4/17/2022).

Japan Sports Association (2016). 日本体育協会「平成27年度コーチ育成のための「モデル・コア・カリキュラム」作成事業」報告書 (Report on the Model Core Curriculum for coach development project in FY2013). https://www.japan-sports.or.jp/Portals/0/data/ikusei/doc/curriculum/modelcore.pdf (in Japanese) (accessed 4/17/2022).

Japan Sport Association (2022). 日本スポーツ協会「公認スポーツ指導者制度の改定について」 (JSPO revision of the Official Sports Coaching System). https://www.japan-sports.or.jp/coach/tabid1198.html (in Japanese) (accessed 4/17/2022).

Kira, T. & Yamashita, T. (2013, February 20). 体罰容認4割 「したことある」6割 中学校教員、春日市教委が調査 (40% approve of corporal punishment, 60% "have used it" Junior high school teachers surveyed by Kasuga City Board of Education), *Asahi Shimbun*, p. 2.

Lara-Bercial, S. & Mallett, C.J. (2016). The practices and developmental pathways of professional and Olympic serial winning coaches. *International Sport Coaching Journal*, 3, 221–239.

Mallett, C.J., Trudel, P. Lyle, J., & Rynne, S. (2009). Formal vs. informal coach education. *International Journal of Sports Science & Coaching*, 4, 325–364.

Martinovic, D. (2009). Being an expert mathematics online tutor: What does expertise entail? *Mentoring & Tutoring: Partnership in Learning*, 17, 165–185.

McQuade, S. & Nash, C. (2015). The role of the coach developer in supporting and guiding coach learning. *International Sport Coaching Journal*, 2, 339–346.

Milistetd, M., Ciampolini, V., Mendes, M. S., Cortela, C. C., & Nascimento, J. V. (2018). Student-coaches perceptions about their learning activities in the university context. *Revista Brasileira de Ciencias Do Esporte*, 40(3), 281–287. https://doi.org/10.1016/j.rbce.2018.03.005.

Milistetd, M., Ciampolini, V., Salles, W. D. N., Ramos, V., Galatti, L. R., & Nascimento, J. V. (2016). Coaches' development in Brazil: Structure of sports organizational programmes. *Sports Coaching Review*, 5(2), 138–152. https://doi.org/10.1080/21640629.2016.1201356.

Milistetd, M., Trudel, P., Mesquita, I., & Nascimento, J. V. (2014). Coaching and coach education in Brazil. *International Sport Coaching Journal*, 1(3), 165–172. https://doi.org/10.1123/iscj.2014-0103.

Miller, A.L. (2013) *Discourses of Discipline: An Anthropology of Corporal Punishment in Japan's Schools and Sports*, Institute of East Asian Studies, University of California.

Nash, C. & Sproule, J. (2009). Career development of expert coaches. *International Journal of Sports Science & Coaching*, 4, 121–138.

Nelson, L.J., Cushion, C.J., & Potrac, P. (2006). Formal, nonformal, and informal coach learning: A holistic conceptualization. *International Journal of Sports Science & Coaching*, 1, 247–259.

Nihon Taiiku Kyoukai (ed.) (2016). 指導者育成50年のあゆみ (50 years of coach development in Japan), Japan Sports Association [in Japanese].

Nippon Sport Science University Coach Developer Academy (ed.) (2021a). *Learning to be a Coach Developer*, Nippon Sport Science University (https://nittaidai.repo.nii.ac.jp/?action=repository_uri&item_id=1731&file_id=37&file_no=1) (2022/4/8 accessed).

Nippon Sport Science University Coach Developer Academy (ed.) (2021b). *Project commissioned by Japan Sports Agency Support for Formation of International Sport Academies 2014–2020 project report*, Nippon Sport Science University (https://nittaidai.repo.nii.ac.jp/?action=repository_uri&item_id=1733&file_id=17&file_no=1) (2022/4/8 accessed).

Paquette, K. & Trudel, P. (2018). Learner-centered coach education: Practical recommendations for coach development administrators. *International Sport Coaching Journal, 5,* 169–175.

Rynne, S. (2014). Fast-tracked and traditional path coaches: Affordances, agent, and social capital. *Sport, Education, and Society, 19,* 299–313.

Salles, W. (2019). *Development of learner centered education: Strategies, perceptions and implications for initial university training in Physical Education.* [Unpublished PhD Thesis]. Federal University of Santa Catarina.

Shiga, H. (2013, August 10). 体罰教員、全国6721人　綿密調査で増大 2012年度 (6,721 teachers having used corporal punishment nationwide in FY2012, number increased according to an in-depth survey), *Asahi Shimbun,* p. 1.

Trudel, P., Milistetd, M., & Culver, D. M. (2020). What the empirical studies on sport coach education programs in higher education have to reveal: A review. *International Sport Coaching Journal,* 7(1), 61–73. https://doi.org/10.1123/iscj.2019-0037.

Turner, D., Nelson, L., & Potrac, P. (2012). The journey *IS* the destination: Reconsidering the expert sports coach. *Quest, 64,* 313–325.

Walker, L.F., Thomas, R., & Driska, A.P. (2018). Informal and nonformal learning for sport coaches: A systematic review. *International Journal of Sports Science & Coaching, 13,* 694–707.

Werthner, P. & Trudel, P. (2009). Investigating the idiosyncratic learning paths of elite Canadian coaches. *International Journal of Sports Science & Coaching, 4,* 433–449.

Wright, T., Trudel, P., & Culver, D. (2007). Learning how to coach: The different learning situations reported by youth ice hockey coaches. *Physical Education and Sport Pedagogy, 12,* 127–144.

4
COACH EDUCATION AND DEVELOPMENT

The What and How to

Kristen Dieffenbach and Stiliani "Ani" Chroni

For as long as sport has existed, there have been people supporting athletes. Identified as trainers, managers, and coaches, these individuals have been tasked with supporting athletic development and performance. For many, the word coach conjures images that often mirror Hollywood icons like Mr. Miyagi from the Karate Kid asking his athlete to 'Wax on, wax off' and Coach Gordon Bombay from the Mighty Ducks turning a diverse group of young ice hockey players into a winning team. Culturally we think we 'know' what a coach is and what a coach does (e.g., male figure with good technical, tactical, disciplinary skills) and by extension we also think we 'know' what it takes to coach (e.g., to know the sport, have played the sport himself). While we are very interested in how coaches do what they do to develop athletes and teams (see literature on coach effectiveness, e.g., Côté & Gilbert, 2009), there has been far less attention paid to how coaches develop themselves. Any reduction of the coaching role to stereotypical views about what a coach is and does undermines the need for a critical examination of the professional development and ongoing learning for individuals tasked with supporting athletic growth and performance.

The International Council for Coaching Excellence (ICCE), an international organization that advocates for and supports the professionalization of coaching through the International Sport Coaching Framework (ISCF) (ICCE, 2013), defines coaching as a complex task and a process. 'A process of guided improvement and development in a single sport and at identifiable stages of development' (p. 14) that requires professional contextual knowledge and skills as well as inter- and intra-personal knowledge and skills and self-awareness of values (Figure 4.1; ICCE, 2013). The ISCF was developed through a process of consultation, development, and collaborative research involving multiple sport organizations and scholars from various countries over a two-year time period to capture how individuals around the world execute the primary tasks of the coaching profession.

DOI: 10.4324/9781003251309-5

Professional Knowledge	The sport
	Athletes
	Sport science
	Coaching theory and methodology
	Foundational skills
Interpersonal Knowledge	Social context
	Relationships
Intrapersonal Knowledge	Coaching philosophy
	Lifelong learning

FIGURE 4.1 Coach knowledge areas (see ICCE, 2013, p. 30).

Sport coaching, however, is often viewed as a calling rather than a vocation (Lu et al., 2022; Ronkainen et al., 2022). Despite the many expectations placed on the sport experience (e.g., Rynne, 2014; Trudel et al., 2020), and by extension the coach (US Department of Health and Human Services, 2019), previous playing experience has been heavily prioritized over intentional and holistic preparation. In both the sporting communities and the literature, the title of 'coach' is seen to infer qualification for the job, with scoreboard outcomes and/or level of participation being used as the litmus test of proof. This has allowed the conversation around coach learning to focus on what individuals prefer and overlook those areas related to what the job requires, despite the growing literature and expectations on long-term development, supportive experiences (Sport for Life Society, 2019), and mental health (Henriksen et al., 2020). This chapter explores what individuals in coaching positions prefer regarding learning, as well as what those in the profession need and what has been found to be effective in supporting initial and ongoing coaching knowledge and skill development.

A Look at Learning

Learning is a central idea within the sports space. Children begin by learning to crawl before they walk and add more fundamental movement skills to their repertoire (e.g., jumping and hopping) before progressing to learning the array of sport-specific movements skills that will open up a lifetime of opportunities to learn the technical, tactical, psychological, and social nuances of their sports. Coaches, as teachers and leaders, are instrumental in supporting athlete learning (Jones, 2006). Coaches, within their role in sport, being a learner and learning themselves, are also crucial to the role of being an effective teacher (Trudel et al., 2013). Learning is a complex process that occurs over time and can be viewed both theoretically and through a practice lens (see Jarvis & Watts, 2017 for a detailed review). Within the context of this chapter, we place emphasis on the practical application of engaging in learning and creating learning environments to support professional development for individuals in sport coaching roles.

The experience of learning can occur formally, non-formally, or informally (Nelson et al., 2006; Walker et al., 2018). All forms of learning require engagement from the learner to move an experience beyond engagement and entertainment to impact on thoughts and behavior growth and/or change. However, not all learning situations are equal. Best practice in learning design supports formal and non-formal modes that are constructed and directed by experts, while informal learning is, by nature, self-directed. Across all three potential modes of learning, it is necessary for the learner to take an active role; engage with ownership and reflect and purposefully translate the lived experiences into knowledge and lessons learned.

How Coaches Learn when Trends Override Science

While traditionally, qualifications to coach have been unimportant with exception of playing time and experience in the sport, recent research findings challenge us to revisit what kind of and how experiences of the past are brought into one's coaching practice. For instance, McMahon et al. (2020) challenge us on how toxic coaching practices can be recycled and Denison et al. (2017) describe outdated styles of play being socially reproduced without being questioned. In English, when a word's meaning changes due to capitalization it is known as a capitonym (MacMillan Dictionary, 2022). The impact of the capitalization of the word 'Coach' can be seen not only within teams but also in broader communities where a 'Coach' can take on celebrity (or villain) status. The cultural 'you played, therefore you can coach' convention (Lyle, 2020) contributes to an individual mindset that influences learning expectations and values that is supported by ego- and sociocentric beliefs that prior experience is sufficient. This same mindset has been noted in sports organizations, with the fast tracking of retiring athletes into the coaching realm with minimal preparation beyond playing time (Rynne, 2014). This trend of elite athletes retiring from competitive sport and transitioning to coaching roles, oftentimes high-performance roles via a fast-track pathway that national governing bodies provide, is widespread across many sports and countries and has attracted the attention of researchers whose findings contest the affordance of past playing experiences for the coaching role (see Blackett et al., 2021; Chroni et al., 2021; Mielke, 2007). Furthermore, the trend appears to create inequalities for coach development. In Norway, coaches perceived more coach development opportunities being provided to elite athletes (Chroni et al., 2018) while Rynne's (2014) research on fast-tracking shed light to a luxury that is not afforded to coaches without a competitive-athletic background. The emphasis on experience as the sole coaching requirement can also be seen in the carry over into coach practices where opportunities to intern, shadow, or assist a renowned coach are prioritized (Bertz & Purdy, 2011; Mesquita et al., 2014; Turner & Nelson, 2009).

The early and limited examinations of coach learning focused on the preferences of individuals in existing coaching roles (e.g., Chroni et al., 2018;

Dieffenbach, 2003) or on coach learning as a mediator for the athlete's learning and/or experience (Sheehy et al., 2019). Outside of formal organizational learning spaces, coaches have reported attending sport-specific conferences, seeking out books and internet topics to explore solutions or gather new ideas, and personal interactions with others (their athletes included), also informal mentorship as strategies to support their own learning (e.g., Chroni, et al., 2018; Wright et al., 2007). In the largest national profiling study conducted to date (Chroni et al., 2018), a majority of the 5,977 individuals coaching in Norway indicated a desire to expand their knowledge and skills, with primary focus on their sport-specific knowledge. Informal knowledge sources, like shadowing other coaches, athlete feedback and reflection were reported as most impactful for improving coaching practices. Interestingly, while the coaches reported lack of time as a key obstacle for advancing their knowledge and skills, they preferred in person weekend courses that require more time than online courses. Such findings suggest the value and possible trust of a relational coaching community and the preference for informal learning among peers. Interestingly, these coaches believed that the best thing in coaching were the opportunities to stimulate enjoyment in their athletes yet when asked what knowledge and skills they want to expand, they said sport-specific ones and not inter- or intra-personal, revealing a lack of clarity and knowledge on skills that support their work. This suggests that desired knowledge may not always align with necessary knowledge to support best practices.

What Coaches Need: Science to Override Empiricism

In their integrated definition of sport coaching that brought together the importance of expertise and effectiveness, Côtè and Gilbert (2009) highlight the value of considering the knowledge an individual has, the context in which they work, and the expectations for athlete impact or outcomes. The ISCF (ICCE, 2013) using this definition as a foundation identified the primary functions of a coach as: (1) to set a vision and strategy, (2) to shape the environment, (3) to build relationships, (4) to conduct practices and prepare for competition, (5) to read and react to the field, and (6) to learn and reflect. The breakdown of the responsibilities of the coaching role creates a foundation for knowledge and skill needs. The ISCF categorizes these knowledge and skills into three larger areas, inter-personal, intra-personal, and professional, that support building relationships, self-reflection, as well as 'what' to and 'how to' teach, respectively, all informed and guided by an individual's values, goals, and philosophy (Figure 4.2).

The ISCF knowledge and skill-based model (ICCE, 2013) for the sport coaching profession also stresses the importance of context. The model recognizes that, while there are common roles and responsibilities that span levels of play and groups of participants, the knowledge, and skills a coach needs to execute their responsibilities will be different depending on the setting within which one is coaching. For example, understanding the developmental needs

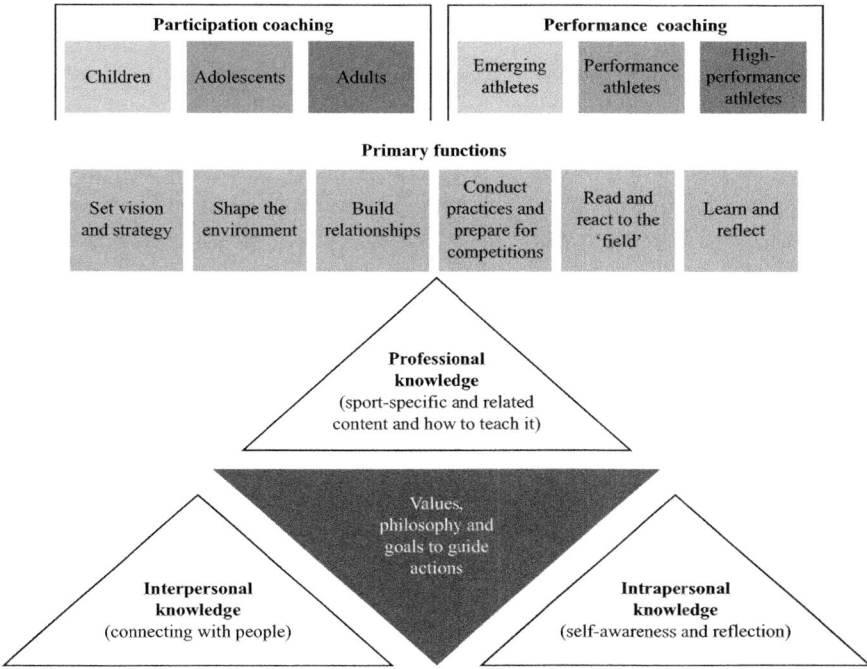

FIGURE 4.2 International Sport Coaching Framework (see ICCE, 2013, p. 31).

of elementary school multicultural participants and the cultural competencies and skills to build effective relationships will be different from those needed to effectively coach competitive adults (Chroni & Kavoura, 2020; Kontos, 2009; Sarkar et al., 2015; Schinke et al., 2012). Each sport context may bring together multiple cultures related to the athlete(s) or team's sport, ethnic backgrounds religions, genders, sexual orientation, and other social factors that differentiate people. Cultural awareness and sensitivity knowledge and skills can aptly support a coach's reflexivity, communication, relations, and coaching practices (see Chapter 14). Considering that cultural sport coaching is an underdeveloped area, one would need to borrow knowledge and skills from the sport psychology literature (e.g., see Chroni & Kavoura, 2020; Kontos, 2009; Sarkar et al., 2015; Schinke et al., 2012). Similarly, beyond social development, the sport setting influences physical, tactical, and technical readiness expectations and development needs as do variables like level of competition, the participant's chronological age, number of years in sport training, physical and psychological maturation, competitive interest, motivation, cultural background, and goals. The complexities of having the knowledge and skills to coach effectively in any given context suggest that the initial and continuing education to coach requires breadth and depth beyond a linear model of preparation focused on the beginner through elite sport continuum.

Another important area for examination when considering education within the profession is the distinctions between 'what to' and 'how to' coach. Content knowledge, the 'what to' is informed not only by sport-specific knowledge but also by the underlying sport sciences such as exercise physiology and sport psychology (see Figure 4.1). Designing appropriate training plan designs requires both an understanding of the sport-specific demands as well as an understanding of physiology and how to elicit appropriate change to meet those demands. Coaching also requires making corrections to help shape athlete development and performance. The knowledge of what 'good' looks like needs to be supported by an understanding of how and what to focus on (observation) as well as an understanding what to correct (decision-making and prioritization for short-term and long-term skill development) and how. The 'how' of correction to provide appropriate and meaningful feedback, at the right time, and in a supportive manner is also an essential and learned professional skill (Figure 4.3). A recent meta-analysis of 78 studies looking at the impact of negative feedback on the intrinsic motivation of children and youth reported that while positive feedback was more motivating, compared to neutral and no feedback. However, negative feedback had no effect on one's intrinsic motivation when '(a) the feedback statement included instructional details on how to improve, (b) criterion-based standards were used to provide feedback, and (c) feedback was delivered in-person' (Fong et al., 2019, p. 121).

When considering the educational needs within the profession of coaching, it is also essential not to lose sight of the learners themselves, beyond the content and skills. An individual's investment in their own learning is an essential part of growth and development. However, it cannot be assumed that all potential learners place the same value on learning both as a process and for the knowledge and skill content to be gained. It also cannot be assumed that all potential learners will have the skills and personal resources to do so, particularly if the

Biomechanics	Organizational psychology	Sport pedagogy
Education	Pedagogy	Sport philosophy and ethics
Exercise physiology	Physical education	Sport psychology
Motor control	Physiology	Sports medicine
Motor development	Psychology	Sport nutrition
Motor learning	Psychology of coaching	Sport sociology
Nutrition	Sport history	Strength and conditioning

FIGURE 4.3 Sciences supporting best practices in sport coaching.

current educational structure is limited. An environment that presents an optimal level of personal challenge, supports the development of learning strategies, and encourages individuals in examining the 'why' behind their decisions is as critical as the information itself.

An Emerging Profession

Since the publication of Coleman Griffith's book *Psychology of Coaching* in 1926, the exploration of the role of the coach within the sport has grown. Coaches are an asset to athlete development (e.g., Blom et al., 2013; Conroy & Coatsworth, 2006) and are central to positive outcomes (McCullick et al., 2009). Countless trade books that present coaching formulas for success through a focus on drills, practice plans, and the 'what' of coaching can be found online and in bookstores. Biographies about the practices of highly revered coaches like John Wooden, Phil Jackson, Pat Summit, Eddie Jones, and Jürgen Klinsmann are top sellers. Discussions about 'how' to coach, and to the point of this chapter, how best to develop coaching skills and knowledge, are only beginning to become a mainstream conversation.

Despite the recognized complexities of sport performance and growing fields of knowledge within sport science focused on optimizing growth, the need for preparation and the practice of coaching itself have historically been presented and summarized through platitudes and reported 'best practices' of revered individuals from high-profile sport settings. More recently, a conversation about professional development and recognition of coaching as a profession has begun to emerge (Davis, 2003; Duffy et al., 2011). The increased focus on evidence informed coaching (Stodter, 2021), long-term athletic development (e.g., Bergeron et al., 2015; Pichardo et al., 2018), positive youth development through sport (Fraser-Thomas, et al., 2005), and athlete well-being (see Campbell et al., 2021; Giles et al., 2020) have been a part of the call for the professionalization of sport coaching (Duffy et al., 2011; North et al., 2019). The goal within this movement is to recognize and support the value of quality coaching practices as well as to support the individuals within those roles and their preparation and ongoing development.

The role of education within the sports realm with an emphasis on the role of the sport coach as a teacher was examined in the book *The Sport Coach as Educator: Re-conceptualizing Sport Coaching* (Jones, 2006). While conceptually the classification of the 'coach as teacher' and thus the need for clear preparation guidelines is well reasoned, this paradigm shift is challenging for the applied sporting community. Steeped in tradition, sport has fiercely loyal fans (see Coombs & Osborne, 2022) and strong programmatic cultures (Blackett, 2017; Blackett et al., 2021) that compounds the natural human resistance to change (Jost, 2015). Calls for the professionalization of the sport coaching role have also discussed broader cultural and system changes needed to support this evolution (see Dieffenbach, 2019; Duffy et al., 2011; Lara-Bercial & Bales, 2022; North et al., 2019). Within sport spaces there are opportunities to educate parents, athletes, coaches, and administrators about current best practices that support quality coaching. Increased education is needed about what quality coaching both looks like and requires. System changes are needed as well to provide and support contextual focused coaching and to support knowledge application and replication in the field (see Chapters 11 and 12).

Standards of Professionalism and Professional Development

Standards of professionalism within coaching are becoming more and more prominent. Many sport federations and governing bodies have developed coaches' codes of ethics or professional standards of behavior (e.g., Fédération Internationale de Football Association, 2020; Sports Coach UK, 2009; World Rowing, 2021). Guiding professional documents like the *National Standards for Sport Coaches*, 3rd Edition (Society of Health and Physical Educators, 2019), the *Standards for Higher Education: Sport Coaching Bachelor Degrees* (International Council for Coaching Excellence, 2016), and *Universal Standards on Sport Integrity: Youth Development and Child Protection* (Sport Integrity Global Alliance, 2020) provide guidance on essential areas of knowledge and skill for coaches. Additionally, many sport organizations have requirements for coaches. However, these requirements can range from strict children sport regulations of Norway (Norges Idrettsforbund, 2015) to more sophisticated levels of training such as an academic degree in Brazil (Milistetd et al., 2014) to the Union of European Football Associations (UEFA, 2021) coaching license levels to minimal, and even no requirements within many youth sport settings.

Beyond the formal standards being developed by countries and organizations and across the sport industry, there are also less formal but no less important occupational socialization standards (for an overview of occupational socialization theory, see Pennington, 2021). The occupational 'norm' for coaching will vary in different settings and can either reinforce or hinder individual's learning valuation and investment within the profession. The development of a strong professional philosophy can help individuals clarify their personal beliefs and identity as a coaching professional which can assist them in navigating within the broader landscape of sport. A professional philosophy should clarify who an individual aspires to be as a professional and the teaching behaviors and leadership style that they plan to espouse within a given context.

Universal Learning Needs within the Coaching Profession

Despite the differences between the sports themselves, the foundational sport science information that guide skill acquisition, training plan design, relationship building, and many other core coaching responsibilities share a lot of coaching overlap. The shared knowledge and skills needed for coaching suggest opportunities for cross sport collaborations in both creating and engaging in professional development.

Universal or shared learning needs should also be considered based on the adult classification of most coaches, both volunteer and paid ones. Recognizing these individuals as adult learners, the principles of adult learning (see Knowles et al., 2015; Merriam & Bierema, 2013) can be used to support the development of engaging and impactful educational experiences. Providing an opportunity for learners to draw on personal experiences and construct new knowledge, adult learning focuses on supporting learning through environment construction in formal and informal spaces as well as skill development for learning to continue in non-formal spaces. Among adult learners, learning experiences have been found to be most impactful when they are self-directed, solve or address recognizable challenges or problems, and align with the individual's motivation and readiness to engage.

Côté and Gilbert (2009) as well as Gilbert and Côté (2013) thoroughly discussed the universal need for coaches to develop knowledge based on experience, self-awareness, and reflection. Reflection is the process that renders experience into knowledge (Dewey, 1997; Gilbert & Trudel, 2001; Kolb, 1984; Schön, 1983, 1987). Reflective learning via critical reflection practices appears to be a suitable and effective approach for providing coaches with both content- and context-related understanding, particularly when the latter is socially derived (see Knowles et al., 2005; Peel et al., 2013). Critical reflection practices are performed purposely *on* action, *in* action (see Schön, 1983, 1987) as well as *for* action (Dixon et al., 2013) supporting the translation of a mere experience to implicit and explicit knowledge depending on the experience, one's aims, and levels of awareness. Experiential learning requires self-awareness, providing the coaches with insight into who they are, why they behave as they do, and giving them direction for self-improvement. Both reflection and awareness skills are teachable and form a robust foundation for coach development (ICCE, 2013).

Contextual Learning Needs within the Coaching Profession

The previous section highlighted universal learning considerations related to both the common responsibilities across sport contexts and common best practices within adult learning. There are, of course, also contextual differences to consider in the professional learning experiences of coaches. Specific contextual situations that should be examined include the needs of the novice versus more experienced coach. Across a continuum that Schempp and colleagues (2006) categorized as ranging from novice to proficient to expert, the depth of possible learning related to each context and the unique needs of 'within' sport transition.

Understanding the athlete level and the sport setting will help both the learner and those responsible for constructing learning environments to comprehend the challenges and expectations experienced when coaching within a given context. Educational experiences that align with the learner's experiences will both enhance engagement and ownership and support development of meaningful and applicable knowledge.

Traditionally, sport education for coaches has been considered as a linear journey from youth/beginner information up through high-performance knowledge. Programs and individuals following this model begin with an entry level course, with each subsequent educational opportunity focusing on progressively higher levels of sport engagement. This approach has overlooked several important elements relative to the contextual education needs within the sport coaching profession (ICCE, 2013) by failing to recognize that value of developing knowledge depth within a set context. Engaging in development opportunities that help an individual move beyond a novice stage toward professional competency and proficiency requires greater knowledge and a more nuanced and skilled ability to apply what is known (Schempp et al., 2006).

Moving Toward Evidence-Informed Coaching in the Aftermath of Trends and Traditions

At the center of the professional learning conversation in coaching is the individual who coaches. Recognizing the individual who is seeking to grow their knowledge and skills to be more effective and efficient helps break the assumptions of title-inferred preparation. Developing coach-related sciences further and breaking free from stereotypes, trends, and traditions of the past appears to be the way forward. What coaches need based on the existing literature may sometimes challenge what coaches want and prefer and how national governing bodies prepare their coaches. In national profiling studies conducted in Finland, Norway, and the UK (see Chroni et al., 2018; Hämäläinen & Blomqvist, 2016; McIlroy, 2015) coaches' preferences call for a more content-driven approach (i.e., sport-specific) and less competency-driven (i.e., inter- and intra-personal) to their learning and development. Nonetheless, the 'how to' is equally important with the 'what to' while it can also ensure that coaching as a profession walks away from old styles or toxic styles of coaching. The simplistic convention 'you played; therefore, you can coach,' is being contested by sport sociologists, psychologists, and coach education scholars from both the individual and the system lens. From the individual standpoint, knowledge and competence supported by personal athletic experience are not enough (Chroni et al., 2020; Rynne, 2014), and the past appears to be challenging on one's coaching identity and philosophy (Blackett et al., 2017, 2021). From the system standpoint, the wish of governing bodies to preserve the culture of their environment (i.e., playing and coaching philosophies) by recruiting their retiring athletes as coaches (Blackett, 2017; Chroni & Dieffenbach, 2022) is challenged by what the literature suggests about coaches' needs (knowledge and skills) for performing the coaching role tasks as well as the idea of breaking away from old styles of coaching.

While we acknowledge the benefit, even advantage, for coaches who possess past athletic experiences of their own, we firmly believe that raw past experiences cannot rightly serve the tasks of the coach. One's athletic experience of the past needs to be revisited and reflected upon for it to be translated into knowledge and competency, and for the individual to step away from the identity of the past and step into the identity of the present, the coaching one. The individual needs to let go of the embodied knowledge and skills developed through experience and move into science-informed coaching with the advantage of enhanced understanding because of past athletic experiences. More research is needed to better understand both the individuals and the system and what keeps coaching stereotypes, trends, and traditions alive. Stereotypes, trends, and traditions impede science-informed coach education, development, and practice and delay progress in the professionalization of the coaching profession.

References

Bergeron, M. F., Mountjoy, M., Armstrong, N., Chia, M., Côté, J., Emery, C. A., Fagenbaum, A., Hall, G., Kriemler, S., Léglise, M., Malina, R. M., Pensgaard, A. M., Sanchez, A., Soligard, T., Sundgot-Borgen, J., van Mechelen, W., Weissensteiner, J. R., & Engebretsen, L. (2015). International Olympic Committee consensus statement on youth athletic development. *British Journal of Sports Medicine, 49*(13), 843–851. https://doi.org/10.1136/bjsports-2015-094962.

Bertz, S., & Purdy, L. (2011). Coach education in Ireland: observations and considerations for high performance. *Journal of Coaching Education, 4*(3), 29–43. https://doi.org/10.1123/jce.4.3.29.

Blackett, A. (2017). *Understanding the 'fast-track' transition between elite athlete and high-performance coach in men's association football and rugby union: A grounded theory* (Doctoral dissertation, University of Lincoln).

Blackett, A. D., Evans, A., & Piggott, D. (2017). Why 'the best way of learning to coach the game is playing the game': Conceptualising 'fast-tracked' high-performance coaching pathways. *Sport, Education and Society, 22*(6), 744–758. https://doi.org/10.1080/13573322.2015.1075494.

Blackett, A. D., Evans, A. B., & Piggott, D. (2021). Negotiating a coach identity: A theoretical critique of elite athletes' transitions into post-athletic high-performance coaching roles. *Sport, Education and Society, 26*(6), 663–675. https://doi.org/10.1080/13573322.2020.1787371.

Blom, L. C., Visek, A. J., & Harris, B. S. (2013). Triangulation in youth sport: Healthy partnerships among parents, coaches, and practitioners. *Journal of Sport Psychology in Action, 4*(2), 86–96. https://doi.org/10.1080/21520704.2012.763078.

Campbell, N., Brady, A., & Tincknell-Smith, A. (Eds.) (2021). *Developing and Supporting Athlete Wellbeing: Person First, Athlete Second*. Routledge. https://doi.org/10.4324/9780429287923.

Chroni, A., Dieffenbach, K., & Pettersen, S. (2021). An exploration of recruitment of elite athletes to coaching within federations. *International Sport Coaching Journal, 8*(3), 315–327. https://doi.org/10.1123/iscj.2020-0056.

Chroni, S., & Kavoura, A. (2020). Cultural praxis. In D. Hackfort & R. Schinke (Eds.), *The Routledge International Encyclopedia of Sport and Exercise Psychology* (pp. 227–238). Routledge.

Chroni, S., Nilsen, D. A., Medgard, M., Sigurjonsson, T., & Solbakken, T. (2018). Profiling the coaches of Norway: A national survey report of sports coaches and coaching. Elverum, NOR: Inland Norway University of Applied Sciences. Accessed at https://brage.bibsys.no/xmlui/handle/11250/2569671.

Chroni, S. A., & Dieffenbach, K. (2022). Facilitating and supporting the elite athlete-to-coach transition: Lessons learned from Norwegian coaches and federations. *Journal of Sport Psychology in Action, 13*(1), 27–39. https://doi.org/10.1080/21520704.2020.1861145.

Chroni, S. A., Pettersen, S., & Dieffenbach, K. (2020). Going from athlete-to-coach in Norwegian winter sports: Understanding the transition journey. *Sport in Society, 23*(4), 751–773. https://doi.org/10.1080/17430437.2019.1631572.

Conroy, D. E., & Coatsworth, J. D. (2006). Coach training as a strategy for promoting youth social development. *The Sport Psychologist, 20*(2), 128–144. https://doi.org/10.1123/tsp.20.2.128.

Coombs, D. S., & Osborne, A. C. (Eds.) (2022). *Routledge Handbook of Sport Fans and Fandom*. Routledge. https://doi.org/10.4324/9780429342189.

Côtè, J. & Gilbert, W. (2009). An integrative definition of coaching effectiveness and expertise. *International Journal of Sports Science & Coaching, 4*(3), 307–323. https://doi.org/10.1260/174795409789623892.

Davis, P. (2003). Why coaches education? *The Olympic Coach, 15*(4), 16–17.

Denison, J., Mills, J.P., & Konoval, T. (2017). Sports' disciplinary legacy and the challenge of 'coaching differently'. *Sport, Education and Society, 22*(6), 772–783. https://doi.org/10.1080/13573322.2015.1061986.

Dewey, J. (1997). *Experience and Education*. Touchstone. (Original work published 1938)

Dieffenbach, K. (2008). Exploring learning among USA cycling licensed coaches. *Journal of Coaching Education, 1*(2), 19–37. https://doi.org/10.1123/jce.1.2.19.

Dieffenbach, K. (2019). Frameworks for coach education and development. In K. Dieffenbach & M. Thompson (Eds.), *Coach Education Essentials* (pp. 3–16). https://doi.org/10.5040/9781718206694.ch-001.

Dixon, M., Lee, S., & Ghaye, T. (2013). Reflective practices for better sports coaches and coach education: Shifting from a pedagogy of scarcity to abundance in the run-up to Rio 2016. *Reflective Practice, 14*(5), 585–599. https://doi.org/10.1080/14623943.2013.840573.

Duffy, P., Hartley, H., Bales, J., Crespo, M., Dick, F., Vardhan, D., Nordmann, L., & Curado, J. (2011). Sport coaching as a 'profession': Challenges and future directions. *International Journal of Coaching Science, 5*(2), 93–123.

Fédération Internationale de Football Association (2020). *FIFA Code of Ethics*. Retrieved from https://digitalhub.fifa.com/m/174b40d0256de722/original/upxpc0qzxqdgipiiejuj-pdf.pdf.

Fong, C.J., Patall, E.A., Vasquez, A.C., & Stautberg, S. (2019). A meta-analysis of negative feedback on intrinsic motivation. *Educational Psychology Review, 31*, 121–162 https://doi.org/10.1007/s10648-018-9446-6.

Fraser-Thomas, J. L., Côté, J., & Deakin, J. (2005). Youth sport programs: An avenue to foster positive youth development. *Physical Education & Sport Pedagogy, 10*(1), 19–40. https://doi.org/10.1080/1740898042000334890.

Gilbert, W., & Côté, J. (2013). A focus on coaches' knowledge. In P. Potrac, W. Gilbert & J. Denison (Eds.), *Routledge Handbook of Sports Coaching* (pp. 147–159). Routledge.

Gilbert, W. D., & Trudel, P. (2001). Learning to coach through experience: Reflection in model youth sport coaches. *Journal of Teaching in Physical Education, 21*(1), 16–34. https://doi.org/10.1123/jtpe.21.1.16.

Giles, S., Fletcher, D., Arnold, R., Ashfield, A., & Harrison, J. (2020). Measuring well-being in sport performers: Where are we now and how do we progress? *Sports Medicine, 50*(7), 1255–1270. https://doi.org/10.1007/s40279-020-01274-z.

Griffith, C. (1926). *Psychology of Coaching: A Study of Coaching Methods from the Point of Psychology*. Scribner.

Hämäläinen, K., & Blomqvist, M. (2016). A new era in sport organizations and coach development in Finland. *International Sport Coaching Journal*, 3(3), 332–343. https://doi.org/10.1123/iscj.2016-0075.

Henriksen, K., Schinke, R., McCann, S., Durand-Bush, N., Moesch, K., Parham, W. D., Larson, C., Cogan, K., Donaldson, A., Poczwardowski, A., Noce, F., & Hunziker, J. (2020). Athlete mental health in the Olympic/Paralympic quadrennium: A multi-societal consensus statement. *International Journal of Sport and Exercise Psychology*, 18(3), 391–408. https://doi.org/10.1080/1612197X.2020.1746379.

International Council for Coaching Excellence (2013). *International Sport Coaching Framework Version 1.2*. Human Kinetics.

International Council for Coaching Excellence (2016). *ICCE Standards for Higher Education: Sport Coaching Bachelor Degrees*. Retrieved from https://www.icce.ws/_assets/files/icds-draft-4-final-november-23.pdf.

Jarvis, P., & Watts, M. (Eds.). (2017). *The Routledge International Handbook of Learning*. Routledge. https://doi.org/10.4324/9780203357385.

Jones, R. L. (2006). *The Sports Coach as Educator: Reconceptualizing Sport Coaching*. Routledge. https://doi.org/10.4324/9780203020074.

Jost, J. T. (2015). Resistance to change: A social psychological perspective. *Social Research*, 82(3), 607–636. https://doi.org/10.1353/sor.2015.0035.

Knowles, M. S., Holton, E., & Swanson, R. (2015). *The Adult Learner: The Definitive Classic in Adult Education and Human Resource Development* (8th ed.). Elsevier.

Knowles, Z., Borrie, A., & Telfer, H. (2005). Towards the reflective sports coach: Issues of context, education and application. *Ergonomics*, 48(11–14), 1711–1720.

Kolb, D. A. (1984). The process of experiential learning. In D. A. Kolb (Eds.), *Experiential learning: Experience as the Source of Learning and Development* (pp. 20–38). Prentice-Hall, Inc.

Kontos, A. P. (2009). Multicultural sport psychology in the United States. In R. J. Schinke & S. J. Hanrahan (Eds.), *Cultural Sport Psychology* (pp. 103–116). Human Kinetics.

Lara-Bercial, S., & Bales, J. (2022). The challenge of doing coach education and development in the 21st century: Past, present, and future trends. In K. Petray & J. de Jong (Eds.), *Education in Sport and Physical Activity: Future Directions and Global Perspectives* (pp. 10–23). Routledge. https://doi.org/10.4324/9781003002666-3.

Lu, W. C., Lin, S. H., Cheng, C. F., & Wu, M. H. (2022). When coaching is a calling: A moderated mediating model among school sports coaches. *International Journal of Sports Science & Coaching*, 17(5), 964–973. https://doi.org/10.1177/17479541221103778

Lyle, J. (8 May 2020). Getting it right for everyone: Sport coaching and the adult participation domain. *The Sport Journal*, 21(3): 1–18. Retrieved from https://thesportjournal.org/article/getting-it-right-for-everyone-sport-coaching-and-the-adult-participation-domain/.

MacMillan Dictionary (2022). Capitonym. Retrieved from https://www.macmillandictionary.com/us/buzzword/entries/capitonym.html.

McCullick, B., Schempp, P., Mason, I., Foo, C., Vickers, B., & Connolly, G. (2009). A scrutiny of the coaching education program scholarship since 1995. *Quest*, 61(3), 322–335. https://doi.org/10.1080/00336297.2009.10483619.

McIlroy, J. (2015). The coaching panel 2015: A report on coaches and coaching in the UK. Sport Coach UK.

McMahon, J., Zehntner, C., McGannon, K. R., & Lang, M. (2020). The fast-tracking of one elite athlete swimmer into a swimming coaching role: A practice contributing to the perpetuation and recycling of abuse in sport? *European Journal for Sport and Society*, 17(3), 265–284. https://doi.org/10.1080/16138171.2020.1792076.

Merriam, S. B., & Bierema, L. L. (2013). *Adult Learning: Linking Theory and Practice*. John Wiley & Sons.

Mesquita, I., Ribeiro, J., Santos, S., & Morgan, K. (2014). Coach learning and coach education: Portuguese expert coaches' perspective. *The Sport Psychologist, 28*(2), 124–136. https://doi.org/10.1123/tsp.2011-0117.

Mielke, D. (2007). Coaching experience, playing experience and coaching tenure. *International Journal of Sports Science & Coaching, 2*(2), 105–108. https://doi.org/10.1260/174795407781394293.

Milistetd, M., Trudel, P., Mesquita, I., & do Nascimento, J. V. (2014). Coaching and coach education in Brazil. *International Sport Coaching Journal, 1*(3), 165–172. https://doi.org/10.1123/iscj.2014-0103.

Nelson, L. J., Cushion, C. J., & Potrac, P. (2006). Formal, nonformal and informal coach learning: A holistic conceptualisation. *International Journal of Sports Science & Coaching, 1*(3), 247–259. https://doi.org/10.1260/174795406778604627.

Norges Idrettsforbund (2015). *Children's rights in sport: The provisions on children's sport.* Retrieved from https://www.idrettsforbundet.no/contentassets/482e66e842fa4979902ecc77f0c05262/36_17_barneidrettsbestemmelsene_eng.pdf.

North, J., Piggott, D., Lara-Bercial, S., Abraham, A., & Muir, B. (2019). The professionalisation of sport coaching. In R. Thelwell & M. Dicks (Eds.), *Professional Advances in Sports Coaching* (pp. 3–21). Routledge. https://doi.org/10.4324/9781351210980-2.

Peel, J., Cropley, B., Hanton, S., & Fleming, S. (2013). Learning through reflection: Values, conflicts, and role interactions of a youth sport coach. *Reflective Practice, 14*(6), 729–742. https://doi.org/10.1080/14623943.2013.815609.

Pennington, C.G. (2021). Concepts in occupational socialization theory. *Curriculum and Teaching Methodology, 4*, 1–3. https://www.clausiuspress.com/article/658.html.

Pichardo, A. W., Oliver, J. L., Harrison, C. B., Maulder, P. S., & Lloyd, R. S. (2018). Integrating models of long-term athletic development to maximize the physical development of youth. *International Journal of Sports Science & Coaching, 13*(6), 1189–1199. https://doi.org/10.1177/1747954118785503.

Ronkainen, N. J. Ryba, T. V., McDougall, M., Tod, D., & Tikkanen, O. (2022). Hobby, career or vocation? Meanings in sports coaching and their implications for recruitment and retention of coaches. *Managing Sport and Leisure, 27*(4), 381–396. https://doi.org/10.1080/23750472.2020.1803108.

Rynne, S. (2014). 'Fast track' and 'traditional path' coaches: Affordances, agency and social capital. *Sport, Education and Society, 19*(3), 299–313. https://doi.org/10.1080/13573322.2012.670113.

Sarkar, M., Hill, D. M., & Parker, A. (2015). Reprint of: Working with religious and spiritual athletes: Ethical considerations for sport psychologists. *Psychology of Sport and Exercise, 17*, 48–55. https://doi.org/10.1016/j.psychsport.2014.09.001.

Schempp, P. G., McCullick, B., & Mason, I. S. (2006). The development of expert coaching. In R. Jones (Ed.), *The sports coach as educator: Reconceptualizing sport coaching* (pp. 163–179) Routledge. https://doi.org/10.4324/9780203020074.

Schinke, R. J., McGannon, K. R., Parham, W. D., & Lane, A. M. (2012). Toward cultural praxis and cultural sensitivity: Strategies for self-reflexive sport psychology practice. *Quest, 64*, 34–46. https://doi.org/10.1080/00336297.2012.653264.

Schön, D.A. (1983). *The Reflective Practitioner. How professionals think in action.* London: Temple Smith.

Schön, D. A. (1987). *Educating the Reflective Practitioner: Toward a New Design for Teaching and Learning in the Professions.* Jossey-Bass.

Sheehy, T. L., Dieffenbach, K., & Reed, P. (2019). An exploration of coaching research in Journal of Applied Sport Psychology from 1989 to 2017. *Journal of Applied Sport Psychology, 31*(3), 352–365. https://doi.org/10.1080/10413200.2018.1494642.

Society of Health and Physical Educators (2019). *National Standards for Sport Coaches* (3rd ed.). Retrieved from https://www.shapeamerica.org/standards/coaching/.

Sport for Life Society (2019). Long term development in sport and physical activity 3.0. https://sportforlife.ca/wp-content/uploads/2019/06/Long-Term-Development-in-Sport-and-Physical-Activity-3.0.pdf.

Sport Integrity Global Alliance (2020). *SIGA Universal Standards on Sport Integrity: Youth Development and Protection in Sport*. Retrieved August 1, 2022, from https://siga-sport.com/youth-development-child-protection/.

Sports Coach UK (2009). *Code of Practice for Sports Coaches*. Retrieved from https://www.cambridge.gov.uk/media/3147/code-of-practice-for-sports-coaches.pdf.

Stodter, A. (2021). *Myths about Learning Styles in Sport Coach Education*. Sequoia Books.

Trudel, P., Culver, D., & Werthner, P. (2013). Looking at coach development from the coach-learner's perspective: Considerations for coach development administrators. In P. Potract, W. Gilbert, & J. Denison (Eds.), *Routledge Handbook of Sports Coaching* (pp. 375–387). Routledge.

Trudel, P., Milestetd, M., & Culver, D. M. (2020). What the empirical studies on sport coach education programs in higher education have to reveal: A review. *International Sport Coaching Journal*, 7(1), 61–73. https://doi.org/10.1123/iscj.2019-0037.

Turner, D., & Nelson, L. (2009). Graduate perceptions of a UK university based coach education programme, and impacts on development and employability. *International Journal of Coaching Science*, 3(2), 3–28.

US Department of Health and Human Services. (2019). *National Youth Sport Strategy*. Retrieved from https://health.gov/sites/default/files/2019-10/National_Youth_Sports_Strategy.pdf.

UEFA (2021). *UEFA coaching licenses: Every course for which UEFA sets minimum criteria*. Retrieved from https://www.uefa.com/insideuefa/news/0268-11ef810e73fb-f340214d3d91-1000–uefa-coaching-licences-every-course-for-which-uefa-sets-minimum/.

Walker, L. F., Thomas, R., & Driska, A. P. (2018). Informal and nonformal learning for sport coaches: A systematic review. *International Journal of Sports Science & Coaching*, 13(5), 694–707. https://doi.org/10.1177/1747954118791522.

World Rowing (2021). *Appendix S11: By-laws to article 58: World Rowing code of ethics*. Retrieved from https://worldrowing.com/wp-content/uploads/2021/03/2021-World-Rowing-Code-of-Ethics.pdf.

Wright, T., Trudel, P., & Culver, D. (2007). Learning how to coach: The different learning situations reported by youth ice hockey coaches. *Physical Education and Sport Pedagogy*, 12(2), 127–144. https://doi.org/10.1080/17408980701282019.

5
TRANSITIONS INTO COACH DEVELOPMENT

You Coached So You Can Develop

Kristen Dieffenbach and Stiliani "Ani" Chroni

This chapter explores the role and ways of development of the coach developer as well as the knowledge and skills they need to support the preparation and ongoing development of sport coaches. Task responsibilities for the coach developer role range from creating and providing coaching education programming and resources through high-performance team management and individual executive leadership consultation. Given the importance placed on the coaching role within sport, the coach developer role has emerged as a valuable supporting profession for supporting high-quality coaching practices and the individuals within the profession. Through their work with coaches, coach developers also play an important role in creating healthy, safe, and productive experiences for the athletes, the coaches, and the sport in general. The emerging understanding and recommendations for best practice for providing coach development, in preparing coach developers, and embedding them within the sport systems, are also discussed and future research recommendations are offered.

Like many professions that initially emerged organically to meet identified needs within an industry, the role of the coach developer evolved differently within different organizations to address issues such as coach recruitment and retention, coaching assignment management, coach training, and coaching performance evaluation and assessment. The foundation for the current coach developer role discussions in the literature and in the sport settings can be seen across the wide range of titles given to the position that supports and manages those in the coaching role such as coach educator, coaching director, or coaching education manager. In many cases the role of the coach developer is not a stand-alone position, instead coach development related tasks are embedded within the job descriptions of positions such as talent director or athlete development coordinator. Consequently, there is currently no common background or pathway for becoming a coach developer within most sport settings (see Chapter 2). While individuals fulfilling these

DOI: 10.4324/9781003251309-6

roles commonly possess some level of coaching experience, the multiple roles they are asked to perform as educators, facilitators, presenters, mentors, and assessors (ICCE, 2013) bring attention to the need for preparation beyond coaching experience as the coach developer role requires a level of expertise in learning and in optimizing opportunities for others to learn (Stodter & Cushion, 2019).

The Emerging Coach Developer Role

The use of the term "coach developer", as an umbrella term for a continuum of professional support responsibilities, has been increasingly common as the conversation about quality, scalable coach preparation, assessment, and development continues to grow. While coaching has long been practiced as an informal apprenticeship profession (Cassidy & Rossi, 2006; Cushion et al., 2003; see Chapter 7), increasingly organizations are recognizing the need for both foundational preparation and ongoing professional growth support that is based on evidence-informed best practice guidelines, raising the preparation expectations beyond personal athletic experiences and peer mentorship in coaching (McQuade & Nash, 2015).

The role of the coach has been identified as central to supporting development, potential, and well-being of the athletes, and prior athletic experience has been recognized as being insufficient and not a reliable indication of proper preparation to coach (Rynne, 2014). While many organizations have a long-standing history of offering educational programs, for example, UK Sport coaching courses, National Federation of High School Sports Coaching Principles courses, that provide content-based "what to" knowledge. This has elicited concerns about how to create quality sport experiences focusing on ensuring that coaches develop not only proper "what" to knowledge, but also the "how to" skills necessary to support age, stage, and contextually appropriate training, positive youth development, and holistic well-being (e.g., US Department of Health and Human Services, 2019). Thus, the role of the coach developer is emerging as a central position capable of bridging the gap between content and application to support individuals as they develop and coach.

It can be tempting to view the coach developer as an all-inclusive position responsible for all aspects of coach education and development with a singular set of guidelines, similar to the view of coaching. The growing call for preparation suited to the demands of the coaching position and the needs of the athletes (Dieffenbach, 2019) necessitates an expansion of thinking when considering the preparation and contextualization (knowledge and skills) of the coach developer role. Developing a clear understanding of the coach developer position requires us to also consider some different preparation pathways that recently emerged around the world which we shall do further in this chapter.

Defining the Coach Developer Role

Despite the cultural value placed on coaching and the calls for professionalization (North et al., 2019), coaching as a profession is still an emerging one (Moustakas et al., 2022). Alongside, the role of coach developer is evolving as

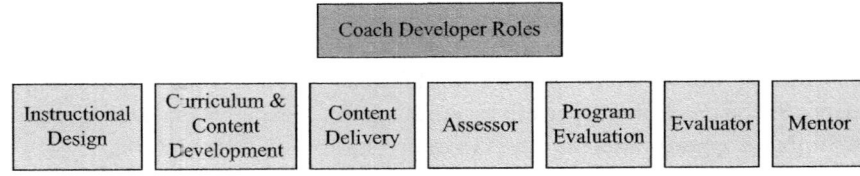

FIGURE 5.1 Coach developer roles.

well, creating an opportunity to consider the central tasks and responsibilities of the role, the frameworks of operation, and the intersectional knowledge necessary to build and support a sustainable standard of professionalism within sport coaching systems.

The ICCE formally defined the coach developer role in the *International Coach Developer Framework* (2014). Bales and colleagues (2019) updated the coach developer role as being "to engage, facilitate, educate and support coaches' learning and behavioural change through a range of opportunities, and many include leading organisational change in coach education programmes and coaching systems" (p. xix). The first professional standard for coach developers published in 2021 by the UK-based Chartered Institute for the Management of Sport and Physical Activity highlights the responsibility of the coach developer to have a style that is "flexible and adaptable" such that supportive and "caring relationships" can be formed and where the nature of the relationship is educational and developmental support (p. 4). Figure 5.1 shows some of the central roles currently associated with the coach developer position (Dieffenbach et al., 2019).

The Coach Developer within the Sport System

Although coach developers can fulfill a variety of roles within a sport system, the position itself represents only one piece of a very complex system (Edwards et al., 2020) that works with and impacts coaches. Understanding how and where the coach developer position fits within the sport system helps identify areas of knowledge and the skills an individual needs to acquire and practice to be effective and impactful as a professional (see Chapters 11 and 12).

At the highest levels of sport, such as national governing sport organizations and international sport federations, coach developers support the coaches directly and indirectly through coaching education systems. From a leadership perspective, an organization's coaching education system should be based on best practice recommendations and often provides resources and certification pathways for a broader sport system (Chroni et al., 2020; Rynne, 2014). More directly, coach developers work with high-performance coaches, providing educational and developmental support and opportunities. Additionally, coach developers play an important role in the design and delivery of fast-track programs that create a career entry pathway for athletes making a within-sport transition into coaching. At a more grassroots level, within regional and local sport organizations, coach developers are commonly tasked with delivering the coaching education workshops within the border coach credentialing programs offered by governing bodies. Depending on the nature and type of organization, coach developers may also support coaches through field assessments, ongoing professional development workshops, and one-on-one mentoring. This complexity can create challenges for the coach developer surrounding the role clarity and expectations one holds.

Contextualizing the Coach Developer Role

The recognition of the breadth and depth of sport settings across which coaches may perform in and thus need preparation support for and development support within highlights the need to understand the range of knowledge and skills a coach developer needs to be effective. The sport continuum spans from participation to performance environments that encompass recreational and development opportunities as well as high-performance and competitive experiences for individuals across the lifespan (Ellerton, 2019). While there is overlap, the different coaching contexts require unique knowledge and skill sets that need to be taught and supported. Clarifying the contextual range of coaching skills and knowledge to be taught creates a foundation for considering the educational preparation necessary to be an effective coach developer.

The 2019 IMG Academy's Leaders Performance Institute report "Coaching the Coaches" explored the responsibilities of coach developers working within high-performance sport. In the report the coach developer was defined as a leadership role that provides the "right level of both support and challenge for coaches to ensure time is provided to learn and opportunity is provided to grow" (p. 3). Denison (2019) supports this approach to coach development in his identification of a key coach developer role that supports individuals to think beyond the parameters of their own sporting experience.

Who the Coach Developer Develops

Within the broad picture of sport, the coach developer might work with anyone coaching across the continuum of sport. However, most positions will occur within a particular environment, allowing the responsibilities of the coach developer to be targeted within a specific context. In high-performance settings, the professional nature of coaching positions means individuals in coaching roles are adults. For career professionals in high-performance coaching, the pathway appears to begin shortly after completing their athletic career (Blackett et al., 2021; Chroni et al., 2020) with some transitioning on their own and others being identified and fast tracked by their sport federations (e.g., Chroni et al., 2021). These individuals commonly have high levels of sport experience from the athlete perspective but have not had an opportunity to develop the knowledge and understanding necessary to coach (Chroni et al., 2021) creating an opportunity for coach developers to assess and individualize development.

Similar to the high-performance space, the majority of the coaching positions in youth sport are filled by individuals over the age of 18. Large-scale sport landscape projects designed to gain a better understanding of the sport coaching workforce (see Chroni et al., 2018; Dieffenbach & Villalon, in press; Hämäläinen & Blomqvist, 2016; McIlroy, 2015) suggest that the average age of individuals who coach can be classified as middle aged and that coaching is a secondary and/or volunteer role as opposed to a full-time position. Unlike in high-performance settings, in the developmental sport context, it is not uncommon for individuals volunteering to coach to have had an extended gap of time since their playing days, lower level or even no experience with the sport prior to coaching, therefore requiring different types of coach development support. Additionally, a majority of youth sport volunteers coach their child's team (Busser & Carruthers, 2010; Silverberg et al., 2001) suggesting a different motivation than individuals who are following a professional career pathway, further supporting the importance of contextually relevant coach developer knowledge and skill development.

Regardless of the setting, overlap does exist across coaching contexts requiring coach developers to have a working knowledge of educational theory and sport-specific knowledge, as well as the skills to appropriately assess needs as well as select and utilize the appropriate learning strategies. For example, a coach developer needs to understand both pedagogy, the applied teaching practices that should inform the coaching practices of those working with youth and adolescent athletes, as well as adult learning theory which focuses on supporting the ongoing development of experienced individuals, such as is commonly seen in the workplace.

Coach Developer: Essential Knowledge

Understanding where coach developers operate and who they support gives a foundation for identifying the essential knowledge areas a coach developer needs to have at their disposal to adequately support the professional development of sport coaches. It is also helpful to consider the primary responsibilities of the sport coach, regardless of context: (1) setting a vision and strategy, (2) shaping the environment, (3) building relationships, (4) conducting practices and preparing for competitions, (5) reading and reacting to the growth of the sport, and (6) learning and reflecting as a professional, identified in the *International Sport Coaching Framework* (ICCE, 2013). Essential coach developer knowledge areas to support coach learning include educational design, adult learning, sport sciences and kinesiology, sport and exercise psychology, and meta-cognition and reflection as well as an understanding of the sport system itself.

Educational Design

Coaching education has often used a content knowledge approach, providing information through lectures and manuals that focus on knowledge sharing to prepare novice and support experienced coaches within many credential or certification models. Alternately, Schempp and McCulloch (2006) drew on the best practices master teacher preparation literature to suggest that concurrent knowledge and skill development are necessary to progress from early career (foundational) coaching to the levels of competency and proficiency that are seen in highly effective educators (coaches). Teacher preparation models (see Clandinin & Husu, 2017) provide guidance for a "train the trainer" framework coach developers can utilize in shaping the sport coaching environment. Within this framework the coach is the learner being trained and the coach developer is the individual responsible for training or supporting coach learning and development both directly (e.g., classroom) and indirectly (e.g., field assessment). Although the core principles of coaching are universal, the age of the student (athlete) and the nature of the subject matter (sport) require different coach preparation models. For example, both the content (what is taught) and skills of teaching (how it is taught) are different for a primary youth sport coach versus a high-performance coach, requiring coach developers to have the knowledge and skills to appropriately adjust their teaching and support strategies.

Adult Learning Theory

Within education, adult learning theory (Merriam, 2018) focuses on the unique needs of learners, recognizing that an individual's maturity and life experience influence what they need and want from learning opportunities, the strategies that best support ongoing development, and the role the individuals themselves play within the process. The seven essential principles of adult learning have been identified as: self-directed, transformational, mental orientation to learning, experiential, mentorship, motivational, and readiness to learn. Understanding the principles and being able to design and implement learning strategies to support professional development helps create a learner-centered environment that will serve the age group with which the coach is working.

Sport Science and Kinesiology

Modern coaching is informed by the expanding body of knowledge from the sport science and kinesiology disciplines such as exercise physiology, strength and conditioning, motor development, and motor learning as well as the sub-disciplines that examine these areas contextualized for environments with children, youth, high performance, and older participants. As a coach developer, it is not necessary to be an expert across the sport science disciplines. However, having a broad understanding of the disciplines supports efforts to develop a coach's "what" and the "how" knowledge and skills.

Sport and Exercise Psychology

Sometimes considered a sub-discipline within the area of sport science and kinesiology (in the US), sport psychology can be viewed both for the work associated with participants' development and performance as well as the coaches as performers themselves. Understanding how individuals impact the sporting experience and the sporting experience impacts individuals, as well the various complexities of interactions within sport environments are essential parts of the inter- and intrapersonal areas of knowledge that Côté and Gilbert (2009) identified as foundational knowledge and skill areas for sport coaches. For the coach developer, a working knowledge of the essential principles and theories of sport psychology that inform what a coach does (human behavior and actions) as well as an understanding of the psychology of coaching (human performance) are critical areas of knowledge.

Decision-Making and Reflection

Understanding the development and application of both decision-making and reflection skills supports the coach developers' growth as professionals and informs the work they do to support the coach's development. Grounded in critical thinking (see Lai, 2011a; Lyons & Ward, 2017) and meta cognitive theory (Lai, 2011b), the decision-making process is central to providing feedback and making leadership and teaching choices. The study of reflection, in particular self-reflection for professional development and growth (see Schön, 2017), provides insight into understanding the impact of facilitating reflection to support others in making meaning of knowledge and experiences.

Sport System

While common themes exist across the kinesiology disciplines that inform modern coaching practices, the settings within which coaches and coach developers work have unique cultures. Thus, similar to coaches (Blackett et al., 2019), to best navigate the environment coach developers need to have or develop organizational structure knowledge, as well as understand the relationships between sports organizations and federations, key players, programs and policies, and the micro politics within the systems. This idea is further supported by Walsh and Carson (2019) in their call for the use of signature pedagogies, particularly when constructing appropriate to the context-learning experiences for new or novice coaches.

Coach Developer: Essential Skills

Recognizing the necessary disciplinary and principle knowledge central to creating and cultivating professional development environments for others highlights the need to also consider the skills a coach developer needs to develop for supporting learning facilitation. Figure 5.2 provides an overview of essential teaching and facilitation skills to fulfill the coach developer role.

Transitions into Coach Development   75

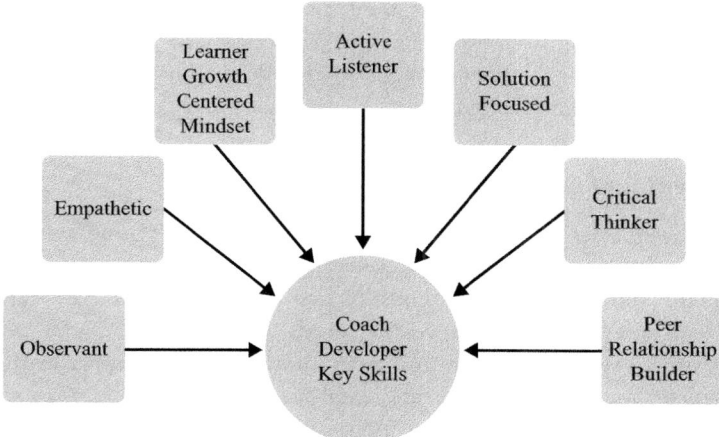

FIGURE 5.2   Sciences supporting best practices in sport coaching.

Facilitation of Learning

Ultimately, learning is the acquisition of knowledge that results in a change in behavior and/or knowledge of the learner, however the environment created for learning does play a role in the quality and ultimately the impact of the experience (Mostafa, 2017). Learning, of course, occurs across a wide range of formal, informal, and non-formal settings. Within the scope of the coach developer role, one is responsible for being able to construct and adapt learning environments that best suit the content to be learned and the needs of the learner (coach).

The emerging literature on the practice of developing coaches explores a range of strategies and skills coach developers can employ to create effective learning experiences. Dray and Howells (2019) explored the use of e-portfolios as a learning communication and reflection tool which they found to be effective in supporting student coaches within an academic program. At the other end of the spectrum, when working with high-performance coaches, Rodrigue and colleagues (2019) placed an emphasis on the importance of the interpersonal relationship between a coach and the coach developer to facilitate the trust necessary for personal development. This recommendation was supported by Dohme and colleagues (2019) where the ability to shape professional motivation to learn in others was associated with creating inclusive and welcoming environments, supporting the development of a personal "why" and by personally being approachable and supportive.

Facilitating within a community of practice setting is another opportunity to shape and support a learning environment that will enrich learning opportunities (Culver et al., 2019). In their examination of large-scale use of a community of practice design to support coaching education, Culver and colleagues discussed the challenges of balancing covering necessary content and focusing on the learner's needs. The implications for coach developer skill development suggest that ongoing in-action reflection is necessary to adequately attend and adjust to relevant environmental cues as well as be able to adjust and adapt delivery strategies to suit available time.

Assessment and Evaluation

The responsibilities of the coach developer to support learning are not always limited to the classroom. Coach development is also done using observation, assessment, and evaluation methods. When utilizing subjective strategies to consider progress, the coach developer needs to have a clear understanding of the assessment rubric as well as understand how to properly apply it. Best practice models should be used to create templates that support the prioritization of feedback to optimize learning. In more direct or one-to-one facilitation, the parameters of performance or process evaluations need to be transparent with the learning goals being set by the coach to be supported by the coach developer.

Mentoring

Despite the frequent casual use of the word mentoring, it is important to clearly define mentorship within the scope of the coach developer role (see Stodter & Cushion, 2019; Trudel et al., 2013). Mentorship responsibilities of the coach developer role can be informal or formal depending on the context and the expectations within the sport system. Formally, mentorship pairings may be assigned or requested to support a coaching transition or professional development. Informally, ongoing relationship building within a sport system creates opportunities for providing situational support and guidance. In their examination of coach mentors within the sport coach developer context, Leeder and colleagues (2019) suggest that these individuals have "a crucial role in the development of sports coaches, through co-constructing new knowledge, exchanging ideas, and encouraging the use of reflective practice" (p. 270). Doing so requires the ability to develop interpersonal relationships as well as a professional identity that embraces the responsibility of the mentor relationship.

Coach Developer Development: System Approach, Individual Journeys, and Missing Links

The past decade has seen a crystallization of the conversation among researchers and practitioners around the role of the coach developer bringing together the need for evidence-informed and applied knowledge from both the sport science literature and the sport context. This cross collaboration has resulted in an emerging area of literature that examines the strategies and models that have been developed to enrich coach learning and support through the coach developer role. We share here three examples of such models that underline diversity and multiplicity as these models emerged within national and international contexts.

Perhaps one of the better-known models within the field has been Nippon Sport Science University's National Coach Developer Academy (NCDA) that was funded by 2020 Tokyo Legacy fund, Sport for Tomorrow, and supported by the ICCE. Over a six-year period, the NCDA Coach Developer Program (CDP) brought together 110 professionals from 42 countries (National Coach Developer Academy, 2021), with a roughly even split between academics, sport governing bodies and international federation professionals who identified with the conceptual role and work associated with coach development. The result of this program includes a growing global community of practice of coach developers that operates both virtually and meets in person, an increase in research related to coach developers and development, and the expansion of the coach developer role within sport leadership organizations (for instance, delivering joint sessions at coaching conferences like the ICCE, USCCE, etc., and conducting research together like Callary et al., 2020). The NCDA CDP also created the opportunity for the founding of the United States Center for Coaching Excellence, a nationally based nonprofit organization that supports coach developers and builds upon the coaching education accreditation process in the United States (USCCE, 2017).

According to Campbell and colleagues (2020), the most valued experiences of the NCDA program for its participants were building a team, practicing together, gaining clarity, and shaping practices back home. Alike teacher education programs (Desimone, 2011), Campbell et al. (2020) concluded that effective CDP are interactive, collaborative, located in practice, and spread over a longer duration. Earlier on, Campbell and Waller (2020) had reviewed 56 studies on CDP and found that majority of them took place within a national accreditation system (38%) followed by CDPs that were part of research initiatives (30%) and then of educational curricula (18%). Majority of the programs were also less than a day long and addressed various sports and coaching contexts (participation, performance, children, youth, adults), leading the researchers to question the impact they may have on coach development. Stodter and Cushion (2019) also addressed coach developers' knowledge and preparations with particular focus on limited learning frameworks used with coach developers (CDs) and how often they rely on self-taught knowledge and come to feel underprepared and restricted in developing others.

Considering the limitations of coach development programs that focus heavily on content-based professional knowledge, the Sport New Zealand Coach Developer Training Program steered its attention toward a competency-driven approach focusing more on the development of interpersonal and intrapersonal skills (Walters et al., 2019). In particular, they recognized that self-regulation exists at the origin of both interpersonal and intrapersonal competencies and used the Self-Determination Theory needs of autonomy, competence, and relatedness (Deci & Ryan, 1985) as the backbone of the NZ CD training program. Based on the premise that meeting one's needs leads to improved self-regulation and higher intrinsic motivation thus better professional engagement, opportunities for meeting one's basic psychological needs are reflected in the activities undertaken and the behaviors modeled within the CD training program (Walters et al., 2019).

In Brazil, coaches need to complete an undergraduate degree in PE that gives them general education on coaching topped by sport-specific coach education offered by sport governing bodies. Brazil's sport governing bodies have not formalized a particular learning pathway for Brazilian coach developers, yet in the case of surfing, the establishment of some sport organizations (e.g., Brazilian Institute of Surf and Santa Catarina Association of Surf Schools & Surfing Specialists) along with the consolidation of knowledge and competences by certain coaches, facilitated the transition from coach-to-coach developer (Brasil et al., 2018). For the Brazilian surfing coach developers, their role is related to sharing knowledge, helping new coaches to develop, and supporting other ones toward professional certification. According to Brasil et al. (2018), the process of becoming a coach developer is a slow one and is mainly envisioned and led by the individual; it is the "movement toward fuller, mature participation; and therefore, the development of skills, understandings, and an identity, [that] led to growing responsibility and participation in different surf-related practices that involved a range of roles until they became coach developers" (p. 357). Aligned with the person-led Brazilian path of becoming a coach developer, Ciampolini et al. (2020) shared how Mille transitioned from being an athlete, to becoming a coach, a coach developer, and lastly a master trainer in rugby. It was his own life events that led Mille in making decisions for evolving in his roles as his personal and professional development was driven by internal and external challenges he created for himself. Mille, like the surfing coach developers of Brasil et al. (2018), took on the challenge of becoming a coach developer upon recognizing the importance he could have toward the growth and development of others.

Implications for the Coach Developer Footprint

As an emerging field tasked with supporting the evolution and professionalization of sport coaching, the role of the coach developer requires investment from both the systems and the individuals within it. Lara-Bercial and Bales (2022) assert that before coach education can be created, delivered, or assessed, it is necessary to assess the function the coach developer will fulfill as well as to identify their competence, knowledge, and values related to coach development and coach education. It appears that the assumption, "You coached, therefore you can develop coaches", is not rich enough for the coach developer role.

This chapter elaborates on the transition into the coach development role considering the coach developer tasks, context, and essential elements for capitalizing on it. Despite the emergence of the role as an important one within the coaching education system, Watts and colleagues (2021a,b) found that adopting and fulfilling this role is not without challenge, depending on the size and scope of the organization in which coach developers work. Their preliminary look at the job realities suggested that further research is needed to assess the pressures that coach developers experience and the strategies for managing these contextual issues. Research has also suggested that further study is needed to examine the strategies of coach developer education that will best support the development of their identity as a learning facilitator (Vinson et al., 2022).

So far, no studies on coach developers, coach developer education, and systems have considered the cultural context within which coach developers exist and perform, and the role it might play when for instance the national culture intertwines with the international, national, or local sport cultures and subcultures (see Skille & Chroni, 2018). The cultural praxis heuristic for research and application (see Chroni & Kavoura, 2020; Ryba & Wright, 2010) is an approach that has not informed coaching, coach development, or coaching science in general. To this day, coaching research and practice are still approached and delivered based on Western ethnocentric cultural assumptions considering that the majority of knowledge and practice advances comes from North America and Europe. According to Ryba and Wright (2010), cultural praxis as a heuristic model has the potential to bridge local with global, monoculture with multiculture, national with international, academic with applied, and theory with practice. Through cultural praxis, scholars and practitioners are encouraged to consider all elements that constitute culture (i.e., race, ethnicity, gender, sexual orientation, religion, community, etc.) not as categorical grouping variables, but as shifting and intersecting discourses that shape one's values, beliefs, and behaviors (see Chroni & Kavoura, 2020; Ryba & Schinke, 2009), which in our case are essential for the role of the coach developer (Lara-Bercial & Bales, 2022). The voices from the field, brought to light by Callary and Gearity (2019b), attest to how novel the coach developer role is, the absence of one-ways-fits all, and the different challenges encountered by those practicing in South Africa, Bhutan, Lesotho, and every other place, indicating how the cultural context can shed light on improved contextualized understanding of, preparation, and support for the coach developer's role and tasks.

References

Bales, J. D., Crisfield, P. M., Ito, M., & Alder, J. P. (2019). Foreword. In B. Callary & B. T. Gearity (Eds.), *Coach Education and Development in Sport: Instructional Strategies* (pp. xvii–xix). Routledge.

Blackett, A. D., Evans, A. B., & Piggott, D. (2019). "They have to toe the line": A Foucauldian analysis of the socialisation of former elite athletes into academy coaching roles. *Sports Coaching Review*, 8(1), 83–102. https://doi.org/10.1080/21640629.2018.1436502.

Blackett, A. D., Evans, A. B., & Piggott, D. (2021). Negotiating a coach identity: A theoretical critique of elite athletes' transitions into post-athletic high-performance coaching roles. *Sport, Education and Society*, 26(6), 663–675. https://doi.org/10.1080/13573322.2020.1787371.

Brasil, V. Z., Ramos, V., Milistetd, M., Culver, D. M., & Nascimento, J. V. (2018). The learning pathways of Brazilian surf coach developers. *International Journal of Sports Science & Coaching, 13*(3), 349–361. https://doi.org/10.1177/1747954117739717.

Busser, J. A., & Carruthers, C. P. (2010). Youth sport volunteer coach motivation. *Managing Leisure, 15*(1–2), 128–139. https://doi.org/10.1080/13606710903448210.

Callary, B., Brady, A., Kiosoglous, C., Clewer, P., Resende, R., Mehrtens, T., Wilkie, M., & Horvath R. (2020). Making sense of coach development worldwide during the COVID-19 pandemic. *International Journal of Sport Communication, 13*(3), 575–585. https://doi.org/10.1123/ijsc.2020-0221.

Callary, B., & Gearity, B. (2019b). Voices from the field: Q&A with coach developers around the world. *International Sport Coaching Journal, 6*(3), 366–369. https://doi.org/10.1123/iscj.2019-0070.

Campbell, S. M., Fallaize, A., & Schempp, P. (2020). Most valued experiences in an international coach developer training programme. *International Sport Coaching Journal, 8*(1), 130–135. https://doi.org/10.1123/iscj.2019-0063.

Campbell, S., & Waller, S. (2020). Systematic review of the contemporary research on coach development programs. *International Journal of Coaching Science, 14*(1), 3–38.

Cassidy, T., & Rossi, T. (2006). Situating learning: (Re) examining the notion of apprenticeship in coach education. *International Journal of Sports Science & Coaching, 1*(3), 235–246. https://doi.org/10.1260/174795406778604591.

Chartered Institute for the Management of Sport and Physical Activity (2021). CIMPSA Professional Standard: Coach Developer. https://www.cimspa.co.uk/globalassets/document-downloads-library-all/education-and-training/prof-standards-and-mts/cimspa-ps-coach-developer-v1.0.pdf.

Chroni, A., Dieffenbach, K., & Pettersen, S. (2021). An exploration of recruitment of elite athletes to coaching within federations. *International Sport Coaching Journal, 8*(3), 315–327. https://doi.org/10.1123/iscj.2020-0056.

Chroni, S., & Kavoura, A. (2020). Cultural praxis. In D. Hackford & R. J. Schinke (Eds.), *The Routledge International Encyclopedia of Sport and Exercise Psychology* (pp. 227–238). Routledge.

Chroni, S., Nilsen, D. A., Medgard, M., Sigurjonsson, T., & Solbakken, T. (2018). *Profiling the coaches of Norway: A national survey report of sports coaches and coaching*. Elverum, NOF: Inland Norway University of Applied Sciences. Accessed at https://brage.bibsys.no/xmlui/handle/11250/2569671.

Chroni, S. A., Pettersen, S., & Dieffenbach, K. (2020). Going from athlete-to-coach in Norwegian winter sports: Understanding the transition journey. *Sport in Society, 23*(4), 751–773. https://doi.org/10.1080/17430437.2019.1631572.

Ciampolini, V., Tozetto, A. V., Milan, F. J., Camiré, M., & Milistetd, M. (2020). Lifelong learning pathway of a coach developer operating in a national sport federation. *International Journal of Sports Science & Coaching, 15*(3), 428–438. https://doi.org/10.1177/1747954120912384.

Clandinin, D. J., & Husu, J. (Eds.) (2017). *The SAGE Handbook of Research on Teacher Education*. Sage.

Côté, J., & Gilbert, W. (2009). An integrative definition of coaching effectiveness and expertise. *International Journal of Sports Science & Coaching, 4*(3), 307–323. https://doi.org/10.1260/174795409789623892.

Culver, D. M., Werthner, P., & Trudel, P. (2019). Coach developers as 'facilitators of learning' in a large-scale coach education programme: One actor in a complex system. *International Sport Coaching Journal, 6*(3), 296–306. https://doi.org/10.1123/iscj.2018-0081.

Cushion, C. J., Armour, K. M., & Jones, R. L. (2003). Coach education and continuing professional development: Experience and learning to coach. *Quest*, *55*(3), 215–230. https://doi.org/10.1080/00336297.2003.10491800.

Deci, E. L., & Ryan, R. M. (1985). *Intrinsic Motivation and Self-Determination in Human Behavior.* Plenum Press.

Denison, J. (2019). What it really means to 'think outside the box': Why Foucault matters for coach development. *International Sport Coaching Journal*, *6*(3), 354–358. https://doi.org/10.1123/iscj.2018-0068.

Desimone, L.M. (2011). A primer on effective professional development. *Phi Delta Kappan*, *92*(6), 68–71. https://doi.org/10.1177/003172171109200616.

Dieffenbach, K. (2019). Frameworks for coach education and development. In K. Dieffenbach & M. Thompson (Eds.), *Coach Education Essentials* (pp. 3–16). Human Kinetics.

Dieffenbach, K., Thompson, M., Low, L., & McQuade, L. (2019). Coaching development within the USA Hockey coach education system. A presentation for USA Hockey. Denver. Colorado.

Dieffenbach, K., & Villalon, C. (in press). National Sport Report. United States Center for Sport Coaching & Center for Applied Coaching and Sport Sciences at West Virginia University.

Dohme, L. C., Rankin-Wright, A. J., & Lara-Bercial, S. (2019). Beyond knowledge transfer: The role of coach developers as motivators for lifelong learning. *International Sport Coaching Journal*, *6*(3), 317–328. https://doi.org/10.1123/iscj.2019-0034.

Dray, K., & Howells, K. (2019). Exploring the use of e-portfolios in higher education coaching programs. *International Sport Coaching Journal*, *6*(3), 359–365. https://doi.org/10.1123/iscj.2018-0082.

Edwards, J., Culver, D., Leadbetter, R., Kloos, K., & Potwarka, L. (2020). "One piece of a big puzzle": Understanding the roles of coach developers through interorganizational relationships in Canada's coach education system. *International Sport Coaching Journal*, *7*(1), 102–108. https://doi.org/10.1123/iscj.2019-0014.

Ellerton, H. (2019). What is the LTAD model and should you be using it? Human Kinetics. https://humankinetics.me/2019/04/12/ltad-model/

Hämäläinen, K., & Blomqvist, M. (2016). A new era in sport organizations and coach development in Finland. *International Sport Coaching Journal*, *3*(3), 332–343. https://doi.org/10.1123/iscj.2016-0075.

International Council for Coaching Excellence (2013). *International Sport Coaching Framework*. Human Kinetics.

International Council for Coaching Excellence (2014). *International Coach Developer Framework*. Version 1.1. ICCE.

Lai, E. R. (2011a). Critical thinking: A literature review. *Pearson Research Reports*, *6*(1), 40–41.

Lai, E. R. (2011b). Metacognition: A literature review. *Always Learning: Pearson Research Report*, *24*, 1–40.

Lara-Bercial, S., & Bales, J. (2022). The challenge of doing coach education and development in the 21st century: Past, present, and future trends. In K. Petry & J. de Jong (Eds.), *Education in Sport and Physical Activity* (pp. 10–23). Routledge.

Leeder, T. M., Russell, K., & Beaumont, L. C. (2019). "Learning the hard way": Understanding the workplace learning of sports coach mentors. *International Sport Coaching Journal*, *6*(3), 263–273. https://doi.org/10.1123/iscj.2018-0069.

Lyons, J., & Ward, B. (2017). *The New Critical Thinking: An Empirically Informed Introduction.* Routledge.

McIlroy, J. (2015). The coaching panel 2015: A report on coaches and coaching in the UK. Leeds: National Coaching Foundation. Sport Coach UK.

McQuade, S., & Nash, C. (2015). The role of the coach developer in supporting and guiding coach learning. *International Sport Coaching Journal*, 2(3), 339–346. https://doi.org/10.1123/iscj.2015-0059.

Merriam, S. B. (2018). Adult learning theory: Evolution and future directions. In K. Illeris (Ed.), *Contemporary Theories of Learning* (2nd Edition) (pp. 83–96). Routledge. https://doi.org/10.4324/9781315147277-6.

Mostafa, A. R. A. (2017). Creating a positive learning environment for adults. *International Journal of Learning and Teaching*, 9(3), 378–387. https://doi.org/10.18844/ijlt.v9i3.525.

Moustakas, L., Lara-Bercial, S., North, J., & Calvo, G. (2022). Sport coaching systems in the European Union: State of the Nations. *International Journal of Sport Policy and Politics*, 14(1), 93–110. https://doi.org/10.1080/19406940.2021.1987291.

National Coach Developer Academy (2021). *Learning to be a Coach Developer*. Nippon Sport Science University.

North, J., Piggott D., Lara-Bercial, S., Abraham, A., & Muir, B. (2019). Professionalization of sport coaching. In R. Thelwell and M. Dicks (Eds.), *Professional Advances in Sport Coaching* (pp. 3–21). Routledge. https://doi.org/10.4324/9781351210980-2.

Rodrigue, F., Trudel, P., & Boyd, J. (2019). Learning from practice: The value of a personal learning coach for high-performance coaches. *International Sport Coaching Journal*, 6(3), 285–295. https://doi.org/10.1123/iscj.2018-0078.

Ryba, T. V., & Schinke, R. J. (2009). Methodology as a ritualized Eurocentrism: Introduction to the special issue. *International Journal of Sport and Exercise Psychology*, 7(3), 263–274 https://doi.org/10.1080/1612197X.2009.9671909.

Ryba, T. V., & Wright, H. K. (2010). Sport psychology and the cultural turn: Notes toward cultural praxis. In G. Tennenbaum & R.J. Schinke (Eds.), *The Cultural Turn in Sport Psychology* (pp. 3–28). Human Kinetics.

Rynne, S. (2014). "Fast track" and "traditional path" coaches: Affordances, agency, and social capital. *Sport, Education and Society*, 19(3), 299–313. https://doi.org/10.1080/13573322.2012.670113.

Schempp, McCullick, B. A., Busch, C. A., Webster, C., & Mason, I. S. (2006). The self-monitoring of expert sport instructors. *International Journal of Sports Science & Coaching*, 1(1). 25–35.

Schön, D. A. (2017). *The Reflective Practitioner: How Professionals Think in Action*. Routledge.

Silverberg, K. E., Marshall, E. K., & Ellis, G. D. (2001). Measuring job satisfaction of volunteers in public parks and recreation. *Journal of Park and Recreation Administration*, 19(1), 79–92.

Skille, E. Å., & Chroni, S. A. (2018). Norwegian sports federations' organizational culture and national team success. *International Journal of Sport Policy and Politics*, 10(2), 321–333. https://doi.org/10.1080/19406940.2018.1425733.

Stodter, A., & Cushion, C. J. (2019). Layers of learning in coach developers' practice-theories, preparation, and delivery. *International Sport Coaching Journal*, 6(3), 307–316. https://doi.org/10.1123/iscj.2018-0067.

Trudel, P., Culver, D., & Werthner, P. (2013). Looking at coach development from the coach-learner's perspective: Considerations for coach development administrators. In P. Potrac, W. Gilbert & J. Denison (Eds.), *Routledge Handbook of Sports Coaching* (pp. 375–387). Routledge.

US Department of Health and Human Services (2019). National Youth Sport Strategy. https://health.gov/sites/default/files/2019-10/National_Youth_Sports_Strategy.pdf.

USCCE (2017). Who we are. Retrieved July, 15, 2022, from https://uscoachexcellence.org/who-we-are/.
Vinson, D., Simpson, H. & Cale, A. (2022). 'I felt I'd lost myself – not really knowing who I was': coach developer learning as negotiating identity through engagement, imagination and alignment. *Sport, Education and Society*. https://doi.org/10.1080/13573322.2022.2038126.
Walsh, J., & Carson, F. (2019). Searching for a signature pedagogy in novice coach education. *International Sport Coaching Journal*, 6(3), 349–353. https://doi.org/10.1123/iscj.2018-0049.
Walters, S., Rogers, A., & Oldham, A. R. (2019). A competency-based approach to coach learning: The sport New Zealand coach developer program. In B. Callary & B. Gearity (Eds.), *Coach Education and Development in Sport* (pp. 154–165). Routledge. https://doi.org/10.4324/9780429351037-13.
Watts, D. W., Cushion, C. J., & Cale, L. (2021a). Exploring professional coach educators' realities, challenges and workplace relationships. *Sport, Education and Society*, https://doi.org/10.1080/13573322.2021.2019696.
Watts, D. W., Cushion, C. J., & Cale, L. (2021b). Exploring professional coach educators' journeys and perceptions and understandings of learning. *Sport, Education and Society*, 27(5), 632–646. https://doi.org/10.1080/13573322.2021.1887115.

SECTION II
Approaches to Developing Coaches

In this section the authors consider the different learning environments and methods that coach developers can utilise. We have moved away from the traditional approach of developing the tactical/technical/fitness knowledge of the coach to a more complex view of coaching. This is further complicated by the amount of information readily available, so coaches and coach developers need to become critical consumers, sifting the evidence to improve their practice. This section starts with knowledge auditing – how to identify development needs – and ends with how to accelerate expertise.

All of these chapters emphasise the expertise approach to coach development, encouraging coach developers to engage coaches in their learning. Coaches need to develop deep transferable knowledge structures along with metacognitive and self-regulation skills, and we offer some suggestions of how this can be achieved.

6
KNOWLEDGE AUDITING FOR COACHES

Where Are the Gaps?

Miguel Crespo and Rafael Martínez-Gallego

Introduction

Coaches are generally knowledgeable about their sport, the skills, and drills or Xs and Os. In both coach education and development programmes, difficulties usually arise around the non-technical aspects of coaching; the how-to-coach skills. One of the challenges faced by coach developers is providing the best environment possible for effective coach learning and development (see Chapter 2) even in challenging and uncommon scenarios (Kay, Mason, & Hartley, 2022). To do so, it is crucial the appropriate strategies, content, and delivery methods are put in place using comprehensive, holistic, and well-rounded approaches. In this scenario, understanding the individuals coaches interact with, appreciating their needs, and using leadership skills and team management strategies to select appropriate content and methods to help them unleash their potential as coaches are of paramount importance for coach developers (Dempsey et al., 2021). As mentioned in Chapter 1, an initial needs analysis is recommended to identify these demands and the existing support network for coach developers. Knowledge auditing (KA) can help identify the gaps in this process.

In this chapter we encourage readers to see the big picture and appreciate the long-term benefits a sound coach developer strategy based on KA principles will provide, while we "go small" and dive into individual case studies to provide practical examples of how this process can be implemented by coach developers. The aim of this chapter is to present coach developers with several examples of programmes of practice and case studies illustrating progress, display evidence of real, credible achievements, improvements, and positive outcomes that remain current and reflect the needs of our discipline, supported by narratives and facts, and explained in easy-to-understand terms.

The term knowledge auditing originated in business management and organisational domains. Organisations, regardless of their remit, strive to gain strategic advantage that will put them at the forefront of their ecosystems. Organisational knowledge is an asset, when efficiently managed, that can assist in achieving this goal. KA is considered as the first step of the knowledge management (KM) strategic process organisations can use to understand, among other relevant aspects, the knowledge needed and how to manage it (Sohal, Ragsdell, & Hislop, 2017; Sohal, Ragsdell, Hislop, & Brown, 2020).

KA initiatives may be used as a tool by coach developers to understand where coaches are at present, what they want (see Chapter 4), and what they need. These initiatives will help coaches identify what is most appropriate for them, and how the knowledge required can be generated and shared. It has been argued that KA will help provide an understanding of the culture and context of both the organisation and the individual in complex and dynamic environments such as that of sport coaching (Jones, Bailey, & Thompson, 2013).

Knowledge Auditing for Coach Developers

As mentioned in Chapter 2, coach development based upon a needs analysis is a challenging scenario. Due to the complex, dynamic, and multifaceted nature of the sport coaching environment, a comprehensive understanding of the standards, competences (skills and knowledges), and key roles of the coach developers is essential. Research has shown that one of the key tasks of the coach developer is to establish a positive interaction with the coaches, which will help to analyse their skills and knowledge and their competence in delivering their job and assist the coach to implement a personal development plan to address the possible gaps (North, 2010). To assist coach developers in this task, KA may be applied by evaluating four key concepts; self-awareness, accountability, leadership from within, and mastering team dynamics. KA will report on the current skills and knowledge the coaches have, and, consequently, it will also identify any gaps and highlight interventions required to address them. Once KA has identified the knowledge strengths and weaknesses within coaches, what they do and don't prefer, and what is needed or not, coach developers can make an action plan to plug the gaps (Pill, Agnew, & Abery, 2022).

One of the challenges in this process is the access to and management of the available information and its transfer into meaningful and applicable knowledge. Several decades ago the challenge for coach developers was finding any information, due to its scarcity, whereas nowadays the challenge is processing the vast amount of information and content available to coach developers (see Chapter 8). One of the key roles of coach developers is to share information with the coaches on aspects such as the current trends in athlete development, latest advances in sports sciences, recent trends in pedagogy, methodology or skill acquisition, as well as the experiences of the most successful coaches that are relevant to their daily work (Callary & Gearity, 2019). Coach developers should do this by adapting and presenting the information according to the needs identified, not by telling coaches what to do, but by assisting them in learning how to identify the most relevant information for their requirements and those of their athletes.

Coaches love to acquire new knowledge about how to help their athletes for several reasons. On the one hand, knowing more increases the coaches' self-esteem and confidence and they feel more useful in helping their athletes. On the other hand, new knowledge can also elicit emotions, feelings, and behaviours, enabling coaches to be better equipped to share their passion for the sport, the enjoyment of being involved in an activity they love, and the necessary commitment to strive for maximum effort and to give 100%. This is what coaches want to pass on to their athletes; their feelings of belonging to a sport that, in many cases, forms a big part of their lives. In this context, coach developers have acted as motivators for life-learning by inspiring coaches to exceed their roles (Dohme, Rankin-Wright, & Lara-Bercial, 2019).

We might think that, thanks to today's advances, coach developers and coaches are better equipped to know and understand what is available to them, but information overload – also called "infoxication" or "infopollution" – leads to confusion and the creation of false news due to the many unreliable and unverified data sources. This over-information has the pernicious effect of preventing us from thinking for ourselves as the avalanche of news, which is short-lived, makes it impossible to have time for reflection and analysis. Sometimes this information overload can lead us to believe we are thinking for ourselves, which becomes the height of manipulation. Coach developers should forget the clamour of information and focus on what knowledge/information is required. It seems anyone can have access to data, but not everyone is equipped to understand and effectively apply the information contained in the data (see Chapter 8).

It is crucial coach developers make use of the KA principles to assess where coaches can improve and adapt the learning process to their needs. By doing so, coaches will view the learning process they are undertaking as meaningful and inspiring. This, in turn, will make them aware of the importance of their role as coaches in the development process of their athletes.

Self-Awareness: Know Yourself, Your Strengths, Your Strategies, Your Motives

Self-awareness is step one of the KA processes. When applied to organisations it could be internal and/or external and it consists of analysis such as SWOT (strengths, weaknesses, opportunities, and threats), PESTEL (political, economic, social, technological, environmental, and legal), or 360° review. This process should start with the coaches or coach developers asking themselves "why" they work. This requires the individual to adopt an attitude based on clarity and honesty to provide a "reality check" that reflects on the motives for their choice, their current situation, and their personal and professional trajectory. The individual needs to recognise the hard hits and ups and downs and openly address the hard "truths". However, the coach developer needs to provide reassurance by explaining how to resolve the different personal and professional challenges. This will instil confidence showing their development is in good hands and that "the person is on it". This critical evaluation, as emphasised by authors such as Vangrunderbeek et al. (2022), demonstrates the use of realistic self-reflection skills is important (see Chapter 15).

Some authors (North, 2016) have suggested realistic evaluation is a process that will help coach developers understand their roles are enacted in systems complicated by their interpersonal relations with coaches, important others, institutions such as their families or clubs, and with higher systems such as the relevant governing bodies (federations, councils) media, sponsors, and so on. In the process of KA, coach developers should understand the cognitive structure of coaches: the academic, professional, and coaching background, previous knowledge, skills and competences, prior learning activities, motivation and approach to learning and development, current expectations, limitations and challenges, future perspectives, and so on. They should also understand their feelings, thoughts, and behaviours to facilitate meaningful learning and experiences (Santos, Camiré, & MacDonald, 2021). Studies have highlighted many coaches feel the current system of formal coach education fails to meet their needs and preferences. Coach developers are recommended to use multiple strategies to assist coaches to increase their self-awareness. Communities of practice (that is, observing, interacting, and communicating with their peers) and other social learning methods (that is, using online blogs to become a reflective practitioner) can complement formal education (Stoszkowski & Collins, 2014). Appreciative self-reflection and inquiry has also been proposed as a useful process for developing coach self-awareness (McCarthy & Brady, 2017) with the use of video-based feedback as a recommended tool for coach development (Mead, Spender, & Kidman, 2016).

Coaches tend to learn best what they want to learn, so it is essential that coach developers try to know their coaches better, finding the various learning methods preferred by coaches. Whether this is the traditional face-to-face, the online and distance deliveries, or the blended or hybrid programmes offering the best of both mediums, the people that help coaches develop should be at the forefront of the most relevant and appropriate instructional strategies to achieve their goals. Some authors have discussed the relevance of engagement, imagination, and alignment as useful tools to better understand learning. For example, the individualised identities of the coach developers play a relevant role when shaping their experiences (Vinson, Simpson, & Cale, 2022).

Coach development opportunities in various forms are provided by sport organisations, higher education institutions, private companies, at local, national, and international level, to coaches who deal with novice athletes up to the high-performance professional levels of all sports and disciplines (see Chapters 11 and 12). These development opportunities are designed for all populations regardless of gender, physical or mental abilities, or geographical location. When delivering coach development and education services to coaches from different backgrounds and cultures, it is important to understand the sociocultural, historical, and organisational context of the individuals (Lafrenière, 2015; see Chapter 14). However, there are no set formulas for facilitating this self-awareness and coach developers should be aware that respect, understanding, and empathy are key components in this process.

The first case study presents the example of a digital tool designed to assist coaches and coach developers in understanding more about their knowledge, what they know, and how much they think they know about some key aspects of their coaching practice. Then, by using advanced machine learning, the platform provides coaches with suggestions on how to address the gaps identified. Coach developers can also use this tool to have a better understanding of their knowledge and that of the coaches they interact with.

CASE STUDY 1

Name: ITF Tennis Academy
Organisation: International Tennis Federation (ITF)

Background

The ITF Academy is the official online education platform from the ITF and offers a variety of short courses ranging from general sport to tennis-specific topics. The short courses are presented through text, images, video, audio, as well as animations to ensure the content is interesting and engaging. It also contains a library where coaches will find high-quality videos from conferences around the world, articles as well as scientific research papers to provide for all their information needs.

The available certification courses are made up of various online and face-to-face courses, all of which must be completed to achieve the final certification. The users should click on the course name to be taken directly to the course enrolment page.

Guided learning pathway

This section of the ITF Academy engages the users to embark in a guided learning pathway which will be individually designed for them using an artificial intelligence tool available in the platform. Therefore, instead of registering in the Academy and following the courses directly available in the landing page or searching the web to find the appropriate course according to the interest of the user, the guided learning tool consists of the following steps:

- **What do I want to know? – Selection of the area of interest**: The users indicate their interest from a list which consist of the different levels of players they may be working with; beginner, intermediate, advanced, and high performance.
- **How much do I know? – Knowledge self-assessment**: The platform proposes a survey based on your level of tennis the users wish to focus their learning. The surveys will ask around 30 questions divided into three main areas of coaching competency: training, competition, and management. An updated series of proposed questions will be provided each time the users take the survey.
- **What should I know? – Content recommendation**: Based on the users' responses the platform will propose a series of recommended courses through advanced machine learning. This recommended list will be suggested to the user on completion of any of the surveys available for any area of interest.
- **How often can I take this? – Continuous professional development**: The users can come back to this section of the ITF Academy at any time to view their list of recommended courses and progressively work through completing each of these. They can also retake the survey at any time. Furthermore, an updated list of recommended courses will be provided in each instance which may be different to what had been recommended in the past.

Anecdotally, coaches using this system consider it to be of use; however, once the system has become operational for a period of time, a review would be useful to evaluate the effectiveness.

Accountability: Know Your Job, Do Your Job

The multiple demands specifically placed on coach developers in their role of supporting and guiding coach learning have attracted considerable attention, especially around accountability (McQuade & Nash, 2015). Their workplace relationships have been described as challenging, repetitive, and pressurised, thus creating conflicting experiences. Watts, Cushion and Cale (2022) highlight that coach developers understanding their realities, knowing their job, and doing their job is key. The multiple roles of coach developers have been identified by organisations and individuals. For example, the ICCE (2014) distinguished between (1) leader; (2) facilitator; (3) mentor, (4) assessor, and (5) course designer and evaluator. Horgan and Daly (2015) differentiated between programme developers (i.e., designers) and programme deliverers (i.e., tutors, facilitators … you name them) and Abraham (2016) identified their behaviours, skills, and knowledge in six domains: (1) understanding club and federation context, strategy, and politics, (2) understanding the coach, (3) understanding adult learning and development, (4) understanding coaching curriculum, (5) understanding self, and (6) process and practice.

Having said that a lack of consistency on how these roles (that is, professional skills and required knowledge) are applied in different sports and contexts has been noted. Professional development should be based around the guiding principle of helping coach developers be better at assisting coaches. For this reason, having quality coach developers is crucial in attracting and retaining coaches (Lafrenière, 2015).

The learning pathway and transition from coach to coach developer (see Chapter 5) include a series of steps. These are the accumulation of experience as an athlete, the growth of the sport in their context, the professional certification and qualification acquired, the need to align sport coaching with the professional domain and pursuing continuous interaction with significant others (Brasil et al., 2018). Lifelong learning is a process that coach developers should embrace and engage with (Ciampolini et al., 2020) since it will foster their passion and desire to assist others by sharing their knowledge and experience.

Coach developers have identified an absence of opportunities for continuous professional development (training, accessing information, etc.), important for practising and capturing learning and interaction with the organisations as well as a lack of strategic leadership. In this case, personal drive and individual motivation need to be supported by clear directions and actions from the organisations (Norman, Rankin-Wright, & Allison, 2018).

Coach developers should be accountable, but a key aspect of their role is holding others (athletes, administrators, media) accountable for their behaviours and actions. There are also collective obligations where everyone should be accountable – for example, safeguarding, integrity, inclusivity, or gender equality (see Chapter 13). In the initial stages, coaches are more focused on the tangible aspects of coaching practice and pay less attention to their coaching philosophy. This may be caused by a lack of integrated understanding of what it means to develop a coaching philosophy (Nash et al., 2008). It is difficult for novice coaches to have a clear idea of what their responsibilities are, so it is important for coach developers to review this dimension of KA bearing in mind the coaches' awareness of their own philosophy and accountability. This will allow these issues to be addressed in a much more specific and individualised way, as coaching philosophy is individual, complex, and context-dependent, so general models cannot be applied (Nash et al., 2008). Understanding your coaching philosophy and how this relates to your role and developmental process is critical to the authentic sport coach.

Accordingly, coach developers should facilitate coaches becoming a force for good by engaging them in practices and self-reflections that benefit their athletes.

They should track improvements and observe signs that players are meeting development goals. Developers should recognise and reward the coaches who are leading the way. The call to action is for coaches to do their job with passion and effectiveness, with care and professionalism. Coaches should be assisted in the task of setting personal and programme Key performance indicators (KPIs), commit to them, and keep them at the forefront. One of the best approaches here is to write their coaching strategy and base it on a solid philosophy that will help them along the journey. This is not optional. Coach developers should clearly show that they are there to support the coaches.

Leadership from within: Successful Teams Have Great Leaders

Coach developers have been identified as "the most important link in the chain" of coach education and development (Eade & Reid, 2015, p. 350). This emphasises the importance of coach developers and coaches demonstrating confidence, without being defensive, showing empathy and positivity. When engaging in the coach development process, all parties should strive to create a learning environment that involves truthfulness, transparency, and trust.

Leading is about influencing others. To achieve this coach developers need to present their authentic self thus generating credibility and respect from the coaches (Jones & Santos, 2011). The role of the coach developer as a dedicated leader has been identified by strategies such as appreciative inquiry (AI), especially in its discovery stage, by keeping members of the community of practice engaged and active. Here the coach developer is seen as a facilitator sustaining coach buy-in (Bertram, Gilbert, & Culver, 2016). The leadership role of coach developers is demonstrated by their design of quality coach learning and education programmes to convey their expertise and knowledge (inter-, intra-personal, and professional). Approaches that favour flexible, comprehensive, progressive, and open-minded deliveries will ensure the growth of necessary skills in the coaches (Callary & Gearity, 2019).

The early leadership constructs in sports coaching were built around traits, through the consideration of personalities, behaviours, situations, and contingencies, to the contemporary approaches based on charisma, transaction, resonance, and transformation. Coach developers, as leaders, should use growth-based and strengths-based approaches to generate a positive learning climate, based on self-reflection and appreciative inquiry that will boost their vision, mission, and desire for change (Trudel, Gilbert, & Rodrigue, 2016).

A personal learning coach can assist high-performance coaches translate learning to practice as well as challenging perceptions of leadership (Rodrigue, Trudel, & Boyd 2019). The idea of the coach developer as the super-leader, who can facilitate others to lead themselves, may be appropriate when educating and developing coaches. Case study 2 exemplifies the development of a super-leader within coach development in tennis and how she transitioned through the organisation.

CASE STUDY 2

Name: Edita Liachoviciute (Lithuania)
Position: National Tutor (Lithuanian Tennis Union – LTU)

Background

I am the Technical Director of the LTU, and I deliver coach education courses nationally. I am a former professional player and Billie Jean King captain. I have a university degree in Sport Science, and I am an ITF Coach of High-Performance Players certified coach, and a graduate of the Women in Sport Leadership (WSLA) programme.

The coach developer as a leader

I feel that, more than what I say or do, it is my profile as coach developer what is instrumental to my role as leader and coach developer. As a leader, I try to understand that my key task is to facilitate and develop practice and knowledge. One of the challenges I have faced is the lack of available time that many coaches may have for their development and education. Therefore, the coach developer should try to produce a considerable impact on the coaches within a limited contact time. That is why many of our programmes have short courses and workshops to address the time, and in many cases, the financial challenges that the coaches face.

My experiences, education, background, trajectory, and biography influence the way I act as a coach developer, the way I lead the group, the type of interactions I have with the coaches, and my interpretation of which content to deliver and how it should be shared with them. To this end, leading with example has proven to be a good strategy to engage coaches. Being hands on, providing practical coaching both on- and off court, having sound behaviours, and motivating coaches to use their previous knowledge and experiences as sources of learning and development.

Another experience I can mention is that of sharing with the coaches not only the best practices I have from my experience but, in many cases, and most importantly, those who are examples of scenarios that did not work too well ... the worst practices. I present these situations as case studies, using narrative coaching as the tool to present the story as close as possible to their individual circumstances. And then I ask the group, which would have been their decisions and actions in their case. This usually starts an open, frank, and sometimes heated debate, which is generally full of interventions of all the members of the group who share their views and experiences related to other scenarios and situations that are worth discussing with the fellow coaches.

I also emphasise to the coaches that the leader, and the coach, cannot have all the answers. I discuss with them the value of saying in some cases: "I don't know" to players, parents, coaches, managers, etc. In this context, I reinforce the benefit of being humble, and thoughtful in opposition to the dominating image of the leader (or coach) that has answers to all questions whether they are correct or not and solutions to all problems, no matter if they are appropriate or not. In a challenging environment as that of tennis coaching, not everything goes, and many aspects are closer to the grey palette than to the bright white or dark black.

The multidimensional nature of leadership is more present than ever when I assist in the delivering of courses to groups of international coaches. In these situations, my approach as a leader is to look for the commonalities in the group. I try to find out the aspects that are common to all of us: the passion for our sport, our desire to teach, our love for the players, the hard work on court, and the internal rewards of the job that is well done. However, at the same time, I aim to discover the things that differentiate the group and how they can get us closer together by sharing aspects that can help coaches to empathise with their peers and learn from them.

Leading using technological advances

In trying to design and deliver the best learning environment for coaches, I feel that coach developers should use all means available to achieve this goal. Since it is known that coaches learn through many different learning situations, I believe that we should lead in the pathway of understanding their needs and provide them with the relevant environment that will facilitate their self-development. Therefore, even though before pandemic times, we were using some online methods to deliver our programmes, it has been during and post COVID-19 times, when the implantation of blended or hybrid delivery options has become a must. I have found that asking coaches to reflect and thus consolidate their learning when delivering courses online is usually more challenging than when using face-to-face methods.

Most important takeaway

I feel that coach developers, as leaders, should put the coaches at the centre of the learning process. Furthermore, this will allow the coaches to imagine, create, and construct their own knowledge. Building on their experiences and those of their colleagues they can generate the skills needed for their individual circumstances. Leading is multifaceted, since it combines observation, analysis, guidance, assistance, and support, among other many aspects that will empower the coaches to deal with the dynamic and challenging nature of the sport coaching ecosystem.

Mastering Team Dynamics – What's Best for the Team

The relational nature of coaching and coach development implies that coach developers should also excel at mastering team dynamics by always facilitating what is best for the team (Stodter & Cushion, 2019). In this context, the team can be understood as a community of practice which comprises people that share values, beliefs, visions, and missions, all encompassed by a history and a culture that shares ways of doing things and talking about them. Coaches and coach developers will generally be part of a number of teams with the dynamic varying for each. Here what is best for the team may reflect the particular focus and aim of each group and may be counter intuitive.

There are strategies that can be used to create team identity and cohesion; these include:

- **Consistency:** treat everyone the same
- **Open lines of communication:** be clear about responsibilities and expectations
- **Role clarity:** everyone on team knows their job
- **Create a team identity:** a feeling of belonging to the team

People working together for a common purpose is an outcome of team dynamics and cohesion, and this can be manipulated by deliberate intervention by the coach or coach developer (Kozlowski & Ilgen, 2006).

Research has shown that coach developers recognise the importance of ensuring adequate time for questions and reflection to enable deep learning from the group members while facilitating learning (Culver, Werthner, & Trudel, 2019). This is in line with the calls for a shift in the paradigm from an "instructional" to a "learning" approach in coach development to better assist coaches in getting ready for the complexity and challenging nature of their job. Therefore, when dealing with the team, coach developers should be able to position the coaches at the centre of the learning process through engagement, interaction, and reflection (Ciampolini et al., 2019). Case study 3 highlights how a coach developer in tennis manages team dynamics.

CASE STUDY 3

Name: Armando González (Colombia)
Position: International Tutor (ITF)

Background

I am the Director of Development for the Colombian Tennis Federation (FCT). I manage and deliver the coach education programme of the FCT, which is recognised by the ITF as a "Gold" nation, self-sufficient to deliver coach education at all levels of the game. I have a master's degree in physical education, and I am an ITF Coach of High-Performance Players certified coach, and an ITF international tutor. I have been delivering coach certification courses both nationally and internationally for over two decades.

How I deal with team dynamics

When working with coaches in the different courses, I start by thinking that my presence and my actions are for the benefit of the coaches on court, in the room or virtually. I force myself to provide plenty of opportunities to involve them in discussions and Q&As. If we are a team of tutors delivering the programme, we make sure that the coaches feel that all the coach developers are talking to them, with them, for them, and that those who have "stepped up" and share their views are recognised and feel gratified.

How I recognise what is best for the team

My experience has shown that working together is what works best for the teams. Throughout the narrative, show that when coach and coach developers align effort and aggregate assets, we innovate, create new knowledge streams, and applied value. We drive progress, will drive more and better athletes and make more impact when we advance as a unified global body: Not "us", but 'we".

Successes in coaching are a direct result of aggregation thanks to the eco-system we generate in our interactions. This is because the sum of all our parts creates global competitive advantage: the people (athletes, coaches, support teams, administrators, managers, parents, fans, etc.), the organisations (clubs, federations, companies, media), the events (tournaments, trainings, competitions) … all pushing towards the same direction…that of achieving the best one can do.

How to mobilise the group

I am quite a fan of storytelling in coach education and development. I am a firm believer that it is very important to draw on the emotions of the coaches with compelling stories. Similarly, I try to voice specific calls to action, stating clearly and simply what the coaches need and are asking for. In this case, I always try to provide evidence and cite numbers and deadlines. For example, how many nations have players in the pro rankings. Which ones? How many? Why? How many more nations can we expect to have players ranked? Why do nations need to adopt and implement a long-term player development strategy? I urge coaches to be clear about what is needed, why, and why now.

A key message is to include stories, data and proof points that acknowledge where coaches and coach developers have contributed – whether delivering coaching sessions, attending tournaments, travelling with players, being team captains, implementing programmes at different levels of the sport, gathering meaningful data, or resolving complex challenges. In this process, it is instrumental to demonstrate in our words and our actions that we are confident about the decisions we have made, that the systems and methods that we are using show that are useful to athletes because they help them to progress and develop, and that our transformation as coaches is bearing fruit and bringing benefits. As coach developers, we should provide the facts that prove this.

Acknowledging the power of the group

At the heart of our story as coach developers is the message that the coaches and the coach developers form a global powerhouse and as such can be a force to be reckoned with. We achieve more and greater things and we are all stronger, smarter, and more efficient when we join forces and work together for the benefit of our athletes and our sport.

What this means for the coach developer is to take the coaches through the different contents of the syllabi or the course programme with confidence and empathy – within the dynamic context and changing ecosystem of challenges that coaches should face due to the intrinsic nature of their job, but also point to the opportunities that always arise as a result.

Most important takeaway

Each coach education or development activity provides an opportunity to communicate positively about what the coaches are achieving and acknowledge the important role they actively play when supporting the athletes and the whole sports community in navigating uncharted waters: providing expertise and assets, facilitating engagement, contributing to progress, challenging others, all this enables them to have an individual impact with global consequences. As coach developers, we need to encourage coaches to fully get on board. We need to be very clear on what we want, why we want it, what's in it for them, and where they sign up.

As coach developers our language should be succinct, clear, and honest to share a message that is positive and humble in which coaches can feel engaged and proud of their profession.

In Summary

This chapter deals with the importance and main characteristics of KA as applied to the work done by coach developers in their different roles across a range of organisations. KA has been shown as a powerful tool to identify the knowledge needed by coaches and coach developers, as well as the gaps that need to be addressed.

Once these gaps have been identified, we have tried to provide several options for the coach developer to identify development opportunities for the coach to plug these gaps. Understanding the reasons why, collecting information about the coach, understanding their issues and needs, and determining how to best assist the coach can be a complex process. A strong case conceptualisation, as defined by the biological, psychological, and social contexts of the coach, provides a framework for the coach developer to condense and synthesise multiple pieces of information into a coherent and well-developed narrative (Table 6.1).

TABLE 6.1 Summary of the strategies coach developers can use to implement KA

	Strategies
Self-Awareness: Know yourself, your strengths, your strategies, your motives	• Providing access to information and signposting (i.e., workshops and formal or informal mentoring opportunities) • Observing sessions and providing feedback • Using communities of practices and other social learning methods (i.e., interactions with other coaches – using online reflective blogs) • Engaging coaches in self-directed learning experiences • Emphasising critical thinking and self-reflection on past athletic experiences and current practice (i.e., using r-cards) • Implementing appreciative inquiry practices
Accountability: Know your job, do your job	• Formal learning: Coach Certification programmes, University degrees • Nonformal learning: Apprenticeship, professional certificates, vocational training, clinics, and conferences • Informal learning. Mentors, key coaching collaborators, coaches, athletes, entourage members, family, etc. • Generating a commitment to continuous learning and professional development • Continue to evolve the delivery style • Adopt a holistic approach to your job
Leadership from within: Successful teams have great leaders	• Personalise and individualise your approach • Be independent and self-directed in the learning • Recognise that coaches learn and should be led in different ways • Keep the members engaged by facilitating activity and practice • Use a personal learning coach to co-create knowledge • Raise coaches' aspirations by increasing their sense of purpose and duty
Mastering team dynamics – What's best for the team	• Focus on leading the team while supporting the person • Use strategies such as narrative coaching to facilitate interaction with the team • Be coach-centred, flexible, and facilitate the co-construction of knowledge and experiences • Foster cohesiveness to create a sense of belonging to and identity of the team • Be available, approachable, and supportive • Embrace the idea of: "We are on a journey together to create!"

While some areas are still in transition with results yet to come, coach developers and coaches should be left in no doubt that the achievements made have been possible thanks to collective effort, knowledge sharing, research findings, and positive engagement. For the upcoming future, coach development and education strategies based on knowledge audit are without question the scalable roadmap and guide for all. In this scenario, cooperation between practitioners and academics is instrumental to better understand the needs of coaches, coach developers, and coach development programmes.

References

Abraham, A. (2016). Task analysis of coach developers: Applications to the FA youth coach educator role. In W. Allison, A. Abraham, & A. Cale (Eds.) *Advances in coach education and development* (pp. 73–85). London: Routledge.

Bertram, R., Gilbert, W., & Culver, D. (2016). Using appreciative inquiry to create high-impact coach learning: Insights from a decade of applied research. *AI Practitioner, 18*(2), 59–65.

Brasil, V. Z., Ramos, V., Milistetd, M., Culver, D. M., & Nascimento, J. V. (2018). The learning pathways of Brazilian surf coach developers. *International Journal of Sports Science & Coaching, 13*(3), 349–361.

Callary, B., & Gearity, B. (2019). Coach developer special issue: Global perspectives in coach education for the coach developer. *International Sport Coaching Journal, 6*(3), 261–262.

Ciampolini, V., Milistetd, M., Rynne, S. B., Brasil, V. Z., & Nascimento, J. V. (2019). Research review on coaches' perceptions regarding the teaching strategies experienced in coach education programs. *International Journal of Sports Science & Coaching, 14*(2), 216–228.

Ciampolini, V., Tozetto, A. V., Milan, F. J., Camiré, M., & Milistetd, M. (2020). Lifelong learning pathway of a coach developer operating in a national sport federation. *International Journal of Sports Science & Coaching, 15*(3), 428–438.

Culver, D. M., Werthner, P., & Trudel, P. (2019). Coach developers as 'facilitators of learning' in a large-scale coach education programme: One actor in a complex system. *International Sport Coaching Journal, 6*(3), 296–306.

Dempsey, N. M., Cope, E., Richardson, D. J., Littlewood, M. A., & Cronin, C. J. (2021). Less may be more: How do coach developers reproduce "learner- centred" policy in practice? *Sports Coaching Review, 10*(2), 203–224.

Dohme, L. C., Rankin-Wright, A. J., & Lara-Bercial, S. (2019). Beyond knowledge transfer: The role of coach developers as motivators for lifelong learning. *International Sport Coaching Journal, 6*(3), 317–328.

Eade, A., & Reid, B. (2015). The role of the coach developer in supporting and guiding coach learning: A commentary. *International Sport Coaching Journal, 2*(3), 350–351.

Horgan, P., & Daly, P. (2015). The role of the coach developer in supporting and guiding coach learning: A commentary. *International Sport Coaching Journal, 2*(3), 354–356.

International Council for Coaching Excellence. Association of Summer Olympic International Federations, & Leeds Metropolitan University (2014). *International coach developer framework v1.1.* Leeds, UK: International Council for Coaching Excellence.

Jones, R. L., Bailey, J., & Thompson, A. (2013). Ambiguity, noticing and orchestration: Further thoughts on managing the complex coaching context. In P. Potrac, W. Gilbert, & J. Denison (Eds.) *Routledge handbook of sports coaching* (pp. 271–283). Routledge.

Jones, R. L., & Santos, S. (2011). *Who is coaching? Understanding the person of the coach.* Keynote lecture given at the 'Sports and Coaching; Pasts and futures' Conference, Manchester Metropolitan University, Cheshire, June 25–26.

Kay, C., Mason, C., & Hartley, T. (2022). Co-producing desistance opportunities with women in prison: Reflections of a sports coach developer. *Journal of Prisoners on Prisons, 31*(1), 40–64.

Kozlowski, S. W. J., & Ilgen, D. R. (2006). Enhancing the effectiveness of work groups and teams. *Psychological Science in the Public Interest, 7*(3), 77–124.

Lafrenière, L. (2015). The role of the coach developer in supporting and guiding coach learning: A commentary. *International Sport Coaching Journal, 2*(3), 347–349.

McCarthy, L., & Brady, A. (2017). Coaching the coaches: Appreciative reflection and appreciative inquiry in the development of sport coaches. In A. Brady & B. Grenville-Cleave (Eds.) *Positive Psychology in Sport and Physical Activity* (pp. 232–242). Routledge.

McQuade, S., & Nash, C. (2015). The role of the coach developer in supporting and guiding coach learning. *International Sport Coaching Journal, 2*(3), 339–346.

Mead, S., Spencer, K., & Kidman, L. (2016). Video self-reflection and coach development in New Zealand, Asia-Pacific. *Journal of Health, Sport and Physical Education, 7*(2), 139–156.

Nash, C. S., Sproule, J., & Horton, P. (2008). Sport coaches' perceived role frames and philosophies. *International Journal of Sports Science & Coaching, 3*(4), 539–554.

Norman, L., Rankin-Wright, A. J., & Allison, W. (2018). "It's a concrete ceiling; It's not even glass": Understanding tenets of organizational culture that supports the progression of women as coaches and coach developers. *Journal of Sport and Social Issues, 42*(5), 393–414.

North, J. (2010). Using 'coach developers' to facilitate coach learning and development: Qualitative evidence from the UK. *International Journal of Sports Science & Coaching, 5*(2), 239–256.

North, J. (2016). Benchmarking sport coach education and development: Using programme theories to examine and evolve current practice. In W. Allison, A. Abraham, & A. Cale (Eds.) *Advances in coach education and development: from research to practice* (pp. 17–29). Routledge.

Pill, S., Agnew, D., & Abery, L. (2022). Analysis of a community club coach developer project. *Physical Education and Sport Pedagogy,* 1–16. DOI: 10.1080/17408989.2022.2125944.

Rodrigue, F., Trudel, P., & Boyd, J. (2019). Learning from practice: The value of a personal learning coach for high-performance coaches. *International Sport Coaching Journal, 6*(3), 285–295.

Santos, F., Camiré, M., & MacDonald, D. (2021). Coaching the coaches: A coach developer's experiences creating and implementing a positive youth development coach education program. *International Journal of Sport Psychology, 52*(1), 1–27.

Sohal, D., Ragsdell, G., & Hislop, D. (2017, September). Towards Sustainable Knowledge Management in High-Performance Sport. In *European Conference on Knowledge Management* (pp. 1212–1219). Academic Conferences Int. Limited.

Sohal, D., Ragsdell, G., Hislop, D., & Brown, P. (2020, December). Revisiting the knowledge management audit: Learning from practice in a high-performance sport organisation. In *European Conference on Knowledge Management* (pp. 747–XXII). Academic Conferences Int. Limited.

Stodter, A., & Cushion, C. J. (2019). Layers of learning in coach developers' practice-theories, preparation and delivery. *International Sport Coaching Journal, 6*(3), 307–316.

Stoszkowski, J., & Collins, D. (2014). Communities of practice, social learning and networks: Exploiting the social side of coach development. *Sport, Education and Society, 19*(6), 773–788.

Trudel, P., Gilbert, W., & Rodrigue, F. (2016). The journey from competent to innovator: Using appreciative inquiry to enhance high performance coaching. *AI Practitioner*, *18*(2), 4–5.

Vangrunderbeek, H., De Backer, M., McCarthy, L., Buelens, E., & Ponnet, H. (2022). Developing critical reflection skills in a formal coach education program. *International Sport Coaching Journal*, *1*(aop), 1–16.

Vinson, D., Simpson, H. J., & Cale, A. (2022). 'I felt I'd lost myself–not really knowing who I was': Coach developer learning as negotiating identity through engagement, imagination and alignment. *Sport, Education and Society*, 1–17. DOI: 10.1080/13573322.2022.2038126.

Watts, D. W., Cushion, C. J., & Cale, L. (2022). Exploring professional coach educators' journeys and perceptions and understandings of learning. *Sport, Education and Society*, *27*(5), 632–646.

7
APPRENTICESHIP AND COACHES' DEVELOPMENT

The Potential of Recognizing the Workplace as Learning Organizations

Michel Milistetd, William das Neves Salles and Heitor de Andrade Rodrigues

Introduction

The concept of continuing education in sports coaching is traditionally associated with the concept of removing the coach from the professional environment to be educated in formal environments (Ciampolini et al., 2019). Although common, this practice has little impact, since the contents and strategies adopted in coach education programs (CEPs) are decontextualized from the coaches' reality – their own coaching environment (Nash & Sproule, 2012; Trudel et al., 2013). This limitation of formal programs leads coaches to perceive their main sources of knowledge come from informal learning contexts such as interaction and observation of other coaches, without intentionality toward professional development. In this sense, to reach a desired level of articulation between the practical reality and the preparation of coaches, Walker et al. (2018, p. 11) suggest that "formalized informal coach development programs would provide an ideal site for accelerating coaches' knowledge development" (see Chapter 10 for further detail). Apprenticeship programs can be an interesting option to formalize learning opportunities that occur informally in the coaches' workplaces, as they make visible (subject to observation, analysis and systematization) processes, tasks, and knowledge previously considered abstract and therefore unknown. These programs help apprentices represent and learn the skills and knowledge underlying the work of experts in different areas (Collins et al., 1991). They also seek to use the daily demands of work as opportunities to accelerate the process of adapting coaches to the organizational culture of their workplace, as well as to foster the development of certain professional skills and the idea of lifelong learning (Cassidy & Rossi, 2006). In fact, considering sports coaching as a continuous process of learning and development, both for the individual and for the organizations (Trudel et al., 2021), it is therefore necessary to change

DOI: 10.4324/978-1-003251309-9

the coaches' workplaces from implicit-only learning environments to authentic *learning organizations* (Milistetd et al., 2021). Implicit-only learning environments are the contexts where the coaches learn from their own experience, through the observation of colleagues or even discussions without the focus on learning. On the other hand, a learning organization is a skilled organization for systematic problem solving, experimentation with new approaches, learning from experience, learning from the best practices of others, and transferring knowledge quickly and efficiently throughout the organization (Garvin, 1993).

In addition to workplace reconfiguration toward a philosophy and structure more aligned with the concept of learning organization, the coach developer has a pivotal role in this context. Among different functions, the coach developer needs to identify the characteristics of the environment and the coaches' learning needs to plan, conduct, and evaluate the most appropriate strategies to stimulate coach development. Considering the predominantly adult profile of sports coaches, andragogy principles must be at the foundation of the learning process. Valuing the coaches' previous experiences and daily professional practices should be used to stimulate interactions, discuss dilemmas and challenges, introduce new concepts and stimulate the coaches' reflection on their own practice. The understanding resulting from the discussions and reflections may help them to solve the practical challenges of their daily practice (Trudel et al., 2013).

This chapter aims to explore the role of learning organizations as promoters of sports coach development, situating apprenticeship in the authentic learning environment and the role of the coach developer to unlock the learning potential of sports settings, creating deliberate learning strategies. The purpose is not to suggest partnerships between Sports Federations and Sports Clubs or other coaching workplaces to certify coaches, but rather to explore the potential of these environments as learning organizations and legitimate fields of professional development.

Theoretical Foundation

Contributions of Andragogy to Promote Coach Learning

One of the aspects to consider when promoting coach development initiatives is to understand the characteristics of the coaches, making it possible to identify their potential and development needs. In this sense, the programs need to be developed based on the andragogical perspective, which differs from pedagogic assumptions (teaching children and youth) because the nature of learning and motivations for learning are different between these groups (Knowles et al., 2005). In pedagogy, a "top-down" approach is prioritized, in which a central figure (teacher/instructor) has (almost) total control over the child's learning process. In this scenario, it is assumed children have few resources (life experiences, capacity for abstraction, and reflection), as well as being more dependent on external stimuli (for example, grades, approvals) to learn. In andragogy, on the other hand, learners (adults) usually want to see the immediate benefits of learning – especially how it will help them in their jobs and daily tasks. Moreover, adults already have better conditions (life experiences, reflective capacity, intrinsic motivation) to take responsibility for their own learning and development. As such, instructors might use the adults' own experiences as raw material for reflection and construction of new understandings, which will help them to solve everyday problems (Knowles et al., 2005).

The simple participation of coaches in experiences and other learning activities is not enough to encourage active learning, at levels deep enough to transform the coaches' identity and actions; the role of the coach developer is important to mediate/facilitate this process (McQuade & Nash, 2015). In addition to understanding the coaches' needs and stimulating their interactions, the coach developer must support coaches to build and reflect on their knowledge base according to the new information, to provide feedback that will support lifelong learning (Dohme et al., 2019).

The constructivist perspective based on andragogical principles has been suggested as one of the main ways to improve the quality of coach development (Mesquita et al., 2014; Nelson et al., 2012; Trudel et al., 2013). The popularization of the constructivist paradigm is justified by the increase in the professional recognition of sports coaches, in addition to the information available through the internet today (see Chapter 8). As a result, programs have sought to develop coaches' continuous and autonomous learning skills, in addition to internalizing specific knowledge for professional interventions (Ciampolini et al., 2019).

Usually, the constructivist approach in CEPs seek to promote interaction between coaches through discussions and opportunities for reflection. The performance of interactive activities is essential to sustain collaborative learning environments (Pritchard & Woollard, 2010). Through contact with the perspectives and experiences of colleagues, learners can develop negotiation skills and relinquish their own interests in favor of the collective goals (Morgan et al., 2013). Collaborative negotiation provides knowledge legitimacy and creates a sense of connectivity and belonging among coaches as it is not defined or prescribed by an external source (Wenger, 1998). In studies carried out in Canada (Hussain et al., 2012; Paquette et al., 2014) and the United Kingdom (Jones et al., 2012; Morgan et al., 2013), there was a positive result from the use of active learning strategies in formal programs. McCullick et al. (2005) reported the use of teaching strategies based on the coaching reality in the United States favored the development of pedagogical skills such as organization of the training environment, the guidance of training sessions, and the leadership of athletes. The support of coach developers is essential on these occasions to initiate discussions, reflect on experiences, and promote meaningful learning (Jones et al., 2012; Morgan et al., 2013).

Reflective practice has been used as a support for critical analysis of the participating coaches' beliefs, knowledge, and decision-making skills (Gilbert & Trudel, 2006; Trudel et al., 2013). Strategies such as self-assessment and assessment focused on the pedagogical action of coaches can encourage them to reflect on their own practice, stimulating professional learning (Paquette et al., 2014). The use of feedback in coaching intervention is also recognized as effective for the development of coach learning in the UK (Turner & Nelson, 2009). These strategies are perceived as fundamental by the coaches themselves, to situate their professional practice and encourage them to reflect on their decisions (McCullick et al., 2005).

Despite the growing evidence of andragogical principles in coach development programs, the impact of these initiatives on the daily intervention of sports coaches after the end of the training period has not been properly investigated (Ciampolini et al., 2019). It is important to carry out longitudinal investigations to monitor and compare the performance of sports coaches before and after their participation in these programs, to identify changes in behavior in daily routines after the intervention period. Finally, for the learning process to be effective, the workplace must be configured as an authentic learning environment, in which there is a philosophy that supports continuous professional development.

Apprenticeships: Characteristics, Specificities, and Models for Improving Coach Development

Faced with the recommendations and demands for contextualizing the learning of sports coaches, the concept of apprenticeship emerges as a learning perspective with potential to contribute to the coach's development initiatives. Apprenticeships are recognized as traditional training practices that articulate work and learning in an integrated manner. In other words, a form of learning embedded in the authentic work context. Commonly, apprenticeship presupposes the apprentice as learner, craft knowledge sharing, the master as teacher and the idea that learning in workplaces is context dependent. Learning is conceived as a socialization process, which involves observation and assimilation over time without any intentional, planned or systematic training intervention. It is predominantly based on the sharing and development of tacit knowledge; learning by doing that promotes the appropriation of an implicit procedural knowledge (Gessler, 2019; Pratt, 2016).

According to Fuller et al. (2015), apprenticeship is historically associated with the preparation and occupational inclusion of youth. However, in the last 15 years, government funding of adult apprenticeships has become more common, due to policies that help workers extend their working lives within an ever-changing labor market. These and other changes in the world of work and employment, such as the requirements to strengthen the skill base of a future workforce, the emergence of a literature on learning organizations and individuals as lifelong learners has contributed to the renewal of the academic debate and apprenticeship proposals (Guile & Young, 1998).

The contemporary debate recognizes the relevance of this formative role, while identifying its limits. Guile and Young (1998), for example, warn of the inconsistencies of transposing the traditional concept of apprenticeship to any trade or profession, disregarding the nature of work and the knowledge and expertise associated with professional practice. For them, it is necessary to consider the complex interrelationships between cognition and the work contexts, which cannot be accomplished with the generalization of the traditional principles of apprenticeship. This requires a review of the learning models associated with this concept. For instance, Collins et al. (1991) proposed the concept of cognitive apprenticeship, a model of instruction adapted to teaching and learning of cognitive skills. The authors suggest a framework for designing learning environments, involving choices and adjustments of content and method, including modeling, coaching, scaffolding, articulation, reflection, and exploration strategies.

An apprenticeship is widely viewed as one of the predominant forms of training in sports coaching. The accumulated experience as an athlete, observing and working with more experienced coaches, are learning opportunities highly valued by coaches (Cushion et al., 2003; Trudel & Gilbert, 2006). Despite the appreciation, it is recognized as an unreflective approach to learning, restricted to the reproduction of known practices and with limited ability to promote critical analysis, new knowledge, and innovative practices. There is also a tendency toward instrumental analysis of coaching practice, neglecting, or ignoring its complexity as a social practice (Cassidy & Rossi, 2006).

Given these aspects, Cassidy and Rossi (2006) consider: "The challenge we face in coaching and coach education is to find ways of utilizing the positive aspects of the apprenticeship [...] while being cognizant of their weakness (as well as having it informed by current educational/adult learning research)" (p. 239). The authors subsequently propose a (re)examination of the notion of apprenticeship through the lenses of social learning theory (Lave & Wenger, 1991; Wenger, 1998). The authors highlight learning as a process of social participation, a phenomenon that goes beyond the accumulation of information and skills and involves the constitution of an identity. From the concept of Communities of Practice, it is the idea of becoming a member of a community, which involves mutually engaged in a joint enterprise in which they have a shared repertoire (Wenger, 1998).

In coaches' development initiatives these principles can inform the design, implementation, and evaluation of training programs (Cassidy & Rossi, 2006). Cassidy and Rossi (2006) suggest designing programs for learning and valuing coach education as a process of identity construction. For the authors, it is essential to place the learning process in the work context, where the coach participates in a community and performs a work activity. In this context, having the support of a mentor or coach developer, to deal with the uncertain and changing situations of professional practice, can facilitate learning and the process of becoming a coach (identity construction). In this process of becoming a coach, the sense of membership is crucial, as it enables participation in social practice and, consequently, the development of the ability to choose and make decisions in the real world.

The renewal of the apprenticeship concept can revitalize the coaches' development initiatives, placing the training proposals in a close relationship with the workplace environment. At this point, the perspective of learning organizations can enable initiatives in line with the principles described above.

Learning Organizations

Learning organizations are recognized as structures that develop from their members' learning needs. The individuals themselves support their structure, sharing beliefs, ideas about specific needs that are imposed in the context of practice, and consequently, they expand their work capacity, developing new strategies in their contexts (Jarvis, 2007). According to Örtenblad (2018, p. 151), learning organization is a complex concept embracing not only the concept of individual learning in the organization but also the whole organization that learns. Hence, Örtenblad (2018) focuses attention to key aspects of the learning organization:

- **The organization as a facilitator:** Instead of sending professionals to take formal courses, the organization opts for learning at work. The organization offers tools and opportunities for learning to both individuals and groups. The professionals are encouraged to experiment, reflect upon the outcomes, understanding that failures are a learning opportunity.
- **The organization as a learning unit:** As individuals learn and share, an organizational memory is continuously updated and functions as a basis for conducting work tasks and further learning.
- **The organization as an end process:** As a learning organism, professionals learn about the functions, tasks, and challenges of colleagues from other departments. The organization develops a flexibility to deal with problems and perform in the best way.

When implemented, the learning organization is characterized as a promising way of evaluating the practices and cultural elements of the organization that support continuous learning, which contributes to the professionals' understanding of what has been experienced in formal learning or other situations (Ions & Minton, 2012). In addition, if the learning organization is a promoter of continuous development they should consider how to avoid learning from occurring simply by chance or as a result of mistakes that may occur in the professionals' decision-making (Garvin, 1993). To operationalize the complex concept of learning organizations, Garvin et al. (2008) proposed a framework based on three building blocks with distinct components (Table 7.1). The building blocks represent broad factors that are essential for organizational learning and continuous adaptability.

A supportive learning environment is considered as a space in which people can share perspectives, respecting differences without the fear of making mistakes. The relations of power are decreased, promoting engagement and ownership of participants. Participants share a mutual trust in new ideas that can bring

TABLE 7.1 Dimensions of learning organizations (adapted from Garvin et al., 2008)

Building blocks	Subcomponents
Supportive learning environment	• Psychological safety
	• Appreciation of differences
	• Openness to new ideas
	• Time for reflection
Concrete learning processes and practices	• Experimentation
	• Collection and analysis of information
	• Education and training
	• Information transfer
Leadership that reinforces learning	• Recognition of limitations
	• Invitation of inputs
	• Incentive to identify and solve problems

a process of innovation into the organization. Personal experience is appreciated as part of a collective wisdom.

Concrete learning and practices represent deliberate strategies for learning. Through conscious cycles of experiential learning, participants can create a deep understanding of the results of their practice. As a result, more information is available to be shared in distinct levels of the organization using several resources of dissemination to improve the current practices. Moreover, specific training can be undertaken in certain departments to enhance the quality of the work.

Finally, a leadership that reinforces learning is required to support a safe learning environment and the ongoing strategies for learning. Leaders have the crucial role of continually promoting the learning culture of the organization. Consequently, to recognize vulnerability and be open to continuous feedback from the participants is necessary as a leader. According to Garvin et al. (2008, p. 4), "organizations do not perform consistently across the three blocks, nor across the various subcomponents. That fact suggests that different mechanisms are at work in which building block area and that improving performance in each is likely to require distinct supporting activities". Therefore, a deep understanding of an organization's philosophy and its current practices is crucial to address strengths and weaknesses to promote a contextualized continuous learning enhancement.

Recently, Tozetto et al. (2019) analyzed a Brazilian soccer club recognized for its long-term athlete development model and the financial capital the club achieved selling players from youth age teams. In this study, three deliberate strategies were identified as a learning organization: (a) Club Philosophy – long-term goals, coaches' job insurance, coaches' ongoing evaluation; (b) financial support for continuing education; (c) mentoring and meeting – assistance among coaches, discussions with coaching staff, and free theme meetings. The initiatives allowed coaches an ongoing learning in a supportive environment (incentive and security) in which coaches could focus on players' development instead of just winning at all costs. The possibilities of learning in the workplace raise the quality and the level of practice among coaches integrating new knowledge in their contextual reality working under the same club philosophy (Solana-Sanchéz et al., 2016).

The Role of Coach Developers in Helping Nurture Learning Organizations

Assuming learning organizations as an environment that promotes apprenticeship and professional development, the creation of departments or defining professionals with specific functions that promote the ongoing learning into the organization is imperative. In the sports coaching settings, the coach developer is the one recognized to support coaches' learning (ICCE, 2014). However, as traditionally coach developers operate in formal contexts of learning, the roles of coach developers are related to instruction, facilitation, mentoring, assessment, and course design (McQuade & Nash, 2015). More recently, a few studies supported through social learning theories have been positioned coach developers with a new function or expanding its role to a system convener in informal contexts such as sports federations and multisport clubs (Duarte et al., 2021; Milistetd et al., 2021). A system convener according to Wenger-Trayner and Wenger-Trayner (2015, p. 100) works "unlocking unexplored spaces, forging promising partnerships, building bridges, resetting boundaries, challenging established colonies, and creating new settlements".

Based on the engagement of coaches and other professionals, the coach developers should create legitimate learning opportunities from coaching practice (Trudel et al., 2021). Therefore, coach developers are critical conduits in creating learning organizations in sport setting and they need to enhance their knowledge and competences to the capacity of influencing people, read the field, translate knowledge, create learning communities, provide contextualized support, engage leaders to the ongoing learning perspective, among other functions explored in the next section of this chapter.

As an example of the new role of coach developers within sports organizations, Duarte et al. (2021) illustrated the process of framing a learning environment to wheelchair curling coaches from Curling Canada. The coach developers had to play distinct roles in different levels of the organization focusing on:

- Building trust and meaningful relationships among coaches and technical leaders
- Opening new learning opportunities through offering a range of learning activities and formats that could facilitate coaches' access to knowledge
- Balancing power relationships enabling coaches from different "status" to share and learn from each other
- Facilitating learning to improve coaches' knowledge in specific topics that they choose
- Brokering strategic conversations between coaches and the Curling Canada to enhance learning opportunities and working conditions

In another study, Milistetd et al. (2021) presented a coach development initiative in a multisport club with more than 100 coaches and 6,000 athletes from participation to professional teams in eight sports in Brazil. The coach developer started working with the sport organization 12 months before to start the learning activities for coaches. During this period, several meetings, presentations, and connections were tailored to enhance the learning capability of the multisport club. Moreover, meetings with different departments and stakeholders occurred to understand the local culture, the coaches' routine and learning needs based on the multisport club philosophy. After agreement with different stakeholders the coach development initiative started based on different themes addressed from the participants using multiple learning strategies linked to the coaches' daily activities. As the project ended the authors provided reflections on the limitations of the learning activities if not aligned and tailored in all levels of the club and especially when it is not planned in a sustainable way as part of the coaching routines.

Promoting Learning Organizations in Sports Settings

Although the learning organizations concept has been present in business for the last three decades (Senge, 2006), there is a paucity of evidence in sports coaching toward enhancing coaches' learning and development. Garvin et al. (2008) reveal the main barriers to operationalizing the learning organizations' concept into practice are:

a. The concept is aimed to senior executives, hindering the conditions to managers and ground professionals to apply it
b. A lack of implementation mechanisms
c. The absence of assessment tools

To address possibilities for sports organizations to become learning organizations and support apprenticeship and coach development, suggestions are presented below using the principles of andragogy, apprenticeship, and learning organizations to design, implement, and evaluate a learning environment to foster the coaches' development.

Designing a Learning Environment

The promotion of workplaces with the characteristics of learning organizations in sports settings does not only depend on creating training strategies for the coaches but also in developing a learning culture in which all stakeholders assume responsibility to nurture it in different ways. The first challenge for a coach developer is to apply the andragogical approach and understand the structure and members of the organization with which they are working, to identify its knowledge potential and learning readiness. Sometimes, for example, the implicit values might be different from the explicit values transposed in the organization statements. The immersion in the managerial culture, power relationships, and work routines are fundamental to this mapping. This process of approximation and contact with the members of the organization – through interviews, observations, and meetings with different groups – is essential to establish a trustworthy environment.

An external perspective is important to identify implicit behaviors or practices that can be improved. However, it is essential to look at the potential the organization and its members have to share with other participants. Research shows that part of the knowledge of coaches is tacit and learned unintentionally. This capital might be explored by applying some strategies such as focus groups to stimulate the sharing of practices, knowledge, and values. This in turn can serve as raw material to subsequently define areas of expertise that coaches have and create deliberate learning strategies to help them.

It is important to consider the position each coach occupies in the organization. Information regarding training, experience accumulated within the organization, functions and positions held allow identification of the coach's position within the community. In possession of this information, it is possible to distinguish those who are at the center (old-timers) from those who are on the periphery (newcomers) of the work processes. In general, old-timers accumulate knowledge about the organization and professional practice in that context, so they occupy a strategic place in the development of the learning environment. In turn, newcomers seek to integrate into the work context through the sharing of daily work practices and are usually dependent on old-timers.

The coach developer assumes a role of creating bridges between coaches of different levels or from distinct sports, considering they share common experiences and dilemmas linked to their workplace. Technical coordinators or managers must also participate in these actions, aware they must promote safe environments for learning, reinforcing the andragogical message that there is valuable knowledge among the organization's members. This message might stimulate everyone to share their expertise, especially as they work under the same institutional philosophy and possibly have already solved issues others may be going through.

When establishing favorable environments for shared learning, the organization could recognize, through incentives such as the provision of workload, financial compensation, or other forms of stimulation, that strategies for professional development are part of the coaching routine, and therefore the coaches will not have to "study" in the extra time. These conditions promote the psychological safety needed for engaging participants, which is aligned with the andragogical goal of facilitating the learner's intrinsic motivation to learn. Considering the organizational alignment, clear goals that can be evaluated and measured are required, evidencing outcomes of the learning process. This establishment of clear criteria for all participants allows the design of a learning agenda based on the organization's strengths, coaches' learning needs, and goals to be achieved through continuous learning.

Implementing the Learning Activities

Once the learning agenda is established, coach developers should be responsible for structuring the learning activities, as well as selecting content and people who are recognized as experts in different topics. Learning activities must be designed in collaboration with technical coordinators and Human Resources members. For instance, if meetings are planned with coaches from different departments or even the formalization of a mentoring process from a head coach to a coach of his/her team, the apportioning of agendas, roles, and responsibilities must be clear to all involved, avoiding establishing learning activities as extra-time work. According to the principles of andragogy, meetings between coaches allow genuine exchanges about content that are part of their routines, exploring personal experiences and opening space for joint reflection and problem solving. However, it is essential to be open to innovative ideas, especially due to social instability and constant challenges present today in coaches' routines.

Access to scientific materials and the use of knowledge translation tools are essential to design learning materials. In addition, coaches must develop critical skills for accessing quality information to avoid accepting untested fads or myths in their coaching (see Chapter 8). The expansion of a knowledge repertoire is essential for coaches, but above all, the search for change in their behavior should also be the focus of learning actions. Cycles of planning, doing, checking and acting (PDCA) are fundamental to understanding how new actions can be implemented in an organization.

Evaluating the New Learning Practices

Learning assessment is always challenging in any context. In line with the perspective of learning organizations, the idea here is not to identify whether individual trainers' knowledge has accumulated, but to establish a continuous assessment that can sustain lasting changes within the organization itself. The definition of success criteria, aligned with the organization's philosophy, can guide deliberate reflection supported by tools that help coaches to monitor their practices and routines. Instruments such as recording practices (see Stodter & Cushion, 2019) and use of reflective cards (see Rodrigue & Trudel, 2018) or video diaries (see Jones et al., 2015) are essential to make explicit moments in which new practices are experienced and subsequently evaluated individually or collectively.

Based on the information extracted from these activities, individual and collective feedback can be prepared with coaches and other stakeholders to enhance practices or highlight necessary changes. This ongoing process of organizational feedback allows for the establishment of similar practices to be adopted by different coaches in a move toward innovation. Once new routines are defined, summits or training can be held with all stakeholders, enabling the systematic transfer of the new knowledge to the whole organization.

The organization's leaders such as sport directors, managers, and head coaches are fundamental pillars for the achievement of organizational learning. Depending on their responsibilities and powers linked to their positions, they should promote continuous learning and coach engagement by facilitating deliberate moments of learning. The invitation to continuous reflection and promotion of a culture of mutual help and sharing among different professionals must be also developed among the leaders themselves to reduce barriers and to use the organization's potential to enhance its learning capability.

Final Considerations

This chapter explored the role of learning organizations as promoters of coach development, based on the discussion of the role of the coach developer in the articulation of andragogy principles with the apprenticeships' work-learning integrative proposal. Apprenticeships are explored in coach education due to the high value the coaches attribute to learning in the workplace and with more experienced colleagues. Moreover, some coach development initiatives have been applying andragogical principles to implement coach training programs, mainly through interactions and reflection opportunities.

In contrast, some limitations are highlighted in the current state of discussions and practices in this area. Firstly, it is recognized that apprenticeships still suffer from a predominantly prescriptive approach, which lack further reflective depth to transform current practices. In this sense, it is necessary to implement the systematic reflective practice to create meaningful exchange of experiences in the workplace. Secondly, coach development initiatives that apply andragogical principles still need to transform these specific moments into permanent processes of the organization, making it possible to monitor their effectiveness in the coaches' development on a daily basis.

The coach developer is one of the key actors for the design, implementation, and evaluation of apprenticeships in sports coach learning organizations. In addition to having specific andragogical skills to develop teaching in an appropriate manner for the participating coaches, this professional needs to act as a system convener, to bring together the different members of the organization (managers, coaches, support team, etc.) in the learning journeys within the coach workplace.

The effective insertion of the coach developer in the workplace is, in fact, complex. One of the issues to be considered is the background of the coach developers who will play the role of system conveners. If these professionals already belong to the organization, it may be easier to gain the trust of sports managers and coaches and to subsequently lead the program. On the other hand, they may have a biased comprehension of the organization's characteristics, and not see potential opportunities for lifelong learning as they are already used to/ influenced by certain procedures and daily practices established. If, in turn, the coach developers are external to the organization, they may have difficulties in gaining the trust of people inside or may not be able to adequately understand the current institutional culture. In this sense, more time is needed to understand the context and build trust relationships before developing the project.

The most important challenge is the search for the dissemination of the apprenticeship in the workplace culture among many individuals, ensuring the process does not depend exclusively on one person (coach developer). This requires the complete transformation of the coach workplace into a learning organization. This process, although potentially slow and gradual, needs to be implemented to allow the maintenance of the philosophy and culture of lifelong learning, essential for aligning coach development initiatives with the demands of contemporary society.

References

Cassidy, T., & Rossi, T. (2006). Situating learning: (Re)examining the notion of apprenticeship in coach education. *International Journal of Sports Science & Coaching*, 1(3), 235–246. https://doi.org/10.1260/174795406778604591.

Ciampolini, V., Milistetd, M., Brasil, V. Z., & Nascimento, J. V. (2019). Teaching strategies adopted in coach education programs: Analysis of publications from 2009 to 2015. *Journal of Physical Education*, 30(1), e3006. https://doi.org/10.4025/jphyseduc.v30i1.3006.

Collins, A., Brown, J. S., & Holum, A. (1991). Cognitive apprenticeship: Making thinking visible. *American Educator*, 15(3), 6–11, 38–46.

Cushion, C. J., Armour, K. M., & Jones, R. L. (2003). Coach education and continuing professional development: Experience and learning to coach. *Quest*, 55, 215–230. https://doi.org/10.1080/00336297.2003.10491800.

Dohme, L.-C., Rankin-Wright, A. J., & Lara-Bercial, S. (2019). Beyond knowledge transfer: The role of coach developers as motivators for lifelong learning. *International Sport Coaching Journal*, 6(3), 317–328. https://doi.org/10.1123/iscj.2019-0034.

Duarte, T., Culver, D. M., & Paquette, K. (2021). Framing a social learning space for wheelchair curling. *International Sport Coaching Journal*, 8(2), 197–209. https://doi.org/10.1123/iscj.2019-0095.

Fuller, A., Leonard, P., Unwin, L., & Davey, G. (2015). *Does apprenticeship work for adults? The experiences of adult apprentices in England: executive summary*. UCL Institute of Education.

Garvin, D. E. (1993). Building a learning organization. *Harvard Business Review*, 71(4), 78–91.

Garvin, D. A., Edmondson, A. C., & Gino, F. (2008). Is yours a learning organization? *Harvard Business Review*, 86(3), 109–116.

Gessler, M. (2019). Concepts of apprenticeship: Strengths, weaknesses, and pitfalls. In *Handbook of vocational education and training* (pp. 677–709). https://doi.org/10.1007/978-3-319-94532-3_94.

Gilbert, W., & Trudel, P. (2006). The coach as a reflective practitioner. In R. L. E. Jones (Ed.), *The sports coach as educator: Re-conceptualising sports coaching* (pp. 113–129). Routledge.

Guile, D., & Young, M. (1998). Apprenticeship as a conceptual basis for a social theory of learning. *Journal of Vocational Education & Training*, 50(2), 173–193. https://doi.org/10.1080/13636829800200044.

Hussain, A., Trudel, P., Patrick, T., & Rossi, A. (2012). Reflections on a novel coach education program: A narrative analysis. *International Journal of Sports Science & Coaching*, 7(2), 227–240.

International Council for Coaching Excellence. (2014). *International Coach Developer Framework*. Version 1.1. ICCE.
Ions, K., & Minton, A. (2012). Can work-based learning programmes help companies to become learning organisations? *Higher Education, Skills and Work-Based Learning*, 2(1), 22–32. https://doi.org/10.1108/20423891211197712.
Jarvis, P. (2007). *Globalisation, lifelong learning and the learning society: Sociological perspectives*. Routlegde.
Jones, R. L., Fonseca, J., De Martin Silva, L., Davies, G., Morgan, K., & Mesquita, I. (2015). The promise and problems of video diaries: building on current research. *Qualitative Research in Sport, Exercise and Health*, 7, 395–410. http://dx.doi.org/10.1080/2159676X.2014.938687.
Jones, R. L., Morgan, K., & Harris, K. (2012). Developing coaching pedagogy: Seeking a better integration of theory and practice. *Sport, Education and Society*, 17(3), 313–329. https://doi.org/10.1080/13573322.2011.608936.
Knowles, M. S., Holton, E. F., & Swanson, R. A. (2005). *The adult learner: The definitive classic in adult education and human resource development*. Elsevier.
Lave, J., & Wenger, E. (1991). *Situated learning: Legitimate peripheral participation*. Cambridge University Press.
McCullick, B. A., Belcher, D., & Schempp, P. G. (2005). What works in coaching and sport instructor certification programs? The participants' view. *Physical Education & Sport Pedagogy*, 10(2), 121–137. https://doi.org/10.1080/17408980500105015.
McQuade, S., & Nash, C. (2015). The role of the coach developer in supporting and guiding coach learning. *International Sport Coaching Journal*, 2(3), 339–346. https://doi.org/10.1123/iscj.2015-0059.
Mesquita, I., Ribeiro, J., Santos, S., & Morgan, K. (2014). Coach learning and coach education: Portuguese expert coaches' perspective. *The Sport Psychologist*, 28(2), 124–136. https://doi.org/10.1123/tsp.2011-0117.
Milistetd, M., Trudel, P., Culver, D., Cortela, C. C., Tozetto, A. V. B., Lima, C. O., & Souza, V. G. (2021). A second look at a 24-month collaborative initiative to develop coaches in a multisport club. *Journal of Sport Pedagogy and Research*, 7(6), 1–12.
Morgan, K., Jones, R. L., Gilbourne, D., & Llewellyn, D. (2013). Changing the face of coach education: Using ethno-drama to depict lived realities. *Physical Education and Sport Pedagogy*, 18(5), 520–533. https://doi.org/10.1080/17408989.2012.690863.
Nash, C., & Sproule, J. (2012). Coaches perceptions of their coach education experiences. *International Journal of Sport Psychology*, 43, 33–52. https://doi.org/10.7352/IJSP.2012.43.033.
Nelson, L., Cushion, C. J., Potrac, P., & Groom, R. (2012). Carl Rogers, learning and educational practice: Critical considerations and applications in sports coaching. *Sport, Education and Society*, 19(5), 513–531. https://doi.org/10.1080/13573322.2012.689256.
Örtenblad, A. (2018). What does "learning organization" mean? *The Learning Organization*, 25(3), 150–158. https://doi.org/10.1108/tlo-02-2018-0016.
Paquette, K. J., Hussain, A., Trudel, P., & Camiré, M. (2014). A sport federation's attempt to restructure a coach education program using constructivist principles. *International Sport Coaching Journal*, 1(2), 75–85. https://doi.org/10.1123/iscj.2013-0006.
Pratt, D. D. (2016). Conceptions of Teaching. *Adult Education Quarterly*, 42(4), 203–220. https://doi.org/10.1177/074171369204200401
Pritchard, A., & Woollard, J. (2010). *Psychology for classroom: Constructivism and social learning*. Routledge.
Rodrigue, F., & Trudel, P. (2018). A college football coach's experience of using reflective cards as internal learning situations. *LASE Journal of Sport Science*, 9(1), 39–59.

Senge, P. M. (2006). *The fifth discipline: The art & practice of the learning organization.* Currency Doubleday. New York, London.

Solana-Sánchez, A., Lara-Bercial, S., & Solana-Sánchez, D. (2016). Athlete and coach development in the Sevilla Club de Fútbol Youth Academy: A values-based proposition. *International Sport Coaching Journal, 3*(1), 46–53. https://doi.org/10.1123/iscj.2015-0085.

Stodter, A., & Cushion, C. (2019) Evidencing the impact of coaches' learning: Changes in coaching knowledge and practice over time. *Journal of Sports Sciences, 37*(18), 2086–2093. https://doi.org/10.1080/02640414.2019.1621045.

Tozetto, A. V. B., Galatti, L. R., Nascimento, J. V., & Milistetd, M. (2019). Strategies for coaches' development in a football club: A learning organization. *Motriz: Revista de Educação Física, 25*(2). https://doi.org/10.1590/s1980-6574201900020010.

Trudel, P., Culver, D. M., & Werthner, P. (2013). Looking at coach development from the coach-learner's perspective: Considerations for coach development administrators. In P. Potrac, W. Gilbert, & J. E. Denison (Eds.), *Routledge handbook of sports coaching* (pp. 375–387). Routledge. https://doi.org/10.4324/9780203132623.ch30.

Trudel, P., & Gilbert, W. (2006). Coaching and coach education. In D. Kirk, D. Macdonald, & M. E. O'Sullivan (Eds.), *The handbook of Physical Education* (pp. 516–539). SAGE. https://doi.org/10.4135/9781848608009.n29.

Trudel, P., Paquette, K., & Lewis D. (2021). The Process of "Becoming" a Certified High-Performance Coach: A Tailored Learning Journey for One High-Performance Athlete. *International Sport Coaching Journal, 9*(1), 133–142.

Turner, D. J., & Nelson, L. (2009). Graduate perceptions of a UK university based coach education programme, and impacts on development and employability. *International Journal of Coaching Science, 3*(2), 3–28.

Walker, L. F., Thomas, R., & Driska, A. P. (2018). Informal and nonformal learning for sport coaches: A systematic review. *International Journal of Sports Science & Coaching, 13*(5), 694–707. https://doi.org/10.1177/1747954118791522.

Wenger, E. (1998). *Communities of practice: Learning, meaning, and identity.* Cambridge University Press.

Wenger-Trayner B., & Wenger-Trayner, E. (2015). Systems conveners in complex landscapes. In E. Wenger-Trayner, M. Fenton-O'Creevy, S. Hutchinson, C. Kubiak, & B. E. Wenger-Trayner (Eds.), *Learning in landscapes of practice: Boundaries, identity, and knowledgeability in practice-based learning* (pp. 99–118). Routledge.

8
THE IMPORTANCE OF CRITICAL THINKING IN COACHING

Separating the Wheat from the Chaff

Loel Collins and Chris Eastabrook

Effective coaching has been described as being evidence-informed by Cope and Cushion (2020). Implying that coaches must, therefore, be able to select and appraise knowledge sources, make meaningful sense of their own experiences, those of their colleagues and athletes and to be able to consider the relevance to their coaching. Each of these tasks presents opportunities for the coach, but the sheer volume of readily available information means that the first step, selecting and appraising *relevant* knowledge, is daunting. One practical way to manage this challenge is to develop critical thinking skills (Al-Kumaim et al., 2021). Critical thinking enables the coach to focus on the most appropriate sources of information, highest-quality evidence, and knowledge to inform their practice. Logically, then, critical thinking is a goal for coach development. Therefore, there is a need to foster a coaching culture that includes critical thinking and supports coaches in being critical: A willingness to 'throw stones at false idols!'.

This chapter explores, how critical thinking skills could be developed in coaches and Coach Developers (CD), so they can identify appropriate information and knowledge to inform their practice. In it we will propose a set of dispositions that the coach and CD can apply to aid in sifting *the wheat from the chaff*. We start by outlining the context and exploring the need for critical thinking as an essential, ethical, and professional part of Evidence-Informed Coaching (EIC) before considering how those dispositions may enhance criticality in coaches.

Part 1: Critical Thinking?

Culver and colleagues (2019) have highlighted the need for a well-educated, well-informed, and professional coaching workforce. We contend that a well-informed workforce has to be suitably critical of the knowledge, and knowledge sources it uses to inform its practices (Stoszkowski et al., 2020; Tiller et al., 2022).

In particular, EIC requires coaches and CD to be critical consumers of a wide range of knowledge from a range of sources (Stoszkowski et al., 2020). This section explores criticality, coaches as critical consumers, and the challenges coaches face as evidence-informed practitioners.

What Is Criticality?

Conceptions of critical thinking vary. For example, Dewey (1938) limited critical thinking to thinking about one's observations, experiences, and experiments. While others, such as Bailin et al. (1999) and Ennis (1962), include the products of that consideration, Ennis (2015) takes critical thinking to cover both the 'thinking about' and appraisal of the 'products' of critical thinking. In the same spirit, critical thinking can be conceived as *just* a judgment (Dewey, 1938; Lipman, 1987). However, once again, Ennis (2015) and Bailin et al. (1999) see both actions *and* beliefs as the logical endpoint of a process of critical thinking. Therefore, Bailin et al. (1999) propose that critical thinking is characterised as having:

1. a purpose,
2. an accuracy – a precision and focus to the thinking process on that purpose rather than *just* generally about the coaching and
3. a threshold to *critically* think on rather than *just* thinking about – there is a point at which the thinking becomes critical, it is incisive, honest, accurate, and accurate.
   In addition, we propose a fourth:
4. in coaching contexts – an intention to act.

Being critical *of* and thinking critically on a particular aspect of their practice enables the coach to analyse and evaluate different information and its sources. Stanovich and Stanovich (2010) ground critical thinking in the thinker's rationality, in particular, fitting the thinkers beliefs of their world to optimise goal fulfilment. Stanovich and Stanovich highlight the 'propensity' to override the suboptimal with their 'autonomous mind' (p. 227), in short, the ability to recognise the ineffective, theorise as to a possible solution with the 'tools' at hand, apply those new or adapted 'tools', and evaluate their application. Therefore, criticality can be viewed as using and questioning information rather than simply accepting, absorbing, or replicating it. As such, we consider criticality is not just an individual or set of processes but a set of dispositions that can be enhanced by the CD to shape a coach's practice.

Coaches as Critical Consumers

A critically thinking coach can position information and ideas in the bigger picture. By being critical of what they have discovered or have had presented they are able to comprehend its strengths and weaknesses and identify evidence that supports or contradicts its potential application. Importantly the critically thinking coach can problem-solve, adapt to changing circumstances, and thus is pedagogically agile. In sort be an adaptive expert (Mees et al., 2020).

Several authors have identified that coaches prefer to learn informally (Nelson et al., 2006; Sinfield et al., 2020; Stoszkowski & Collins, 2014). However, there are some nuances within this assertion. Voluntary and inexperienced coaches prefer less formal coach education, while professional coaches and those with greater experience appear to recognise a value in more formal opportunities (Sinfield et al., 2020; Stoszkowski & Collins, 2014). In either situation, it is an advantage, if not essential, for the coach to be critical of the information and knowledge they digest if they are to be able to apply such knowledge effectively.

We know coaches are critical via different approaches integrated and nested into their coaching process (Nash et al., 2022). For example, recognising the effectiveness of an intervention based on observed performance is a critical evaluation, as is identifying the optimum aspect of a technical performance that requires adaptation. At another level, the coach selects from various approaches based on advice from other coaches or in discussion with the learner. This advice is, at least, viewed as worthy of trial, a critical appraisal before the critique of its effectiveness if applied. An essential component is the evaluation of any information's appropriateness based on its intended use, how the information has been derived, interpreted, and presented.

The Challenge for the Critical Coach

We live in an 'information-rich world' (Stoszkowski et al., 2020, p. 7) where coaches and CD have access to vast amounts of un-sifted information. This knowledge has been described as either evidence or opinion based (Rushall, 2003). Coaching practice combines both, a spectrum of either. The challenge for the coach and CD is to understand the balance in each situation, the proportions probably reflecting the coaches' knowledge, experiences, values, and beliefs.

Furthermore, learning and coaching is ripe with myths and folklore (Cope & Cushion, 2020). Some of this becomes convention or received wisdom if left unchallenged, which once entrenched becomes orthodoxy (see Visual, Aural, Read/write and Kinaesthetic [VARK] as described by Nancekivell et al., 2020 or Neurolinguistic Programming (NLP) as discussed by Passmore and Rowson, 2019) and therefore difficult to challenge. While criticality is the norm in research, coaches and CD also need to be critical of the research itself and its application (Collins & Collins, 2019). Criticality is part of the practical wisdom needed by the coach and is the essential aspect of EIC.

What Is Evidence-Informed Coaching?

Understanding and exploiting the synergy of theory and practice lies at the heart of coach development (Collins & Collins, 2019). The last two decades have seen

TABLE 8.1 The components and importance of EIC

Component	Importance
1 The integration of the current best available research and its evaluation	That generates credible knowledge by applying scientific principles of proof and reliability (Baillie et al., 2019)
2 The coaches and CD's expertise (knowledge and skills)	Evidence from the coaching process and development of expertise
3 The experiences of those being coached	Practical wisdom derived from the delivery of coaching in context (Schwartz, 2011)

a consensus emerge that research *if critically applied*, improves coaching (Abraham & Collins, 2011). In contrast, Hattie et al. (2015) identify that action research, for example, has had no impact on teaching. It seems the *critical* application is essential. Thus, EIC has emerged in contrast to evidence-*based* practice (Franks, 2002; Greenhalgh, 2001). EIC has three components, as shown in Table 8.1.

Blending these sources is advantageous because it enables knowledge to be constructed by the coach in a contextually driven, conditional, and evolving manner (Nutley et al., 2013). Such approaches facilitate innovation and adaptation in response to multiple interrelated factors. Additionally, EIC considers the cultural context, the preferences and values of those being coached, and significantly, for the coach and CD, factors influencing the application of research. Thus, effective EIC and its development hinge on the coach having a practical wisdom, being a critical thinker, a scientist-practitioner (Lane & Corrie, 2002) who undertakes professional enquiry as part of a career-long development and growth (Cochran-Smith & Lytle, 2009; Menter et al., 2010). Sternberg (1985) views this as a practical intelligence and describes adapting, shaping, and selecting to achieve a contextual fit between the individual, their actions, and their environment. *Adaptation*: a change within oneself to better adjust to the context. *Shaping*: changing their environment to better suit their needs. And *Selection*: moving to or creating a new environment. Sternberg also highlights the need to apply analytic skills to typical situations as a critical aspect of practical intelligence. This practical wisdom is manifest in the knowledge of what practices work best in a specific context. We content this conditional knowledge, practical wisdom, is built up over time. Therefore, in line with our fourth characteristic of critical thinking, as intention to act, Part 2 offers four dispositions to guide coach and CD thinking.

Part 2: Enhancing Criticality; The Coach's Dispositions

Via the agile coaching process mentioned earlier, we suggest that coaches have the fundamental skills to be critical. However, the development of these skills requires scaffolding, mentoring, and coaching from the CD. One challenge in articulating how to develop and enhance critical thinking is the risk of proposing 'a method', in doing so running the risk of it being decontextualised and thus misunderstood, miss-applied, or misused. At worst, becoming one of the memes we criticised earlier or being relegated to the 'lip service' we see paid to reflective practices in many coach development programmes.

Rather than a model, we propose and address, in turn, five interlinked dispositions that scaffold critical thinking for the coach: (1) the lens of criticality; a coach's values and beliefs, (2) understanding potential sources of knowledge, (3) making sense of the coaching experience, (4) the curious coach: an enquiring mind, and (5) adding to the conversation. Each disposition is now presented and discussed in turn.

The Lens of Criticality; A Coach's Values and Beliefs

A coach's values and beliefs about coaching and learning shape their practice (Perry, 1981). Importantly, any critical thinking is compared using those values and beliefs, forming the basis of how knowledge is integrated into practice. Understanding how those values and beliefs link to practice is key if the coach and CD are to avoid potential bias. There is contention as to whether this branch of philosophy and epistemology should consider views purely about knowledge or also integrate beliefs about learning (Schommer-Aikins, 2004). From a coaching and coach development perspective, we perceive the two are interlinked.

Both Perry (1981) and Schommer (1994) conceive of a coach's values and beliefs as being on a continuum between naïve or sophisticated. A naïve perspective accepts knowledge as clear, distinct, specific, fixed, grounded in accepted and prescribed models and reinforced by authority sources. Consequently, this position supports a notion that those skills can be learnt rapidly. In contrast, a sophisticated perspective holds knowledge as complex, changing, dynamic, and learnt gradually via cognitive processes (Howard et al., 2000; Schommer, 1994). Consequently, learning is constructed through reasoning, reflection and can also be learned (Howard et al., 2000).

A coach's beliefs and values have five interrelated dimensions: (1) the validity and source of information, (2) its certainty and reliability, (3) the structure and complexity, (4) potential speed of learning, and (5) the ability and capacity for learning (Schommer-Aikins & Easter, 2006). These dimensions develop at different rates (Schommer, 1994), however do provide the basis for critical consideration. While the coaches' and CDs' overall positions can be viewed as between naïve or sophisticated, each coach also holds different positions for each dimension and can be highly personalised (Schommer-Aikins, 2004).

A coach's values and beliefs link to their coaching in a metaphorical chain. Several authors have identified this chain (Christian et al., 2020; Grecic & Collins, 2013) as a consistent, logical relationship with a rationale and justification – a demonstration of their beliefs in action. Recently, authors have also suggested these metaphorical chains connect the coach to the values and developmental philosophies of the body that certifies or employs them, 'the

FA way, the RYA way, the BASI way', for example. An approach Nelson et al. (2006) suggested could be little more than indoctrination. Certainly, Mees et al. (2020) identify a link between an employer's educational philosophies and the development and evaluation of its coaches. Logically, it seems unlikely that a coach could qualify or be employed without a shared mental model of coaching practice of their organisation. Negatively, a coach simply replicates 'the way' to qualify and the CD only needs to present 'the way' during training.

Furthermore, if those values and beliefs are poorly formed or the chain unclear, i.e., not manifest in what the organisation teaches to its coaches, there is a disconnect between training, evaluation and practice, and a lack of constructive alignment (Biggs & Tang, 2009). Mees et al. (2020) have identified a disconnect between an organisation that employs coaches and the National Governing Body that initially certified its coaches, as the organisation has a very well-established educational philosophy. This incoherence may have significant implications for quality, safety, effectiveness, evaluation, and certification (cf. Collins et al., 2012). Clearly this requires addressing if a body training and certifying coaches is to ensure those coaches are employable in the long term.

However and positively, a void between a coaches belief and action (Collins et al., 2015) may indicate that the coach is developing their own beliefs but may lack the pedagogic skills to enact their newly forming values. Indeed, such a disconnect may be required and even desirable as an aspect of the coach's development. This represents a challenge for the CD, the awarding body or employer.

Understanding Potential Sources of Knowledge

A clear source of potential knowledge is literature. Peer-reviewed research and more accessible and digestible grey sources (Benzies et al., 2006) of information such as magazine articles, some books, blogs, social media, case studies, and reports offer a vast range of potential influences. Understanding the quality of these sources is clearly a deposition and accumulation of critical thought.

Dagenais et al. (2012) and Collins and Collins (2019) found that teachers and coaches with an inquiring mindset took a positive view and engaged with research to inform their practice. The teachers and coaches viewed research and researchers as different, however, frequently overplayed the significance of research in their own practice. Dagenais et al. and Collins and Collins also noted that some teachers and coaches are 'turned off' by research, the term itself forming the obstacle, consequently, they discounted research as alien, irrelevant, and even threatening. In EIC encouraging and embracing an enquiring mindset may be an essential philosophical 'shift', for some coaches, CD and awarding bodies. Certainly, a shift away from the 'formal' approach, single method and any didactic tendencies of some coach development would seem essential. What seems clear is that a meaningful translation requires a healthy criticality of the research and its application via EIC.

Not All Sources Are Created Equal

Coaches and CDs will require the skills to consider different sources. It is important to know where your information is coming from, some sources are more credible than others. Eaton (2018) offers a hierarchy with examples presented in Table 8.2 that can guide CD and coaches in how to view that information.

The Reality of Research: Expectation Management

Research rarely answers the BIG questions or provides *the* answer, it frequently generates more questions, this is challenging as many coaches seek the answer to the challenges they face at that moment. Indeed, when a source proposes other avenues of investigation and interpretations of its results, it is, overall, a good thing. However, research findings rarely exist as absolutes in coaching and coach

TABLE 8.2 Not all sources are created equal adapted from Eaton (2018)

Credibility	Description	Example
Most credible	Scientific sources that have gone through a peer review process. Peer review reviews the quality of investigation, its interpretation, and any findings. Peer review is frequently blind and uses multiple experts to review a paper in a cycle until the quality and rigour required for publication are met	Journal papers, conference presentations, and proceedings
Credible	Scholarly articles found in books from experts. These books are frequently a collection of invited articles edited by a coordinating editor	Academic books. These are typically published by academic publishing houses (e.g., Sage, Routledge, university presses)
Acceptable	Contains accurate information that is supported by evidence or can be verified from trusted sources. Good articles in this category frequently cite their original sources, typically one of the above	Publications from academic presses, professional and trade magazines, encyclopaedias, government websites (.gov), and educational websites (.edu)
Less acceptable	Few or no references or supporting evidence, resources with outdated information or are vague about what the authors intend	Newspapers, journalism, magazine articles. Books from non-academic sources or that are self-published, websites, and podcasts
Untrustworthy	These sources have other intentions than the presentation of un-bias knowledge	Social media. Commercial websites (.com), organisations' websites (.org). Wikipedia

development terms; any claims, implied or otherwise, must be viewed with high degrees of criticality. The scientific method isn't to question any grand generalisable or universal theory. Here the coach's values and beliefs play a role in what they expect from research, how fixed are the research findings? The CD has a role in expectation management. Being critical of any research is essential, as the context is likely to be different from the coach's or CD's own.

In all reading, there is potential for naturalistic generalisation (Smith, 2018). If narrative or findings 'ring true' to the reader's own values, beliefs, and experiences, it becomes relatable and has a greater value to that reader. The readers inherent bias can be exacerbated, for example by using social media as a source of coaching knowledge – the algorithms seek out similar posts that 'ring true' to find more, similar content. In reality, the opposite should be sought – 'What other explanations exist?'. Different views help criticality by strengthening any usefulness of that knowledge whilst also being mindful of any confirmation, cognitive or availability bias. As such, having a true understanding of a coach's values, beliefs, and experiences and that of their learners is also an essential deposition to more fully understand all forms of literature.

Making Sense of the Coaching Experience

The ability for a coach to learn by understanding their experiences facilitates insight into their own and other practices (Nelson et al., 2006). This process, called reflection, enables the coach to make links from one experience to the next and is a fundamental aspect of EIC. Nash et al. (2022) report that many coaches do not perceive themselves as reflecting on their practice, a point we concur with based on our observations and experiences with coaches. Coaches are, perhaps, more involved in 'in-action' thinking, addressing the problem at hand cited earlier, rather than the 'on-action' (Schön, 1983) reflection academic models offer (Collins & Collins, 2019). Consequently, coaches may not perceive a value in 'on action' models like those often espoused on development programmes. At the heart of critical thinking is an assumption that practice can always be improved, that a single approach is insufficient because the performer and context differ. In essence, the coach questions and challenges their assumptions and those around them. This questioning enables the coach to problem-solve by recognising the need for new solutions, internally justifying, and rationalising their decisions and thus becoming more agile and coherent to their beliefs and values. Good coaches place significance on this aspect of practice and create time and space within their session to think, on-action while in-context, adopting coaching approaches that create 'time to think' (Collins & Collins, 2016; Schön, 1983). The coach becomes creative, imaginative, and resourceful and is ready to adapt to new ways and methods of thinking and practice, adaptably applying the resources they have at hand.

In practice there are five key attributes to effective critical appraisal of a coaching session: (1) a clear purpose, (2) an experience that has relevance to that purpose – potential to learn, (3) 'capturing' that experience – the experience is impactful or can be described in sufficient richness, depth, and detail, (4) having sufficient comprehension to understand the relationships of the different parts of that experience, and (5) distilling the learning into key actionable parts.

Coaching has been considered a collaborative affair between coach and learner (Jowett & Slade, 2021). The learner's perspective of the coaching experience would seem essential. Becker (2009) suggests the learners perspective is under-represented. Understanding the learner's perspective may yield insight into how a performance is understood, how independent practice might be created, or how future learning objectives may be created. These aren't about whether the coaching was good or not but are more nuanced, investigating the impact and perceptions of different practices at different times and in different contexts. The flaw in seeking a learner perspective is that coaches may teach for praise (Black & Weiss, 1992), as such, and previously noted, a blend of different information sources is required. After receiving feedback, you can either, act on it, have an intention to act differently next time, store the information and gather more, figure out what to do with it, or chose to ignore it when if it is ill informed, contradictory, over played or just nonsense.

The Curious Coach: An Enquiring Mind

New information need not be limited to those discussed above. However, in an effort not to absorb and replicate or change for the sake of change (think fads), there might be a need to 'test' out new knowledge within a coach's or CD's practice. Therefore, CDs could find it advantageous to encourage their coaches to conduct a form of practitioner inquiry of any new information. Indeed, we echo Hattie et al. (2015) that coaches (teachers) aren't researchers but they do have the power to be evaluators of their own impact. As such, a critical mind would consider what the new information impact might have and did have on the process and outcome of their coaching. The coach formulates a hypothesis on the impact of the new knowledge in a similar fashion to the coach anticipating the impact of a particular intervention (Eastabrook & Collins, 2021). For example, observation of an athlete's performance leads the coach to propose an intervention based on what they ascertain is required to improve that performance. The coach observes the effect of that intervention and measures the impact against an anticipated change in performance, their beliefs, and values before creating a subsequent intervention, a cycle of hypothesis, theory generation, and testing. New information can be treated similarly as the coach seeks to understand what has and has not worked in their practice. The key aspect with new information, as with assessing the impact of a coaching intervention, is to attempt to isolate the variable that you anticipate changing. Once the change is identified, a suitable method can be used to test its impact in practice while also being robust enough to provide the coach with confidence in that new information. The goal is to test out any new information and its suitability for the individual coach and the specific context. The focus for CDs is to encourage coaches to be open to new information, be critical of its source and to then test it out in practice and against their beliefs.

Adding to the Conversation

At times, coaching development has a frustrating cyclical nature! The CD should aim to encourage an upward spiral rather than an unbroken cycle. One way to achieve this is to engage within a Community of Practice (CoP), otherwise we risk all, separately, trying to figure out the same things or repeatedly rediscovering the same thing, over a 40-year career I have had the same 'fact' presented to me four times as new essential information for technical understanding on coach education courses each eight years apart! There is value in critically sharing experiences, information, and considerations while also being open to new sources and experiences. The SECI spiral model (Nonaka & Toyama, 2003) offers one such approach in which experiences and information is Socialised (S) through practice, guidance, and observation and dialogue with other who have those skills. That knowledge is the Externalised (E), converted from being tacit, uncodified, to explicit, codified, and shared among members in the CoP; once codified that knowledge is Combined (C) and converted into accessible sources like books, documents, manuals, and papers. Finally, that knowledge is Internalised (I) converted into tacit knowledge and modified for an individual to use. Unshared, the knowledge base does not move forward. The CDs aim to encourage sharing and robust debate that challenges assumptions and practices as the norm described by Bailey (2011) as the Zone of Uncomfortable Debate (ZOUD).

There is something inherently valuable in sharing the findings from practitioner inquiry, a simple logic of seeking a larger sample and robust criticality. Without which any new 'thing' can be overhyped, prone to confirmation, cognitive or blind spot bias. The CD needs to avoid the 'next big thing' or the very illusive coaching silver bullet when small progressions act as unique selling points in a commercial or competitive market.

Within these professional conversations coaches and CDs should be open and willing to share (1) source(s) of new information, (2) thoughts and notes on how that information might be useful, (3) details of any inquiry, both practitioner or academic; the variable and anticipated changes, a rational and explanation of the methods used – why, who, and how many were tested, and (4) outcome of inquiry including what didn't work. Sharing is extremely useful but, without criticality, can contribute to more chaff. Equally, in critique of our own title, with effective sharing, particularly consider things that might not have worked what one coaches might perceive as 'wheat' might be another's 'chaff', sharing in a critical manner help others decide for themselves what might work in their context. As Mees et al. (2022) find, 'the ability to do the right thing, in the right place and right time with the right people'.

Implications for Coach Development: Developing Critical Thinking

Coach development programmes that facilitate and encourage criticality would therefore have several characteristics. CD and training bodies would comprehend their own views and beliefs in relation to coaching, there would be a clear rationalised chain linking those beliefs to what is being taught and developed on a programme – a coherence between beliefs and practice. This relationship would be clear and shared across all developmental programmes, at all levels, for all coaches, CDs and the organisation 'this is what we think good coaching is … because ….'. These beliefs act as an underpinning theme, exemplified early in each programme 'what do our coaching values and beliefs look like in this context?'.

Those values and beliefs are, in turn, reflected in the course content and delivery. Using a broad range of approaches and tools that enable learning in both formal and informal settings, creating independent learners. Sources of information need to be acknowledged so the CD or organisation are not the owners and managers of that knowledge, the pro and cons of different approaches acknowledged and when an approach has advantages over another.

Importantly the CD role is to acknowledge and grasp the complexity of coaching practice, explaining it as simply as possible but not making it simplistic. Memes, folklore, and assumptions should be challenged and addressed, 'throwing stones at false idols'. This latter aspect requires a current, updated, and open-minded CD workforce. Great coaching and coach development works best when we are thoughtful and critically scrutinise claims carefully.

Concluding Remarks

We have identified that there are advantages for coaches and CDs to be critical consumers of literature and the practice of their peers and selves. Criticality supports an EIC practice that would aid coaches and CDs and improve their practice by finding information that is relevant to their practice more easily. To aid the development of EIC, we propose a set of dispositions. We prefer the notions of dispositions as they offer concurrent thoughts that can be integral to the coaching process avoiding the perception of criticality as separate to the coaching process – avoiding the trap 'reflection' find itself in, rather than prescribing a set way of thinking about thinking. A set of dispositions are flexible and adaptable to different practices, literature, beliefs, and organisations. Finally, the logical outcome of developing EIC is the development of practical wisdom.

References

Abraham, A., & Collins, D. (2011). Taking the next step: Ways forward for coaching science. *Quest, 63*, 366–384. https://doi.org/10.1080/00336297.2011.10483687.

Al-Kumaim, N. H., Hassan, S. H., Shabbir, M. S., Almazroi, A. A., & Al-Rejal, H. M. A. (2021). Exploring the inescapable suffering among postgraduate researchers:

information overload perceptions and implications for future research. *International Journal of Information and Communication Technology Education, 17*(1), 19–41. https://doi.org/10.4018/IJICTE.2021010102.

Bailey, C. (2011). Working through the ZOUD. *Management Focus, 30*(Spring), 14–15. http://dspace.lib.cranfield.ac.uk/handle/1826/5687.

Bailin, S., Case, R., Coombs, J. R., & Daniels, L. B. (1999). Conceptualizing critical thinking. *Journal of Curriculum Studies, 31*(3), 285–302. https://doi.org/10.1080/002202799183133

Baillie, L., Carrick-Sen, D., Marland, A., & Keil, M. F. (2019). In S. Llahana, C. Follin, C. Yedinak, & A. Grossman (Eds.), *Research and Evidence-Based Practice: The Nurse's Role BT – Advanced Practice in Endocrinology Nursing* (pp. 1321–1337). Springer International Publishing. https://doi.org/10.1007/978-3-319-99817-6_69.

Becker, A. J. (2009). It's not what they do, it's how they do it: Athlete experiences of great coaching. *International Journal of Sports Science & Coaching, 4*(1), 93–119. https://doi.org/10.1260/1747-9541.4.1.93.

Benzies, K. M., Premji, S., Hayden, K. A., & Serrett, K. (2006). State-of-the-evidence reviews: Advantages and challenges of including grey literature. *Worldviews on Evidence-Based Nursing, 3*(2), 55–61. https://doi.org/10.1111/j.1741-6787.2006.00051.x.

Biggs, J., & Tang, C. (2009). Applying constructive alignment. In *Training Material for "quality teaching for learning in higher education" Workshop for Master Trainers* (pp. 23–25). Ministry of Higher Education.

Black, S. J., & Weiss, M. R. (1992). The relationship among perceived coaching behaviors, perceptions of ability, and Motivation in competitive age-group swimmers. *Journal of Sport & Exercise Psychology, 14*, 309–326. https://doi.org/10.1123/jsep.14.3.309.

Christian, E., Hodgson, C. I., Berry, M., & Kearney, P. (2020). It's not what, but where: How the accentuated features of the adventure sports coaching environment promote the development of sophisticated epistemic beliefs. *Journal of Adventure Education and Outdoor Learning, 20*(1), 68–80. https://doi.org/10.1080/14729679.2019.1598879.

Cochran-Smith, M., & Lytle, S. L. (2009). Practitioner inquiry: Versions and variance. In M. Cochran-Smith & S. L. Lytle (Eds.), *Inquiry as Stance Practitioner: Research for the Next Generation* (pp. 37–59). Routledge.

Collins, D., Abraham, A., & Collins, R. (2012). On vampires and wolves – Exposing and exploring reasons for the differential impact of coach education. *International Journal of Sport Psychology, 43*(3), 255–271.

Collins, L., & Collins, D. (2016). Professional judgement and decision-making in adventure sports coaching: The role of interaction. *Journal of Sports Sciences, 34*(13), 1231–1239. https://doi.org/10.1080/02640414.2014.953980.

Collins, L., & Collins, D. (2019). The role of 'pracademics' in education and development of adventure sport professionals. *Journal of Adventure Education and Outdoor Learning, 19*(1), 1–11. https://doi.org/10.1080/14729679.2018.1483253.

Collins, L., Collins, D., & Grecic, D. (2015). The epistemological chain in high-level adventure sports coaches. *Journal of Adventure Education and Outdoor Learning, 15*(3), 224–238. https://doi.org/10.1080/14729679.2014.950592.

Cope, E., & Cushion, C. (2020). A move towards reconceptualising direct instruction in sport coaching pedagogy. *Impact – Journal of Chartered College of Teachers, 1*, 10.

Culver, D. M., Werthner, P., & Trudel, P. (2019). Coach developers as 'facilitators of learning' in a large-scale coach education programme: One actor in a complex system. *International Sport Coaching Journal, 6*(3), 296–306.

Dagenais, C., Lysenko, L., Abrami, P. C., Bernard, R. M., Ramde, J., & Janosz, M. (2012). Use of research-based information by school practitioners and determinants of

use: A review of empirical research. *Evidence and Policy, 8*(3), 285–309. https://doi.org/10.1332/174426412X654031.
Dewey, J. (1938). *Experience and education.* New York: Macmillan Company.
Eastabrook, C., & Collins, L. (2021). Ethical considerations and limited guidance for research in adventure sports coaching. *Journal of Adventure Education and Outdoor Learning, 22*(3), 239–249. https://doi.org/10.1080/14729679.2021.1925563
Eaton, S. E. (2018). Educational research literature reviews: Understanding the hierarchy of sources. *Journal of Educational Thought, February, 22*(3), 239–249.
Ennis, R. H. (1962). A concept of critical thinking. *Harvard Business Review, 23*(4), 462–472.
Ennis, R. H. (2015). Critical thinking: A streamlined conception. In *The Palgrave Handbook of Critical Thinking in Higher Education* (pp. 31–49). Palgrave Macmillan.
Franks, I. M. (2002). Evidence-based practice and the coaching process. *International Journal of Performance Analysis in Sport, 2*(1), 1–5. https://doi.org/10.1080/24748668.2002.11868256.
Grecic, D., & Collins, D. (2013). The epistemological chain: Practical applications in sports. *Quest, 65*(2), 151–168. https://doi.org/10.1080/00336297.2013.773525.
Greenhalgh, T. (2001). *How to Read a Paper: The Basics of Evidence Based Medicine* (Second Edition). Wiley and Sons Ltd.
Hattie, J., Masters, D., & Birch, K. (2015). *Visible Learning into Action: International Case Studies of Impact.* Routledge.
Howard, B. C., McGee, S., Schwartz, N., & Purcell, S. (2000). The experience of constructivism: Transforming teacher epistemology. *Journal of Research on Computing in Education, 32*(4), 455–465. https://doi.org/10.1080/08886504.2000.10782291.
Jowett, S., & Slade, K. (2021). Understanding the coach-athlete relationship and the role of ability, intentions and integrity. In C. Heaney, N. Kentzer, & B. Oakley (Eds.), *Athletic Development: A Psychological Perspective* (pp. 1–25). Open University publication chapter.
Lane, D., & Corrie, S. (2002). *The Modern Scientist.* Routledge.
Lipman, M. (1987). Critical thinking: What can it be? *Analytic Teaching, 8*(1), 5–12.
Mees, A., Sinfield, D., Collins, D., & Collins, L. (2020). Adaptive expertise – a characteristic of expertise in outdoor instructors? *Physical Education and Sport Pedagogy, 25*(4), 423–438. https://doi.org/10.1080/17408989.2020.1727870.
Mees, A., Toering, T., & Collins, L. (2022). Exploring the development of judgement and decision making in 'competent' outdoor instructors. *Journal of Adventure Education and Outdoor Learning, 22*(1), 77–91. https://doi.org/10.1080/14729679.2021.1884105.
Menter, I., Hulme, M., Elliot, D., & Lewin, J. (2010). Literature review on teacher education in the 21st century. In *Scottish Government Social Research*. https://dera.ioe.ac.uk/1255/1/0105011.pdf.
Nancekivell, S. E., Shah, P., & Gelman, S. A. (2020). Maybe they're born with it, or maybe it's experience: Toward a deeper understanding of the learning style myth. *Journal of Educational Psychology, 112*(2), 221–235. https://doi.org/10.1037/edu0000366.
Nash, C., MacPherson, A. C., & Collins, D. (2022). Reflections on reflection: Clarifying and promoting use in experienced coaches. *Frontiers in Psychology, 13*(May). https://doi.org/10.3389/fpsyg.2022.867720.
Nelson, L. J., Cushion, C. J., & Potrac, P. (2006). Formal, nonformal and informal coach learning: A holistic conceptualisation. *International Journal of Sports Science & Coaching, 1*(3), 247–259. https://doi.org/10.1260/174795406778604627.
Nonaka, I., & Toyama, R. (2003). The knowledge-creating theory revisited: knowledge creation as a synthesizing process. *Knowledge Management Research & Practice, 1*(1), 2–10. https://doi.org/10.1057/palgrave.kmrp.8500001

Nutley, S., Powell, A., & Davies, H. (2013). What counts as good evidence? Provocation paper for the alliance for useful evidence. In *Research Unit for Research Utilisation (RURU)*. https://doi.org/10.1007/BF00187010.

Passmore, J., & Rowson, T. S. (2019). Neuro-linguistic-programming: A critical review of NLP research and the application of NLP in coaching. *International Coaching Psychology Review*, *14*(1), 57–69. https://centaur.reading.ac.uk/91275/%0AIt.

Perry Jr, W. G. (1981). Cognitive and ethical growth: The making of meaning. *College Student Development and Academic Life: Psychological, Intellectual, Social and Moral Issues*, *1*(234), 48–55.

Rushall, B. S. (2003). *Coaching development and the second law of thermodynamics (or belief-based versus evidence-based coaching development)*. http://coachsci.sdsu.edu/csa/thermo/thermo.htm.

Schommer, M. (1994). Synthesizing epistemological belief research: Tentative understandings and provocative confusions. *Educational Psychology Review*, *6*(4), 293–319. https://doi.org/10.1007/BF02213418.

Schommer-Aikins, M. (2004). Explaining the epistemological belief system: Introducing the embedded systemic model and coordinated research approach. *Educational Psychologist*, *39*(1), 19–29. https://doi.org/10.1207/s15326985ep3901_3.

Schommer-Aikins, M., & Easter, M. (2006). Ways of knowing and epistemological beliefs: Combined effect on academic performance. *Educational Psychology*, *26*(3), 411–423. https://doi.org/10.1080/01443410500341304.

Schön, D. (1983). *The Reflective Practitioner: How Professionals Think in Action*. Ashgate.

Schwartz, B. (2011). Practical wisdom and organizations. *Research in Organizational Behavior*, *31*, 3–23. https://doi.org/10.1016/j.riob.2011.09.001.

Sinfield, D., Allen, J., & Collins, L. (2020). A comparative analysis of the coaching skills required by coaches operating in different non-competitive paddlesport settings. *Journal of Adventure Education and Outdoor Learning*, *20*(2), 170–184. https://doi.org/10.1080/14729679.2019.1609998.

Smith, B. (2018). Generalizability in qualitative research: misunderstandings, opportunities and recommendations for the sport and exercise sciences. *Qualitative Research in Sport, Exercise and Health*, *10*(1), 137–149. https://doi.org/10.1080/2159676X.2017.1393221.

Stanovich, K. E., & Stanovich, P. J. (2010). A framework for critical thinking, rational thinking, and intelligence. In *Innovations in Educational Psychology: Perspectives on Learning, Teaching, and Human Development* (pp. 195–237). Springer Publishing Company.

Sternberg, R. J. (1985). Implicit theories of intelligence, creativity, and wisdom. *Journal of Personality and Social Psychology*, *49*(3), 607–627.

Stoszkowski, J., & Collins, D. (2014). Communities of practice, social learning and networks: Exploiting the social side of coach development. *Sport, Education and Society*, *19*(6), 773–788.

Stoszkowski, J., MacNamara, Á., Collins, D., & Hodgkinson, A. (2020). "Opinion and Fact, Perspective and Truth": Seeking truthfulness and integrity in coaching and coach education. *International Sport Coaching Journal*, *8*(2), 263–269. https://doi.org/10.1123/iscj.2020-0023

Tiller, N. B., Sullivan, J. P., & Ekkekakis, P. (2022). Baseless claims and pseudoscience in health and wellness: A call to action for the sports, exercise, and nutrition – science community. *Sports Medicine*. https://doi.org/10.1007/s40279-022-01702-2.

9
SENSEMAKING FOR THE COACH DEVELOPER

Jamie Taylor and Christine Nash

Introduction

As the genesis of this book highlights, the role of the coach developer (CD) is generating increasing interest, both in literature and practically, within sporting organisations and grass root clubs. In practice, the role of CD has been conceptualised as: "expert support practitioners who plan for, implement, and sustain strategies and interventions in support of skilled performance in sport coaching… it will also be collaborative, contextually situated, and concerned with helping coaches to develop active, critical knowledge and skills" (CIMSPA, 2021, p. 4). As a distinct role framing, CDs have been conceptualised as needing to incorporate elements of other roles in the coach education workforce, for example: coach educator (Cushion et al., 2019) and coach mentor (Grecic & Collins, 2013; Leeder & Sawiuk, 2021). Yet, despite the role of CD becoming more prevalent amongst sporting organisations and a wealth of literature offering critical insight into coach education practice (e.g., Downham & Cushion, 2020), there remains limited conceptual or empirical work 'for', rather than 'of' CD practice (cf. Cushion et al., 2006).

This appears especially important given that discussions about the professionalisation of sport coaching and dissatisfaction about the quality of coach education are widespread (Lyle & Cushion, 2017). Although much research has been conducted in the UK this can be viewed a global issue, where developed coach education systems operate. For example, Hedlund and colleagues (2018) highlight the global need to improve coach education while Stewart and Koch (2020) highlight the difficulties faced by US college coaches accessing quality coach education. As such, the domain remains without a strong grounding, or evidence, to guide the progress of professionals. At the time of writing the domain is dominated by approaches that are grounded in executive coaching, often devoid of the specific knowledge bases required to inform CDs (Nash & Collins, 2006) and missing the complexity of the coaching process (Cushion, 2007). In contrast, both in literature (Abraham et al., 2013; McQuade & Nash, 2015) and professional standards (CIMSPA, 2021), the role of CD has been built on the conceptual base of Professional Judgment and Decision Making (PJDM).

PJDM explicitly recognises the complexity of coaching practice and puts a significant weighting on the decision-making capability of the individual practitioner and advocates for an expertise approach in practice (Nash et al., 2012). Taking this reasoning a step further, the dynamic nature of coaching requires coaches to develop adaptive expertise rather than routine (Mees et al., 2020). This 'it depends' approach, although critiqued as being over ambiguous (Garner et al., 2022), puts greater weighting on the needs of the individual and context than conforming to a rigid methodology. It begins with the identification of intentions for impact, before formulating and flexibly implementing a plan to support the target change (Collins et al., In Review; Martindale & Collins, 2007). As such, the approach represents a research-informed approach to practice, one that draws on the best available evidence, needs of context and experience of practitioner (Neelen & Kirschner, 2020). Supportive of enhancing the practical application of a PJDM approach for the CD, in this chapter we seek to address the conceptual gap by considering the value of sensemaking to the CD.

Knowledge and Its Application

The first area for consideration is the critical role of knowledge as it pertains to the coach and to the CD. The role of knowledge in the coaching process is well established, as is the need for a significant knowledge base across a range of domains (Abraham et al., 2006). Nash and Collins (2006) suggested that coaches needed to be able to integrate knowledge from three specific domains: sport specific, the 'ologies' (psychology, physiology, etc.), and pedagogy. In addition, to flexibly deploy declarative knowledge in the right manner, understanding the complex causal relationships between knowledges (Anderson, 2000). This deep conceptual knowledge appears to be a significant vehicle for transfer and the ability for a coach to be able to think in an abstract manner and move towards the level of adaptive expertise that is likely necessary to be effective in the complex milieu presented to the coach (Mees et al., 2020). Given the inherent complexities of the coaching process, there is a growing recognition of PJDM as an appropriate approach for the development of coaches (CIMSPA, 2019). It is this abstract thinking that should be a target for efficacious CD practice, especially taking account of the inherent complexities of the coaching process, where knowledge is both flexibly used and generated in a contextually situated manner. This flexible use of knowledge and the associated epistemological basis is something that has been explored in the role of the coach mentor (Grecic & Collins, 2013). Epistemology has been identified as fundamental to thinking and the ability to understand the acquisition and development of knowledge, an important component of CD, as knowledge is fundamental to the role. A key feature of coach mentoring is supporting the coach in developing a 'sophisticated epistemology', recognising the tentative nature of knowledge (Schommer, 1994). Therefore, whilst both procedural and declarative knowledge are critical, the latter is likely to be essential for truly flexible practice (Anderson, 1983). This flexibility is a growing feature of wider educational practice, where there is growing recognition of the need for evidence-informed (rather than evidence-based) practice, which takes account of the best available evidence, practitioner experience, and the needs of the context (Neelen & Kirschner, 2020).

Elsewhere, various other categories of knowledge have been linked to the development of expertise, including: perceptual skills, a sense of typicality, routines, and mental models (Klein & Militello, 2004). This was later operationalised in the coaching domain by Nash et al. (2012) who suggested that these skills, along with others, characterised expert coaching practice. So therefore, building a knowledge base and the coach's ability to generate further knowledge in the future should therefore be a core feature of CD work (Stoszkowski et al., 2020). Yet, given that the operationalising of knowledge appears to be an essential feature of practice and that coaching is a messy, complex domain, there remains the question of how coaches and CDs make optimum use of knowledge. Knowledge is of course necessary for flexible practice, but clearly not sufficient. For coaches and CDs to be truly impactful, there is a need for application (Nash & Collins, 2006).

Sensemaking

It is against this backdrop that we propose the concept of sensemaking offers the potential to underpin the practice of the CD. This is especially so, given the need for applying knowledge in the complexity of the coaching process. Although a variety of framings of sensemaking have been offered in the literature, it has been conceptualised as the "deliberate effort to understand events" (Klein et al., 2007, p. 114) and "turning circumstances into a situation that is comprehended explicitly in words and that serves as a springboard into action" (Weick et al., 2005, p. 409). It is, in essence, a practical activity that should lead to action on the behalf of a professional.

Models of Sensemaking

There are a number of different conceptions of sensemaking, established from divergent fields with contrasting approaches and outcomes, illustrated by the differences in spelling (sensemaking, sense-making, and sense making) – as will be made clear later in this chapter, we have chosen to use sensemaking. Despite these differences, sensemaking is commonly understood as the processes through which people interpret and give meaning to their experiences. In the interests of the flexible approach we advocate, we have provided a brief overview of some common models.

Dervin Sensemaking

This particular approach was proposed by Brenda Dervin (1980) and focuses on the individual – a form of human information behaviour. Within many contexts, people encounter situations where there is a gap in their knowledge. In order to move on, individuals must 'make sense' of the situation to move past or cross the gap. This theory provides little insight as to how individuals 'cross the gap' but does provide some strategies as examples.

Madsbjerg's Sensemaking

This approach may appeal to coaches and CDs alike as it takes a stance against 'number crunching' based processes that according to Madsberg (2017) now dominate business practices – the power of big data. His model accentuates the importance of deep, nuanced engagement with the culture, language, and history of individuals in order to make sense in the modern world.

Cynefin Framework

The Cynefin framework developed by Snowden (2020) is a sensemaking tool used to help individuals, usually in leadership positions, think through a problem or situation to find a solution. It breaks down problems into four domains: Obvious, Complicated, Complex, and Chaotic. This framework encourages decision-making by focusing on the important elements of each context.

Weick

From a social constructivist perspective, Karl Weick proposed sensemaking as a socially mediated activity that emphasises the role of metaphor. This view sees sensemaking as "the ongoing retrospective development of plausible images that rationalise what people are doing" (Weick et al., 2005, p. 409). It is the process by which individuals attempt to create order and understand past events. Whilst it is the individual that does the making of sense, this is inherently socially mediated (Weick, 1995). More recently, although perhaps portrayed as a purely cognitive phenomena, the action-based components of sensemaking have been emphasised (Weick, 2020). This perspective challenges the assumption that sensemaking is internal and individual in nature, focusing on the social construction of meaning. Weick's account has also been critiqued as putting too much weighting on building retrospective coherence for the purpose of future action (Snowden, 2010).

Wayfinding

Ingold (2000), followed by Raubal (2008), introduced the concept of wayfinding, an ecological model, that enables individual to make sense of where they are and where they need to go. This 'bottom up' approach (emphasising action) suggests that learners self-regulate through emergent problems. Ecological perspectives on Wayfinding have emphasised the need for search and action in environments and de-emphasised the role of representations or knowledge. Simply put, the CD would design learning opportunities for the coach to engage in search and exploration. In turn, the CD would likely navigate their way through the role without a clear end point, or knowledge base to inform action, instead of being attuned to the environment (Woods et al., 2020). Effective sensemaking and wayfinding are interdependent but also require capabilities such as flexibility, agility, and continuous improvement. As information is discovered and knowledge is built, short learning cycles enable faster iteration increasing the likelihood of success.

Abductive Approaches

Despite the value and insight offered by the above models, for the purpose of practical application, this chapter will focus on abductive approaches to sensemaking. Firstly, through the lens of Predictive Processing (PP) (e.g., Friston, 2018; Williams, 2020) latterly and, in more depth, the Data Frame (DF) model of sensemaking (Klein et al., 2006a). Although conceptually distinct, with the former considered a meta-theory, the abductive basis for both suggests the need to understand sensemaking as both a top-down and bottom-up process. In essence, a circular process and interaction between top-down knowledge structures (generative models, frames, knowledge) and bottom-up perception of stimuli/data (Clark, 2016). In essence, whilst being strongly action oriented, there is a need to recognise the "pro-active neural strategy keep(ing) us poised for action" (Clark, 2016, p. 52). Our reasoning for this focus is twofold, firstly, the context of the work of the CD is often as an individual and with an individual and secondly, it is inherently a practical activity. For the CD working in an alternative capacity, they may wish to consider group models of sensemaking (e.g., Klein et al., 2010).

DF is a view of sensemaking framed within the study of macrocognition, a holistic view of human functioning in complex and dynamic real-world situations (Klein et al., 2003). Or, more simply, it can be thought of as understanding how people make decisions under messy conditions, clearly an important feature of CD work. Macrocognition has been contrasted with microcognition, as the discreet investigation of mental events. This view suggests the CD fits data to a mental structure (the frame) and this frame is used to account for data and guide the search for further data. The frames we hold will shape and define what we perceive to be relevant data. In addition, data will change our frames (Klein et al., 2006b). Similar to PP, DF is very much grounded in representational accounts of human functioning (cf. Constant et al., 2021). The DF model runs counter to explanations from early models of information processing that posit a cascade from data, to information, to knowledge, and to understanding (Klein et al., 2006a). Importantly, DF also suggests that sensemaking is typically initiated by surprising, or difficult circumstances, whereby individuals will choose to find the data to elaborate an existing frame or will reframe entirely if the data doesn't fit. At a practical level therefore, commitment to a particular frame must be coupled by the motivation to test the frame for inaccuracies (Klein et al., 2006b). In essence, in addition to using frames to make sense of incoming sense data, humans also use frames as a means of defining what data actually matters in the first place

Sensemaking for CDs and Coaches

We would suggest that the DF model, along with the other discussed models of sensemaking, has significant capacity to influence CD practice. Specifically, DF suggests a number of functions of sensemaking, all of which are especially relevant to the role of the CD:

- Problem detection
- Connecting dots and making discoveries
- Forming explanations
- Anticipatory thinking
- Project future states
- Find the levers
- See relationships
- Problem Identification (Klein et al., 2007)

People will aim to explain events based on data (from the bottom-up), in conjunction with an organising frame (top-down). Frames are considered conceptual approximations, rather than referring to a more formal notion of the construct (Hoffman, 2013). Where there is a mismatch between data and frame, the individual will begin a process of questioning of the frame, by tracking anomalies, finding inconsistency, making judgements about plausibility and the quality of data. Following the questioning of a frame, individuals will either follow a path of re-framing (Klein et al., 2021), by seeking alternative explanations or elaborate an existing frame with data (Klein et al., 2007). Schön (1983) considered the frame to be the perspective from which interpretations are formed and if the frame was adjusted it allowed individuals to view events from a different perspective.

Surprise

Typically, sensemaking is initiated by the experience of surprise, a failure of expectations, the uncovering of contradictory beliefs, or data inconsistent with existing frames (Friston et al., 2020; Hutton, 2019). It is often this that encourages the questioning of an existing frame, when one seeks to: "connect what is observed with what is inferred, to explain and to diagnose, to guide actions before routines emerge for performing tasks, and to enrich existing routines" (Klein et al., 2007, p. 114). That is, when confronted with surprise, sensemaking

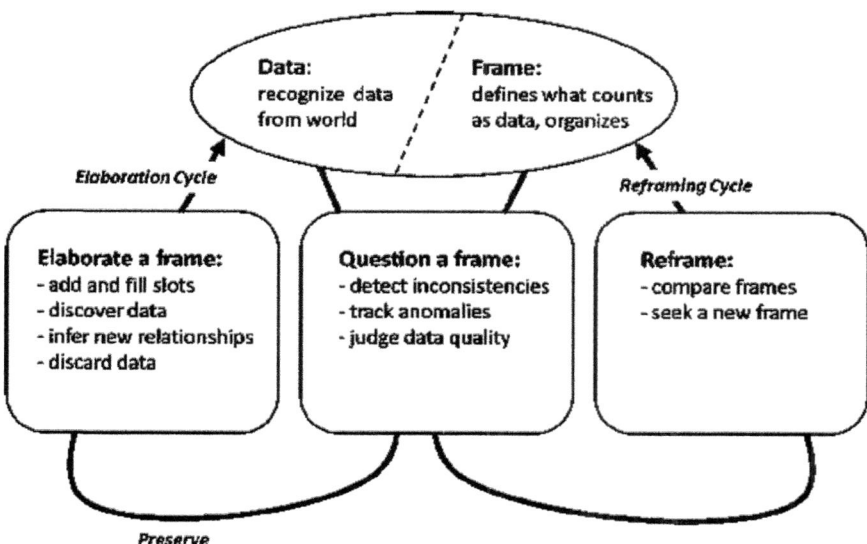

FIGURE 9.1 Data Frame model (see Klein et al., 2006b, p. 89).

aims to identify relationships explaining past events and enhancing future expectancies (see Figure 9.1).

It is therefore during this process that systematic analysis of existing frames will likely occur (Moore & Hoffman, 2011). It is this systematic analysis that may be of significant utility to the CD working 'in situ' with the coach. By taking steps to support the active process of sensemaking, when encountering surprise or when the CD deliberately challenges the coach, there is an opportunity for learning/growth. It is from this point where the existing frame can be preserved, elaborated, or reframed entirely. The experience of surprise, or a discrepancy between expectation and outcome, is important. Elsewhere in the literature it has been identified as a critical feature of learning experiences (Taylor & Collins, 2020; Woolley & Fishbach, 2022). Separately it has been conceptualised as the experience of desirable difficulty (Bjork & Bjork, 2020), a disorienting dilemma (Mezirow, 1978), confusion (Dewey, 1910; Schön, 1983) amongst others. It is also coherent with PP accounts of human functioning that suggest that the difference between prior expectation and data is the source of learning (Constant et al., 2021; Linson et al., 2018).

It is this learning from confusion or doubt that we turn to next. The ability to move beyond an initial frame may be a matter of skill and experience (Moore & Hoffman, 2011), but a challenge for both coach and CD. This is partly because errors in practice, or surprising circumstances, are often not that visible, especially if a coach works on their own. Whilst in high-performance sport, the big win or loss may yield periods of deep reflection (Lara-Bercial & Mallett, 2016) and one of the key challenges for the coach and CD is that opportune errors, or 'surprises', may not be especially obvious, at least over the short term. As an example, we frequently see coaches judging their effectiveness by the improvement (or otherwise) of their athletes in a single session. When compared with the learning literature, we know this to be an ineffective marker (Soderstrom & Bjork, 2015). In essence, there is an opportunity for the mundane to become an opportunity for deep reflection and sensemaking. Importantly, whilst the DF model suggests that sensemaking will typically be initiated by a level of 'surprise', this is not always the case. Nor does it suggest that there is necessarily a beginning or end to the process. Sensemaking can commence at any point and doesn't suggest a clear end point (Hoffman, 2013). This has significant implications for the CD because whilst 'surprise' might not necessarily be a common feature of practice, it is easier to identify and address than the more usual everyday practice of an experienced coach.

Frames

This of course raises an important question about frames and one that we would suggest is fundamental to coaching and CD practice. The frames used in the process of sensemaking can rest on internal representations or mental models that reflect causal structures (Hutton, 2019). Therefore, effective sensemaking relies on coaches and CDs holding appropriate mental models to frame incoming data. Mental models are regarded as a description of a system's form, explanation of functions that allow us to predict future states (Rouse & Morris, 1986), knowledge of limitations, and typical errors (Borders et al., 2019). Or, mental models can be how we simplify complexity, why we consider some things more relevant than others, and how we reason. Importantly, experts and novices do not appear to use distinct approaches to sensemaking, what does appear to distinguish expert and non-expert populations are the quality of mental models and knowledge bases. That is, experts will generate inferences in the same way, but those inferences will be different based on deeper knowledge bases and high-quality mental models (Sieck et al., 2007). The depth and quality of mental models will support the individual's ability to judge credibility of the data and make plausibility judgments. If the frame of the coach is short-term sessional improvement, or for the CD witnessing a coach reproducing a socially approved behaviour (Downham & Cushion, 2020; Stoszkowski et al., 2020), there is likely an issue. It is for this reason Klein et al. (2007) suggest the need for practitioners to build a richer and deeper repertoire of frames. This has significant implications for CD practice in suggesting that CDs should possess rich mental models of coaching practice and are unlikely to be effective if the CDS do not have this repertoire.

Importantly, of course, coaching does not take place in the abstract, it is highly contextualised and socially situated, as with any other professional practice. This, we would argue, doesn't mean that coaches and CDs need to adopt 'bottom up' approaches like 'wayfinding' which would suggest that coaches find a way, acting based on sources of information and deploying a specific methodological approach (Woods et al., 2020). It also contrasts with 'top down' sensemaking approaches such as OODA loop (observe, orient, decide, act – Osinga, 2005) based on waterfall models of information processing. Instead, the approach advocated by this chapter seeks to move the discourse towards a middle way. The DF approach is reciprocal, top-down, and bottom-up, where data is fitted to a frame and the frame is fitted around the data. Neither of these processes is considered to be more important (Hutton, 2019). It is therefore inherently pragmatic in nature and focused on supporting and developing action in the real world, rather than for the purpose of theory (Hoffman, 2013; Sieck et al., 2007).

Practical Application for the Coach

We will now consider two levels at which sensemaking is important in the work of the CD. Previously we have highlighted the complexity of the work, so there is a need for the CD to engage in a twin process of sensemaking, both for coach and their own CD work. Firstly, as it pertains to the support of the coach and how CDs might go about supporting the sensemaking of the coach. Given a core role of the CD to promote the long-term development of the coach, we would suggest that sensemaking appears to be critical in that the CD may want to deliberately exaggerate particular data or manipulate certain situations to encourage sensemaking and the questioning of a coach's frames. This of course requires a level of caution for the CD, given the risk of reinforcing faulty frames or simply promoting a given ideological stance (Downham & Cushion, 2020). Yet, there is also the opportunity for the CD to be truly impactful and shape the ongoing learning of the coach. By supporting effective sensemaking, the CD can help the coach challenge and subsequently adjust existing frames. It is through the adjustment, which may allow the coach to notice a clash between expectations and events as they happen, as a means of reframing problems and considering alternative strategies for action (Schön, 1983). This is a strategy shown to be an effective feature of CD practice and an overt emphasis on the ability of the coach to engage in sensemaking appears to offer more opportunity to recognise learning opportunities and the update of frames (Nash et al., 2022). Indeed, this may be especially important given the proliferation of social media as the knowledge source of choice (Stoszkowski et al., 2020). This suggests that the application of sensemaking may be crucial in influencing the criticality of the coach (see Chapter 8) and, in turn, supporting their future learning and development.

Practical Application for the Coach Developer

In addition to use with the coach, there are also important implications for the CD, therefore, we would also emphasise the need for the CD to spend time in case of conceptualisation, understanding the needs of the coach, and forming rich mental models of the coach's current knowledge and skillset (Hoffman, 1998). This will help to mitigate against a coach's 'knowledge shields' or the mental manoeuvres used to rationalise existing beliefs without changing a view (Hoffman et al., 2014). Without this first step, there is a real risk that CD practice can become a series of nice chats, without serious developmental action. In essence, this is the critical step that allows the CD to conceptualise intentions for impact, then plan for the types of experiences that will likely be of benefit to the coach (Martindale & Collins, 2005). It is from this point that the CD can anticipate the types of input that they can offer and the types of experience that are likely to be useful for the coach. Importantly, we would suggest that this suggests a sensemaking process for the CD and encourages the notion that experts will likely spend longer examining a situation than novice counterparts (Klein et al., 2003; Schön, 1983). As such, to truly make the most of learning in context, maximising the benefit of sensemaking we would advocate for coaches and CDs to deliberately articulate their intentions of impact (Martindale & Collins, 2005), along with identifying markers of success that can then be used as a means to prompt sensemaking (Collins & Collins, 2020). In essence, a lack of clarity on what you are trying to achieve may prevent the initiation of sensemaking.

Tools in Use

In response to the complex challenge presented to the CD, a variety of tools have been developed that aim to scaffold CD sensemaking. Firstly, the use of competency check lists, which for so long have remained the tool of choice for many sporting organisations to quickly and cheaply assess the competency of coaches. This approach has obviously been subject to significant criticism from multiple sources (Collins et al., 2015), but unfortunately remains the bedrock of much practice. Cynically, this may be because it meets the needs of human resource departments and an agenda that cares less about coach quality and more about sheer volume of coaches that can be developed quickly and easily.

In response to the limitations of the check list approach, Cushion et al. (2012) developed the Coach Analysis and Interventions System (CAIS), a behavioural inventory that can be used to 'objectively' measure features of coaching practice in action. It also allows for an understanding of when behaviours happen and the direction of specific behaviours (Cushion et al., 2012). As a tool, it has gained traction in the wider CD community and a number of practitioners are using the approach as a frame to define and filter data in the coaching session. Based on the notion that coaches struggle to coach in a manner aligned to their intentions (Partington & Cushion, 2013), it has also been used as a tool to generate surprise for the coach. Yet, if the tool is naively used as the whole solution to coach observation, there are a number of issues (Cope et al., 2017). Firstly, it misses coaching activities that takes place away from the field/court/track/pitch, something that is increasingly recognised as a critical element of coaching (Bjørndal & Ronglan, 2018; Taylor & Collins, 2022). In addition, whilst taking a purely behavioural approach to coaching practice may be useful for the purpose of identifying *what* happened, it doesn't emphasise *why* a coach behaves in a particular way (Abraham & Collins, 2011a). When coupled with the assumption that there is a 'right way' to coach and all the user needs to do is to count behaviours (Lyle & Cushion, 2017), there is a serious risk of stunting the development of the coach. Anecdotally in practice, we have witnessed coaches being presented with infographics of coaching behaviour, which make recommendations to the coach devoid of context, such as: 'coach should ask more questions'. Similarly, feedback to coaches that praises them for using a behavioural repertoire that has been linked to a specific pedagogic approach (cf. Kidman, 2010). Taking either of these approaches assumes that coaches *should* behave in a particular way, regardless of athlete needs and absent of any sensemaking of the data. Behavioural instruments also ignore the significant work that many coaches engage in away from practice time (Richards et al., 2017). In essence, tools of this nature are only as effective as the user's sensemaking process and subsequent decision-making. None can be used effectively without reference to an understanding of the decision-making process of the coach and the context in which they are working. In short, understanding why they are doing what they are doing, we propose that the missing link is sensemaking.

In response, taking an alternative approach explicitly embedding PJDM, Taylor et al. (in review) have proposed the 3Ps approach (Procedure, Process, and Planning) to the observation of coaching practice: procedure being the basic procedures used by the coach (positioning, organisation, time management); process being the more intuitive decisions made by the coach (Collins et al., 2016); and planning being a focus on the enactment of the slower more thoughtful decisions made in the lead up to the session (Abraham & Collins, 2011b). The 3Ps strongly emphasise the need for sensemaking from the CD throughout their work. Indeed, this approach encourages what Crandall and colleagues described with reference to understanding expertise:

> When the tasks that people are doing are complex, it is not enough to simply observe people's actions and behaviours – what they do. It is important to find out how they think and what they know, how they organise and structure information and what they seek to understand better.
> *Crandall et al. (2006, p. 3)*

In essence, regardless of the approach taken to gathering data on coaching practice, rather than the tool, it is the extent to which the CD is able to make sense of the complexity of the coaching process. There is a need for the CD to use observation of the coach across multiple contexts, beyond training or competition, to identify specific features that could be used to initiate sensemaking for the coach based on a longer term nested agenda (cf. Abraham & Collins, 2011b).

It is not just session observation whereby the CD needs to engage in sensemaking. This should be interwoven into every element of practice: case conceptualisation, nested planning for the coach, coach observation, and intervention strategies. The following Case Study exemplifies our operationalisation of sensemaking in the CD context.

CASE STUDY

A CD working with a boxing coach discovers through early needs analysis that the coach holds a limited conceptualisation of learning. By engaging in early discussions about her practice, then observing interactions with other coaches in a planning meeting, it appears the sole target of her practice are short-term changes to motor skill within a session (cf. Schmidt & Bjork, 1992). As part of a broader strategy focused on helping the coach to develop a richer knowledge of learning, the CD asks the coach to pull together video footage of a particular boxer and the changes made to their ability to parry a jab against a south paw opponent over three sparring sessions separated by three months. Generating moderate surprise for the coach, over that time period, limited change has been made, despite it being a core focus for their work and the fighter being highly motivated to make the change. The CD then offers to film a coaching session, gathering video and audio data for the coach. In session, the coach appears to be getting significant short-term improvement with the fighter being asked to parry jabs in highly blocked, massed practice formats. When the CD debriefs the session with coach, they begin a conversation regarding different approaches to practice design. This allows the CD to present a variety of different practice formats to the coach, discussing their relative strengths and weaknesses (navigating knowledge shields and offering new frames). The coach is then asked to review the session and analyse their practice set against each of the practice forms (e.g., Williams & Hodges, 2005). The next debrief session asks the coach to describe the practice forms they have used and why they have been chosen. At this stage, it is clear to the coach that they are not sure why they are doing what they are doing. In essence, the CD has initiated sensemaking and has skilfully engineered a situation where the coach is motivated to deepen knowledge of her practice. The coach and CD then agree to spend some time developing a base of declarative knowledge of the differential effects of different approaches to practice design (Skurvydas et al., 2020). The CD also encourages the coach to creatively consider alternative courses of action by using 'the Big 5' reflective question set (Collins & Collins, 2020). Significantly, the CD and coach work together to apply this knowledge to the specific contextual demands of boxing, taking account of their personal experience and generate alternatives for practice (Neelen & Kirschner, 2020). The outcome of the approach being the extension of the coach's frames and declarative knowledge supporting enhanced future sensemaking and criticality.

Conclusion

Coach development is entering an interesting stage, whilst there is clear recognition of its overall value to the coach, across a number of domains, there remains an anti-intellectual approach to knowledge in many coaching communities (Cushion et al., 2019; Stoszkowski & Collins, 2016). This in some cases lends itself to procedurally hungry coaches (Nash & Collins, 2006), who lack criticality and prefer working to recipes than from a declarative base (Abraham et al., 2009; Stoszkowski et al., 2020). The clear implication of the work and application presented by this chapter suggests the need for a greater focus on the expertise of CDs and their focus on developing expertise in the wider coaching workforce. We would suggest that if coaching is to make progress as a profession (Woodman, 1993), we need to be more sophisticated in our understanding and development of coaches.

We hope that this chapter has highlighted the potential that sensemaking processes may hold for the CD and for coaching as a complex multifaceted endeavour. One of the things we have sought to emphasise throughout this chapter is the critical application of sensemaking as a concept for the CD. We suggest that a primary role of the CD is to deliberately initiate a process of sensemaking for the coach, with the ultimate end of enhancing their PJDM, in essence: "helping coaches to develop active, critical knowledge and skills" (CIMSPA, 2021, p. 4). To do this, there is an additional layer of sensemaking that the CD needs to engage with by making sense themselves.

Steps to encourage coaches to hold more sophisticated frames or models for their practice would seem to be a critical area to support long-term development. This seems especially important given the drive towards oversimplification, whether it be through the uncritical application of concepts from outside of sport (e.g., Taylor et al., 2022) or approaches that advocate for random coaching interventions. Approaches like this are highly questionable, given that they appear explicitly antithetical to the development of expertise in coaches and prevent active sensemaking. Knowledge and the application of knowledge would seem to be an area that is routinely referenced in literature but is routinely de-emphasised in the applied world. By highlighting the promise of sensemaking, we also suggest that declarative knowledge is an essential pre-requisite for the CD to do their work.

References

Abraham, A., & Collins, D. (2011a). Effective Skill Development – How Should Athletes' Skills be Developed. In D. Collins, A. Button, & H. Richards (Eds.), *Performance Psychology: A Practitioner's Guide* (pp. 207–230). Elsevier.

Abraham, A., & Collins, D. (2011b). Taking the Next Step: Ways Forward for Coaching Science. *Quest*, 63(4), 366–384. https://doi.org/10.1080/00336297.2011.10483687.

Abraham, A., Collins, D., & Martindale, R. (2006). The Coaching Schematic: Validation through Expert Coach Consensus. *Journal of Sports Sciences*, 24(6), 549–564. https://doi.org/10.1080/02640410500189173.

Abraham, A., Collins, D., Morgan, G., & Muir, B. (2009). Developing Expert Coaches Requires Expert Coach Development: Replacing Serendipity with Orchestration. In A. Lorenzo, S.J. Ibanez, & E. Ortega (Eds.), *Aportaciones Teoricas Y Practicas Para El Baloncesto Del Futuro*. Wanceulen Editorial Deportiva.

Abraham, A., Morgan, G., North, J., Muir, B., Duffy, P., Allison, W., Cale, A., & Hodgson, R. (2013, 21–24 May 2013). Task analysis of coach developers: Applications to the FA youth coach educator role. Proceedings of the 11th international conference on naturalistic decision making (NDM 2013), Marseille, France.

Anderson, J. R. (1983). *The Architecture of Cognition*. Lawrence Erlbaum Associates.

Anderson, J. R. (2000). *Learning and Memory: An Integrated Approach* (2nd ed.). John Wiley & Sons Inc.

Bjork, R. A., & Bjork, E. L. (2020). Desirable Difficulties in Theory and Practice. *Journal of Applied Research in Memory and Cognition, 9*(4), 475–479. https://doi.org/10.1016/j.jarmac.2020.09.003.

Bjørndal, C. T., & Ronglan, L. T. (2018). Orchestrating Talent Development: Youth Players' Developmental Experiences in Scandinavian Team Sports. *Sports Coaching Review, 7*(1), 1–22. https://doi.org/10.1080/21640629.2017.1317172.

Borders, J., Klein, G., & Besuijen, R. (2019). An operational account of mental models: A pilot study. International Conference on Naturalistic Decision Making, San Francisco, CA.

CIMSPA. (2019). *Coaching in High Performance Sport V1.7*. Retrieved 2nd November from https://www.cimspa.co.uk/standards-home/professional-standards-library?cid=18&d=463

CIMSPA. (2021). *Coach Developer Standard V1.0*. Retrieved 2nd November from https://www.cimspa.co.uk/standards-home/professional-standards-library?cid=18&d=485

Clark, A. (2016). *Surfing Uncertainty: Prediction, Action and the Embodied Mind*. Oxford University Press. https://doi.org/10.1093/acprof:oso/9780190217013.001.0001.

Collins, D., Burke, V., Martindale, A., & Cruickshank, A. (2015). The Illusion of Competency Versus the Desirability of Expertise: Seeking a Common Standard for Support Professions in Sport. *Sports Medicine, 45*(1), 1–7. https://doi.org/10.1007/s40279-014-0251-1.

Collins, D., & Collins, L. (2020). Developing Coaches' Professional Judgement and Decision Making: Using the 'Big 5'. *Journal of Sports Sciences, 39*(1), 115–119. https://doi.org/10.1080/02640414.2020.1809053.

Collins, D., Collins, L., & Carson, H. J. (2016). "If It Feels Right, Do It": Intuitive Decision Making in a Sample of High-Level Sport Coaches [Original Research]. *Frontiers in Psychology, 7*(504). https://doi.org/10.3389/fpsyg.2016.00504.

Collins, D., Taylor, J., Ashford, M., & Collins, L. (In review). It Depends Coaching – The most fundamental, simple and complex principle or a dangerous copout? *Sports Coaching Review*. https://doi.org/10.1080/21640629.2022.2154189.

Constant, A., Clark, A., & Friston, K. J. (2021). Representation Wars: Enacting an Armistice through Active Inference [Hypothesis and Theory]. *Frontiers in Psychology, 11*. https://doi.org/10.3389/fpsyg.2020.598733.

Cope, E., Partington, M., & Harvey, S. (2017). A review of the Use of a Systematic Observation Method in Coaching Research between 1997 and 2016. *Journal of Sports Sciences, 35*(20), 2042–2050. https://doi.org/10.1080/02640414.2016.1252463.

Crandall, B., Klein, G., & Hoffman, R. R. (2006). *Working Minds: A Practitioner's Guide to Cognitive Task Analysis*. MIT Press.

Cushion, C. (2007). Modelling the Complexity of the Coaching Process. *International Journal of Sports Science & Coaching, 2*(4), 395–401. https://doi.org/10.1260/174795407783359650.

Cushion, C. J., Armour, K. M., & Jones, R. L. (2006). Locating the Coaching Process in Practice: Models 'for' and 'of' Coaching. *Physical Education and Sport Pedagogy, 11*(1), 83–99. https://doi.org/10.1080/17408980500466995.

Cushion, C. J., Griffiths, M., & Armour, K. (2019). Professional Coach Educators in-situ: A Social Analysis of Practice. *Sport, Education and Society, 24*(5), 533–546. https://doi.org/10.1080/13573322.2017.1411795.

Cushion, C., Harvey, S., Muir, B., & Nelson, L. (2012). Developing the Coach Analysis and Intervention System (CAIS): Establishing Validity and Reliability of a Computerised Systematic Observation Instrument. *Journal of Sports Sciences, 30*(2), 201–216. https://doi.org/10.1080/02640414.2011.635310.

Dervin, B. (1980). Communication gaps and inequities: Moving toward a reconceptualization. *Progress in Communication Sciences, 2*, 73–112.

Dewey, J. (1910). *How We Think*. D.C. Heath & Co Publishers.

Downham, L., & Cushion, C. (2020). Reflection in a High-Performance Sport Coach Education Program: A Foucauldian Analysis of Coach Developers. *International Sport Coaching Journal, 7*(3), 347–359. https://doi.org/10.1123/iscj.2018-0093.

Friston, K. (2018). Does Predictive Coding Have a Future? *Nature Neuroscience, 21*(8), 1019–1021. https://doi.org/10.1038/s41593-018-0200-7.

Friston, K. J., Parr, T., Yufik, Y., Sajid, N., Price, C. J., & Holmes, E. (2020). Generative Models, Linguistic Communication and Active Inference. *Neuroscience & Biobehavioral Reviews, 118*, 42–64. https://doi.org/10.1016/j.neubiorev.2020.07.005.

Garner, P., Roberts, W. M., Baker, C., & Côté, J. (2022). Characteristics of a Person-centred Coaching Approach. *International Journal of Sports Science & Coaching, 7*(4), 722–733. https://doi.org/10.1177/17479541221077052.

Grecic, D., & Collins, D. (2013). The Epistemological Chain: Practical Applications in Sports. *Quest, 65*(2), 151–168. https://doi.org/10.1080/00336297.2013.773525.

Hedlund, D.P., Fletcher, C. A., Pack, S. M., & Dahlin, S. (2018). The Education of Sport Coaches: What Should They Learn and When Should They Learn It? *International Sport Coaching Journal, 5*(2), 192–199.

Hoffman, R. (2013). *An Integrated Model of Macrocognitive Work and Trust in Automation*. https://www.aaai.org/ocs/index.php/SSS/SSS13/paper/view/5724/6002.

Hoffman, R. R. (1998). How Can Expertise Be Defined? Implications of Research from Cognitive Psychology. In R. Williams, W. Faulkner, & J. Fleck (Eds.), *Exploring Expertise: Issues and Perspectives* (pp. 81–100). Palgrave Macmillan UK. https://doi.org/10.1007/978-1-349-13693-3_4.

Hoffman, R. R., Ward, P., Feltovich, P. J., DiBello, L., Fiore, S. M., & Andrews, D. H. (2014). *Accelerated Expertise: Training for High Proficiency in a Complex World*. Psychology Press.

Hutton, R. (2019). Macrocognitive Models of Expertise. In P. Ward, J. M. Schraagen, J. Gore, & E. M. Roth (Eds.), *The Oxford Handbook of Expertise*. Oxford University Press. https://doi.org/10.1093/oxfordhb/9780198795872.013.9.

Ingold T. (2000). *The Perception of the Environment: Essays on Livelihood, Dwelling and Skill*. Taylor & Francis Group.

Kidman, L. (2010). *Athlete-Centred Coaching: Developing Decision Makers*. IPC Print Resources.

Klein, G., Jalaeian, M., Hoffman, R. R., & Mueller, S. T. (2021). *The Plausibility Gap: A Model of Sensemaking*. https://doi.org/10.31234/osf.io/rpw6e.

Klein, G., & Militello, L. (2004). The knowledge audit as a method for cognitive task analysis. In H. Montgomery, R. Lipshitz, & B. Brehmer (Eds.), *How Professionals Make Decisions*. Lawrence Erlbaum Associates.

Klein, G., Moon, B., & Hoffman, R. R. (2006a). Making Sense of Sensemaking 1: Alternative Perspectives. *IEEE Intelligent Systems*, *21*(4), 70–73. https://doi.org/10.1109/MIS.2006.75.

Klein, G., Moon, B., & Hoffman, R. R. (2006b). Making Sense of Sensemaking 2: A Macrocognitive Model. *IEEE Intelligent Systems*, *21*(5), 88–92. https://doi.org/10.1109/MIS.2006.100.

Klein, G., Phillips, J. K., Rall, E. L., & Peluso, D. A. (2007). A data-frame theory of sensemaking. In R. R. Hoffman (Ed.), *Expertise Out of Context: Proceedings of the Sixth International Conference on Naturalistic Decision Making* (1st ed.). Psychology Press. https://doi.org/10.4324/9780203810088.

Klein, G., Ross, K. G., Moon, B. M., Klein, D. E., Hoffman, R. R., & Hollnagel, E. (2003). Macrocognition. *IEEE Intelligent Systems*, *18*(3), 81–85. https://doi.org/10.1109/MIS.2003.1200735.

Klein, G., Wiggins, S., & Dominguez, C. O. (2010). Team Sensemaking. *Theoretical Issues in Ergonomics Science*, *11*(4), 304–320. https://doi.org/10.1080/14639221003729177.

Lara-Bercial, S., & Mallett, C. J. (2016). The Practices and Developmental Pathways of Professional and Olympic Serial Winning Coaches. *International Sport Coaching Journal*, *3*(3), 221–239. https://doi.org/10.1123/iscj.2016-0083.

Leeder, T. M., & Sawiuk, R. (2021). Reviewing the Sports Coach Mentoring Literature: A Look Back to Take a Step Forward. *Sports Coaching Review*, *10*(2), 129–152. https://doi.org/10.1080/21640629.2020.1804170.

Linson, A., Clark, A., Ramamoorthy, S., & Friston, K. (2018). The Active Inference Approach to Ecological Perception: General Information Dynamics for Natural and Artificial Embodied Cognition [Hypothesis and Theory]. *Frontiers in Robotics and AI*, *5*. https://doi.org/10.3389/frobt.2018.00021.

Lyle, J., & Cushion, C. (2017). *Sport Coaching Concepts: A Framework for Coaching Practice*. Routledge.

Madsbjerg, C. (2017). *Sensemaking: The Power of Humanities in the Age of the Algorithm*. Hachette Books.

Martindale, A., & Collins, D. (2005). Professional Judgment and Decision Making: The Role of Intention for Impact. *The Sport Psychologist*, *19*(3), 303–317. https://doi.org/10.1123/tsp.19.3.303

Martindale, A., & Collins, D. (2007). Enhancing the Evaluation of Effectiveness with Professional Judgment and Decision Making. *The Sport Psychologist*, *21*(4), 458–474. https://doi.org/10.1123/tsp.21.4.458

McQuade, S., & Nash, C. (2015). The Role of the Coach Developer in Supporting and Guiding Coach Learning. *International Sport Coaching Journal*, *2*(3), 339–346. https://doi.org/10.1123/iscj.2015-0059.

Mees, A., Sinfield, D., Collins, D., & Collins, L. (2020). Adaptive Expertise – A Characteristic of Expertise in Outdoor Instructors? *Physical Education and Sport Pedagogy*, *25*(4), 423–438. https://doi.org/10.1080/17408989.2020.1727870.

Mezirow, J. (1978). Perspective Transformation. *Adult Education*, *28*(2), 100–110. https://doi.org/10.1177/074171367802800202.

Moore, D. T., & Hoffman, R. R. (2011). Data-Frame Theory of Sensemaking as a Best Model for Intelligence. *American Intelligence Journal*, *29*(2), 145–158. http://www.jstor.org/stable/26201963.

Nash, C., & Collins, D. (2006). Tacit Knowledge in Expert Coaching: Science or Art? *Quest*, *58*(4), 465–477. https://doi.org/10.1080/00336297.2006.10491894.

Nash, C., MacPherson, A. C., & Collins, D. (2022). Reflections on Reflection: Clarifying and Promoting Use in Experienced Coaches [Original Research]. *Frontiers in Psychology*, *13*. https://doi.org/10.3389/fpsyg.2022.867720.

Nash, C., Martindale, R., Collins, D., & Martindale, A. (2012). Parameterising Expertise in Coaching: Past, Present and Future. *Journal of Sports Sciences, 30*(10), 985–994. https://doi.org/10.1080/02640414.2012.682079.

Neelen, M., & Kirschner, P. (2020). *Evidence-Informed Learning Design: Use Evidence to Create Training Which Improves Performance.* KoganPage.

Osinga, F. P. B. (2005). *Science, Strategy and War: The Strategic Theory of John Boyd.* Eburon Academic Publishers.

Partington, M., & Cushion, C. (2013). An Investigation of the Practice Activities and Coaching Behaviors of Professional Top-level Youth Soccer Coaches. *Scandinavian Journal of Medicine & Science in Sports, 23*(3), 374–382. https://doi.org/10.1111/j.1600-0838.2011.01383.x.

Raubal, M. (2008). *Wayfinding: Affordances and Agent Simulation.* s.l.:University of California at Santa Barbara.

Richards, P., Collins, D., & Mascarenhas, D. R. D. (2017). Developing Team Decision-making: A Holistic Framework Integrating Both On-field and Off-field Pedagogical Coaching Processes. *Sports Coaching Review, 6*(1), 57–75. https://doi.org/10.1080/21640629.2016.1200819.

Rouse, W. B., & Morris, N. M. (1986). On Looking into the Black Box: Prospects and Limits in the Search for Mental Models. *Psychological Bulletin, 100*(3), 349–363. https://doi.org/10.1037/0033-2909.100.3.349.

Schmidt, R. A., & Bjork, R. A. (1992). New Conceptualizations of Practice: Common Principles in Three Paradigms Suggest New Concepts for Training. *Psychological Science, 3*(4), 207–218. https://doi.org/10.1111/j.1467-9280.1992.tb00029.x.

Schommer, M. (1994). Synthesizing Epistemological Belief Research: Tentative Understandings and Provocative Confusions. *Educational Psychology Review, 6*(4), 293–319. https://doi.org/10.1007/BF02213418.

Schön, D. A. (1983). *The Reflective Practitioner: How Practitioners Think in Action.* Harper Collins.

Sieck, W. R., Klein, G., Peluso, D. A., Smith, J. L., & Harris-Thompson, D. (2007). *Focus: A Model of Sensemaking.* United States Army Research Institute for the Behavioral and Social Sciences.

Skurvydas, A., Satas, A., Valanciene, D., Mamkus, G., Mickeviciene, D., Majauskiene, D., & Brazaitis, M. (2020). "Two sides of the same coin": Constant Motor Learning Speeds Up, Whereas Variable Motor Learning Stabilizes, Speed–accuracy Movements. *European Journal of Applied Physiology, 120*(5), 1027–1039. https://doi.org/10.1007/s00421-020-04342-4.

Snowden, D. (2010). Naturalizing Sensemaking. In K. L. Mosier & U. M. Fischer (Eds.), *Informed by Knowledge: Expert Performance in Complex Situations* (pp. 223–234). Taylor & Francis.

Snowden, D. & Rancatti, A. (2021). *Managing Complexity (and Chaos) in Times of Crises. A Field Guide for Decision Makers Inspired by the Cynefin Framework.* Publications Office of the European Union.

Soderstrom, N. C., & Bjork, R. A. (2015). Learning Versus Performance: An Integrative Review. *Perspectives on Psychological Science, 10*(2), 176–199. https://doi.org/10.1177/1745691615569000.

Stewart, F. & Koch, A. (2020). Educational Preparation of College Coaches: "Are We Winning Yet?" *The Physical Educator, 77*(1), 15–28

Stoszkowski, J., & Collins, D. (2016). Sources, Topics and Use of Knowledge by Coaches. *Journal of Sports Sciences, 34*(9), 794–802. https://doi.org/10.1080/02640414.2015.1072279.

Stoszkowski, J., MacNamara, À., Collins, D., & Hodgkinson, A. (2020). "Opinion and Fact, Perspective and Truth": Seeking Truthfulness and Integrity in Coaching and

Coach Education. *International Sport Coaching Journal*, 1–7. https://doi.org/10.1123/iscj.2020-0023.

Taylor, J., & Collins, D. (2020). The Highs and the Lows – Exploring the Nature of Optimally Impactful Development Experiences on the Talent Pathway. *The Sport Psychologist*, *34*(4), 319–328. https://doi.org/10.1123/tsp.2020-0034.

Taylor, J., & Collins, D. (2022). The Talent Development Curriculum. In C. Nash (Ed.), *Practical Sport Coaching* (2nd ed.). Routledge.

Taylor, J., Collins, D., & Ashford, M. (2022). Psychological Safety in High Performance Sport: Contextually applicable? [Perspective]. *Frontiers in Sports and Active Living*, *4*. https://doi.org/10.3389/fspor.2022.823488.

Weick, K. E. (1995). *Sensemaking in Organizations* (Vol. 3). Sage.

Weick, K. E. (2020). Sensemaking, Organizing, and Surpassing: A Handoff*. *Journal of Management Studies*, *57*(7), 1420–1431. https://doi.org/10.1111/joms.12617.

Weick, K. E., Sutcliffe, K. M., & Obstfeld, D. (2005). Organizing and the Process of Sensemaking. *Organization Science*, *16*(4), 409–421. https://doi.org/10.1287/orsc.1050.0133.

Williams, D. (2020). Predictive Coding and Thought. *Synthese*, *197*(4), 1749–1775. https://doi.org/10.1007/s11229-018-1768-x.

Williams, A. M., & Hodges, N. J. (2005). Practice, Instruction and Skill Acquisition in Soccer: Challenging Tradition. *Journal of Sports Sciences*, *23*(6), 637–650. https://doi.org/10.1080/02640410400021328.

Woodman, L. (1993). Coaching: A Science, an Art, an Emerging Profession. *Sport Science Review*, *2*(2), 1–13.

Woods, C. T., Rudd, J., Robertson, S., & Davids, K. (2020). Wayfinding: How Ecological Perspectives of Navigating Dynamic Environments Can Enrich Our Understanding of the Learner and the Learning Process in Sport. *Sports Medicine – Open*, *6*(1), 51. https://doi.org/10.1186/s40798-020-00280-9.

Woolley, K., & Fishbach, A. (2022). Motivating Personal Growth by Seeking Discomfort. *Psychological Science*, *33*(4), 510–523. https://doi.org/10.1177/09567976211044685.

10
ACCELERATING EXPERTISE

Principles for Coach Developers

Christine Nash

Much of this book focusses on developing expertise, in this context with coach developers, who in turn pass on their experience to sports coaches supporting them as they gain expertise. Many of the chapters highlight the skills and knowledge required to build the proficiency required for expertise, such as sensemaking (Chapter 9), critical thinking skills (Chapter 8) and transitions (Chapter 5). This chapter examines concepts associated with accelerating expertise and discusses whether this would be effective in the field of coach development. The theory and models presented in the Hoffman, Ward, Feltovich, DiBello, Fiore and Andrews (2014) book *Accelerated Expertise*, provides the starting point and context for this chapter.

Accelerated Expertise was produced to address military training requirements, to shorten the amount of time for new recruits to complete basic training, be assigned to the most appropriate branch of the military and then focus on their particular tasks until they became 'useful'. Although there are clearly differences in contexts between the requirements of the military and coach developers, many of the principles are worthy of consideration within the sport coaching environment. Most notably the military recognised it required a different, more modern, approach and decided to implement an expertise model of development. This, in my view, is a much-needed direction for sport coaching and coach development. This chapter will include some examples illustrating how this has been achieved.

Researchers in coach development and coach developers agree if the performance of coaches, and subsequently athletes, is worthy of investment of time and money, then coach development frameworks need to change and recognise the dynamic and complex nature of coaching and the reality of everyday coaching practice (Nash, 2014, Nelson, Cushion & Potrac, 2013). Coach learning should be recognised and accepted as a critical driver of improving performance, so placing the coach at the centre highlights the importance of an effective coach development programme (Lara-Bercial & Mallett, 2016). As research into expertise portrays learning to coach should be considered as a lifelong endeavour, however, we need to recognise that while expertise is a long-term goal for both coaches and coach developers, it is not achievable by all (Nash, Culver, Koh, Thompson, Galatti & Duarte, 2019).

Accelerated expertise has been used in other domains, not just the military; for example, business, teaching, construction and medicine. DiBello and colleagues (2009) report on the success of a 'natural laboratory' in a biotech company, where the principles of simulated training harness the knowledge and expertise of front-line workers to solve a short-term issue. Within teaching, there is an emphasis on working knowledge as distinct from professional knowledge (Markauskaite & Goodyear, 2014), which is dynamic, context specific and designed to make things work in classroom situations, leading to an 'intuitive pedagogy'. This intuitiveness can be acquired only by association with those who already possess it. However, because of their expertise, this intuitiveness has become automatised and therefore difficult to communicate. Within construction, Austin, Pishdad-Bozorgi and de la Garza (2016) examine the practice of fast-tracking, a method employed to attain speed of completion while maintaining the quality of building practice. They used examples from other industries to streamline the engineering, procurement and construction processes enabling the systems to communicate effectively.

Excellent coaches use adaptive expertise. Effective coaching is a highly individualised, differentiated and contextualised process. Consequently, good coaching is facilitated by effective judgement and decision-making, underpinned by critical reflection. This requires the coach to have a full comprehension of the context and the biopsychosocial factors influencing the coaching process. Coach developers must understand the complexity of the coaching role, identify where coaches need help and support and have the skills to implement interventions. This may allow coach developers to accelerate coach expertise although they require their own expertise in learning and development to analyse individual situations, integrate the appropriate learning approach and evaluate the outcomes.

How Do We Capture Expert Knowledge in Coaching?

Many companies and organisations have realised when long-term employees leave, whether through retirement or changing jobs, they are losing valuable contextual knowledge about how to perform their role. This is often referred to as tacit knowledge. Tacit knowledge has been used to characterise the knowledge gained from everyday experience that has an implicit, unarticulated quality (Sternberg, 2003). It has been referred to as implicit knowledge, practical intelligence and working knowledge (Vereijken & Whiting, 1990; Wood, Bandura & Bailey, 1990). As tacit knowledge is often not openly expressed or stated, individuals must acquire such knowledge through their own practice, as evidenced by many in the coaching world. Often, the individual is unaware they possess this knowledge (Nash & Collins, 2006). Polanyi (1983, 1974) pioneered work in this area, recognising the importance of first-hand experience during training, for example, student teacher training. He also proposed more complex skills could not be taught through traditional methods.

Given that coaches in the high performing domain, as well as volunteer coaches working at a variety of levels, do not always enjoy longevity in their sport coaching 'careers', how do organisations and coach developers encourage long-term engagement? Is this part of their organisational culture/remit? If not, I would argue it should be. Unless coaches are involved and engaged on a long-term basis, there is little opportunity for them to develop expertise, let alone accelerate expertise. The evidence would suggest we are not good at capturing expert knowledge in sport coaching. Coaches with many years of coaching experience may have accumulated many nuggets of practical wisdom that are not collected captured and, as a result, often lost to the coaching context when they leave their sport.

Perhaps, like many other industries and organisations dealing with employees leaving their jobs in the next few years, we should be taking steps to capture this valuable knowledge. Every organisation should have a way of passing on this highly contextual and relevant knowledge, so it is not lost for current and future employees. To achieve this, organisations need to identify individuals who have both the skills, motivation and ability to transfer this knowledge; it is not just about time served! The following section will examine the areas where coach developers can have the most impact when encouraging coaches to develop and accelerate expertise.

How to Structure Learning to Optimise Expertise

One of the best examples I have heard of came from the IT industry. A group of system engineers were attending a week-long course designed to familiarise them with new software so that they could support such systems back in their own workplace. This is comparable to coaches undertaking development with their peers, rather than in their own coaching environment. Back to the engineers. Before the lunch break on the last day, the course instructor dismissed the class for an extended break, citing an urgent request by the facilities staff to repair a faulty air-conditioning unit in the class room. Unknown to the engineers, the instructor spent the time altering the configuration on each workstation ensuring it would not start when switched on. The engineers arrived back after their extended lunch break and, anticipating a final presentation from the instructor, tried to switch on the workstations; none of them would start and each reported a different error message. Confused, the engineers reported the errors to the instructor who sat back, smiled and confessed his part in the unfolding drama. The instructor then gave the students one hour to identify the problem with the configuration of their workstation and if possible correct the errors.

The final session turned into a time-boxed, hands-on practical workshop, with each engineer applying their recently acquired theoretical knowledge to repair their workstation without any input from the instructor or reference to a manual. This is an excellent example of how learning can be structured to simulate the real-world scenarios these system engineers would encounter in their workplace, allowing them to develop the expertise required to fulfil their roles.

However, in a domain such as sport coaching there are ethical and practical difficulties associated with embedding similar scenarios into coaching practice. Perhaps this highlights the need for coach developers to consider more complex conceptualisations of coaches' requirements and, therefore, adapt their input to reflect real coaching issues and scenarios. The only scenario that I have used is the airport lounge, where the coach is waiting with an athlete or team to head to a competition. There are options that can be added – plane delays, cancellations and how the coach cope with issues such as nutrition, hydration, sleep and practice schedules. I have to say I have actually been in a similar situation when travelling to Paris with a football team and everything that could possibly go wrong did happen – it certainly challenges coaches.

Practice Environments

Larkin, Barkell and O'Connor (2022) consider the practice environment to be the optimum learning opportunity for athletes. Is this the same for coaches? The practice field is the place where coaches can have the time to put their structured plans into practice and should provide the option to examine their preparations and receive feedback from others including coach developers. I would suggest this will only happen if coaches are motivated to continue learning and improving. To achieve or accelerate expertise, the practice environment should be as close to the competitive environment as possible. Consider the 'Top Gun' approach used by the United States Navy where the top naval aviators were selected to attend the United States Navy Strike Fighter Tactics Instructor programme. The success behind this programme is the instructors, knowledgeable fighter tacticians with specialist knowledge in one specific field of expertise, who are also able to devise practice sessions to hold the attention and motivate the best pilots in the US Navy. Key to accelerating expertise is the constantly evolving programme, considering new technology and making adjustments according to critiques and varying points of view, as well as credible threat assessments.

Surgeons are another distinct group who must develop expertise before operating on 'live' patients and they achieve this expertise through several methods, practising on animals or cadavers, mechanical simulators or, more recently, e-learning. A recent systematic review concluded within surgery e-learning tools are limited to teaching cognitive processes; for example, the knowledge base necessary to develop mental models, or the cognitive elements necessary to perform psychomotor tasks, but required to be supplemented by other methods

(Maertens, Madani, Landry, Vermassen, Van Herzeele & Aggarwal, 2016). More recently, the impact of COVID and subsequent lockdowns prompted trainee surgeons to use other, more remote, methods of training. Structured virtual reality training was shown to be effective in improving surgical skills, particularly the more complex the situation and was not dependent on prior virtual reality experience (Sommer, Broschewitz, Huppert, Sommer, Jahn, Jansen-Winkeln, Gockel & Hau, 2021).

The types of practice exemplified by these domains and others may not be directly applicable to coaching and accelerating expertise. However, the following important points should be considered for coach development:

- The US Navy using 'expert' fighter pilots to lead courses. How much thought goes into the recruitment process for those developing coaches? Can we develop or accelerate expertise if we do not have the 'correct' individuals in place? Many coach developers are in place as a result of self-nomination or selection based on their background as a coach, or even a player.
- The Top Gun approach is exemplified by a constantly evolving programme/curriculum. How often does the curriculum of coach education/development programmes change? If/when it does change, what is the basis of that change? Feedback? Critical reflection? Consider the pace of change within professional practice.
- The competition/real-life arena illustrated by the military and surgeons are where they put their expertise into practice, either in combat or the operating theatre, both requiring a level of precision that could mean the difference between life and death. This is not the case within sport coaching. However, do coaches have to 'up their game' at major championships or has the work already been done? How do coach developers differentiate between practice versus competition coaching? Or do they?
- The virtual or online environment may offer valuable opportunities for several domains to practice skills in a controlled and safe setting. There are other advantages associated with online learning, such as lower costs, timing and convenience. COVID forced many organisations to switch to an online environment; how many coaches are now regularly embracing this as a method for gaining knowledge and developing expertise? Are coach developers sufficiently skilled or motivated enough to embrace new technologies and devise different developmental programmes other than podcasts? The structure of these types of opportunities, as well as the delivery mechanisms, are likely to affect the success of this approach.

Evidence from other domains would suggest that learning situations can be manipulated deliberately to build expertise by developing mental models, moderately abstract conceptual representations and anticipatory thinking skills (Klein & Snowden, 2011; Zeitz, 1997). It would be useful to reflect on these principles in coach development.

Feedback

How the coach chooses to communicate with athletes during competition and training has been shown to have a significant impact on performance (Otte, Davids, Millar & Klatt, 2020). Feedback gives coaches the opportunity to inform athletes how they are performing in relation to their expectations and much research has been carried out about the timing and type of feedback coaches should provide (Amorose & Nolan-Sellers, 2016; Mason, Farrow & Hattie, 2020). However, while coaches must be skilled in offering feedback, they also need to receive feedback on their practice to improve. Nash and colleagues (2017) categorised the types of feedback used by coaches as including the use of their network, the opinions of participants, their use of critical thinking skills and support systems they were able to use. More experienced coaches with established networks of like-minded coaches seemed to be more open to constructive feedback, but how challenging will like-minded colleagues turn out to be? Peer feedback quality depends on the expertise of the person providing feedback. There is limited research into the provision and effectiveness of feedback offered to coaches, much may be explained by the nature of the coaching environment; many coaches work on their own and do not have the opportunity for informal peer feedback and support. This is where the coach developer can assist.

Higgins and colleagues (2013) maintain effective feedback directs attention to the intended learning and/or success criteria, pointing out strengths and offering specific information to guide improvement. Whatever the form of the feedback, it should be explicit about the learning goals and success criteria. Conversely, the coach needs to have a clear idea of their aim/objective for the session as well as the criteria to judge success against. Although this may seem obvious, quality sessions should consist of more than a collection of drills and contribute to the overall aim. If we are to accept feedback in a frequently used and high-impact strategy to progress a learner from current to goal performance (Hattie, 2009) how can coach developers use feedback to enhance coaching performance?

Questions as Feedback

Questions serve many purposes when eliciting feedback and can:

- Provide the coach developer (questioner) with an overview of the coach's thoughts, a sense of mood, willingness to engage with the process and a starting point for discussion.
- Assist the coach to reflect on the session against the criteria for success.
- Develop metacognitive skills.
- Encourage new ideas.
- Reinforce the notion that coaches should be an active participant in their own development. This can also allow the coach to become their own source of feedback, by using similar questions while on their own.

Debrief as Feedback

The military have a long history of debriefing, not just as an aftermath following active service. Bartone and Adler (1995) provided an early template that was used in both active service and training. Critical elements are to review the chronology of events, to give soldiers an opportunity to clear up any confusion and to allow a healthy understanding, acceptance and integration of their experiences. Hammett (2018) explains how this approach can be used in business, reframing the debrief as an After Action Review (AAR). He highlights three principles that can be helpful to everyone seeking feedback:

1. **Involve everyone:** Every person who was involved in the activity, from leader and key personnel to supporting players, should be actively included and feel able to contribute to the breakdown and analysis of the strengths and weaknesses. This level of inclusivity contributes to a knowledgeable organisation.
2. **Leave rank at the door:** To allow everyone to feedback objectively there can be no hierarchy of individuals. Leaders generally tend to lead debriefs, but, in these situations, where each opinion is of equal weight, it may be helpful to use an external individual.
3. **Finish with action points:** There are two components determining whether a debrief will be effective in enhancing future activities. Firstly, the organiser should encourage questions from all involved. Secondly, they should provide a summary of the debrief, including the agreed action points that will be implemented.

Challenge of Feedback

There are many instances of people receiving feedback they do not want to hear or they disagree with – how does this influence the development of expertise? Often this can be an emotional response from the coach, perhaps reflecting the feedback delivery methods rather than the feedback itself. The debrief referred to above is designed to be a challenging, rather than a cosy conversation. If coaches genuinely wish to improve, this issue of facing uncomfortable feedback needs to be addressed. In Chapter 9 on sensemaking we discussed knowledge shields, barriers individuals erect to avoid considering information contrary to their beliefs or that upset their mental models.

How do coach developers handle these situations? I'm sure we all recognise there are some individuals that require more time, effort and thought than others. Many coaches will embrace change willingly and want to become highly effective coaches, no matter where or who they are coaching. Coach developers need to assess coaches and identify the main areas for growth (Chapter 6). Table 10.1 contains some examples for reflection.

TABLE 10.1 Coach development vignettes

Vignette	Description	Actions
1	Coach 1 is male and in his 50s with considerable experience in his field. He considers himself to be a great teacher, with considerable expertise in this area so his opinion is the right opinion. He would rather spend hours explaining why you are wrong, rather than explore the possibility that there might be another way to do things. He also thinks he is a leader but when asked to put this into practice, shies away from any responsibilities. He believes he is best placed to find faults and expose what he perceives to be organisational incompetence.	Explain your initial conversation with this coach to broach the subject. How would you break down the shields?
2	Coach 2 is female and in her 30s. She started coaching after she retired from her sport and is of similar age to some of her athletes. She has well-developed observational skills and can explain exactly what her athletes and team need to improve. She struggles to put these thoughts into action, partly as she feels this would be a big change to training. She is unconvinced that the senior players would welcome the change to the routine and is not sure she could handle this challenge effectively.	What do you think is the best place to start? How would you encourage the coach to meet their challenges?
3	Coach 3 is working with a team of coaches, overseeing their plans and progressions and tasked with driving the coaching programme forward. Coach 3 likes to pay attention to detail and expects all the coaches' paperwork to be comprehensive with every element complete. Coach 3 takes pride in the systems and processes in place and holds weekly meetings to review and update. Coach 3 cannot understand why the team of coaches are not equally invested in this meticulous routine and struggles to motivate them to contribute to the weekly meetings.	What actionable steps could you suggest to foster development?

Transferability

Transferring knowledge from one domain to another or from one context to another is one of the skills attributable to experts. Many coaches report difficulties incorporating information presented at coaching clinics into their own coaching environments so how can coach developers facilitate this knowledge transfer? Transferability provides the opportunity to critically evaluate coaching sessions (see Chapter 8 on critical thinking) and reach conclusions on what is best to apply to each scenario (see Chapter 9 on sensemaking). The transferability, or otherwise, can be dependent upon the type of knowledge and most tend to be considered generic rather than sport-specific; for example, leadership, problem-solving, influencing, teamworking and planning (Ramos, Ng, Sung & Loke, 2013). According to Sternberg (2005) skills cannot be easily transferred between different contexts as skills develop within a specific context and are bound to this context. Individual, social and contextual factors determine the actual transfer of skills (Sternberg, 2003). More recently, Saks and colleagues (2014) note skill transfer can be assisted by the environment; for example, a supportive organisational climate (see Chapter 7).

There are several factors coach developers should be aware of that can affect the ease of transfer:

- **Superficial level of understanding:** If coaches do not have an adequate depth of knowledge about a particular area or approach, they will struggle with transfer. Consider how coach developers can enable this depth of understanding – I would argue this can be developed in multiple discussions/meetings over an extended period of time rather than the one day or three hour 'shot' of coach education that still occurs. This would suggest coach development should be a more individual process. As well as time constraints, coach developers should be aware of how to develop these deeper understandings, as well as recognising when coaches are, or are not, developing beyond the superficial.
- **What needs to be transferred:** There is considerable difference in ease of transfer between forms of skills and learning, the more complex the task, the harder the transfer. Consider the difference in the transmission of factual knowledge or simple skills versus procedural rules and more complex skills. The more intricate the knowledge, the more opportunities exist for mistakes to occur.
- **Breadth of use:** Generally, especially when knowledge and skills are newly acquired, coaches tend to view them in one dimension. This focus tends to mean coaches will only use this information in specific situations, imitating the situational context presented by the coach developer. As concepts are easier to transfer to different situations, coach developers should emphasise principles rather than specifics to allow coaches to consider future use and adapt the theory to real-world scenarios. Kaiser, Jacobs and Cichy (2022) maintain abstract conceptual representations are critical for the development of human intelligence although, despite their importance, they are not well understood and applied.
- **Variations in context:** As coaching is a complex activity involving individuals, teams and varying levels of ability, necessitating a highly flexible and adaptable sport coach, there are considerable differences in coaching environments. Generally, when the transfer context is dissimilar from the learning context, coaches may not see how their knowledge is relevant or how their current knowledge can be applied to the new situation. Coach developers cannot be expected to cover all the situational variables that exist within coaching environments but should encourage coaches to consider how variations in context could affect the delivery. These variations could, for example, include age, skill level of participants, experience of coach and type of sport.
- **Opportunities to practice:** Although skills and knowledge become embedded the more they are used, it must be emphasised the transfer of trained tasks is more than a function of the quality of the training programme.

Coaches must take or engineer opportunities to practice new techniques in a variety of coaching environments. This is important as each opportunity will differ and require an individual approach, allowing the coach to develop expertise. It would be advantageous to the coach if they had access to feedback, especially from a coach developer.

Transfer of learning is the process of applying acquired knowledge to new situations. Research consistently highlights coaches have difficulty applying acquired knowledge and skills to situations where they are appropriate. Apprenticeship programmes, especially cognitive apprenticeships as suggested by Collins, Brown and Holum (1991), can facilitate the transfer of skills (see Chapter 7), as can mentoring programmes (McQuade, Davis & Nash, 2015). To facilitate developing expertise these programmes must build on situated learning in real-life coaching environments, activating deep learning. Nash, MacPherson and Collins (2022) also demonstrated critical reflection is useful in both the transfer and application of learning as well as the acceleration of expertise.

Retention

Knowledge retention is the process of absorbing information over time and the ability to access and apply it when needed, another skill attributed to expertise (Nash & Collins, 2006). Unfortunately, traditional rote memory techniques mean information can be retained for a short period of time and then forgotten. The most successful way to retain information is to be involved and engaged with the learning process. Within medicine, skill retention has been shown to decline within three months of training (if not used within those three months) (de Ruijter, Biersteker, Biert, van Goor & Tan, 2014) which is worrying as the research was carried out in life-saving techniques. However, more recently Offiah and colleagues (2019) found using simulation-based training aided retention and was effective as a retraining technique, again in the medical profession.

Bodilly and colleagues (1986, p. 28) share this thought that should be worthy of note to coach developers, saying 'The training method which produces the highest original performance will produce the best retention over time'. This places the onus on the coach developer in planning, delivering and evaluating the 'training method' they select and clearly links back to the earlier section on practice environments. Much research has been conducted around the learning and retention of motor skills in sport as a function of the type of instructional method (cf Bobrownicki, MacPherson, Collins & Sproule, 2019), but little has been carried out in coaching – perhaps a missed opportunity.

Of course, the best way to retain skills and knowledge is to keep using them – practice does keep skills fresh. Consider the words of this elite field hockey coach in the following case study. This coach had a long career in the sport but remains motivated, engaged and keen to continue learning.

CASE STUDY: NATIONAL OLYMPIC HOCKEY COACH

How did I get to be where I am in coaching? I guess by taking advantage of each and every learning opportunity that I had. I also did not wait for opportunities to be given to me – I actively sought them out and not just in hockey or sport. For example, I wanted to know more about physical conditioning, so I went and spent some time with track and field coaches. I wanted to understand how to interact better with players and understand their difficulties, so I enrolled on a counselling course. I'm guessing that not many coaches bother to do that but it is a case of recognising what you are not good at and chasing opportunities to improve, develop. I was also very motivated and single minded – I wanted to succeed BUT you need a plan to make that happen. What is the next step? How do you get there? Who or what do you need to help? And I guess the key question I was asking myself was 'am I good enough' but I never let anyone else know that I was having doubts.

Am I an expert? I don't know about that! I am at the top and there are not many challenges left – apart from winning that gold medal! I love the challenge. I've been coaching hockey at various levels but I still have things to learn. I think that is why I'm still involved in hockey, what keeps me turning up, what motivates me to keep trying. I'm clear that gold medal is beyond me now but I have a lot to share and we need to win at that level. If I can light the fire in the next generation, and assist them to succeed then that is good for me. It also keeps me on my toes, working with younger, hungrier coaches – I'm not allowed to forget!

How do I explain my success? When I started coaching, I was really fixed on the results! That was the only thing that mattered to me and I reckon that was made clear to the players – you either won or you got dropped. I kept losing players so I did a 180 and came to realise that I needed not to fixate on the results. Let's look at the performance, let's work on quality practice and supporting my guys to succeed – that's when it all changed for me. I guess it also helped me with my coaching. If I focussed on results, I either won or lost, succeeded or failed, so I evaluated my coaching on that basis. When I moved to focus on performance there was so much more to reflect on. I could actually move my coaching forward, make gains.

What was my interaction with coach developers? I have to say that when I started coaching it was because of my reputation as a player – I was headhunted. So I guess I thought I was there! I knew it all! My initial experience of coaching instruction was very negative – I knew more than the instructors or so I thought. As I matured, or maybe grew up, and was able to admit I did not know it all, I started to trust some educators. The bond was important, I could not communicate my thoughts, fears, dilemmas and uncertainty with anyone. I needed to trust them and to understand my vulnerability. I guess as I progressed in my coaching I got more one-on-one support and that proved

> really useful. I guess I didn't really consider this coach development at the time as I was kinda bouncing ideas and plays off of different folk, trying to get a sense of what would work. That's still what I do now but I have to say other coaches are bouncing ideas off me now.
>
> What do I still need help with? It's the situations that arise that I haven't come across before – especially the ones where I need to react quickly. Usually that happens in games but not always – practice can throw up some headaches too. I'm getting better at recognising difficult situations before they happen and kinda heading them off at the pass but that is something that is difficult.

Adaptive Expertise

The term expertise is used frequently in everyday life but what does it mean? Expertise and experts are important; consider how many critical decisions are routinely delegated to so-called experts in different spheres of influence (Selinger & Crease, 2002). Much of the debate surrounding expert studies has centred on the definition of expertise or an expert (Nowotny, 2000). More recently in the UK and USA there has been a deliberate denigration of expertise in favour of sound bites, media spin and hostility towards intellectuals (Nichols, 2017). Do we still need to develop expertise in coaching? To face the increasing demands of organisations and the availability of knowledge, there is now a distinction between the routine expert and the adaptive expert. I would argue the coach and coach developer require to be adaptive experts. Ward, Gore, Hutton, Conway and Hoffman (2018, p. 36) 'differentiate the adaptive nature of expertise from routine or everyday skill, and attempt to redress the balance between the what (i.e., components of expertise) and when (i.e., when the important components matter most) of expertise' and so 'expertise is a process of continual learning and development—required, in part, because the work itself is constantly changing. From this perspective, expertise is a process of adaptation and the ability to deal with change' (p. 37).

Grotzer, Forshaw and Gonzalez (2021) posited six key components of adaptive expertise:

1. **Cognitive flexibility:** This refers to seeing beyond the traditional applications of types of knowledge; the transfer I mentioned earlier. It is the ability to view knowledge and skills as principles or concepts; doing so makes it is easier to use them in differing ways.
2. **Metacognitive self-regulation:** Metacognitive processes are central to expertise in the sport context and in this case reflective skills are key. However, self-regulation coupled with reflection can be of great use to the coach and coach developer by removing emotion from any feedback given or received.
3. **Seeking future-oriented feedback:** Coach developers should be encouraged to provide not just feedback on coaching they have viewed and evaluated

but also 'feedforward' on how the coach can continue to learn and develop. Individuals who seek this type of feedback demonstrate a genuine desire to improve. This will sometimes require coaches to ignore the emotion highlighted above when feedback is poorly delivered.
4. **Building progressive learning paths:** A learning path or a professional development plan would seem a valid exercise for coaches at any level. However, the more accomplished individuals become in their domain, the more it becomes increasingly difficult to build that path as it may require trying things that have never been done before and involve failure as a learning opportunity. This requires commitment and motivation from both coach and coach developer.
5. **Developing a user's manual to one's mind:** This involves collating knowledge on how the brain works, but more importantly how or own brain functions best. In other words, understanding the types of approaches and strategies that will work best for us as individuals. This will be important for coach developers to appreciate how different individuals learn best as a result of their cognitive structures and motivations, but also the differences between individuals at similar levels of achievement.
6. **Capacity for navigating cultures:** Organisational culture often dictates the amount of support individual can expect in learning situations. However, being able to navigate the cultures and subcultures surrounding sport and coaching is very challenging (see Chapter 14).

Grotzer and colleagues (2021) further contend this adaptive expertise can only occur within learning organisation (see Chapter 7) and the philosophy of the organisation must align with the coach and coach developer approach.

In Summary

We need to identify the critical components of coaching that allow sport coaches to develop expertise, using evidence gathered from the observation and analysis of coaching practice. I have cited examples from other domains in this chapter, such as medicine and the military, to illustrate how this has been undertaken elsewhere. Specifically:

- **Keep learning:** There are numerous free sources available allowing coaches and coach developers to accelerate their learning and stay one step ahead of the opposition. One caveat: use critical thinking skills to separate the wheat from the chaff (Chapter 8).
- **Challenge yourself:** This is where the coach developer can help, providing that push, asking the difficult questions and making you feel uncomfortable. This is often not a pleasant experience, but coach developers need to develop the skills required to manage these challenging conversations. Remember the knowledge shields in Chapter 9.

- **Embrace failure:** With challenge added to the continuous learning, there is always the possibility of failure. An organisation I previously worked with refused to accept coaches may fail in some activities but handled correctly could be a useful learning experience. They insisted failure was not part of their vocabulary. However, consider the approach of the US military; in the 1v1 scenarios they engineer there is always a successful pilot and an unsuccessful pilot. However, with the debriefs and the AARs the potential for success in the future is enhanced.
- **Embrace uncertainty:** Adaptive expertise builds confidence to deal with the unknown and the unexpected and certainly sport coaching has been classed as 'messy' and 'complex'. The capacity to identify and work with ambiguity is the norm within coaching, so there is no 'right' answer. Coaching is a complex activity and coach developers need to understand those complexities. Athletes are individuals and we encourage coaches to coach the individual. Should we not adopt the same approach for coach developers?
- **Look at the big picture:** Identify what are you trying to achieve and work backwards. Big picture thinking is the ability to grasp abstract concepts and ideas but also to set priorities and plan how they are to be achieved. It also means you avoid getting bogged down in minutiae.

References

Amorose, A.J., & Nolan-Sellers, W. (2016). Testing the moderating effect of the perceived importance of the coach on the relationship between perceived coaching feedback and athletes' perceptions of competence. *International Journal of Sports Science & Coaching, 11*(6). 789–798.

Austin, R.B., Pishdad-Bozorgi, P., & de la Garza, J.M. (2016). Identifying and prioritizing best practices to achieve flash track projects. *Journal of Construction Engineering and Management, 142*(2). https://doi.org/10.1061/(ASCE)CO.1943-7862.0001061.

Bartone, P.T., & Adler, A.B. (1995). *Event-Oriented Debriefing Following Military Operations: What Every Leader Should Know.* A Special Foreign Activity of the Walter Reed Army Institute of Research. U.S. Army Medical Research Unit-Europe.

Bobrownicki, R., MacPherson, A.C., Collins, D., & Sproule, J. (2019). The acute effects of analogy and explicit instruction on movement and performance. *Psychology of Sport and Exercise, 44*, 17–25.

Bodilly, S., Fernandez, J., Kimbrough, J., & Purnell, S. (1986). Individual ready reserve skill retention and refresher training options. Rand Note, Rand National Defense Research Institute, Contract No MDA903-85-C-0030.

Collins, A., Brown, S.J., & Holum, A. (1991). Cognitive apprenticeship: Making thinking visible. *American Educator, 15*, 1–18.

de Ruijter, P.A., Biersteker, H.A., Biert, J., van Goor, H., & Tan, E.C. (2014). Retention of first aid and basic life support skills in undergraduate medical students. *Medical Education Online, 19*, 24841.

DiBello, L., Missildine, W., & Struttman, M. (2009). Intuitive expertise and empowerment: the long-term impact of simulation training on changing accountabilities in a biotech firm. *Mind, Culture, and Activity, 16*(1), 11–31.

Grotzer, T.A., Forshaw, T., & Gonzalez, E. (2021). Developing Adaptive Expertise for Navigating New Terrain: An Essential Element of Success in Learning and the Workplace. The Next Level Lab at the Harvard Graduate School of Education. President and Fellows of Harvard College: Cambridge, MA.

Hammett, G. (2018). Military Leaders Know the Power of Reflection. Here's How You, Too, Can Use the Debrief in Business. *Inc.* https://www.inc.com/gene-hammett/military-leaders-know-power-of-reflection-heres-how-you-too-can-use-debrief-in-business.html. Accessed 22/08/2022.

Hattie, J.A.C. (2009). *Visible Learning*. Routledge.

Higgins, S., Katsipataki, M., Kokotsaki, D., Coleman, R., Major, L.E., & Coe, R. (2013). *The Sutton Trust – Education Endowment Foundation Teaching and Learning Toolkit*. Manual. Education Endowment Foundation.

Hoffman, R.R., Ward, P., Feltovich, P.J., DiBello, L., Fiore, S.M., & Andrews, D.H. (2014). *Accelerated Expertise: Training for High Proficiency in a Complex World*. Psychology Press.

Kaiser, D., Jacobs, A.M., & Cichy, R.M. (2022). Modelling brain representations of abstract concepts. *PLoS Computational Biology*, 18(2), e1009637. https://doi.org/10.1371/journal.pcbi.1009637.

Klein, G., & Snowden, D. (2011). Anticipatory Thinking. *Informed by Knowledge Expert Performance in Complex Situations*. https://doi.org/10.4324/9780203847985.

Lara-Bercial, S., & Mallett, C.J. (2016). The practices and developmental pathways of professional and olympic serial winning coaches. *International Sport Coaching Journal*, 3(3), 221–239.

Larkin, P., Barkell, J., & O'Connor, D. (2022) The practice environment—How coaches may promote athlete learning. *Frontiers in Sports and Active Living*, 4. https://doi.org/10.3389/fspor.2022.957086.

Maertens, H., Madani, M., Landry, T., Vermassen, F., Van Herzeele, I., & Aggarwal, R. (2016). Systematic review of e-learning for surgical training. *British Journal of Surgery*, 103, 1428–1437.

Markauskaite, L., & Goodyear, P. (2014). Tapping into the mental resources of teachers' working knowledge: Insights into the generative power of intuitive pedagogy. *Learning, Culture and Social Interaction*, 3(4), 237–251.

Mason, R.J., Farrow, D., & Hattie, J.A.C. (2020). Sports coaches' knowledge and beliefs about the provision, reception, and evaluation of verbal feedback. *Frontiers in Psychology*, 11, https://doi.org/10.3389/fpsyg.2020.571552

McQuade, S., Davis, L., & Nash, C. (2015). Positioning mentoring as a coach development tool: Recommendations for future practice and research. *Quest*, 67(3), 317–329.

Nash, C. (2014). How coaches learn and develop. In C. Nash (Ed.), *Practical Sports Coaching* (pp. 177–189). Routledge/Taylor & Francis Group.

Nash, C., & Collins, D. (2006). Tacit knowledge in coaching: Science or art. *Quest*, 48, 234–257.

Nash, C., Culver, D., Koh, K.-T., Thompson, M., Galatti, L., & Duarte, T. (2019). The coaching journey: Learning as lifelong and life-wide. In R. Thelwell & M. Dicks (Eds.), *Professional Advances in Sport Coaching: Research and Practice*. 1st ed. Routledge.

Nash, C., MacPherson, A.C., & Collins D. (2022) Reflections on reflection: Clarifying and promoting use in experienced coaches. *Frontiers in Psychology*, 13, https://doi.org/10.3389/fpsyg.2022.867720.

Nash, C., Sproule J., & Horton, P. (2017). Feedback for coaches: Who coaches the coach? *International Journal of Sport Science & Coaching*, 12(1), 92–102.

Nelson, L., Cushion, C., & Potrac, P. (2013). Enhancing the provision of coach Education: The recommendations of UK coaching practitioners. *Physical Education and Sport Pedagogy*, *18*(2), 204–218.

Nichols, T. (2017). *The Death of Expertise: The Campaign against Established Knowledge and Why It Matters*. Oxford University Press..

Nowotny, H. (2000). Transgressive competence the narrative of expertise. *European Journal of Social Theory*, *3*(1), 5–21.

Offiah, G., Ekpotu, L.P., Murphy, S., Kane, D., Gordon, A., O'Sullivan, M., Sharifuddin, S.F., Hill, A.D.K., & Condron, C.M. (2019). Evaluation of medical student retention of clinical skills following simulation training. *BMC Medical Education*, *19*, 263.

Otte, F.W., Davids, K., Millar, S., & Klatt, S. (2020). When and how to provide feedback and instructions to athletes? how sport psychology and pedagogy insights can improve coaching interventions to enhance self-regulation in training. *Frontiers in Psychology*, *11*, https://doi.org/10.3389/fpsyg.2020.01444.

Polanyi, M. (1974). *Personal Knowledge towards a Post-Critical Philosophy*. University of Chicago Press.

Polanyi, M. (1983). *The Tacit Dimension*. Peter Smith

Ramos, C.R., Ng, M.C.M., Sung, J., & Loke, F. (2013). Wages and skills utilization: Effect of broad skills and generic skills on wages in Singapore. *International Journal of Training and Development*, *17*(2), 116–134.

Saks, A.M., Salas, E., & Lewis, P. (2014). The transfer of training. *International Journal of Training and Development*, *18*(2), 81–83.

Selinger, E.M., & Crease, R.P. (2002). Dreyfus on expertise: The limits of phenomenological analysis. *Continental Philosophy Review*, *35*, 245–279.

Sommer, G.M., Broschewitz, J., Huppert, S., Sommer, C.G., Jahn, N., Jansen-Winkeln, B., Gockel, I., & Hau, H. (2021). The role of virtual reality simulation in surgical training in the light of COVID-19 pandemic: Visual spatial ability as a predictor for improved surgical performance: A randomized trial. *Medicine*, *100*(50), 27844.https://doi.org/10.1097/MD.0000000000027844.

Sternberg, R.J. (2005). Intelligence, competence, and expertise. In A.J. Elliot & C.S. Dweck (Eds.). *Handbook of Competence and Motivation* (pp. 15–30).The Guilford Press.

Sternberg, R.J. (2003). *Wisdom, Intelligence and Creativity Synthesized*. Cambridge University Press.

Vereijken, B., & Whiting, H.T.A. (1990). In defence of discovery learning. *Canadian Journal of Sport Sciences*, *15*(2), 99–106.

Ward, P., Gore, J., Hutton, R., Conway, G.E., & Hoffman, R.R. (2018). Adaptive skill as the Conditio Sine Qua Non of Expertise. *Journal of Applied Research in Memory and Cognition*, *7*(1), 35–50.

Wood, R.E., Bandura, A., & Bailey, T. (1990). Mechanisms governing organizational performance in complex decision-making environments. *Organizational Behavior and Human Decision Processes*, *46*, 181–201.

Zeitz, C.M. (1997). Some concrete advantages of abstraction: How experts' representations facilitate reasoning. In P.J. Feltovich, K.M. Ford, & R.R. Hoffman (Edis.), *Expertise in Context: Human and Machine* (pp. 43–65). AAAI Press/The MIT Press.

SECTION III
Systems Approach to Coach Development

In this section we consider a systems approach to developing coaches and by this we mean how all parts of a system contribute to the overall success. This holistic view that systems have a series of building blocks, that everything is interconnected and the more moving parts there are the more complex the system.

We present the opposite ends of this continuum – a sport with no system and no recognition from a national sporting organisation trying to fit the building blocks together in an integrated fashion to grow the participation base of the sport. The opposite end is a well-established high-performance environment that demands success from their athletes and coaches as well as the role of the coach developer in this setting.

Included within this section are areas that sporting organisations need to consider carefully within their remit. How do they address diversity in coach development? What are the cultural barriers that prevent/curtail coaches working globally? How successful are coach education and development programmes in their delivery. Sporting organisations will have to answer these questions to gain or retain their funding so again we offer some thoughts for reflection.

11
VOLUNTEER-LED SPORT (AND COACH) DEVELOPMENT

A Case Study of Pickleball in Scotland

Pippa Chapman, Nanette Mutrie and Sharon MacKechnie

Introduction

This chapter explores the development of a new sport and the work towards establishing a National Governing Body (NGB), by case studying the sport of Pickleball in Scotland. Two of the authors of this chapter are actively involved in Pickleball and therefore draw on their experiences of the sport in Scotland to outline the lived experiences of developing a system for an emerging sport. This section of the chapter introduces the fundamentals of sport development and some of the specifics of the sport of Pickleball and its growing popularity. This is followed by a discussion of the development of a sport organisation and finally the role of people in developing a sport, including establishing leadership and governance for the sport and key aspects of sport development and the role of coaching.

The fundamentals of sport development are generally accepted as being related to the provision of opportunities for people to participate in a certain sport, group of sports or physical activity (Shilbury et al, 2008). Lyle (2012: 498) described sport development as "a layered framework of facilitated sport-related activity", noting in particular that different participant groups have different needs when it comes to how the sport is coached. The nature of provision might vary but there are common features including the need for appropriate and safe space for participation, specific types of equipment or kit in some cases, and knowledgeable leaders to introduce the sport and help people develop their skills, many of whom work in a voluntary capacity. Critical to the development of any sport is the role of NGBs (also known as National Sport Organisations – NSOs).

Pickleball

Pickleball was invented by an American family some 50 years ago and is a central net game, played with paddles and an airflow ball. Pickleball has been a popular sport in the USA for many years, but has only reached Europe and other parts of the world in the past decade. Participation rates are difficult to measure as it remains a relatively unknown sport, but some estimates put the number of regular players in the USA at 5 million, with a further 2 million elsewhere in the world. Pickleball has been played in Scotland for over ten years, and the endeavours of a small group of committed volunteers led to the establishment of an embryonic organisation to lead the sport in 2018. Pickleball Scotland is a wholly voluntary organisation with the sole purpose of promoting and supporting the development of the sport in Scotland and seeking official status as the NGB for Pickleball in Scotland. There are a range of activities focused on growing participation, establishing routes for coaching and organising the sport with good governance and integrity, which are discussed in this chapter.

BOX 11.1

THE FUNDAMENTALS OF PICKLEBALL

Pickleball is a central net game played with paddles (akin to oversize table tennis bats – see Figure 11.1) and an airflow ball (see Figure 11.2) on a small court with a net height of 1 metre. Some say the sport *looks like* a game of mini-tennis but there are important differences. The use of non-strung rackets and a hard ball means that the flight pattern of the ball is very true – players do not need to compensate for playing on a small court by hitting more gently than they would like to, because the ball will go exactly where

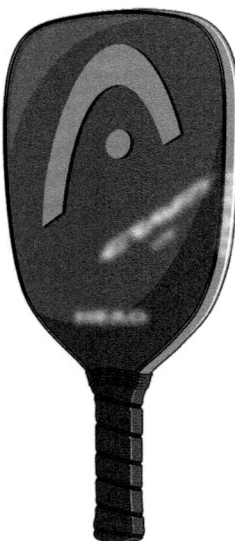

FIGURE 11.1 Fickleball paddle.

Volunteer-Led Sport (And Coach) Development **171**

FIGURE 11.2 Pickleball ball.

and how you want it to go (strung rackets have a lot more rebound, so the balls are less easy to control).

The rules too are an important feature that make this activity unique and accessible. One rule is the 'no-volley zone' – this is the area from the net to a line just behind the badminton service line, 7 feet back from the net (see Figure 11.3), inside which the players are not allowed to play a volley-shot. This

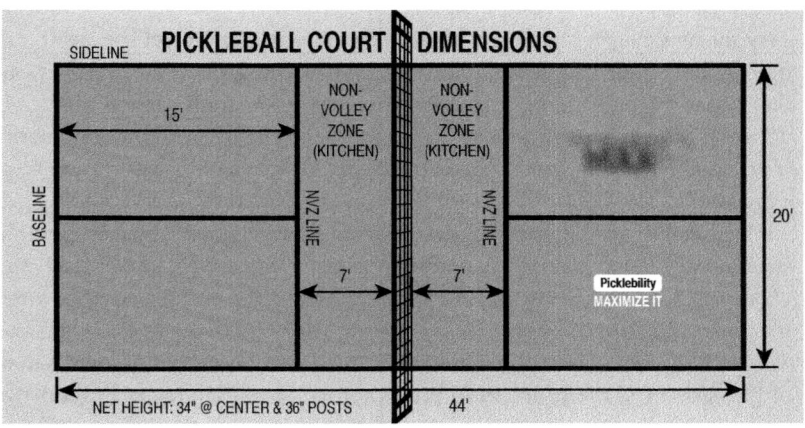

FIGURE 11.3 Pickleball court.

prevents players from being too domineering at the net, and the rule helps to take overly aggressive shots out of the game. The second unique rule is the 'double-bounce' rule. The server must serve underarm from the back of the court and the receiver must let the serve bounce once before playing the return shot (just like tennis); but ... the server must also let this service return shot bounce once before playing their next shot. This prevents the server from playing a serve and volley game and supports rallies to get underway. The nature and rules of the sport mean that there is no need to make adaptations to equipment or playing space, unlike sports such as tennis and badminton.

A key feature of Pickleball is its accessibility and inclusiveness, as discussed in both Boxes 11.1 and 11.2. Inclusion is an important consideration within sport development as understanding different participant groups is crucial for developing a sport and ensuring provision, including facilities and coaching, are appropriate. This can be particularly valuable when considering social groups that are less likely to be engaged in sport, such as older adults. As Jenkin et al (2021) discussed, lower intensity sports can be appealing to older adults and understanding why older adults have chosen to (re-)engage with sport can enable those leading sport to consider ways to develop and deliver sport which is suitable for that demographic.

BOX 11.2

PICKLEBALL AS AN INCLUSIVE SPORT

The popularity of Pickleball is closely linked to its accessibility: it is relatively easy for new players, young and old, to pick up the basics of the sport and quickly become competitive and successful at the sport. The sport is popular amongst older people as it provides an opportunity to be physically active in a directly competitive sport. One enclave of Pickleball popularity is an area known as The Villages in Florida, USA, which is a community of over-50s.

This inclusivity extends to events and competitions. The competition structure enables players to compete against others of similar age and ability – attend any of the larger tournaments and you will see novices, intermediates and experts of all ages competing with others in the same age and ability categories. This competition structure, along with the organic nature of the growth of the sport, makes it a very sociable, friendly and supportive environment in which to enjoy competing at all levels.

Developing an Emerging Sport

As noted in the introduction to this chapter, there are common fundamental components of sport development, and these are important at any stage in a sport's development but particularly as a sport becomes established both in terms of participation numbers and in terms of becoming more formalised in its nature, including the establishment of an NGB. Critical in this process is the role of people with specific skills and a commitment to the sport that means that they are willing to contribute to the development of the sport as volunteers.

Professionalisation and Formalisation

Kikulis et al (1992) identified archetypes of professionalised organisations, specifically the 'kitchen table', which is an organisation with a lack of professionalisation and bureaucracy, the 'boardroom' where there is a bureaucracy and a formal structure and the 'executive office', where the organisation has both bureaucracy and a fully formalised and professionalised set of roles. As Dowling et al (2014) note, this archetype is well utilised in the sport management literature. The formalisation of an organisation's work refers to the standardisation of specific roles and structures within the organisation (Hoye et al, 2015; Nichols et al, 2015) and can be used to increase efficiency and effectiveness of the organisation (Pedras et al, 2020). The extent of professionalisation can in turn impact on formalisation (Dowling et al, 2014). As Pickleball Scotland has developed as an organisation, so there has been a focus on having the staff[1] conducting specific work to contribute to the development of the sport and of the organisation, reflecting the notion of formalisation, drawing on the knowledge and skillsets that the founding members of the organisation possess. This is detailed further later in this chapter.

The increasing professionalisation and formalisation of NGBs in Scotland and the wider UK setting has meant that contemporary research about NGBs tends to focus on their now business-like conduct and the policy decisions and mechanisms that have brought about these conditions (Houlihan and Green, 2009; Tacon and Walters, 2016). This extends to discussions of professionalisation of specific roles in sport, though Dowling et al (2014) noted that research about occupational professionalisation in sport is not as advanced as research relating to organisational professionalisation, and coaching as a profession is often omitted within management-related research. When considering the governance, management and professionalisation of sport in Scotland specifically, there is a dearth of academic literature, in spite of the trajectory of Scottish sport being similar to that in other parts of the UK.

Governance

Governance is an increasingly significant aspect of research related to sports organisations, but there is no fixed definition of what is meant by the term

(Thompson et al, 2022). A systematic review of research by Thompson et al (2022) found that the principles of transparency, accountability and democracy are key features of the discussion of governance in the literature and that governance is multi-level and multi-dimensional and that it is necessary to understand the context of the organisation. In the UK, governance standards for organisations are set out by the sports councils. These standards are designed to ensure that there is good organisational governance amongst organisations that are recognised by the councils and particularly those that are in receipt of public funding as adopting formal practices can be a condition of receiving funding (Nichols et al, 2015). However, meeting these standards can require specific human resources both in terms of time and knowledge in order to develop structures and recruit expertise to an organisation. Walters and Tacon (2018) discuss the adoption of the governance standards as a way for sport organisations to achieve legitimacy, but also a valuable tool in shaping the organisation's work and ensuring accountability.

In Scotland, sportscotland, the national sports council, has good governance as a condition of funding for NGBs, and their framework to guide this aligns with similar standards elsewhere in the UK (sportscotland, 2021). Some aspects of the governance standards that sportscotland set out transcend sport as they are informed by the recommendations of the Nolan Committee, which outlines standards for publicly funded organisations in Scotland, and the framework focuses on key aspects such as accountability through planning and reporting, clearly defined roles and responsibilities within the organisations, and strong leadership (sportscotland, 2021). In order to achieve governance standards, a range of skills are needed to lead a sport: sportscotland (2021) and Nichols et al (2015) noted the importance of matching skills to volunteer and board roles in sport organisations. As will be discussed further later in this chapter, the staff involved in Pickleball Scotland have varied employment and academic backgrounds that collectively lend themselves well to successfully developing and leading the sport.

Achieving Recognition as a Sport

As new sports emerge, become codified and develop national and international structures, there can be risks to their autonomy as decisions are taken as to whether they are distinct sports, or a subsidiary or adapted form of another sport (Box 11.3). As Washington and Patterson (2011) discuss, there can be conflict amongst stakeholders with an interest in a sport and how it is governed, and by whom. This is a challenge that Pickleball Scotland had faced (as discussed in Box 11.4) and has also been an issue in the recent past for the sport of Parkour. In the case of Parkour, the Federation Internationale de Gymnastique (FIG) has sought to bring under its banner, in part so that it can be included as an Olympic discipline, something that has been strongly resisted by Parkour athletes and organisations around the world (Bull, 2018).

BOX 11.3

GAINING RECOGNITION FOR THE SPORT

A key motivator for the founding members of Pickleball Scotland in establishing the NGB and seeking recognition of the sport from the sports councils was to protect the integrity of the sport. The first step in this process was meeting with sportscotland to discuss the process of becoming recognised as the NGB. The founders were informed that the UK sports councils (UK Sport and the home nation sports councils) would first need to be convinced that Pickleball was in fact a distinctive sport and not a subsidiary of one of the established racket sports. Pickleball was already gaining attention and in particular was being considered an alternative to tennis, so there was a concern that Tennis Scotland might be considered a better option for governing the sport. Beyond Scotland, there could be implications for Pickleball organisations and the governance of the sport in the other UK home nations (England, Northern Ireland and Wales) and internationally if a decision was taken that Pickleball was not a sport in its own right.

Fortunately, the CEOs of both Tennis Scotland and Badminton Scotland confirmed that Pickleball should not fall under either NGBs' remits. Furthermore, at this stage, the Pickleball Scotland team moved to work with their counterparts in England to draft a statement of uniqueness and began working through a set of requirements from sportscotland for their recognition, which included building membership within Scotland.

Once again, the proactivity of the Pickleball Scotland team of volunteers has been critical to ensuring the sport is protected as a sport in its own right and is being governed with integrity. There is a clear aim to establish and maintain the organisation and to network with key organisations that can support their endeavours.

In the case of Pickleball, the professionalisation and formalisation of the sport and the work towards establishing an NGB is in its early stages so it is not easy to compare this case with other NGBs and their practices. However, we can explore the nature of the voluntary work being done by staff involved with developing the sport and Pickleball Scotland. It should be noted that the development of the sport and the organisation is not linear: the staff and those with whom they are networked in Scottish sport have experienced tensions and challenges, and it has been necessary to pilot ideas and seek feedback in order to move the development forward. The extensive work of gaining recognition for a new sport and establishing a new NGB, along with the work to develop a system for the sport, cannot be achieved without the input of well-positioned, skilled and knowledgeable individuals. The next section of this chapter will discuss the role of people in developing sport.

The Role of People in Developing a Sport

Institutional Work

Institutional work can be described as the endeavours of individuals or groups to construct, maintain and/or disrupt institutions, be they specific organisations or values and norms that exist within a social space (Lawrence and Suddaby, 2006). Institutional work has been highlighted by scholars such as Dowling and Smith (2016) for its potential for understanding the role of individuals and groups in shaping sport-related institutional settings. Crucially, as Lawrence and Suddaby (2006: 219) noted, institutional work is done by "culturally competent actors with strong practical skills and sensibility who creatively navigate within their organizational fields"; those *doing* the institutional work need to have appropriate knowledge, skills and networks. The work conducted can vary in nature from minor to major (Dowling and Smith 2016): seemingly small, banal activities, such as the writing-up of documents, can be overlooked but are important aspects of institutional work and the shaping of institutions.

A critical aspect of discussions of institutional work is that people engaging in institutional work are active in that process: they are deliberately seeking to influence (through establishment, maintenance and/or disruption) institutions (Lawrence et al, 2011). Being successful in this work requires people to have knowledge of the context and how the current situation has developed, but also to be able to look to the future (Lawrence et al, 2011). The knowledge and skills of the Pickleball Scotland staff and their experiences as participants in the sport make them well equipped and well positioned to carry out the necessary institutional work to establish the NGB and develop the sport in Scotland.

Volunteers

The role of volunteers in sports clubs has been widely discussed in academic literature (for example, Donnelly and Harvey, 2012; Kay and Bradbury, 2009; Taylor et al, 2012) and the significance of volunteering within sport is recognised by sports councils, which also promote volunteering opportunities. Taylor et al (2012: 201) stated, "Volunteers are central to the sport policy context in the United Kingdom" and noted that as well as volunteers being significant in delivery of sport, they are also part of the governance of sport within NGBs. In Scotland, sportscotland promotes volunteering within sport, outlining the benefits of volunteering in terms of developing an individual's skills and knowledge (sportscotland, 2022a). According to the 2019 Scottish Household Survey, approximately 26% of the population in Scotland are engaged in voluntary work (Scottish Government, 2020).

As Nichols et al (2015) note, drawing on the work of Cnann et al (1996), there is a difference between roles with formal and informal volunteering in club settings, with the latter tending to be people who hold specific roles in the club's governance structure or more technical roles such as coaches. Volunteers need to have appropriate skills and qualities and be deployed appropriately (Nichols et al, 2015), thus the work needed to be undertaken in the development of a sport, though reliant on volunteers, needs to have appropriate people engaging in this work. In Scotland, as part of its promotion of volunteering, sportscotland provides role descriptions and case studies of volunteer roles in sport to support people's understanding of the skills that volunteers might need (sportscotland, 2022b).

BOX 11.4

WORK OF PICKLEBALL SCOTLAND 'STAFF'

Three of the founding members of the fledgling Pickleball Scotland NGB came to the table with more than their enthusiasm for the sport. One founding member was a retired accountant who was the Chair of the Finance Committee for Badminton Scotland. The second was the Major Events Operations Manager for Badminton Scotland, with a background in physical education. And the third was the person who brought Pickleball across from the USA, a businessperson with an ability to establish positive networking opportunities with a variety of people who could help the establishment and growth of the organisation – it was she who became and remains the first Chair of Pickleball Scotland.

The networks of the Pickleball Scotland staff were essential: they were able to draw advice from a range of other sports organisations including current and former leaders of other NGBs in Scotland to seek advice and buy-in for the work to become recognised as a stand-alone sport and NGB. The staff have also made use of local connections and had direct discussions with facility owners, including tennis clubs, to make use of those facilities to help build the participant base.

Further work is needed in terms of strategic networking with different stakeholders in the sport industry in Scotland and developing sustainable clubs that can grow their membership and thus help the sport to grow further. There is a dedicated member of the committee to conduct this work who has a strong business background but less knowledge in relation to sport development, though this has not been an issue in developing connections thus far. It is potentially the case that the different perspective she has in *not* coming from a sport-related background is a benefit to the organisation.

Coaching

As noted in the introduction of this chapter, having people with suitable knowledge is vital for the development of sport so that new players can be appropriately and safely introduced to the sport, and those already involved in the sport can develop their skills. As Lyle (2012) highlighted, there are different needs in relation to coaching or leadership depending on the characteristics of the participant group(s).

As a sport becomes formalised and organisations leading the sport look to grow participation levels and build infrastructure for the sport to flourish, developing coaches is often part of that process. For example, as Parkour has become more established, so it has faced these questions of how to develop a coaching system as part of a process of legitimisation of the sport (Sterchele and Ferrero Camoletto, 2017). Developing a coaching system is challenging in Parkour due to the nature of the sport being organic and the importance of, as Sterchele and Ferrero Camoletto (2017: 92) note, "experiential learning" and "peer learning", thus having a formal coach education system in place has been resisted by some groups involved in the sport. Although Pickleball is a more 'traditional' sport than Parkour, the growth in its popularity in Scotland (and indeed elsewhere in the world) has been somewhat organic so there is the potential for existing participants to resist the input of an NGB and a formal coach development system. Traditionally, the national and international federations for a sport are the caretakers of the sport's rules and structures, including competition, and, at a national level, the NGB leads key aspects of the sport's development, such as developing a coaching system. The institutional work of people involved in Pickleball and the NGB becomes critical in this case as they make use of their knowledge of the development of the sport to date, the context in which the NGB is operating and their view of the potential development of the sport, including the development of coaching, as discussed in Box 11.5.

BOX 11.5

PICKLEBALL SCOTLAND AND COACHING

Developing coaches and having a committee member responsible for coaching was a priority for Pickleball Scotland. The first need was to train people in how to introduce the game to people who had never played. The Ambassadors' training package was evolved enabling those who were trained as Ambassadors to grow the game in Scotland. This was also an opportunity to lay the foundations of Pickleball Scotland's approach to developing the game. The five principles evolved for Ambassadors to use were: provide a brief history of the game, be safe, introduce the game bit by bit, ensure games are fun, encourage people to register as players on Pickleball Scotland's website (https://www.pickleballscotland.org) (Figure 11.4).

While it is important to consider the existing participant base when developing a system for the sport, there also needs to be consideration of future players of all ages and experiences. Therefore, Pickleball Scotland took a two-pronged approach: one set of work for engaging adults and another for working with young people.

FIGURE 11.4 Ambassadors in training.

In terms of working with adults, the NGB staff have now written a programme that is of a similar philosophy to the UKCC programme, that is, educating coaches to be reflective practitioners and which equips them with the tools to be adaptive pedagogues. They could have reverted to a more traditional approach to coaching which focuses much more on content-knowledge and a structured skills-based approach. However, in order to make Pickleball Scotland have its own brand and making use of the coaching expertise of the volunteers, the reflective practitioner approach is the one they followed. A key branding aspect here is that after attending the workshop, participants have to complete three reflective journals on three different coaching sessions to then qualify as a club coach. There are also plans to create a performance coach award in the future.

In terms of working with younger people, the NGB has explored how to enable new and younger players to engage with the sport, so they have developed resource for secondary schools that respect current ideas of facilitative teaching approaches. A next step will be to draw the various resources together as they could be used by upper secondary schools and further education establishments to help teach sports leadership, introductory sports coaching and event management. A key challenge for moving this work forwards is money!

There is also a resource to support club and competition organisers, which is freely available on the Pickleball Scotland website.

Getting to this point has been an interesting journey. The key personnel involved with writing the resources, and training courses are highly experienced in their professional fields. However, each of these fields is different, and so it follows that each person's perspective of what these resources and courses should look like differs too. We also came with our own experiences of 'being' coached and taught, and this too had an impact on our individual vision for courses – we all had memories of great, and not so great, courses that we had attended over the years and these, along with our professional and academic understanding of coaching and teaching, influenced our perspectives. The key thing to note is that we all had a shared philosophy of collegiate and reflective practice. This enabled us to work collaboratively to write and test our courses, and after reflection (self-reflection, group reflection and feedback from course attendees), we were able to amend and re-test our courses. This cycle of testing, reflecting and amending will be continuous and will help us to evolve more naturally, and it will also help prevent us from becoming too fixed in our way of thinking and working. This cycle of reflection and re-action is what we ask of our coaching course attendees. Of course, one of the challenges that we need to be cognisant of is how our courses are perceived and valued by others. We are not aligned to a national coaching programme, nor are we offering courses that are accredited by an examining body or even the two Pickleball international federations. So, the question of gaining a 'qualification' through Pickleball Scotland courses is, at the moment at least, in the eye of the beholder! This is potentially another book chapter in its own right – how are sports courses valued and given credence? Who, ultimately, has the authority to decide if a course 'qualifies' an attendee to become a coach?

Concluding Remarks

This chapter has drawn on the experiences of people working in the sport of Pickleball in Scotland to illuminate the challenges and opportunities of developing and new system for sport. With the sport being in the process of becoming formalised in its structures in Scotland and with a growing profile and participant base, volunteers who are leading the sport and beginning the process of establishing a system for developing the sport and considering the role of coach development within this system.

The Pickleball Scotland management board have demonstrated a combined top-down and bottom-up approach to develop this growing sport in Scotland. The responsibilities that the founding members have assumed, and how they have used both their own sets of skills and knowledge and made use of networks in sport in Scotland to create a new organisation that is seeking confirmation as the sport's NGB, show a careful top-down approach to ensure the integrity of the sport and its governing body. They have also ensured that the needs of current and potential players are considered in their planning, and indeed, they are players themselves so they have strong connections to the grassroots of the sport in Scotland.

Moving forward, the development of the sport will rely upon an ongoing increase in the number of regular players and competitors and establishing a secure infrastructure for people to play regularly, including access to appropriate facilities and a calendar of competitions and events to engage those who want to develop their skills and compete in the sport that they enjoy. The further development of a system for developing coaches will aid in growing the sport. For now, the NGB staff continue their institutional work to establish the sport and the organisation governing the sport in Scotland, whilst being mindful of the challenges they face: the primary challenge being having a sustainable income to further the development of the sport.

Note

1 Within this chapter when we refer to 'staff' within Pickleball Scotland, these are not paid individuals but altruistically motivated individuals committing their own time to the sport and to the organisation.

References

Bull, A., 2018. "#weareNOTgymnastics': parkour fights to retain its soul', *The Guardian* (online). https://www.theguardian.com/sport/blog/2018/dec/05/parkour-fight-soul-gymnastics [Accessed 05/06/2022].

Cnaan, R.A., Handy, F. and Wadsworth, M. (1996). Defining who is a volunteer: Conceptual and empirical considerations. *Nonprofit and Voluntary Sector Quarterly*, 25, pp. 364–383.

Donnelly, P. and Harvey, J., 2012. Volunteering and sport. In B. Houlihan and M. Green (eds.) *Routledge Handbook of Sports Development*, Abingdon: Routledge. pp. 71–87.

Dowling, M., Edwards, J. and Washington, M., 2014. Understanding the concept of professionalisation in sport management research. *Sport Management Review*, 17(4), pp. 520–529.

Dowling, M. and Smith, J., 2016. The institutional work of Own the Podium in developing high-performance sport in Canada. *Journal of Sport Management*, 30(4), pp. 396–410.

Hoye, R., Smith, A.C.T., Nicholson, M. and Stewart, B., 2015, *Sport Management: Principles and applications*, 4th Edition. London & New York: Routledge.

Houlihan, B. and Green, M., 2009. Modernization and sport: The reform of Sport England and UK Sport. *Public Administration*, 87(3), pp. 678–698.

Jenkin, C.R., Eime, R.M., Van Uffelen, J.G. and Westerbeek, H., 2021. How to re-engage older adults in community sport? Reasons for drop-out and re-engagement. *Leisure Studies*, 40(4), pp. 441–453.

Kay, T. and Bradbury, S., 2009. Youth sport volunteering: Developing social capital? *Sport, Education and Society*, 14(1), pp. 121–140.

Kikulis, L.M., Slack, T. and Hinings, B., 1992. Institutionally specific design archetypes: A framework for understanding change in national sport organizations. *International Review for the Sociology of Sport*, 27(4), pp. 343–368.

Lawrence, T. B. and Suddaby, R., 2006, 'Institutions and institutional work'. In S. R. Clegg, C. Hardy, T. B. Lawrence, and W. R. Nord (eds.) *Handbook of Organization Studies*, 2nd Edition. London: Sage. pp. 215–254.

Lawrence, T., Suddaby, R. and Leca, B., 2011. Institutional work: Refocusing institutional studies of organization. *Journal of Management Inquiry*, 20(1), pp. 52–58.

Lyle, J., 2012, 'Sports development, sports coaching, and domain specificity'. In B. Houlihan and M. Green (eds.) *Routledge Handbook of Sports Development*, Abingdon: Routledge, pp. 487–500.

Nichols, G., Wicker, P., Cuskelly, G. and Breuer, C., 2015. Measuring the formalization of community sports clubs: Findings from the UK, Germany and Australia. *International Journal of Sport Policy and Politics*, 7(2), pp. 283–300.

Pedras, L., Taylor, T. and Frawley, S., 2020. Responses to multi-level institutional complexity in a national sport federation. *Sport Management Review*, 23(3), pp. 482–497.

Scottish Government, 2020. *Scottish Household Survey 2019: annual report*, available online: https://www.gov.scot/publications/scottish-household-survey-2019-annual-report/ [Accessed 05/06/2022].

Shilbury, D., Sotiriadou, K.P. and Green, B.C., 2008. Sport development. Systems, policies and pathways: An introduction to the special issue. *Sport Management Review*, 11(3), pp. 217–223.

sportscotland, 2021. *SGB Governance Framework*. Available at: https://sportscotland.org.uk/sport-a-z/governing-bodies-of-sport/sgb-governance-framework/ [Accessed 05/06/2022].

sportscotland, 2022a. *Benefits of volunteering*. Available at: https://sportscotland.org.uk/volunteer/benefits-of-volunteering/ [Accessed 05/06/2022].

sportscotland, 2022b. *How to get into volunteering*. Available at: https://sportscotland.org.uk/volunteer/how-to-get-into-volunteering/ [Accessed 05/06/2022].

Sterchele, D. and Ferrero Camoletto, R., 2017. Governing bodies or managing freedom? Subcultural struggles, national sport systems and the glocalised institutionalisation of parkour. *International Journal of Sport Policy and Politics*, 9(1), pp. 89–105.

Tacon, R. and Walters, G., 2016. Modernisation and governance in UK national governing bodies of sport: How modernisation influences the way board members perceive and enact their roles. *International Journal of Sport Policy and Politics*, 8(3), pp. 363–381.

Taylor, P.D., Panagouleas, T. and Nichols, G., 2012. Determinants of sports volunteering and sports volunteer time in England. *International Journal of Sport Policy and Politics*, 4(2), pp. 201–220.

Thompson, A., Lachance, E.L., Parent, M.M. and Hoye, R., 2022. A systematic review of governance principles in sport. *European Sport Management Quarterly*, pp. 1–26.

Walters, G. and Tacon, R., 2018. The 'codification' of governance in the non-profit sport sector in the UK. *European Sport Management Quarterly*, 18(4), pp. 482–500.

Washington, M. and Patterson, K.D., 2011. Hostile takeover or joint venture: Connections between institutional theory and sport management research. *Sport Management Review*, 14(1), pp. 1–12.

12
THE COACH DEVELOPER AS A SYSTEM BUILDER

Maintaining a High-Performing Sport System

Cameron Kiosoglous

Building a High-Performance Sport System – How Important Is the Coach Developer?

This section focusses on how high-performance sport has evolved from the traditional 'athlete–coach' relationship to encompass an increasingly complex and dynamic coaching team, plus additional support staff including physiotherapists, doctors, soft tissue therapists, strength and conditioning coaches, psychologists, physiologists, biomechanists, performance analysts and career lifestyle coaches. Creating and maintaining this coaching infrastructure is problematic as more research is needed to understand the culture in which they operate and improve how these systems work. Specifically, I am exploring strategies and examples of how to integrate these systems to support an athlete's journey and enable coaches to develop the necessary skills. The primary questions to be addressed include:

- **Role:** What is the role of the coach developer within high-performance systems?
- **Value:** How is the coach developer valued within high-performance system?
- **Uniqueness:** What, if anything, differentiates the coach developer in high-performance systems from others?

Evolution and Definition of High-Performance Sport Systems

When we refer to the high-performance sport systems, from a historical perspective, the first documented evidence dates to the 1950s with the onset of the Cold War and sport in the former communist nations and Eastern Bloc. Some nations started to develop a systematic approach, developing athletes to achieve diplomatic objectives (Riordan, 1978). A classic example is how East Germany managed to achieve success on the world stage, known as the sports 'miracle' (Dennis, 2012). During this period, high-performance sport systems saw elite athletes train under the supervision or direction of a coach from their sports federation. However, the approach taken was authoritarian with little place for coach developers (Houlihan & Zheng, 2013). A shift in the 1980s saw 'super teams' evolve, where an athlete had their own team of performance specialists including therapists, psychologists, physiologists, biomechanists and other performance analysts, to guide their success (Collins et al., 2013). The movie Rocky IV, where the Russian character Ivan Drago had a team of super-scientists around him in preparation to fight against Rocky Balboa, illustrated this new approach to supporting athletes. There was still little emphasis on the education and development of sport coaches.

Alder (2015) made the distinction between high-performance and high-performing (HP) contexts. This is an important distinction as these terms are used interchangeably and can cause confusion. A team may be operating in a high-performance environment but that does not mean the team are producing HP results (Collins et al., 2013). HP teams share a belief of producing optimal performance over a sustained and consistent period (Cruickshank & Collins, 2012). According to Alder (2015), high-performance cultures are recognized by the following attributes:

1. High levels of peer challenge with low threat
2. Effective two-way communication
3. Clear task and role acknowledgement
4. Well-managed positive conflict or constructive disagreement
5. A strong and mutual respectful and supportive team ethos
6. Consistency of personnel

The complex, unique and multifaceted nature of the high-performance context is an important driver for producing high-performance results (Cruickshank & Collins, 2013). While not included in this list, high-performance sport requires an increased level of funding, especially when being used as a political tool or statement by a country.

In 2020, sports, especially high-performance sports, grew rapidly with the sports market across North America alone expected to grow from 71.1 billion dollars in 2018 to 83.1 billion dollars in 2023 (McCaffrey et al., 2021), making the North American region the largest sport market in the world. Much of this increase in spending is expected to address the changes, rearrangement and improving operations in response to the impact of the COVID-19 pandemic. One critical area for the future of sport is the use of technology and specifically the precise use of data collection, analysis and application to competition strategy to help optimize athlete performance (Hill, 2021). Although big data provides empirical statistics to help with every aspect of the game, key information for sports systems and coaches relates to injury prevention, improving performance, recruitment and tactics (Clark & Nash, 2021).

High-Performance Systems and Coaching

De Bosscher et al. (2015) found the literature on coach development is less prolific compared to the research on athlete development, for example, Long Term Athlete Development (LTAD) work (Balyi & Hamilton, 2004 and others) and deliberate practice (Ericsson et al., 1993 and others). In terms of coach learning, coaches experience relatively low impact from traditional coach learning and report more worthwhile experiences from mentoring interactions with more experienced coaches and reflections from their experience of being an athlete (Erickson et al., 2007). Lynch and Mallett (2006) reported athletic experience might be useful in developing coaching expertise, but it is not a prerequisite for success in coaching at the international level.

De Bosscher et al. (2015) also noted a strong and significant relationship between quality coaching systems and medal winning success in Olympic sports. Having a clear understanding of what quality coaching looks like in the high-performance context is the foundation to improving the relationship between the systems and athlete performance. Coaches hold a critical role in these sports systems, being the conduit between elite sport policy, government funding, training practice and sporting success (Wicker et al., 2018). As coaches are also closely involved in talent identification, team selection and policy development, they are integral in the system. However, there is little information or research to quantify the role of the coach developer in high-performance systems. Defining quality coaching in this culture will assist in how the coach developer can support and contribute to the coach and athlete's performance. Understanding the value of coach development in the high-performance context is key to improved practice and systems.

As mentioned earlier, coach development has not received much attention and requires more focus to generate the same level of input as other aspects of high-performance systems (De Bosscher et al., 2015). Key to this must be the intensity and challenge of high-performance systems that are different and unique from other sport systems (see Chapter 11). The case studies included later in this chapter highlight some of the different applications of coach development, an important tool in high-performance system development. Success in high-performance does not happen in a vacuum. The interrelated nature of athlete development, coaching education and development, facilities management and resource distribution is a multi-layered environment but sport systems do not lend themselves to an individual approach. Sotiriadou and De Bosscher (2018) suggest to be successful at this level with so many degrees of freedom and choice, treating everyone as an individual is key. The rate of change within high-performance sport can be surprising, especially in the lead up to major championships, which adds to the complexity.

Understanding Complexity

Mowles (2021) highlighted some science disciplines have developed a non-linear model to help explain the nature of complexity in society. The term complexity dates to Aristotle. Occam's Razor is a metaphor to help understand complexity by highlighting the best theory is the simplest theory while still explaining observations (Sober, 2015). Occam's Razor is also referred to as the parsimony rule. For example, an athlete has a headache, goes to the coach and says 'I have a headache, I did some research and it might be a brain tumor.' The coach says, 'let's check with the team doctor' and after asking some questions and further examination, the athlete and coach conclude the headache is better explained by dehydration and training fatigue. The objective is to keep the explanation simple but avoid over-simplification. In most cases the answer is simple (not a brain tumor) but this is not necessarily the case in high-performance sport. The non-linear nature of the context increases the complexity in high-performance sport. Regardless of the amount of work to gather information and reduce the uncertainty, action is still required from the coach, coach developer, athlete and support team (Mowles, 2021). Understanding the different types of complexity typical in high-performance sport will help coach developers and coaches better understand the factors at play. Coaches and coach developers can only influence but never control an uncontrollable context, and the recognition of the unpredictability and the adaptability to deal with unforeseen circumstances determines the success of high-performance sport systems.

Understanding Complexity in High-Performance Sport

Identifying the factors predicting international sporting success is complicated because managing high-performance sport is influenced by a combination of variables located on the macro (country), meso (sport program) and micro (athletes) levels (De Bosscher et al., 2006). Hill (2021) studied different high-performance sport systems in the United States (US) and found the challenges and scenarios facing high-performance sport leaders are unique and different to those faced in other business environments. However, there has been similar research in medical and military contexts highlighting the life-changing challenges and complex decision-making scenarios in life-or-death situations.

Case Study 1 highlights some of the issues facing a coach developer embedded within the high-performance system of a sport in the US.

CASE STUDY 1: AN OLYMPIC SPORT NATIONAL GOVERNING BODY: IS A COACH DEVELOPER IMPORTANT WHEN BUILDING A HIGH-PERFORMANCE SYSTEM?

Complexity n high-performance sport is most noticeable when examining the logistics and administration of coach development within this Olympic sport national governing body in the US. This organization has a history of success at Olympic and World Championships and wants to continue this in the future. However, many Olympic programs in the US and elsewhere around the world have struggled during this unique transition from a long five-year 2020 Olympic cycle to a short three-year 2024 Olympic cycle. Many, if not most, aspects of this complexity were present even prior to the postponement of the Tokyo 2020 Olympics.

The myriad of pressures placed upon high-performance coaches impact the ideal conditions for continued coach learning (Nash et al., 2017). Much of the focus for the coach developer in this context was disproportionately informal interactions and discussions rather than formal systems and interventions. There was an importance placed on the coach developer to meet the coaches, not with any long-term development pathway in mind but simply to resolve the most immediate challenge they were facing at that time (Knowles, 1978). Given the enhanced complexity of the context, a deliberate choice was made by the organization to provide the highest level of support for the coach. Building trust was highlighted as an integral aspect of the working relationship between the coach developer and coaching staff. Highest priority was given to addressing the immediate issues facing the coaches and their athletes.

As an example of how this was implemented, regular meetings were set up to manage the highs and lows related to the global pandemic as this was a major challenge facing all athletes and coaches preparing for Tokyo 2020. Weekly meetings were arranged to discuss athlete health status. The content of these meetings evolved over time and became a forum for coaches to share their insights and thoughts about the challenges they were facing. These meetings evolved over time to become an opportunity to include different performance staff to share their insights and expertise with coaches. These meetings included nutrition, mental performance, physical therapy, medical, coach developer and other performance staff. The coach developer specifically took content and issues discussed in these meetings as an opportunity to follow up with coach learning. The conversations that started with athlete status updates often evolved into more detailed challenges coaches faced as the pressures grew in preparation for the Olympics.

Key questions arising from Case Study 1

How important do you feel the coach developer was in this process?

How valued do you think the coach developer felt in this scenario?

What (if anything) differentiates the coach developer in this context from others?

How much does complexity contribute to this case study?

Think back to Alder's (2015) components of a high-performance environment mentioned earlier. Which elements could apply in this scenario?

Different Models of High-Performance Sport

One unique challenge facing elite sport in the US is the varied use of the term high-performance. Some view high-performance as prioritizing athlete monitoring, others see high-performance as technology-driven services (Hill, 2021). High-performance is often used as a catch-all term. In the US this perception includes concepts of sport sciences driven and performance-enhancing focused, while a research-based model defines high-performance sport in Europe. The two definitions of high-performance sport need more explanation. The European model or Sports Policy factors Leading to International Sporting Success (SPLISS) model was developed and produced the research that has addressed our understanding of elite sport at the Olympic level, as well as the application to other types of competition and professional or commercial sports teams (De Bosscher et al., 2006). It consists of nine pillars:

- **Pillar 1:** Financial support
- **Pillar 2:** Governance, structure and organization
- **Pillar 3:** Sport participation
- **Pillar 4:** Talent identification and development system
- **Pillar 5:** Athletic and post career support
- **Pillar 6:** Training facilities
- **Pillar 7:** Coaching and coach development
- **Pillar 8:** (Inter)National competition
- **Pillar 9:** Scientific research, innovation and technologies

How these elements are emphasized depends on a variety of factors such as the sport, its related context and the leadership involved (Alder, 2015). In this high-performance model, the director is responsible for exercising appropriate financial delegation and monitoring the program's financial operations (Sotiriadou, 2013) (Figure 12.1).

Alternatively, the US approach is best described as one with no, or very limited, government control/financial support as well as the relative infancy of high-performance sport as a structured elite sport management system (De Bosscher et al., 2015). This style of relative autonomy for US-based sport systems provides a freedom and liberty for sport leaders to choose a direction of emphasis for success (Jalili, 2022). High-performance sport systems in the US are often ill-defined entities with a mismatch of factors led by market-driven forces, often privatized, and involve and often require expensive operations when compared to other similar sport systems in other countries (To et al., 2013; Smolianov et al., 2014). The 'model' of high-performance sport in the US consists of these areas:

- **Holistic – supporting athlete development:** career development, media training, sport science, injury prevention and medical advice (Sotiriadou et al., 2013)

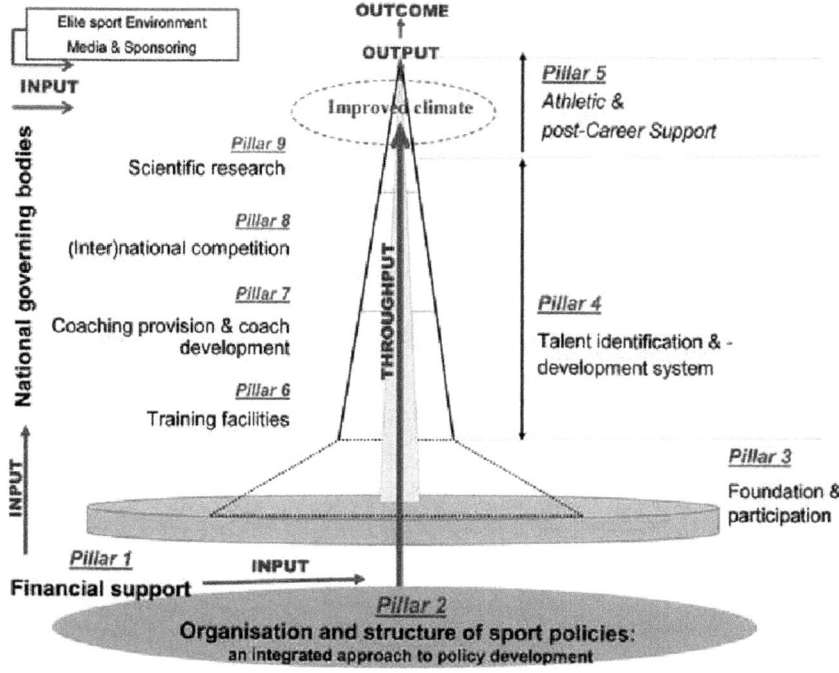

FIGURE 12.1 Representation of the SPLISS pillars.

- **Athlete-centered – addressing athlete needs:** examples include personal and professional development that expand on holistic approach above (Smith & Smolianov, 2016)
- **Collaborative – inclusive communication across groups:** athlete, coach, support staff and administration (Reid et al., 2004)
- **Performance development:** prioritizing athlete growth and improvement as it relates to performance (Sotiriadou et al., 2013)
- **Data analysis, athlete monitoring and technology-driven:** using data (collection, analysis and decision-making) that leads to improving athlete performance (Tenney, 2016)
- **Sport-scientist directed:** subject matter experts who support in improving athlete performance (Hill, 2021)

In the US the role of the high-performance director is often filled by a sport scientist who acquired their training in higher education, including foundational knowledge across the primary disciplines of anthropometry, biomechanics, motor control and learning, physiology, psychology and training methodology, together with advanced, integrated, or applied studies in one or more of these areas (ESSA, 2021). This highlights the scientific approach, characterized by

190 Cameron Kosoglous

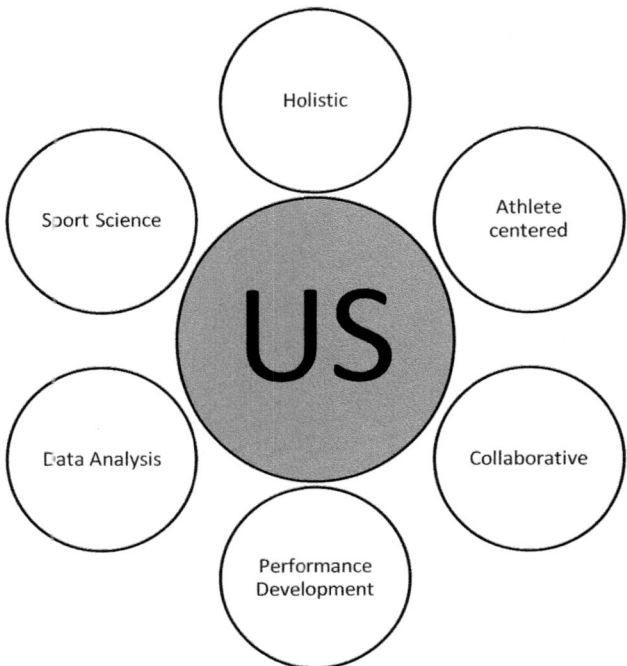

FIGURE 12.2 Representation of the US high-performance sport model.

measurement, training loads and a carefully managed and implemented program (Figure 12.2).

Clarifying this definition of high-performance is important and impacts all aspects of the high-performance system. Significant research and evidence highlight the importance of the competitive advantage that effective management and governance has in optimizing high-performance systems (Sotiriadou, 2013). Collins et al. (2013) emphasized for coaches the high-performance sport environment is always looking for the next cutting edge in advice and solutions for optimal performance, but the source of that information is often hard to access and rely on. Most high-performance systems in the US context do not have a formalized structure, model or framework with job roles and responsibilities, as many organizations and their leaders have little to no idea of what the job entails (Hill, 2021).

Coach Development in High-Performance Sport Settings

The aim of this section is to provide practical lessons through examples of coach development at the high-performance level. While well organized and planned in theory prior to the implementation of these roles, the reality of coach development in the field at the high-performance level is not easy to explain. Rynne and Mallett (2012) identified the specific needs for the development of high-performance coaches in Australian sporting institutes, providing a clear understanding of a modern high-performance coach. Case Study 2 presents some thoughts about how a coach developer in the US can help the high-performance coach enhance their skills and move away from the overly scientific approach.

> **CASE STUDY 2: SUPPORTING COACH'S DEVELOPMENT IN A MULTI-SPORT CONTEXT: IS SPORT-SPECIFIC FORMAL COACH EDUCATION AS IMPORTANT AS DEVELOPING A COACH'S INTERPERSONAL AND INTRAPERSONAL SKILLS**
>
> This example of coach development in the high-performance environment is based on the experiences of a coach developer working with a group of coaches from a variety of sports within a well-organized and funded state (regional) sport high-performance program. Most of the coaches in this program had varying levels of understanding of the coach developer role in both the formal and informal setting. Some of the coaches had worked directly with a coach developer previously, while other coaches had no previous contact with a coach developer in the informal context. These coaches had varied levels of experience working directly with a coach developer. In this situation, the coach developer prioritized working on each coach's intrapersonal and interpersonal skill development. This process of prioritization was conducted through a dialogue with the coach and coach developer in discussions based on questions relating to what was most important to the coach, their context and their coaching needs. The sport-specific coach development was provided by a selected mentor from each coach's sport-specific context. Informal and formal meetings for the coach and coach developer facilitated the process of identifying learning opportunities for the coach including the areas of focus and how they planned to prioritize their development of these skills. These coaches found working with a coach developer to design their learning activities helped develop more targeted learning, enabled them to become intentional about their learning. Feedback from the coaches on key benefits from their work with the coach developer included:
>
> 1. Challenging coach's assumptions about their coaching practices
> 2. Reflecting on coaching practices
> 3. Receiving feedback on communications such as exploring between ways to ask questions and evolve their coaching style
> 4. Coaches value regular and individualized responses to their coaching

The support provided by the coach developer acted as a sounding board to promote the coach in their own self-reflective practice (Winfield et al., 2013). More recently, Nash and colleagues (2022) reported successes with stimulated recall using videos of coaching practice to improve elite coaches' self-reflective skills. In this instance, working one-on-one with a coach developer challenged two commonly held beliefs that coaches hold about their professional development:

1. Coaches prefer formal coach education over individualized coach feedback.
2. Coaches want more sport-specific coaching knowledge when it comes to professional development.

Dispelling these beliefs supports the findings of Wiman (2010) who stated coaching expertise is developed through introspection and gaining self-awareness, however expertise in coaching is characterized by a complex mix of skills, knowledge and ability (see Chapter 10). This case study highlights coach learning is dynamic and this learning approach evolves over time by accepting and rejecting new knowledge through experimenting with new methods in a trial-and-error fashion (Stodter & Cushion, 2017). It also confirmed our understanding about interventions such as coach reflection sessions, and discussions around coaching philosophy helped advance the coaches practices on and off the field of play (Rodrigue et al., 2019). This case study highlights effective coach developer practices, promoting coach learning by prioritizing intrapersonal and interpersonal skill development.

Key questions arising from Case Study 2

How important do you feel the coach developer was in this process?

How valued do you think the coach developer felt in this scenario?

What (if anything) differentiates the coach developer in this context from others?

How much does complexity contribute to this case study?

Think back to Alder's (2015) components of a high-performance environment mentioned earlier. Which elements could apply in this scenario?

Does Investment in Coach Learning Increase Medal Winning Performance?

Much has been written about the impact of hosting an Olympic Games and the resultant increase in medals for the home Olympics and on either side of hosting the Games (Bernard & Busse, 2004; Schlembach et al., 2021). These studies on forecasting Olympic success do not mention the importance of the coach as an integral part of athlete performance. This begs the question is there enough evidence to say the investment in coach development during that period can impact athlete performances and their Olympic medal tally? In recent Olympics both Brazil and Japan have seen an increase their medal tally and their investment in coach development. One explanation of this increase in medal haul is based on home country advantage of hosting the games (Balmer et al., 2003; Singleton et al., 2021). Both nations have made significant strides in establishing programs both in academia and the applied environment to advance the behaviors and performance of their coaches. Perhaps the direct relationship between coach development and medal tally is too difficult to understand at present. The time it takes to see the benefits of coach development can be quick, but in the context of athlete development and performance systems, identifying 'cause and effect' is difficult.

Recommendations

This aim of this chapter is to help inform coach developers and others involved in this high-performance engagement how effective coach developers promote coach learning through a focus on a variety of approaches. Coach development research needs more attention, and this is especially the case at the high-performance level (De Bosscher et al., 2015). The complexity of many moving parts during any given season through a professional team or across the Olympic cycle makes for a difficult discussion. The high-performance environment is hard to fathom on a day-to-day basis, as even then, coaching in this context is often messy and fragmented. Management and organizational decisions can be complicated and hard to describe and understand to an outside observer. The following recommendations from these case studies and the literature are provided for leaders in high-performance sport systems:

- **Defining high-performance:** Creating a common language starts with making sure that all members of high-performance system know what is meant by this term and is a critical part of this process of effective function of the system. This is an important recommendation for coach developers as their role demands they fulfil all the elements in their interactions with coaches.
- **Building trust:** This is critical and applies to coach developers working with coaches in any system. The high-performance context is dynamic and constantly changing; this is reflected in the constantly evolving needs of the group at any point in the preparation for major competition.
- **Establishing effective communication systems:** Regardless of whether the coach developer is working one-on-one in a formal setting with coaches or working with a large team of coaches and other performance staff, the need for creating and sustaining effective communications is also critical.
- **The main thing is to keep 'the main thing the main thing':** Much of the struggle in the complex and ever-changing high-performance sport system is to keep athlete performance the main priority of discussion. Despite

these complexities and the additional areas that need to be addressed, the success of any high-performance system is to keep to the top priorities. Distraction can easily lead to athlete performance not being the area that is given the attention needed to produce world-class performances.

Summary

This chapter provided a background into the high-performance sport systems. This introduction is an attempt to lay the foundation on how coach development has evolved as a part of the high-performance sport system. The evolving role of the coach and the importance of developing the coach's skills and expertise have been highlighted. The challenges for the coach developer in the high-performance context are to identify how to support the coach's growth and development while adjusting to the strains and pressures of the dynamic and fluid high-performance sport context. Some examples from the field have been provided to help highlight best practice and attempts to explain the complexity of this role in the field. Finally, the conclusion to this chapter was to explore if the role of the coach developer is important for the evolution of the high-performance sport system. Some practical recommendations are provided, and future research is required to better understand the value of coach and the coach developer in the high-performance system of the future.

References

Alder, J. P. (2015). *Meaning and sensemaking in high performance sport: managing change in the high-performance unit of a national sport organization* (Doctoral dissertation, Auckland University of Technology).

Balmer, N. J., Nevill, A. M., & Williams, A. M. (2003). Modelling home advantage in the Summer Olympic Games. *Journal of Sports Sciences, 21*(6), 469–478.

Balyi, I., & Hamilton, A. (2004). Long-term athlete development: Trainability in childhood and adolescence. *Olympic Coach, 16*(1), 4–9.

Bernard, A. B., & Busse, M. R. (2004). Who wins the Olympic Games: Economic resources and medal totals. *Review of Economics and Statistics, 86*(1), 413–417.

Clark, J. & Nash, C. (2021). Big data in sport. In C. Nash (Ed.), *Practical Sports Coaching*. 2nd Edition. Routledge/Taylor & Francis Group.

Collins, D., Trower, J., & Cruickshank, A. (2013). Coaching high-performance athletes and the high-performance team. In P. Sotiriadou, & V. De Bosscher (Eds.), *Managing High-Performance Sport* (pp. 205–220). Abingdon: Routledge.

Cruickshank, A., & Collins, D. (2012). Change management: The case of the elite sport performance team. *Journal of Change Management, 12*(2), 209–229.

Cruickshank, A., & Collins, D. (2013). Culture change in elite sport performance teams: Outlining an important and unique construct. *Sport & Exercise Psychology Review, 9*(2), 6–21.

De Bosscher, V., De Knop, P., Van Bottenburg, M., & Shibli, S. (2006). A conceptual framework for analysing sports policy factors leading to international sporting success. *European Sport Management Quarterly, 6*(2), 185–215. https://doi.org/10.1080/16184740600955087.

De Bosscher, V., Shibli, S., Westerbeek, H., & Van Bottenburg, M. (2015). *Successful elite sport policies: an international comparison of the sports policy factors leading to international sporting success (SPLISS 2.0) in 15 nations*. Meyer & Meyer Sport.

Dennis, M. (2012) Securing the Sports 'Miracle': The Stasi and East German Elite Sport. *The International Journal of the History of Sport, 29*(18), 2551–2574

Erickson, K., Côté, J., & Fraser-Thomas, J. (2007). Sport experiences, milestones, and educational activities associated with high-performance coaches' development. *The Sport Psychologist, 21*(3), 302–316.

Ericsson, K. A., Krampe, R. T., & Tesch-Römer, C. (1993). The role of deliberate practice in the acquisition of expert performance. *Psychological Review, 100*(3), 363.

ESSA. (2021). What is an Accredited Sports Scientist (ASpS)? Exercise and sport science Australia. https://www.essa.org.au/Public/Professional_Standards/ESSA_Scope_of_Practice_documents.aspx.

Hill, J. G. (2021). High-performance: Exploratory Study into the High-performance Model and Qualitative Secondary Analysis of Elite Sport Management in the United States. Theses and Dissertations – Education Sciences. 87.

Houlihan, B., & Zheng, J. (2013). The Olympics and elite sport policy: Where will it all end? *The International Journal of the History of Sport, 30*(4), 338–355. https://doi.org/10.1080/09523367.2013.765726.

Jalili, D. P. (2022). Child abuse in the Canadian and American Olympic Movement: Reforming institutional oversight of amateur sports. *Canadian Journal of Family and Youth/Le Journal Canadien de Famille et de la Jeunesse, 14*(1), 207–234.

Knowles, M. S. (1978). Andragogy: Adult learning theory in perspective. *Community College Review, 5*(3), 9–20.

Lynch, M., & Mallett, C. (2006). Becoming a successful high-performance track and field coach. *Modern Athlete and Coach, 44*(2), 15–20.

McCaffrey, M., Fagot, A., Monday, C., Keenan, M., & Panson, S. (2021). (rep.). PwC 2021 sports outlook. (pp. 1–23). San Jose, CA. https://files.stample.co/stample-1520259273817-pwc-sports-outlook-2017.pdf.

Mowles, C. (2021). *Complexity: A Key Idea for Business and Society*. Routledge.

Nash C., MacPherson, A. C., & Collins D. (2022) Reflections on reflection: Clarifying and promoting use in experienced coaches. *Frontiers in Psychology, 13*, https://doi.org/10.3389/fpsyg.2022.867720.

Nash, C., Sproule, J., & Horton, P. (2017). Feedback for coaches: Who coaches the coach? *International Journal of Sports Science & Coaching, 12*(1), 92–102.

Reid, C., Stewart, E., & Thorne, G. (2004). Multidisciplinary sport science teams in elite sport: Comprehensive servicing or conflict and confusion? *The Sport Psychologist, 18*(2), 204–217. https://doi.org/10.1123/tsp.18.2.204.

Riordan, J. (Ed.) (1978). *Sport under Communism: The USSR, Czechoslovakia, the GDR, China, Cuba*. McGill-Queen's Press-MQUP.

Rodrigue, F., Trudel, P., & Boyd, J. (2019). Learning from practice: The value of a personal learning coach for high-performance coaches. *International Sport Coaching Journal, 6*(3), 285–295.

Rynne, S.B., & Mallett, C.J. (2012). Understanding the work and learning of high performance coaches. *Physical Education and Sport Pedagogy, 17*(5), 507–523.

Schlembach, C., Schmidt, S. L., Schreyer, D., & Wunderlich, L. (2021). Forecasting the Olympic medal distribution–A socioeconomic machine learning model. *Technological Forecasting and Social Change, 17*. https://doi.org/10.1016/j.techfore.2021.121314.

Singleton, C., Reade, J. J., Rewilak, J., & Schreyer, D. (2021). *How Big Is Home Advantage at the Olympic Games?* Economics Discussion Papers, Department of Economics, University of Reading. (No. em-dp2021-13).

Smith, J., & Smolianov, P. (2016). The high-performance management model: From Olympic and professional to university sport in the United States. *The Sport Journal*, *500*, 1–19.

Smolianov, P., Zakus, D. H., & Gallo, J. (2014). *Sport Development in the United States: High Performance and Mass Participation*. Routledge.

Sober, E. (2015). *Ockham's Razors*. Cambridge University Press. Chicago

Sotiriadou, P. (2013). The roles of high-performance directors within national sporting organizations. In *Managing High-performance Sport* (pp. 33–46). Routledge.

Sotiriadou, P., & Wicker, P. (2013). Community sports clubs' responses to institutional and resource dependence pressures for government grants. *Annals of Leisure Research*, *16*, 297–314. https://doi.org/10.1080/11745398.2013.853338.

Sotiriadou, P., & De Bosscher, V. (2018). Managing high-performance sport: introduction to past, present and future considerations. *European Sport Management Quarterly*, *18*(1), 1–7.

Stodter, A., & Cushion, C. J. (2017). What works in coach learning, how, and for whom? A grounded process of soccer coaches' professional learning. *Qualitative Research in Sport, Exercise and Health*, *9*(3), 321–338.

Tenney, D. (2015, February). Creating a high performance model in U.S. elite sport [Conference Presentation]. NSCA Coaches Conference, San Antonio, TX. https://www.nsca.com/education/videos/creating-a-high-performance-model-in-u.s.-elite-sport/.

To, W. H., Winston, P. S., & Semotiuk, D. (2013). Comparative high-performance sports models. In *Managing High-performance Sport* (pp. 65–86). Routledge.

Wicker, P., Orlowski, J. & Breuer, C. (2018). Coach migration in German high performance sport. *European Sport Management Quarterly*, *18*(1), 93–111.

Wiman, M. L. (2010). *The development and validation of an expertise development model for sport coaches*. (Unpublished doctoral dissertation). The University of Western Ontario, London, Canada.

Winfield, J., Williams, J., & Dixon, M. (2013). The use of reflective practice to support mentoring of elite equestrian coaches. *International Journal of Evidence Based Coaching & Mentoring*, *11*(1), 162–178.

13
DIVERSIFYING COACH DEVELOPMENT

Diane M. Culver, Siobhan Rourke and Tim Konoval

Sport as an essential social institution has served as a catalyst for social change in the past few decades. In the context of sport, we have seen some positive social change realised through decreases in gender gaps (e.g., Fasting & Sand, 2017), the breaking down of certain racial barriers (i.e., primarily for athletes; Lapchick, 2018), and addressing other issues of inequity. Notwithstanding, the sport domain continues to reinforce damaging social patterns such as racism, gender inequity, homophobia, and the inequitable treatment of other minority groups for both athletes and coaches. The sport workforce continues to lack clear career pathways and opportunities for the development for diverse individuals. The coaching field is not currently capitalising on the talent and skills of the entire population and as a result does not accurately represent the make-up of our society. In this chapter, we will discuss some important barriers regarding the diversification of coach development and offer some suggestions for improving coach development practices through three main sections: diversifying recruitment, diversifying language, and diversifying approaches to learning and development.

The coaching profession has, as a direct result of the socially influenced culture of sport, been largely able-bodied, cisgendered,[1] and settler dominated. Consequently, minority groups and those who are socially constructed as "others" must work harder to prove their ability to hold positions of power (Norman, 2011). There are clear gaps in the literature exploring the experiences of marginalised coaches and the opportunities for diversification. Broadly, diversity refers to the practice of including people who identify with a range of different abilities, social and ethnic backgrounds; and of different genders, sexual orientations, political beliefs, life experiences, etc. Another concept that will be evident across the content of this chapter is intersectionality. The concept of intersectionality was first brought forward by legal scholar Crenshaw

DOI: 10.4324/9781003251309-16

(1989) through the lens of critical race theory to outline the various ways the identities of marginalised groups interact and intersect. Traditionally, coach education has focussed on the content of coaching, without properly considering the learner's identity, the context and the layers within that context. It is important to reflect on what forces influence any unique coaching context and how these intersect with the various components of one's identity. The use of intersectionality allows researchers and practitioners to combat the potentially harmful homogeneity of identity often perpetuated in research about marginalised groups. Thus, in attempting to diversify coach recruitment, there is a need for the application of a systems lens to understand how the forces at societal, organisational, and individual levels interact with a person's intersectional identity and coaching context.

Research has demonstrated that workplace cultures that value diversity are beneficial for all employees, not just those who identify as a minority (Coury et al., 2020). Cultures of similarity have been shown to hurt workplace connection and performance (Bradbury et al., 2021). Despite this, there is a lack of intentionality regarding diversity in coach recruitment, hiring, and development, particularly with regard to a systems-level approach to change (e.g., for gender equity see LaVoi, 2016). In such an approach, each individual actor in the system, whatever their scope of influence, must recognise their contributions and responsibilities regarding the social problem and "once they understand their own responsibility for a problem, they can begin by changing the part of the system over which they have the greatest control – themselves" (Stroh, 2015, p. 18). This chapter will outline the issues related to recruitment, language, and learning at the systemic, organisational, and individual levels for coaches who identify with a minority group. Rather than a systematic review of the factors that exist for all minority groups, we aim to provide a broad overview of the current climate in sport coaching. The use of a system thinking approach allows us to make some practical recommendations with a view to providing "individual contributors to the system an appreciation of the part they [might] play related to the whole" (Culver et al., 2019, p. 304).

Diversifying Recruitment

The use of diverse recruitment practices is necessary to grow the coaching field and increase representation. In this section we will provide a brief overview of the current situations that face several under-represented groups in the coaching domain. While this is not an exhaustive list, we will also address some of the barriers that currently exist for marginalised groups in coaching while providing some suggestions for improving diversity practices. We highlight the Black Female Coach Mentorship Program (BFCMP) in Canada as an example of a programme that is working to increase opportunities to develop historically excluded Black, Biracial, and Indigenous women female coaches in Canada.

Considering Gender

While the implementation of Title IX in the USA successfully increased the number of girls and women participating in sport, gender equity issues persist. In terms of leadership opportunities, before the passing of Title IX roughly 90% of coaches of women's university sports were female (Acosta & Carpenter, 2012). The implementation of Title IX legitimised women's sports (e.g., better salaries for coaches of women's teams) creating greater incentives for men to coach women's teams. To this day, women occupy very few leadership positions, especially in coaching (e.g., see The Tucker Center, 2021). To improve the experiences of women coaches and increase representation at all levels of sport, we must address barriers present at each system level. From an institutional perspective, hiring practices in many sport organisations tend to adhere to homologous reproduction theory (HRT) (Kanter, 1977). HRT asserts that the dominant social group within an organisation either consciously or unconsciously uses their power and privilege to systematically reproduce themselves in their own image, familiar to many as the "Old Boys Club" often seen in sport. Male coaches continue to benefit from the strong, supportive network that has been established over decades. Even as women seemingly garner more opportunities in sport, the discourse of sexism in the coaching field has become more covert, ambiguous, and further embedded in sport structures (Norman & Simpson, 2022). Coaching remains an isolating environment for women and other marginalised groups, often resulting in women experiencing microaggressions when they must perform as the "only" or "token" woman in their context. Microaggressions are defined as "brief and commonplace daily verbal, behavioural, or environmental indignities, whether intentional or unintentional that communicate [derogatory], or negative … slights and insults towards members of oppressed groups" (Nadal, 2008, p. 23). Microaggressions are used by those in power as covert mechanisms that nonetheless are discriminatory. Such aggressions leave women not being seen as the "natural" occupants of leadership roles, thus creating a sense of doubt in their abilities (Norman & Simpson, 2022). Studies have demonstrated the importance of supportive networks for women (Darvin et al., 2019) led by other experienced high-level female coaches, thus providing a safe and welcoming environment for women coaches to learn and develop their coaching skills.

When it comes to the recruiting and hiring of coaches, organisations need to actively seek qualified female coaches since male coaches often rely on experience to make up for a lack of accreditation while women tend not to apply for jobs unless they are confident, they possess the required accreditations (Greenhill et al., 2009; see also Culver, 2021). In fact, a Canadian study (Reade et al., 2009) demonstrated that current women in high-level coaching jobs tended to have more national and international competitive experience than their male counterparts. Increasing the number of women in leadership roles could reduce the negative psychosocial and occupational outcomes for women currently seen in the workplace (Darvin, 2020). According to LaVoi (2016), increasing the number of women would not only help create a sense of belonging for women in sport but also provide more diverse perspectives for athletic departments and improve organisations' overall health.

Considering Race

From the perspective of critical race theory, racism is deeply entrenched in society (Hylton, 2009), and our predominant norms and values perpetuate the status quo of racial minorities firmly remaining in the category of "other" (Cobb & Russell, 2015). Cunningham (2020) articulates that "[t]he institution of sport is largely seen to be White owned and operated, situated within a capitalist economic model and privileges those in power (i.e., white, heterosexual men) and suppressing others (i.e., racial minorities)". This system of oppression remains active today and continues to disadvantage racial minorities and impact their opportunities and experiences in the context of sport. As in their everyday lives, individuals from racial minorities face numerous types of discrimination in the context of sport. Across most professional sport organisations in North America, there is a clear representation gap as racial minorities can participate in sport but not act in leadership roles as evidenced by the larger proportion of racial minority players versus racial minority assistant and head coaches (Cunningham, 2020). A rare response to combat this systemic problem is the National Football League's "Rooney Rule", implemented in 2003 to increase racial diversity among their head coaches. The rule requires teams to interview at least one racial minority when hiring a new head coach or senior-level administrator, and Dubois (2015) found racial minorities were 19–21% more likely to fill a head coach position after its implementation. Despite this fact, there continues to be unconscious bias in decision-making through sport-related and racial stereotypes (Sartore & Cunningham, 2006) and racism evidenced in the recruitment and hiring of coaches (Cunningham et al., 2006), perpetuating the patterns of homologous reproduction within the coaching field (Bradbury et al., 2018). For instance, there continues to be a large research gap concerning Aboriginal sport coaches (Bennie et al., 2019), their perceptions, and experiences as coaches across all sporting contexts. Some research has suggested that Aboriginal coaches play a key role in connecting sport and culture (Thomson et al., 2010; Tynan & Briggs, 2013) and prioritising the inclusion of cultural understandings in policies and practices of sport organisations (Tynan & Briggs, 2013). Aboriginal voices are consistently overlooked in the sport literature because of systemic racism and racialised stereotypes (Bennie et al., 2019) and the narrative that views Aboriginal people as "in need" (Schaefer et al., 2017, p. 275). Notwithstanding, examples of progress are the Aboriginal Coaching Program in Canada, founded to provide culturally relevant professional development for coaches of First Nation, Métis, or Inuit descent. This programme now also provides critical training and tools for non-Indigenous coaches working within Indigenous communities. Another example is the *Aboriginal Sports Coaches, Communities, and Culture* (Marlin et al.,

2020) Australian textbook, the first book to be published with Indigenous sports coaches, in any language, in any settler-colonial context. Overall, many organisational cultures and policies still do not consider how systemic racism limits opportunities for BIPOC coaches in the field (Cunningham, 2020).

Considering Sexuality

Further examining the experiences of minority groups related to coach development, we encounter sexual minorities who also routinely face prejudice and discrimination. Broadly, research regarding sexuality, gender, and sport has focussed most prominently on the experiences of athletes in the 1990s (Cavalier, 2011). While other research has focussed on the experiences of lesbian coaches (Anderson, 2005; Krane & Barber, 2005; Brackenridge et al., 2008; Norman, 2011), research relating to the experiences of sexual minorities in the coaching role is lacking (e.g., Brackenridge et al., 2008). At an organisational level, sport inherently discourages open and progressive dialogues about the issues surrounding sexual identity (Norman, 2011). Coaches are consistently required to monitor, manage, and negotiate their sexuality within the entrenched homophobic and heterosexist social norms of sport (Krane & Barber, 2005), having to comply with these norms while remaining silent about their sexuality (Krane & Barber, 2005). Homophobic and sexist language (see below), very few sexually diverse role models, and a general lack of opportunities for group interaction and/or advice related to sexual diversity are several ways in which repression is perpetuated in sport.

There are also challenges for coaches and athletes in coming out ("The Glass Closet"; Griffin, 1998) as the potential to lose jobs or sponsorships often outweighs the interest in acting as a role model. Furthermore, addressing a broader sense of diversity within coach education curricula and equity training programmes (Norman, 2011) is missing. Finally, there are still harmful assumptions present that lesbian coaches are biologically and culturally deviant. Such sexual prejudice maintains the hegemonic image that coaching is for heterosexual men who are superior leaders. It also perpetuates a culture of "don't ask, don't tell" (Anderson, 2005).

Considering Disability

Disability sport coaches no matter their (dis)abilities face numerous barriers in the coach recruitment, hiring, and educational processes. Research on disability sport coaches has lagged behind while the focus remains almost exclusively on coaches of able-bodied athletes (Rangeon et al., 2012). For one, there is the misconception that coaches need extensive disability-specific knowledge to effectively coach athletes with a disability. Moreover, the standardised knowledge taught in most coaching courses does not address the unique considerations of a disability sport context (Douglas et al., 2018; Wareham et al., 2019). Many resources available for disability sport coach development are underpinned by the medical model of disability where impairment is considered a problem to be solved (Smith & Perrier, 2014) and the goal is to improve performance despite an athlete's limitations (Townsend et al., 2015). These barriers, along with the various social preconceptions and general stigma associated with the disability sport community (Wareham et al., 2019), lead to a lack of coaches. Yet, despite these systemic and organisational barriers, research has shown that disability sport coaches have higher retention rates as compared to able-body sports. Wareham et al. (2019) reported these rates could be due to personal satisfaction, richer interpersonal relationships, and enhanced career progression. Another result of this general lack of coaches in the pipeline is that para-athletes when they do decide to become coaches often ascend quickly and directly through the coaching pathways to national team coaching positions (Douglas et al., 2018; Adam Frost, Talent Identification Coach and Para athlete, Wheelchair Rugby Canada, personal communication, May 24, 2022).

Case Example: Black Female Coach Mentorship Programme

Mentorship programmes are one of the ways to aid under-represented BIPOC women navigate their sport environment (Joseph & McKenzie, 2022). Often, marginalised groups do not see coaching as a viable career due to the lack of representation. Recently, the Black Canadian Coaches Association (BCCA) and the Coaching Association of Canada (CAC) partnered to create the first BFCMP in Canada for historically excluded Black women coaches. The programme has three main objectives: providing Black female mentorship; advancing coach professionalisation for both mentors and mentees; and creating a sustainable, formalised model of mentorship to increase accessibility, support, and leadership development for Black female coaches in Canada. Programme participants come from all sport backgrounds, but for some sports, the Black female coach mentor represents the only current active BIPOC individual at their level thus demonstrating the stark reality of the lack of Black females in coaching and sport leadership positions in Canada (BCCA, 2020). The mentors and mentees, aside developing as leaders, have also voiced experiencing a reduction of their sense of loneliness and increased resilience (Joseph & McKenzie, 2022).

Recommendations for Practice

In this section, we have taken a brief look at various barriers marginalised groups face in the expression of their overlapping identities as human beings and coaches. Despite the separation of these sections based on the research, it is difficult to write this chapter without bearing in mind that diversity is about more than what you can physically see, rather it is about the intersecting components of one's identity (i.e., someone who identifies with multiple marginalised groups). In the quest to diversify coach recruitment, it is important that any strategies address barriers at the systemic, organisational, and individual levels (Joseph & McKenzie, 2022). In the pursuit of a more diverse coaching field where marginalised leaders are supported and actively developed, we must take into consideration not only the unique context in which each coach works and the societal values and norms that are apparent across all sport disciplines but also the specific skills they will need to navigate those diverse spaces. At the systemic level, it has been suggested that intergenerational and peer-to-peer mentorship can positively influence the experiences of marginalised coaches as seen in the BFCMP programme (Joseph & McKenzie, 2022; see above) and for disability sport (Fairhurst et al., 2017).

At the organisational level, it is necessary we actively question the status quo and the current recruitment and employment procedures. Formalising the recruitment process (Schlesinger & Weigelt-Schlesinger, 2013), officially announcing coaching jobs as opposed to using closed channel recruitment (Tugend, 2018), and establishing specific initiatives targeting the recruitment of minority groups are examples of ways to create more equitable recruitment practices. These means may not automatically reduce imbalances but can provide a wider pool of candidates and create a more open hiring process. Tugend (2018) discussed the importance of intentionality when it comes to adapting recruitment and employment practices. Some examples of intentional recruitment include updating recruitment advertisements to demonstrate a commitment to diversity and inclusion and training the search committee through evidence-based research to recognise how the hiring process is impacted by unconscious bias and why the process does not always end in an equitable hire. Formalised support systems such as mentorship programmes can also aid under-represented individuals to navigate their coaching context (Rhode, 2003; Francique & Hart, 2010). Mentorships facilitate development and consider the experiences of minority groups' intersecting identities (Mansfield & Welton, 2016). Targeted action is needed to intentionally build the number of marginalised coaches distributed across the domain (Norman & Simpson 2022); otherwise, coaches from marginalised groups will remain the "only" ones in many contexts thus restricting their ability to develop collective power to affect the coaching culture and shift away from the microaggressions embedded in the field.

At the individual level, research has suggested the practice of reflectivity and introspection to diversify coach development. In the context of disability sport, for example, Allan et al. (2020) found that when coaches focus on building inter- and intra-personal skills, by, for example, reflecting on their own implicit biases and assumptions, there is greater integration of sport, disability-specific information, and greater collaboration between coaches and athletes.

Diversifying Language

In the discussion of diversifying coach development, there is a need to consider language as a device that is not only used for information transfer but also in defining and communicating social categorisations and hierarchies (Maass &

Arcuri, 1996; Koeser & Sczesny, 2014). This section will focus primarily on the current language practices related to gender-exclusive language, disability, and the need for transgender language reform in sport. We also include a short vignette highlighting language best practices for coach developers. Studies have shown that there is a link between the structure of languages used in society and prejudice towards certain social groups (Patev et al., 2019). There is a little understanding of the mechanisms that connect the two, yet according to linguistic hegemony, language can be used as a device for those in power to disempower minorities (Short et al., 2001). Given the close link between language and cognitive representations, the use of gender-exclusive language has had immeasurable effects on the experiences of women and other minority groups in Western societies through the subtle means of gendered pronouns and nouns (e.g. in sport, Segrave et al., 2006). These language devices consciously connect meaning about the people involved with their anticipated dispositions. In sport, a study that analysed word databases of spoken and written media found "man" and "men" mentioned two to three times as many times as "woman" and "women", with the related adjectives being words like "fastest", "strong", and "dominant" for men versus "aged", "married", and "pregnant" for women. Most language used in modern society is gender-biased and the use of masculine generics perpetuates the perception that men hold the power in society thus disempowering women and other minority groups from social narratives (Cameron, 1998). In the 1970s feminists advocated for linguistic reform (Zimman, 2017) but the connection between language use and gender-based prejudice cannot be explained only through the traditional male-female gender binary. Prejudice has also been linked to biased language towards several minority groups including but not limited to lesbian, gay, and bisexual individuals (Patev et al., 2019). As a result, queer linguistics surfaced in the 1990s (Zimman, 2017) to combat not only the inherent misogyny but also the use of biased language stemming from heterosexism, homophobia, and gender normativity. Biased language use can be predicted by the attitudes held towards a marginalised group (Hall & LaFrance, 2007; Chonody et al., 2012). One group that has been relatively excluded from linguistic interventions in language, gender, and sexuality research is transgender non-conforming (TNGC) individuals (Zimman, 2017 see the section "Transgender Language Reform").

When considering disability language reform, using person-first language is currently recommended in communications as it is considered best practice to identify individuals and communities by the terminology with which they identify (e.g., deaf vs. Deaf; Linton, 2006). Many North American journals consider person-first language to be the most respectful terminology, mandating its use (Peers et al., 2014). Person-first language is an explicit strategy used for reconstructing the ways we think about disability (Withers, 2012) issuing from the rights-based approach to disability activism seen in the 1970–90s (Peers et al., 2014). Questions of language in disability are important because the language we use is shaped by the model of disability we follow. Currently, disability scholars in sport and physical education propose the social-relational model. This model, in contrast to the medical model (focussing on the functional limitations of the body; Thomas, 2014) and the social model (which has disability as a social construct enacted by societal structures of exclusion; Thomas, 2014), proposed that disability is socially constructed while also being "given meaning through the relational practices that shape how people experience the world" (Townsend et al., 2015, p. 86). In the context of sport coaching, there is a little research that has examined how coach learners with a disability, or in fact from any minority groups, identify themselves and their language and terminology preferences. Broadly, an individual's language and terminology choices play a fundamental unconscious role in presenting the speaker's beliefs and values (Phipps et al., 2002; Brandt, 2011). As noted by Allan et al. (2020), this is important as what and how coaches interact with athletes will influence their athletes' experiences, no matter how they identify. Deepening our understanding of the use of language is important for sport coaching as reforming our language practices aids in reducing gender stereotypes and increasing the visibility of minority groups.

Transgender Language Reform

Presently, most research focussing on gendered language and equity has concentrated on the traditional man/woman binary, perpetuating the continued exclusion of individuals who diverge from the expected social norms such as those who identify as TNGC (Zimman, 2017). Coupled with the growing interest in creating more trans-inclusive language within key social institutions such as schools and medical providers, there is the opportunity to bring TGNC individuals and their experiences to the forefront of research and coach development. Individuals whose experience of gender is fluid and unstable face barriers in society that often lead to increased discrimination (i.e., homelessness, employment discrimination, health & safety concerns, suicide, hate violence, etc.; Zimman, 2017). As it stands, there are limited terms and meanings to explain gender-related identities and practices that deviate from the norm. The simple creation of a category and relevant pronouns (e.g., hir, s/he) for TGNC individuals also perpetuates the patriarchal nature of language and firmly entrenches peoples' place in the social hierarchy as opposed to providing them with the opportunity to deviate from the "norm". Language remains a central concern for TGNC people as it operates as one of the primary means of constructing gendered identities.

The attitudes one holds towards those who deviate from social norms are one of the largest perceived barriers to using gender-inclusive and trans-inclusive language (e.g., Parks & Roberton, 2004; Zimman, 2017). This lack of use of regular gender-inclusive language can occur for several reasons including one's direct experience with TGNC (Patev et al., 2019) or simply a lack of knowledge. Consequently, coach development must provide learners with this knowledge and instruct them on how to act as cisgender allies in the process of identifying and dismantling current cissexist language practices (Zimman, 2017).

VIGNETTE: Recommendations and Best Practices

This vignette provides several examples of language best practices for coach developers and coaches to use in their practice. Though these examples are broad and applicable across groups, it is important to remember that it is not suitable to use a single language model in all communications.

"Bob" has worked as a coach developer for the past 25 years and recently received feedback about one of his courses that he could include more gender-inclusive practices in his teachings. In the past, Bob has tended to avoid asking for his coaches' genders, instead assuming their gender based on his perceptions of how they physically presented. Mitra, a fellow coach developer who identifies as a queer person with the pronouns they/them, reminds Bob that not all individuals may identify with the gender they seem to present physically. They share with Bob the importance of intentionally allowing people the space to share how they would like to be identified. In Mitra's coaching courses, they begin the sessions by openly talking to the coaches about how they identify and what kind of language they would like other people to use when addressing or referring to them. Mitra allows coaches to self-identify and recommends a best practice for coaches is to not assume heterosexuality. They avoid the use of gendered terminology when it is not relevant. For example, Mitra, in a discussion of parental figures, suggests coaches refer to parents as "your parents", instead of using gendered terminology such as "Mum and Dad". Fast forward two months and Bob has just led another coaching course with a group of 15 coaches. His inclusion of numerous intentional gender-inclusive language practices (i.e., pronoun checks) garnered him positive reviews and allowed him to make his course more inclusive. Bob said, "I had never considered the power of the language I use until I stopped to think about it; now I deliberately practice using gender-inclusive language, trying to provide a welcoming experience for everyone".

Approaches to language should be varied and should not aim to categorise individuals into homogenous groups (Lister et al., 2019) since everyone is a unique individual, no matter how they identify. How we use language has an important impact on those around us, especially when it comes to modelling respect and fairness (Weinberg, 2009). Furthermore, coach developers should bear in mind the "nothing about us, without us" movement coined by Charlton (2000) referring to the disability community. Regardless of the minority group, people have the right to shape the language used to identify them.

Diversifying Approaches to Learning and Development

Much has been written about the different approaches to developing coaches (e.g., Trudel et al., 2013; Callary & Gearity, 2020). It is not our intention to review this literature; rather, we will summarise the key considerations for diversifying approaches to coach learning and development and finish with the advice of one BIPOC coach developer.

For coach learning, arguments about which learning contexts are most impactful for coaches are outdated and unproductive. Indeed, Mallett and colleagues (2009) stated "It is not a matter of which form of education/learning is superior but acknowledging the unique contributions all forms may make to coach development and accreditation" (p. 332). While formal coach education has been critiqued over and over as not meeting coaches' learning needs (e.g., Lyle, 2007), mediated learning (directed by another person; see Werthner & Trudel, 2006) is, while dependent on a coach's stage of learning (Trudel et al., 2016), a necessity. Moreover, many coaches are required to engage in formal coach education making this an ideal place to start introducing coaches to concepts about diversity and inclusion, and equally important, to inclusive learning experiences through modelling (see Vignette in the section above). That said, we also know that coaches learn from and through multiple learning situations including many that are unmediated (learner drives the initiative) such as seeking advice from a colleague, a podcast, or a book. A third learning situation is internal (a reconsideration of one's existing ideas), as through reflection or journal writing.

Formal coach education contexts, adequately designed, can facilitate all three learning situations. However, most curriculum-driven, large-scale programmes have difficulty being truly learner-centred (see Paquette et al., 2014). Thus, short courses and workshops should be supplemented by ongoing support to learners as they wrestle with applying concepts gleaned in formal contexts (through acquisition) into their practice (through participation; Sfard, 1998; Moon, 2001). To address this, action is needed at the systems and organisational levels. Mentoring and various other social learning spaces such as communities of practice should be funded, given their excellent potential for helping coaches learn and change their behaviours (Culver & Trudel, 2006; Stoszkowski & Collins, 2012; Bloom, 2013). Communities of practice have specifically proven effective for helping coaches and sport leaders of minority groups (e.g., Duarte et al., 2021; Kraft et al., 2021). However, success in such initiatives is predicated on organisations supporting the learning of the coach developers who will facilitate them. Trudel and colleagues (2013) provided concrete examples of how this can be accomplished.

An overarching consideration for coach development broadly is summed up in the words of Jenny Moon from Bournemouth University (UK): a "system approach to learning means that the environment is viewed as anything that might influence the learner's learning" (Moon, 2001, p. 47). Therefore, we have noted above the importance of considering factors at the systemic, organisational, and individual levels if diversification is to be fully realised. At these various levels, we have highlighted how recruitment processes and language impact coach learners and the diversification of coach development. Systems and organisations need to be proactive and explicit regarding diversification and inclusion.

An example of this for one organisation is the CAC which, among other initiatives, has posted this statement on their website coach:

> The CAC is committed to developing and fostering an inclusive and diverse coaching environment for coaches and participants across Canada. A diverse coaching environment acknowledges the differences in age, gender, education, and background. It acknowledges individuals' unique life experiences, qualities, and characteristics.
>
> An inclusive coaching culture embraces, respects, and values differences in people regardless of gender, age, racial background, aboriginal background, disability, or sexual orientation.
>
> *CAC, n.d.*

The View of One Coach Developer

We finish this chapter with the perspective of Lee Anna Osei, who is the founder of the BCCA and current Head Coach of the University of St. Francis Xavier women's basketball team in Nova Scotia. With over ten years of coaching experience, Lee Anna is a pioneer in the coaching community empowering and advocating for Black Canadians in sport. She is also behind the CAC's eLearning module "Anti-Racism in Coaching".

Q: What do you most want people to understand about diversifying coach development?

Lee Anna: I want people to understand that we are behind in this process, and it's imperative that we take a look at and hear from groups that have been marginalised or left out of the coach development process to better serve the needs of our entire coach community.

Q: What do you believe needs to change at the systemic, organisational and/or individual level to create more opportunities for minority coaches?

Lee Anna: I believe that standards to ensure equity, diversity, and inclusion in education, hiring processes and workplace environments should be implemented for sport organisations at the recreational, collegiate, and professional level. This would ensure a level of protection and accountability that doesn't just "open" the door for minority coaches; it invites and empowers them in the process.

Q: What indicators would lead you to believe that we are making progress in diversifying coach development?

Lee Anna: There are certain milestones that have been reached from groups leading in advocacy. For example, the CAC, Canada's national coach development organisation, has created Canada's first Anti-Racism in sport e-learning module for sport coaches. In addition, several initiatives have been created and executed at a variety of club, high performance, and collegiate streams in efforts to support diversifying coach development.

Q: *What tangible things can sport organisations work on to create a community that champions equity, diversity, and inclusion?*

Lee Anna: Sport organisations should seek to work with community, education, and sport related groups that intersect with minority and various cultural groups and make it a priority to have representation of diverse members not just a part of their teams, but in leadership positions within their executive administration. Ensuring there is a difference of thoughts related to decision-making from the top creates an environment that is more likely to be inclusive. Sport organisations should also be offering professional development in the areas of Equality, Diversity & Inclusion (EDI) on an annual basis to address safe sport and culture enhancing environments. Lastly, all sport groups should have an interactive set of rules or standards that are part of the onboarding process specific to addressing racist or discriminatory actions, including examples. It is not good enough to just have these written down given the complexity of the subject.

Q: *Is there anything else you would like to add about diversifying coach development?*

Lee Anna: We are headed in the right direction in coach development – but we should not ignore the voices of those who have experienced the lack of support in the process of diversifying coach development. I believe that sport organisations should normalise exit processes for all coaches regardless of background, to implement a method of collecting data about their work experience that informs employers on areas of success and improvement in the culture that they curate for workers. Diversifying coach development is not something that should or can be done once. Just as sport is evolving, we too as a sport society need to think about assessing, reflecting on, and implementing processes that align with the change. As the Founder of the BCCA [I feel] our diverse membership and partners have seen first-hand the great work that can be done if we are willing to work with each other: We are #StrongerTogether!

Acknowledgement

Given the topics discussed in this chapter, we, the authors, feel it is important to acknowledge that we are all white, cisgender, able-bodied individuals who strive to act as allies regarding EDI in sport. That said, we want to thank Coaches Lee Anna Osei and Adam Frost for providing us with their first-hand lived experiences with coach development.

Note

1 Cisgender: "used to describe someone who feels that they are the same gender (= sex) as the physical body they were born with" (Cambridge Dictionary, https://dictionary.cambridge.org/dictionary/english/cisgender).

References

Acosta, R. V., & Carpenter, L. J. (2012). *Women in Intercollegiate Sport: A Longitudinal National Study – Thirty-five year update.* Retrieved May 25, 2021, from http://acostacarpenter.org/AcostaCarpenter2012.pdf.

Allan, V., Blair Evans, M., Latimer-Cheung, A. E., & Côté, J. (2020). From the athletes' perspective: A social-relational understanding of how coaches shape the disability Sport Experience. *Journal of Applied Sport Psychology, 32*(6): 546–564. https://doi.org/10.1080/10413200.2019.1587551.

Anderson, E. (2005). *In the Game: Gay Athletes and the Cult of Masculinity.* State University of New York Press.

Bennie, A., Apoifis, N., Marlin, D., & Caron, J. G. (2019). Cultural connections and cultural ceilings: Exploring the experiences of Aboriginal Australian sport coaches. *Qualitative Research in Sport, Exercise and Health, 11*(3), 299–315. https://doi.org/10.1080/2159676X.2017.1399924.

Black Canadian Coaches Association (2020, October 14). *New mentorship program aims to empower black female coaches in Canada.* Coaching Association of Canada. Retrieved June 8, 2022, from https://coach.ca/new-mentorship-program-aims-empower-black-female-coaches-canada.

Bloom, G. (2013). Mentoring for sport coaches. In P. Potrac, W. Gilbert, & J. Denison (Eds.), *Routledge Handbook of Sports Coaching* (pp. 476–485). Routledge.

Brackenridge, C., Alldred, P., Jarvis, A., Maddocks, K., & Rivers, I. (2008). *A Review of Sexual Orientation in Sport: Sportscotland Research Report no. 114.* Sportscotland.

Bradbury, S., Lusted, J., & van Sterkenburg, J. (Eds.) (2021). *Race, Ethnicity and Racism in Sports Coaching.* Routledge.

Bradbury, S., Van Sterkenburg, J., & Mignon, P. (2018). The under-representation and experiences of elite level minority coaches in professional football in England, France and the Netherlands. *International Review of the Sociology of Sport, 53*(3), 313–334.

Brandt, S. (2011). From policy to practice in higher education: The experience of disabled students in Norway. *International Journal of Disability, Development and Education, 58*(2), 107–120.

CAC. (n.d.). https://coach.ca/diversity-inclusion.

Callary, B., & Gearity, B. (Eds.) (2020). *Coach Education and Development in Sport: Instructional Strategies* (pp. 129–140). Routledge.

Cameron, D. (1998). Representing sociolinguistics? *Journal of Sociolinguistics, 2*(3), 421–431. https://doi.org/10.1111/1467-9481.00054.

Cavalier, E. S. (2011). Men at sport: Gay men's experiences in the sport workplace. *Journal of Homosexuality, 58*(1), 626–646.

Charlton, J. I. (2000). *Nothing about Us without Us: Disability Oppression and Empowerment.* University of California Press.

Chonody, J. M., Rutledge, S. E., & Smith, S. (2012). "That's so gay": Language use and antigay bias among heterosexual college students. *Journal of Gay & Lesbian Social Services, 24*(3), 241–259. https://doi.org/10.1080/10538720.2012.697036.

Cobb, F., & Russell, N. M. (2015). Meritocracy or complexity: problematizing racial disparities in mathematics assessment within the context of curricular structures, practices, and discourse. *Journal of Education Policy, 30*(5), 631–649. http://dx.doi.org/10.1080/02680939.2014.983551.

Coury, S., Huang, J., Kumar, A., Prince, S., Krivkovich, A., & Yee, L. (2020, October 8). *Women in the workplace 2020*. Retrieved May 14, 2021, from https://www.mckinsey.com/featured-insights/diversity-and-inclusion/women-in-the-workplace#.

Crenshaw, K. (1989). Demarginalizing the intersection of race and sex: A black feminist critique of antidiscrimination doctrine, feminist theory and antiracist politics. *University of Chicago Legal Forum, 1*(8), 139–167.

Culver, D. M. (2021). *Rachèle Béliveau: One woman's perspective on three decades of high performance coaching*. coach.ca/sites/default/files/2021-10/CJWC-October2021_EN.pdf

Culver, D., & Trudel, P. (2006). Cultivating coaches' communities of practice: developing the potential for learning through interactions. In R. Jones (Ed.), *Re-defining the Coaching Role and How to Teach It: New Ways of Thinking about Practice* (pp. 97–112). Routledge.

Culver, D. M., Werthner, P., & Trudel, P. (2019). Coach developers as 'Facilitators of learning' in a large-scale coach education programme: One actor in a complex system. *International Sport Coaching Journal, 6*(1), 296–306.

Cunningham, G. B. (2020). The under-representation of racial minorities in coaching and leadership positions in the United States. In S. Bradbury, J. Lusted, & J. van Sterkenburg (Eds.), *'Race', Ethnicity and Racism in Sports Coaching*. Routledge.

Cunningham, G. B., Bruening, J. E., & Straub, T. (2006). The underrepresentation of African Americans in NCAA Division IA head coaching positions. *Journal of Sport Management, 20*(3), 387–413.

Darvin L., Taylor, E., & Wells, J. (2019). Get in the game through a sponsor: Initial career ambitions of former women assistant coaches. *Journal of Issues in Intercollegiate Athletics, 12*, 590–613.

Darvin, L. (2020). Voluntary occupational turnover and the experiences of former intercollegiate women assistant coaches. *Journal of Vocational Behavior, 116*, 103349.

Douglas, S., Falcão, W. R., & Bloom, G. A. (2018). Career development and learning pathways of paralympic coaches with a disability. *Adapted Physical Activity Quarterly, 35*(1), 93–110. https://doi.org/10.1123/apaq.2017-0010.

Duarte, T., Culver, D. M., & Paquette, K. (2021). Assessing the value created in a social learning intervention: Four vignettes of parasport coaches. *International Sport Coaching Journal, 8*(3), 348–361. https://doi.org//10.1123/iscj.2020-0006.

Dubois, C. (2015). The impact of "soft" affirmative action policies on minority hiring in executive leadership: The case of the NFL's Rooney rule. *American Law and Economics Review, 18*(1), 208–233.

Fairhurst, K. E., Bloom, G. A., & Harvey, W. J. (2017). The learning and mentoring experiences of Paralympics coaches. *Disability and Health Journal, 10*, 240–246. PubMed.

Fasting, K., & Sand, T. S. (2017) *Equality in Sport: A Report Focusing on Gender Balance among Employees, Coaches and Leaders in the Sport Associations*. Norwegian Olympic, Paralympic and Confederation of Sports.

Francique, A. R., & Hart, A. (2010). Perspectives of mentoring: The black female student – athlete. *Sport Management Review, 13*, 382–394.

Greenhill, J., Auld, C., Cuskelly, G., & Hooper, S. (2009). The impact of organisational factors on career pathways for female coaches. *Sport Management Review, 12*, 229–240.

Griffin, P. (1998). *Strong Women, Deep Closets: Lesbians and Homophobia in Sport*. Human Kinetics.

Hall, J. A., & LaFrance, B. H. (2007). Attitudes and communication of homophobia in fraternities: Separating the impact of social adjustment function from hetero-identity concern. *Communication Quarterly, 55*, 39–60.

Hylton, K. (2009). *"Race" and Sport: Critical Race Theory*. Routledge.

Joseph, J., & McKenzie, A. I. (2022). Black women coaches in community: Promising practices for mentorship in Canada. *Frontiers in Sports and Active Living, 4*(884239), 1–13.

Kanter, R. M. (1977). *Men and Women of the Corporation*. Basic Books.

Koeser, S., & Sczesny, S. (2014). Promoting gender-fair language: The impact of arguments on language use, attitudes, and cognitions. *Journal of Language and Social Psychology, 33*(5), 548–560.

Kraft, E., Culver, D. M., Din, C., & Cayer, I. (2021): Increasing gender equity in sport organisations: assessing the impacts of a social learning initiative. *Sport in Society*. https://doi.org/10.1080/17430437.2021.1904900.

Krane, V. & Barber, H. (2005). Identity tensions in lesbian intercollegiate coaches. *Research Quarterly for Exercise and Sport, 76*(1), 67–81.

Lapchick, R. (2018). *The 2018 Racial and Gender Report Card*. Institute of Diversity and Ethics. University of Central Florida.

LaVoi, N. M. (Ed.) (2016). A framework to understand experiences of women coaches around the globe: The Ecological-Intersectional Model. In *Women in Sports Coaching* (pp. 27–48). Routledge.

Linton, S. (2006). Reassigning meaning. In L.J. Davis (Ed.), *The Disability Studies Reader*. 2nd Edition. (pp. 161–172). Routledge.

Lister, K., McPherson, E., Coughlan, T., Gallen, A.-M., & Pearson, V. (2019). Towards inclusive language: Exploring student-led approaches to talking about disability-related study needs. In: *Proceedings of the 12th Annual International Conference of Education, Research and Innovation* (ICERI 2019) (pp. 1444–1453). IATED.

Lyle, J., A review of the research evidence for the impact of coach education. *International Journal of Coaching Science*, 2007, 1, 17–34.

Maass, A., & Arcuri, L. (1996). Language and stereotyping. In C. N. Macrae, C. Stangor, & M. Hewstone (Eds.), *Stereotypes and Stereotyping* (pp. 193–226). Guilford Press.

Mallett, S., Trudel, P. Lyle, J., & Rynne, S. B. (2009). Formal vs informal coach education. *International Journal of Sports Science & Coaching, 4*(3), 325–334.

Mansfield, K. C., & Welton, A. D. (Eds.) (2016). *Identity Intersectionalities, Mentoring, and Work–Life (Im)Balance: Educators (Re)Negotiate the Personal, Professional, and Political*. IAP.

Marlin, D., Apoifis, N., & Bennie, A. (Eds.) (2020). *Aboriginal Sports Coaches, Community, and Culture*. Springer.

Moon, J. (2001). *Short Courses and Workshops: Improving the Impact of Learning and Professional Development*. Kogan Page.

Nadal, K. (2008). Preventing racial, ethnic, gender, sexual minority, disability, and religious microaggressions: Recommendations for promoting positive mental health. *Prevention in Counseling Psychology: Theory, Research, Practice, and Training, 2*, 22–27.

Norman, L. (2011). Gendered homophobia in sport and coaching: Understanding the everyday experiences of lesbian coaches. *International Review for the Sociology of Sport, 47*(6), 705–723

Norman, L., & Simpson, R. (2022). Gendered microaggressions towards the "only" women coaches in high-performance sport. *Sports Coaching Review*, Open Access. DOI: 10.1080/21640629.2021.2021031.

Paquette, K.J., Hussain, A., Trudel, P., & Camiré, M. (2014). A sport federation's attempt to restructure a coach education program using constructivist principles. *International Sport Coaching Journal, 1*(2), 75–85. https://doi.org/10.1123/iscj.2013-0006.

Parks, J. B., & Roberton, M. A. (2004). Attitudes towards women mediate the gender effect on attitudes towards sexist language. *Psychology of Women Quarterly, 28,* 233–239.

Patev, A. J., Dunn, C. E., Hood, K. B., & Barber, J. M. (2019). College students' perceptions of gender-inclusive language use predict attitudes toward transgender and gender nonconforming individuals. *Journal of Language and Social Psychology, 38*(3), 329–352.

Peers, D., Spencer-Cavaliere, N., & Eales, L. (2014). Say what you mean: Rethinking disability language in Adapted Physical Activity Quarterly. *Adapted Physical Activity Quarterly, 31,* 265–282. http://dx.doi.org/10.1123/apaq.2013-0091.

Phipps, L., Sutherland, A., & Seale, J. (Eds.) (2002). *Access All Areas: Disability, Technology and Learning.* ALT/TechDis.

Rangeon, S., Gilbert, W., & Bruner, M. (2012). Mapping the world of coaching science: A citation network analysis. *Journal of Coaching Education, 5,* 83–108.

Reade, I., Rodgers, W., & Norman, L. (2009). The under-representation of women in coaching: A comparison of male and female Canadian coaches at low and high levels of coaching. *International Journal of Sports Science & Coaching, 4*(4), 505–520.

Rhode, D. L. (2003). *The Difference "difference" Makes: Women and Leadership.* Stanford University Press.

Sartore, M. L., & Cunningham, G. B. (2006). Stereotypes, race, and coaching. *Journal of African American Studies, 10*(2), 69–83.

Schaefer, L., Lesard, S., & Lewis, B. (2017). Living tensions of co-creating a wellness program and narrative inquiry alongside urban Aboriginal youth. *LEARNing Landscapes, 10*(2), 271–285. Retrieved from http://learninglandscapes.ca/index.php/learnland/article/view/815.

Schlesinger, T., & Weigelt-Schlesinger, Y. (2013). "Coaching soccer is a man's job!" – The influence of gender stereotypes on structures for recruiting female coaches to soccer clubs. *European Journal for Sport and Society, 10*(3), 241–265.

Segrave, J. O., Mcdowell, K. L., & King, J. G. (2006). Language, gender, and sport: A Review of the Research Literature. In L. K. Fuller (Eds.), *Sport, Rhetoric, and Gender* (pp. 31–41). Palgrave Macmillan. https://doi.org/10.1057/9780230600751_3.

Sfard, A. (1998). On two metaphors for learning and the dangers of choosing just one. *Educational Researcher, 27,* 4–13.

Short, J. R., Boniche, A., Kim, Y., & Li Li, P. (2001). Cultural globalization, global English, and geography journals. *The Professional Geographer, 52*(1), 1–11.

Smith, B. M., & Perrier, M. J. (2014). Disability, sport, and impaired bodies: A critical approach. In R. Schinke & K. R. McGannon (Eds.), *The Psychology of Sub-culture in Sport and Physical Activity: A Critical Approach* (pp. 95–106). Psychology Press.

Stoszkowski, J., & Collins, D. (2012). Communities of practice, social learning and networks: exploiting the social side of coach development. *Sport, Education and Society.* https://doi.org/10.1080/13573322.2012.692671.

Stroh, D. P. (2015). *Systems thinking for social change* [Kindle]. Chelsea Green.

Thomas, C. (2014). *Disability and impairment.* In J. Swain, S. French, C. Barnes, & C. Thomas (Eds.), *Disabling Barriers-Enabling Environments* (pp. 9–16). 3rd Edition. Sage.

Thomson, A., Darcy, S., & Pearce, S. (2010). Gamma theory and third-sector-sport-development programmes for aboriginal and Torres Strait Island youth: Implications for sports management. *Sport Management Review, 13,* 313–330.

Townsend, R. C., Smith, B., & Cushion, J. C. (2015). Disability sports coaching: Towards a critical understanding. *Sports Coaching Review*, 4(2), 80–98. https://doi.org/10.1080/21640629.2016.1157324.

Trudel, P., Culver, D., & Werthner, P. (2013). Looking at coach development from the coach-learner's perspective: Considerations for coach development administrators. In P. Potrac, W. Gilbert & J. Denison (Eds.), *Routledge Handbook of Sports Coaching* (pp. 375–387). Routledge.

Trudel, P., Gilbert, W., & Rodrigue, F. (2016). The journey from competent to innovator: Using appreciative inquiry to enhance high performance coaching. *AI Practitioner*, 18(2). dx.doi.org/10.12781/978-1-907549-27-4-5.

The Tucker Center for Research on Girls and Women in Sport. (2021). Women in College Coaching Report Card – 20–21. https://www.cehd.umn.edu/tuckercenter/library/docs/research/WCCRC-Infographic-2020-21.pdf.

Tugend A. (2018). How serious are you about diversity hiring? *The Chronicle of Higher Education*, June 17, 2018. https://www.chronicle.com/article/How-Serious-Are-You-About/243684.

Tynan, M., & Briggs, P. (2013). How culturally competent is the Australian Football League (AFL)? *The International Journal of Sport & Society*, 3, 191–205.

Wareham, Y., Burkett, B., Innes, P., & Lovell, G. P. (2019). Coaches of elite athletes with disability: Senior sports administrators' reported factors affecting coaches' recruitment and retention. *Qualitative Research in Sport, Exercise and Health*, 11(3), 398–415. https://doi.org/10.1080/2159676X.2018.1517388.

Weinberg, M. (2009). LGBT-inclusive language. *English Journal*, 98(4), 50–51.

Werthner, P., & Trudel, P. (2006). A new theoretical perspective for understanding how coaches learn to coach. *The Sport Psychologist*, 20(2), 198–212. https://doi.org/10.1123/tsp.20.2.198

Withers, A. J. (2012). *Disability Politics and Theory*. Fernwood Publishing.

Zimman, L. (2017). Transgender language reform: Some challenges and strategies for promoting trans-affirming, gender-inclusive language. *Journal of Language and Discrimination*, 1(1), 84–105.

14
CULTURAL COMPETENCE AND INTERCULTURAL EFFECTIVENESS IN COACHING AND COACH DEVELOPMENT

Andrea J. Woodburn, Vladislav A. Bespomoshchnov and Mika Saarinen

As coaches and coach developers, we often find ourselves in one of two general scenarios regarding culture; either we are working with someone from another country or culture within our own cultural context, or we are working in a country or culture that is foreign to us. All authors of this chapter have experienced both scenarios during their careers, and better understanding these experiences and improving our current work constituted the impetus for our collaboration in writing this chapter. We realised through our discussions that we had each lived these scenarios without much prior knowledge or explicit preparation in how to navigate them effectively. It quickly became evident that we had a lot to learn in this area ourselves. Our hope for this chapter is that it is as useful to you in its reading as it has been to us in its writing such that we all navigate multi-cultural landscapes of practice with increasing knowledge, competence, and confidence.

Discussion on culture in recent sport literature of late tends to focus on team culture, or how to create positive and effective environments in which individuals and teams thrive. Though bearing some similarities, in this chapter we refer to culture as defined in the Oxford dictionary as "the customs and beliefs, art, way of life, and social organization of a particular country or group". The aims in this chapter are twofold. First, addressed in Part I of this chapter, is to present our current understanding of what it means to be effective when working in coaching and coach education across cultures and introduce the concepts of cross-cultural competence and intercultural effectiveness. Cultural competence is increasingly critical for both work and personal effectiveness in our current world, yet we lack a language and an empirically verified conceptual framework for cultural competence in coaching and coach development. This chapter provides an initial step towards this end. More specifically, we first define the terms *cultural competence and intercultural effectiveness* as they will be used in this chapter. Borrowing from literature in other fields, we then present some conceptual frameworks that can be of use when discussing what might lie at the heart of a person being effective in their work in either of the two scenarios described above.

In preparing Part I we faced a challenge previously outlined by Hall (1989), who pointed out that all theoretical models are incomplete, and it is a common practice to leave certain things out that are at times of similar if not larger importance than the things that have been included. We found many models from different fields that helped us consider the issue through different lenses. We avoided positivist assumptions of a single true reality (see Guba, 1990) and attempts to describe universal truths regarding cultural competence and intercultural effectiveness. Instead, we adopted the pragmatic stance advocated by Morgan (2014), focussing on practical approaches and solutions to the real work of coaches and coach developers. The goal for this chapter is the theory of Part I providing the context for the more practical Part II.

Second, addressed in Part II of this chapter, we aim to move beyond theory and concepts to discuss potential practical applications in coaching and coach development. In this section, we discuss connections we see between cultural competence and some of the literature on coaching effectiveness. The question guiding this second part was *How can we become better at working across cultures in our field?* As a spoiler alert, there are no recipes provided for this. Rather, though raising some key issues and questions, we provide fodder for reflection and conversations with others around this important and current question.

Above all, we hope this chapter approaches cultural competence from the perspectives of love for others and of personal growth. When embarking on a journey towards better cultural competence and intercultural effectiveness in coaching and coach development (CED), hopefully this occurs as a result of genuine curiosity about, interest in, and concern for, others and their well-being. However, as history shows, this journey can also be taken for less noble aims such as to harm, exploit, or convert others to our own ways of thinking and doing. We consider cultural competence foremostly not as a series of skills to be mastered, but rather a central desire to be empathetic and open to other ways of knowing, doing, and being, and as a journey rather than a destination. The aspiration is this quest results not only in better relationships and better working together, but hopefully expands ourselves and our ways of knowing, doing, and being in the process as we move forward in an increasingly interconnected world.

Part I: Cultural Competence and Intercultural Effectiveness

Cultural Competence[1]

The numerous attempts at describing cultural competence, dating back at least to the early 80s, show no consensus on its definition (Gallegos et al., 2018). What follows is a curation of some descriptions we felt captured what was common across all. Gallegos et al. refer to a set of standards for cultural competence in social work practice[2] in which cultural competence is defined as:

> the process by which individuals and systems respond respectfully and effectively to people of all cultures, languages, classes, races, ethnic backgrounds, religions, and other diversity factors in a manner that recognizes, affirms, and values the worth of individuals, families, and communities and protects and preserves the dignity of each.
>
> *(p. 54)*

Notably in this definition, cultural competence can be considered not only a feature of a person but also a feature of a system. From a systems standpoint, cultural competence in practice would constitute the translation of knowledge of others into better outcomes through better informed policies standards, agreed-upon practices, and so on.

When cultural competence is viewed from the standpoint of the individual, cultural competence can also be described as a person's awareness of, and sensitivity to, cultural diversity (Schim & Miller, 1999) and the extent to which that knowledge and attitude informs action. In a systematic review of the literature on cultural competence in health care, Alizadeh and Chavan (2015) identified the lack of consensus in its definition and in the modelling of it or of its components. However, despite the apparent lack of agreement on its definition and the scarcity of empirical evidence and tools for measuring it, they did find a common belief that cultural competence exists and that possessing it can positively affect patient outcomes in health care. Their review revealed, though inconsistently defined, three major elements were consistently present across models of cultural competence; cultural awareness, cultural knowledge, and cultural skills. It was also consistently considered to be more of an ongoing process in continuous development than an endpoint to be attained. The authors proposed defining cultural competence as "the ability to work and communicate effectively and appropriately with people from culturally different backgrounds" (p. e120).

Any conversation on the concept of cultural competence, however, begs an important question – when might the knowledge, skills, and attitudes of a culturally competent person cross the line into what would be more accurately described as stereotyping? Referencing the works of Ashmore and Del Boca (1981) and Miller and Turnbull (1986), Stevens et al. (2018) proposed a stereotype is generally understood to be "those interpersonal beliefs and expectancies that are both widely shared and generally invalid" (p. 653) and stereotyping typically thought of as ignorant behaviour. Stevens et al. (2018) argued cultural competence can be considered a form of what they termed *stereotype rationality*. They defined stereotypes more broadly as "beliefs about the attributes of social groups", identifying stereotypes as one kind of generalisation that is subject to exceptions as "no generalization will ever be 100% accurate" (p. 652). They suggest, in absence of information at the level of the individual, cultural competence

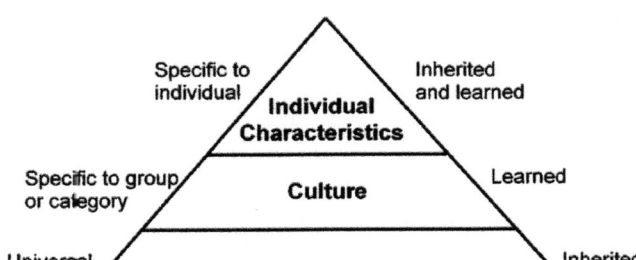

FIGURE 14.1 Three levels of uniqueness in human mental programming (see Hofstede, 1994, p. 6).

requires the reasonable and rational use of stereotypes. However, their central argument is when individual information is available, it is this information that should prevail. In other words, according to Stevens et al. (2018), a culturally competent person is an "accurate social perceiver" who can rationally apply stereotypes when any additional information is unavailable/scarce, reviewing and adjusting as additional information about an individual is increasingly present. Cultural competence implies an awareness of differences between cultural groups yet a course of action based upon the unique characteristics of the individual. Hofstede's model, discussed later in this chapter (see Figure 14.1), provides additional insight into the question of how to both consider group information when it can be helpful without stereotyping at the level of the individual.

Intercultural Effectiveness

Unlike the cloudier concept of cultural competence, intercultural effectiveness can be more easily defined. Simply put, intercultural effectiveness is the output of operationalising cultural competence. It refers to the ability of culturally competent persons to translate their knowledge, skills, and attitudes into better relationships and better work outcomes, to perform effectively with people from other cultures and when they are operating across cultures.

According to Abbe et al., predictors of intercultural effectiveness would include cultural competence (knowledge and cognition, affect and motivation, and skills), culture-specific variables (language and cultural knowledge, and situational and organisational variables), and antecedent variables (a person's dispositions, biography, and identity). Outcomes of intercultural effectiveness can appear in three domains: the work itself, the interpersonal, and the personal (Abbe et al., 2007). Interestingly, these three domains broadly align with those in the definition for coaching effectiveness proposed by Côté and Gilbert (2009), wherein coaching effectiveness is described as "the consistent application of integrated professional, interpersonal, and intrapersonal knowledge to improve athletes' competence, confidence, connection, and character in specific coaching contexts" (p. 316). In the former, the three are discussed as the domains in which cultural competence can be observed, and in the latter the domains in which coaching competence can be acquired.

Conceptual Frameworks for Cultural Competence and Intercultural Effectiveness

Some conceptual frameworks from other fields such as business (for example, Hofstede, 1994), military leadership (for example, Abbe et al., 2007), education (for example, Seeleman et al., 2009), and health care (for example, Tervalon & Murray-García, 1998) may prove helpful, though some caution in using them is warranted. As Alizadeh and Chavan (2015) argue, many have not been empirically verified, and models in one field are not always informed by those in another. What follows is some of the conceptual work that resonated with us in our discussions, where we see potential for advancing our understanding in our field and our own practical work. Each of the three models discussed offers a particular lens though which cultural competence and intercultural effectiveness can be viewed. The first is Hofstede's *Three levels of uniqueness in human mental programming* that, in its operationalisation through Hofstede's tool, considers the potential cultural influence of the country on an individual. The second is Schwartz's *Theory of Basic Values* (1992, 2012), proposing ten values towards understanding human behaviour and transcending geographical boundaries. The third is Abbe et al.'s (2007) *General Framework for Cross-Cultural Competence*, which considers a person's cultural competence and agency towards improving intercultural effectiveness.

Geert Hofstede was among those who pioneered work in the business sector regarding differences among cultures. His work shed light on the differences between countries regarding cross-cultural groups and organisations (Hofstede, 1994). As illustrated in Figure 14.1, Hofstede considered culture to be one of three central components (*levels of uniqueness* in his terminology) influencing how human beings come to think the way they do. Hofstede's model shows a progressive relationship between the three influencing components with one building upon the other, from the broader commonalities shared among humans in general, to those of a particular culture more specifically, and then finally the tip of the pyramid consists of the personal factors of the individual themselves. In this model, culture is considered to bear a central influence on who a person *is*.

Hofstede's (1994) approach is consistent with other attempts to integrate theories of personality and psychology, such as Kluckhohn and Murray's (1953) Tripartite Framework of Personal Identity, Schwartz's (1992) theory of basic human values, and McAdams & Pals' (2006) new Big Five fundamental principles of an integrative science of personality. All are contested, providing evidence of just how difficult it is to accomplish intercultural effectiveness, perhaps even impossible. Kluckhohn and Murray (1953) proposed human beings are shaped by numerous elements from three interconnected areas that are either universal across all human beings, idiosyncratic to each individual and culturally sensitive, and are adaptable across micro and macro timescales. This aligns with Hofstede's (1994) idea that every individual, just like any culture, consists of an interplay of component parts with some more obvious than others. Subsequently, Hofstede developed a tool[3] to provide a snapshot of cultural tendencies across countries. Its potential use is to provide insight when working in cross-cultural settings, with the important caveat once again that there are large differences between individuals that must be considered as overriding any insights generated by the tool, the tool being a starting point only towards understanding cultural tendencies and individual differences.

McAdams and Pals (2006) highlight the complex nature of our existence that has both evolutionary and culturally sensitive components, yet the ongoing debate whether our behaviour is situationally specific or cross-situationally consistent adds to the confusion regarding cultural competence. Nevertheless, the *Theory of Basic Values* by Schwartz (1992) was validated in 82 countries highlighting most societal groups share similar values, yet individuals exhibit considerable differences despite the overwhelming influence of the sociocultural context of our existence (Schwartz & Bardi, 1997; Vaughan et al., 2022). Later, Schwartz (2012) attributed the universality of the values he identified to their relationship with the needs of human existence, namely the "needs of individuals as biological organisms, requisites of coordinated social interaction, and survival and welfare needs of groups" (p. 4). The ten values and the motivations that underpin them may help our conceptualisation of individuals and cultures as seen through the lens of these values.

Figure 14.2 illustrates the ten values comprising Schwartz's theory, with some compatible (adjacent in the figure) and others incompatible with one another (in opposition in the figure). Schwartz (2012) as well as other scholars (for example,

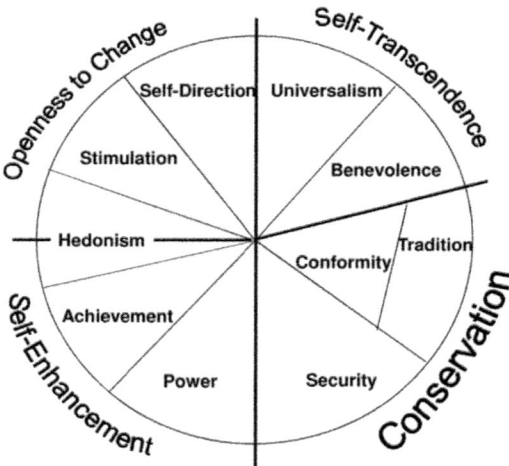

FIGURE 14.2 Theoretical model of relations among ten motivational types of value (see Schwartz, 2012).

Kluckhohn, 1951; Morris, 1956; Allport, 1961; Rokeach, 1973; Feather, 1995) argued values share six common features: they are beliefs, refer to desirable goals, transcend actions and situations, serve as standards, are ordered in importance, and, perhaps most importantly for this discussion, it is the relative importance of multiple values that guides action. Values, according to Schwartz (2012, p. 4), "influence action when they are relevant in the context (hence likely to be activated) and important to the actor".

Although beyond the scope of this chapter to discuss this theory further, it is important to integrate the sciences of personality and psychology; culture is seen as influencing individuals and how they see and act in the world. Huang (1995) ties together Kluckhohn and Murray's (1953) perspective and the essence of Schwartz's theory in the following: "Every man is in certain respects like all other men, like some other men, and like no other man" (p. 110).

Given the importance of understanding cultures to successful military peacekeeping missions (and those with less noble objectives), it is unsurprising that one of the conceptual frameworks for intercultural effectiveness and cultural competence that seems to receive a lot of attention has come from the US army. According to Abbe et al.'s (2007, p. 13) conceptual framework (see Figure 14.3), cultural competence in army leaders includes three principal components as follows:

1. **Knowledge and Cognition:** Cultural awareness, cross-cultural schema, and cognitive complexity
2. **Affect and Motivation:** Attitudes and initiative, empathy, and need for closure
3. **Skills:** Interpersonal skills, self-regulation, and flexibility

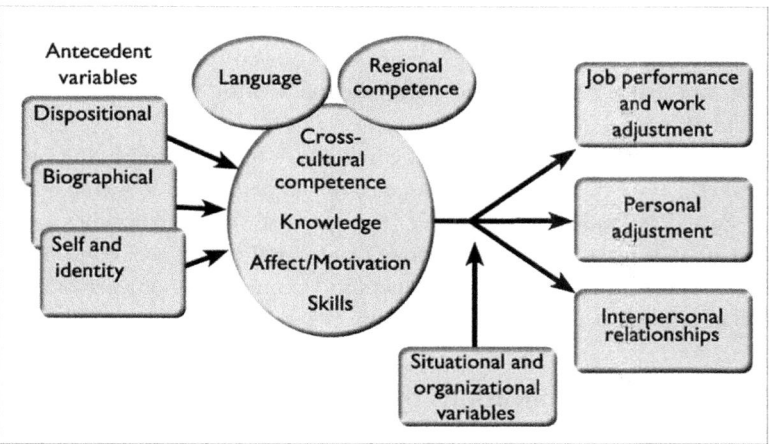

FIGURE 14.3 A general framework for cross-cultural competence in army leaders (see Abbe et al., 2007, p. 2).

In Abbe et al.'s (2007) model, both who we are as well as our biographies are to be considered *antecedent variables*, and the outcome of cultural competence, *intercultural effectiveness*, is mediated by situational and organisational factors. One of the key aspects of this model is the distinction the authors make between specific capability, which they consider to be speaking the language and regional competence (knowing about the country), from cultural competence,[4] which the authors consider to be the general abilities an army personnel would possess regardless of the culture/country within which that person is working. Language and regional competence amplify culture-specific variables, variables that are significant yet not dominant predictors of cultural competence. In other words, and perhaps what most appealed to us in this model was their premise that there is much more to being effective at working in across cultures than simply speaking the language of and knowing about the country.

How can we increase our cultural competence towards improving our intercultural effectiveness as coaches and coach developers when working across cultures? All three models presented in Part I can be contributory towards improving one's understanding of culture and how it comes to bear when operating in both the scenarios outlined at the beginning of this chapter for coaches and coach developers, namely: (1) I am going to work in a country and culture that is not my own, or (2) I am welcoming a person from another country and culture into my own. In absence of other information at the individual level, Hofstede's model and tool provide a starting point in understanding behaviour or ways of seeing based on where a person comes from and the cultural traditions of that country. Swartz's theory reassures us that, though we differ in some ways, we are more similar than different at the very basic level of values and motivations and that how values "play out" in our behaviours tend to change in response to situations and contexts. Abbe et al.'s work frames cultural competence as capabilities that one can improve towards greater intercultural effectiveness. In other words, we have agency over our cultural competence, and we can get better if we are open to doing so and willing to put in the necessary time and effort

How can we increase our cultural competence towards improving our intercultural effectiveness as coaches and coach developers when working across cultures? Part II is framed as a series of five lessons to support coaches and coach developers in translating the knowledge from Part I into practice in our day-to-day work as coaches and coach developers and extending to our personal growth as human beings operating in an increasingly interconnected world.

Part II: Practical Applications for Coaches and Coach Developers

The following lessons are not intended as a typical self-help styled "six steps to achieve cultural competence". Rather, they aim to be used as thought- and discussion-provoking exercises, and their format reflects this end. Together they address the knowledges, attitudes, and skills necessary for developing cultural competence.

Though the relative importance of each lesson will differ for each person, we think their order may prove important. Aligning with Côté and Gilbert's (2009) definition for coaching effectiveness, Lessons 1, 2, and 3 are aimed towards intrapersonal knowledges and start with the self. Lesson 4 targets professional knowledges, or the specific knowledge and skills required for intercultural effectiveness. Finally, 5 and 6 address interpersonal knowledges in the form of practising the two scenarios outlined at the beginning of this chapter – someone's coming from another culture, and I'm going to work in another culture.

- **Lesson 1:** Start with me
- **Lesson 2:** Chose how I want to be
- **Lesson 3:** Explore my values
- **Lesson 4:** Identify what I need to know/learn
- **Lesson 5:** Practise *Someone's coming*
- **Lesson 6:** Practise *I'm going*

Lesson 1: Start with Me

While the authorship is unknown, "γνῶθι σεαυτόν" is a maxim that is generally translated from the original Greek as "know thyself" or "know thy measure". It was popularised by Aeschylus, Socrates, and Plato, and it is inscribed at the Temple of Apollo at Delphi. Two other powerful, relevant, but lesser-known maxims are inscribed below it: "nothing to excess" and "certainty brings insanity".

Guiding question: How does my culture shape me and my ways?

Food for thought from literature from other fields:

- Lu and Wan (2018) spoke of cultural self-awareness as an "individual's metacognitive understanding of culture's influence on the self". In other words, cultural self-awareness is the ability of individuals to understand how their cultural upbringing has shaped who they are. Furthermore, as we know that cultural and human development is a complex process that continuously evolves, this suggests that we critically review our knowledge, beliefs, and attitudes on a regular basis.

Food for thought from coaching and CED literature:

- Côté and Gilbert's (2009) definition of coaching effectiveness includes knowledge (used in its broader sense to include declarative knowledge, skills, and attitudes) in three domains: professional, interpersonal, and intrapersonal knowledges. The intrapersonal domain, they go on to define, is "the understanding of oneself and the ability for introspection and reflection" (p. 311). Viewed in this manner, an effective coach (and coach developers who coach coaches) seeks to better understand themselves as a starting point to then better understand others and the context in which they are working.

Discussion questions:

1. From what culture(s) do I come, in general and in sport (regional, national, global)?
2. How would I tell my own story regarding my culture(s)?
3. How might the culture(s) from which I come influence on my ways of seeing, knowing, and doing?
4. Use Hofstede's tool and enter the country in which you were raised, then ask yourself the following questions: What do I think about what the tool suggests is a potential starting point for another person who knows nothing about me yet to begin to understand me? Where might the tool interfere with understanding me as an individual?
5. Are there aspects related to my cultural influences that I see playing out, for better or for worse, in my work or social relationships?
6. What stereotypes have I found myself thinking or attributing to others with whom I interact for work and social reasons?
7. What can I change tomorrow to improve my ways of interacting with others from different cultures than mine?

Lesson 2: Choose How I Want to Be

"Be curious, not judgemental" is an expression of fictional character Ted Lasso from the comedy television series of the same name. Ted Lasso is an American football coach who has journeyed to England to coach an English football team. In essence, he is adapting to two cultural changes at once – both country and sport. Guiding question: How would I describe a curious person?

Food for thought from literature from other fields:

- Research highlights the importance of your motivation to learn about cultures and tendencies of people with whom you interact and being open-minded to new experiences are likely to enhance your aptitude for intercultural effectiveness (Abbe et al., 2007). For example, Chiu et al. (2000) indicated that high need for certainty and decisiveness is likely to limit a person's ability for intercultural adjustment and, thus, forcing an over-reliance on our existing biases.
- Abbe et al. (2007) stress that knowledge alone is not enough to achieve intercultural effectiveness. It is our intention to apply this knowledge, willingness to understand the perspectives of others and curiosity to discover the pathways of the impact of the culture on the behaviour of individuals. In other words, we all have an opportunity to become interculturally effective if we are curious and willing to study other cultures and individuals from those culture.

Food for thought from coaching and CED literature:

- Research on serial winning coaches highlighted that seeking to understand athletes and those around them was a cornerstone of their coaching philosophies (Lara-Bercial & Mallett, 2016). The authors coined the term *driven benevolence*, defining it as "… a purposeful and determined pursuit of excellence that hinges on an enduring and balanced desire to considerately support oneself and others" (p. 237). Working in a benevolent manner implies an inner curiosity towards others and a desire to better understand the athletes they are coaching, and necessarily involves learning about them and their culture(s).

Discussion questions:

1. What affect and motivation are required for me to grow in cultural competence (e.g., attitudes and initiative, empathy, tolerance for ambiguity)?
2. In what situations do I find myself sliding towards being more judgmental and away from curiosity? Why might that be? Are their situations that justify this or is it always better to steer away from judgement? Why so?
3. Are there any cultures towards which I find myself more judgmental than curious? Why might that be? What might I do to reactivate my curiosity if I feel that is what is required to grow?
4. What have I learned from others with a different cultural background than mine, and how has that influenced my thoughts and actions?
5. What would be important for others to learn about my culture and me to work effectively with me? How might I be forthcoming with this information (i.e., how can help the other know these things about me)?

Lesson 3: Explore My Values

Roy Disney was the lesser-known brother of Walt Disney. Recognised for his business acumen, he was instrumental in the success of the Disney media company. We have chosen one of his quotes for this lesson as it strongly resonates with the content of this lesson: "When your values are clear to you, making decisions becomes easier".

Guiding questions: In what ways do my motivations affect the ways my values are expressed in my actions? How does this increased awareness help me when working across cultures in general and across sport cultures more specifically?

Food for thought from literature from other fields:

- It is important to consider how values play out in our day-to-day actions, how they are influenced by our personal motivations, and how they can shift in importance (and by extension how we end up acting) in response to the context in which we find ourselves at any given moment. Using

Figure 14.2, the graphic representation of Schwartz's (2012) *Theory of Basic Values*, a useful exercise can be to map out our personal profile and use this profile to enhance our understanding of the motives that drive our behaviour (pp. 5–7):

- Self-Direction (independent thought and action, choosing, creating, exploring)
- Stimulation (excitement, novelty, and challenge in life)
- Hedonism (pleasure or sensuous gratification for oneself)
- Achievement (personal success through demonstrating competence according to social standards)
- Power (social status and prestige, control or dominance over people and resources)
- Security (safety, harmony, and stability of society, of relationships, and of self)
- Conformity (restraint of actions, inclinations, and impulses likely to upset or harm others and violate social expectations or norms)
- Tradition (respect, commitment, and acceptance of the customs and ideas that one's culture or religion provides)
- Benevolence (preserving and enhancing the welfare of those with whom one is in frequent, personal contact – the "in-group")
- Universalism (understanding, appreciation, tolerance, and protection for the welfare of all people and for nature)

Food for thought from CED literature:

Research on high-performance coaches highlights the importance of deep reflection to identify core values that reflect their personality, connect to their coaching philosophy and are visible in their actions (Lara-Bercial & Mallett, 2016). Furthermore, Collins (2020) has pointed out that "both your personal belief system and your coaching objectives must also mesh with the philosophy of the agency or organisation with whom you work" (p. 39). Thus, as coaches, we are required to both *zoom in* to consider our characteristics and values and *zoom out* to consider the broader sociocultural setting in which we work to effectively reflect on our core values and their manifestation in our actions. Also, coaches should be mindful of the interplay between own expectations about the coaching process and the expectations that athletes have when it comes to the coach-athlete relationship (Lyle, 2002).

Discussion questions:

For this lesson, there are two sets of discussion questions. This first set comes from Schwartz (2012, p. 20) and aims to stimulate thinking on how your motivations drive your values, using his theoretical model as a framework:

1. Are there any values important to me and that are not part of the basic ten (listed above)? Place them in one of the ten by considering the motivation they express.

2. Hedonism is becoming more important in Western societies. How is this likely to affect the importance of the other values around the circle (see Figure 14.2 in Part I)? Which values are likely to become more important along with hedonism and which ones are likely to become less important?
3. Considering how much cultures differ, how can it be that people in almost all societies organise their values in the same circular structure?
4. How are war, economic depression, or personal crises likely to affect our value priorities? Why?
5. When people talk about values, they usually mean "moral" values. Which values are "moral" and which are not? What makes a value "moral"?
6. People often behave in ways that seem to contradict their values. How can the value circle help to explain this?

This second set of questions aims to extend your thinking more specifically to sport, coaching, and coach development:

1. In all sports, but perhaps more often in team sports, issues can arise when the needs of individuals within a team conflict with the needs of the group. Discuss how Schwartz's model may help to better understand this from a values perspective.
2. Sport can be forum for personal achievement. In what ways might my motivations come into play in my, in the athlete I coach, or in a coach I work with work in my role as a coach developer consider the relative importance I attribute to sport and the role it plays in my live?
3. Is there a relationship between the popularity of certain sports and the ways sport is played and coached in different cultures that can be explained at least in part through Schwartz's model?
4. Have there been times in my work as a coach or coach developer where my motivations changed and shifted the values expressed in my actions?
5. Think about the traditions in the sport(s) in which I work. In what ways might they be (or not be) evolving? Why do I think that might be the case?

Lesson 4: Identify What I Need to Learn

The American author John C. Maxwell, who writes on leadership, reminded us that we cannot learn new things if we feel that our current knowledge is sufficient when he said "Remember, the greatest enemy of learning is knowing, and the goal of all learning is action, not knowledge". With these words, he also stressed the importance of bringing our knowledge to life through our actions. Guiding questions: What can I learn about the cultures of others with whom I work and socialise, and how can I broaden my horizons regarding other cultures? What about the sport cultures in other countries and country history that may have shaped how a particular sport is played or structured? How can this knowledge improve my cultural competence and be seen in my behaviours?

Food for thought from literature from other fields:

- Knowledge of cultural nuances such as history, socio-economic subtleties, and language are important to working more effectively across cultures. This knowledge can be either region-specific or culture-general (Abbe & Halpin, 2009) and represent complementary and necessary starting points for someone who wants to learn about a foreign culture. However, one must consider which of the two is most relevant to the situation at hand. In other words, if you are interested in exploring the tendencies that are foreign to your cultural upbringing in a precise geographical location, then you may aim to improve your region-specific knowledge. However, if you are after general trends and country-to-country comparisons, then you should seek to improve your culture-general knowledge.
- Rasmussen and Sieck (2015, p. 6) identified nine culture-general competencies and how they can be observed in one's actions, as follows:

Competency area	Behavioural indicator
1. Cultural sensemaking	Manages confusion/surprises
2. Perspective taking	Sees events as another sees them
3. Cultural knowledge	Applies cultural facts/theories
4. Self-presentation	Adapts how (to) express themselves
5. Language proficiency	Displays knowledge of language
6. Emotional self-regulation	Controls emotional responses
7. Affect/attitude	Expresses attitude about the culture
8. Withholding/suspending judgement	Withholds moral or value judgement
9. Self-efficacy/confidence	Maintains confidence

Getting better at the behaviours in the right-hand column can be one way to assess whether you are growing in cultural competence.

Food for thought from coaching and CED literature:

- The sport context does not exist independently, rather is influenced by the sports culture of the country. It can differ among countries and can be interpreted through the lens of historic events (Vaughan et al., 2019). Knowledge about a given country's sports culture may prove essential to operating effectively as a coach or coach developer in that country or with people from that country. One example of how this plays out is when considering the playing style of Brazilian football players, known for their flair and creative movement. These players often learned to play through small-sided street games with peers of differing ages and abilities, and often in the poorer communities wherein playing football well could represent a way out of poverty (Uehara et al., 2021). Another example is how both the multi-sport background and socio-economic factors that led to equipment shortages combined to shape the developmental pathways of Soviet ice hockey players (Bespomoshchnov & Caron, 2017; O'Sullivan et al., 2021).

- Culturally competent coaches would proactively embrace systematic reflection (i.e., Hall et al., 2021) to evaluate personal assumptions, current beliefs, and competency when working across cultures. As a complement to this reflection, gaining a better understanding of the historical events or factors that may shape sports in general or a sport more specifically within a particular country or region may help in understanding *why* things are done the way they are done. Nevertheless, while history may provide valuable insights, times, countries, and people change, and so the present sociocultural context, or what may be *currently* influencing sport within a country or region, is also to be considered.

Discussion questions:

1. On what do I currently base my assumptions regarding the behaviours of others and other cultures? Are my assumptions supported with rich experience/exposure?
2. What do I think know about the cultures of the people with whom I work and socialise with on a regular basis? How can I learn more, and how do I distinguish reliable sources from others?
3. How can I test and challenge my assumptions or what I think I know? In other words, what actions might I undertake to challenge my knowledge, beliefs, or assumptions regarding other cultures, and particularly the cultures of those with whom I work and socialise with on a regular basis?
4. How can I distinguish between understanding region-specific tendencies, country-specific tendencies, and stereotyping?
5. What questions could I ask about the traditions and ways of operating that could help me enrich my understanding of sport in other cultures?
6. What strategies could I use to help me understand the shorthand of behaviours and ways of being in other cultures that I might completely miss or misinterpret?
7. In what ways may certain events in my country's history have shaped the importance of a sport of sports in general, how a sport is played, and the importance of winning? How about regarding what is perceived to be effective coaching or coach developer work? How about regarding how sport stakeholders interact (e.g., club administration, athletes, families, fans)?
8. What could be learned from other cultures regarding sport development that could enrich my own?

Lesson 5: Practise "Someone's Coming"

For this lesson, we turn to Nelson Mandela's quote, "A fundamental concern for others in our individual and community lives would go a long way in making the world the better place we so passionately dreamt of". After 27 years of imprisonment and immense personal sacrifice, his quest of uniting the South African nation and her people by ending institutional segregation by race and resulted in South Africa's first non-racial, democratic election in 1994. Mandela lived the conviction he communicated through these words – that a better world starts with our care for one another.

Guiding question(s): What scenarios might be helpful to practise in preparation for welcoming someone from another culture? In other words, what could I think about or do in advance to prepare myself for this happening?

Food for thought from literature from other fields:

- As Kluckhohn and Murray (1953) suggested, we are all made up of aspects that we share with all other human beings, aspects that are culturally sensitive and that we share with some, and aspects that are unique to each of us. In making a new acquaintance from another culture, think first of the multitude of things you are likely to have in common (universal to all human beings), what might be common to others you may have come to know from their culture (being careful not to assume or stereotype), and what might be unique to this person. How might you distinguish between the three and pay attention to all three when trying to help someone who is arriving?

Food for thought from coaching and CED literature:

- Migration of sport coaches to other cultures can present certain challenges, particularly when the two cultures in question are very different from each other regarding social norms and what is regarded as effective coaching and athlete development. Tao et al. (2019) studied the experiences of Chinese migrant coaches hired to work in Australian high-performance sport workplace, two countries that are "very different with respect to sociocultural norms and practice" (p. 3). Among other conclusions, the authors found that, consistent with earlier findings of Schinke et al. (2013), both the coaches and those in the host environment changed because of the arrival of coaches from other cultures through a mutually beneficial interdependence required to achieve successful performances. The desire to be successful that both coaches and athletes shared led to acculturation for both, motivating them to learn from one another. Athletes were able to gain from the sport-specific expertise and training methods of the coaches. The coaches, whose coaching practices were informed by their experiences as athletes and as coaches in China, were able to learn the language and social skills required to be effective in the Australian context.

Discussion questions:

1. How can I help set others up for success when they come to work in my country as a coach or coach developer? Here are some questions to help identify specific actions that I could take to assist others in getting set

up, making friends, and thriving in our culture (both in general and in sport culture):

- Even the basic such as figuring out how to get around, do laundry, and navigate grocery stores can be difficult when arriving in another culture, particularly in a different language. It can also be a challenge to figure out bureaucracy and how systems work when moving or visiting another country of culture, such as accessing medical or legal support if needed. In what ways can I be of assistance in this regard? What would I likely be dealing with if the situation were reversed and I was the one arriving and having to cope with the many stresses of adjusting (i.e., aspects that are universal to all human beings)?
- It can be particularly difficult to fully contribute our best in conversations and even just fit in when communicating in a language other than our first. It often feels like we can't say exactly what we mean, we struggle to pick up on jokes or figures of speech, and so we miss a lot about others, and they miss a lot about us. How could I help another person who has just arrived and who may be experiencing this challenge?
- Think about all the short-hands and idiosyncrasies of my culture that may be invisible or hard to pick up if you are not from it. How can I help make them visible to that person and help them understand how common behaviours may be (mis)interpreted?
- Finally, think about how to truly get to know what is unique to the person arriving, and how to help others see their qualities as well. How can I get to know the person and help others do the same?
- Loneliness is a common feeling when first arriving and can be detrimental to a person's well-being and happiness. How can I play a role in providing a safety net for psychological support and logistical assistance, providing social connection until that person is able to establish their own social circle?

2. When considering sociocultural differences between the culture from which a coach or coach developer is coming and the host country, where might misunderstandings and tensions arise, particularly regarding coaching effectiveness and desirable behaviour? Would there be certain coaching contexts in which this would be particularly problematic (e.g., high-performance versus developmental sport, coaching adults versus coaching children)?
3. Does the sport organisation for which I work have a plan for welcoming a coach or coach developer from another country such that there is benefit through mutual acculturation (i.e., one that aims to help them learn how to adapt to be successful in their host culture while also aiming to learn from them and what they bring)? If not, what can I do to see that one is developed and implemented?
4. How can I learn and grow as a coach or coach developer through learning more about the person arriving and the ways of working in sport in their culture of origin?

Lesson 6: Practise "I'm Going"

"Travelling – it leaves you speechless, then turns you into a storyteller" is a quote attributed to Ibn Battuta, who was a medieval Moroccan Muslim geographer, scholar, and explorer. He travelled more than any other explorer in pre-modern history, documenting his travels over more than 27 years in one of the world's most famous travel logs, the Riḥla. Guiding question(s): What scenarios might be helpful to practise in preparation for going to work in a culture different from my own? In other words, what could I think about or do in advance to prepare myself for this happening?

Food for thought from literature from other fields:

- Travelling to a country with a different culture to our own can be one of the most challenging, simulating, and meaningful opportunities for personal and professional growth as coaches and coach developers. Stevens et al. (2018) caution that when we travel to a foreign culture, we encounter explicit features that we can physically perceive and implicit features that are not as evident and require deeper inquiry. We need to be careful, in other words, not to draw pre-mature conclusions based on the snapshots we get during short-term exposure. Rather, we should strive for a more thorough immersion within a cultural context to become aware of what is initially invisible to us.
- Abbe et al. (2007, p. 20) defined flexibility as "the ability to adjust one's behaviour or cognitive frames of reference in response to situational cues – in particular, in response to cultural cues". Exposure to a foreign culture can be source of dissonance or stress as we face ways of being and doing that challenge those that are familiar to us, and which have informed our own beliefs. This is especially true when we are moving for longer periods of time or even permanently. With stress, however, comes opportunity for growth. Approaching these experiences with an open mind and heart and striving to be flexible and adapt our behaviour and practice are means to this end.

Food for thought from coaching and CED literature:

- When coaches arrive in a new culture, they are required to adjust their practices to coach effectively and to fulfil expectations others have of them in their work (Borges et al., 2015; Kerr & Moore, 2015; Tao et al., 2019). These studies also suggest that navigating cultural difference requires coaches to also consider the culture of their upbring and their sport experiences (as athletes and coaches) to better understand what and how to change.
- In a study of experiences of Russian gymnastics coaches who migrated to New Zealand/Aotearoa (Kerr & Moore, 2015), coaches reported changing behaviours they believed to be effective in their home country to adapt to what they perceived parents and other sport stakeholders expected of them in their host country (e.g., softer speaking and reassurance in lieu of firm instruction). The authors showed that coaches situated the ways they adapted their coaching within what they came to understand as the cultural context of sport for children in New Zealand/Aotearoa.

Discussion questions:

1. What *cultural baggage* regarding my sport as is it played and taught in my culture might be travelling with me? How can I unpack those bags, and how do I decide what may or may not be useful or relevant in my host culture?
2. How can I find out about the *cultural baggage* regarding my sport as is it played and taught in my host culture? What will I do if this culture's approach conflicts with my own values in general, or with my beliefs about teaching and learning in sport more specifically?
3. How do I check how my actions are being interpreted or understood as a coach or coach developer working in a culture different than my own (i.e., by athletes, coaches, other staff, and the organisation)?
4. What would I consider to be flexible in my own behaviours and actions and what would not be? In other words, what would I be prepared to change (or not) to adapt when working in a culture a different than my own?
5. What could I do to maximise my learning/take in all I can when working in a culture different than my own?

Notes

1 Also named cross-cultural competence.
2 NASW Standards for Cultural Competence in Social Work Practice Prepared by the NASW National Committee on Racial and Ethnic Diversity Approved by the NASW Board of Directors, June 23, 2001.
3 https://www.hofstede-insights.com/country-comparison/.
4 They use the term cross-cultural competence.

References

Abbe, A., Gulick, L. M., & Herman, J. L. (2007). *Cross-cultural competence in Army leaders: A conceptual and empirical foundation*. US Army Research Institute for the Behavioral and Social Sciences.
Abbe, A., & Halpin, S. M. (2009). The cultural imperative for professional military education and leader development. *The US Army War College Quarterly: Parameters*, 39(4), 20–31. https://doi.org/10.55540/0031-1723.2491.
Alizadeh, S., & Chavan, M. (2015). Cultural competence dimensions and outcomes: A systematic review of the literature. *Health & Social Care in the Community*, 24(6), e117–e130. https://doi.org/10.1111/hsc.12293.
Allport, G. W. (1961). *Pattern and growth in personality*. Holt, Rinehart & Winston.
Ashmore, R. D., & Del Boca, F. K. (1981). Sex stereotypes and implicit personality theory. In D. L. Hamilton (Ed.), *Cognitive processes in stereotyping and intergroup behavior*. Hillsdale, NJ: Erlbaum.
Bespomoshchnov, V. A., & Caron, J. G. (2017). Coaching philosophy and methods of Anatoly Tarasov: 'Father' of Russian ice hockey. *International Sport Coaching Journal*, 4(3), 305–313. https://doi.org/10.1123/iscj.2017-0058.
Borges, M., Rosado, A., De Oliveira, R., & Freitas, F. (2015). Coaches' migration: A qualitative analysis of recruitment, motivations and experiences. *Leisure Studies*, 34(5), 588–602. https://doi.org/10.1080/02614367.2014.939988.

Chiu, C., Morris, M. W., Hong, Y., & Menon, T. (2000). Motivated cultural cognition: The impact of implicit cultural theories on dispositional attribution varies as a function of need for closure. *Journal of Personality and Social Psychology, 78*(2), 247–259. https://doi.org/10.1037/0022-3514.78.2.247.

Collins, K. (2020). Coaching philosophy. In D. Gould & C. Mallett (Eds.), *Sport coaches' handbook* (pp. 31–49). Human Kinetics.

Côté, J., & Gilbert, W. (2009). An integrative definition of coaching effectiveness and expertise. *International Journal of Sports Science & Coaching, 4*(3), 307–323. https://doi.org/10.1260/174795409789623892.

Feather, N. T. (1995). Values, valences, and choice: The influence of values on the perceived attractiveness and choice of alternatives. *Journal of Personality and Social Psychology, 68*, 1135–1151. http://dx.doi.org/10.1037/0022-3514.68.6.1135.

Gallegos, J. S., Tindall, C., & Gallegos, S. A. (2018). The need for advancement in the conceptualization of cultural competence. *Advances in Social Work, 9*(1), 51–62. https://doi.org/10.18060/214.

Guba, E. G. (1990). *The paradigm dialog.* Sage.

Hall, E. T. (1989) *Beyond culture.* Anchor.

Hall, A. J. A., English, C., Jones, L. W., Westbury, T., & Martindale, R. (2021). The Acculturation Experiences of Elite Rugby Union Coaches. *International Sport Coaching Journal, 9*(1), 30–39. https://doi.org/10.1123/iscj.2020-0103.

Hofstede, G. (1994). The business of international business is culture. *International Business Review, 3*(1), 1–14. https://doi.org/10.1016/0969-5931(94)90011-6.

Huang, K. (1995). Tripartite cultural personality and ethclass assessment. *Journal of Sociology and Social Welfare, 22*(1), 99–119.

Kerr, R., & Moore, K. (2015). Hard work or child's play? Migrant coaches' reflections on coaching gymnastics in New Zealand. *World Leisure Journal, 57*(3), 185–195. https://doi.org/10.1080/16078055.2015.1066601.

Kluckhohn, C. (1951). Values and value-orientations in the theory of action: An exploration in definition and classification. In T. Parsons & E. Shils (Eds.), *Toward a general theory of action* (pp. 388–433). Harvard University Press.

Kluckhohn, C., & Murray, H. A. (1953). Personality formation: The determinants. In C. Kluckhohn, H. A. Murray, & D. M. Schneider (Eds.), *Personality in nature, society, and culture* (2nd ed., pp. 53–69). Alfred A. Knopf.

Lara-Bercial, S., & Mallett, C. J. (2016). The practices and developmental pathways of professional and Olympic serial winning coaches. *International Sport Coaching Journal, 3*(3), 221–239. https://doi.org/10.1123/iscj.2016-0083.

Lu, C., & Wan, C. (2018). Cultural self-awareness as awareness of culture's influence on the self: Implications for cultural identification and well-being. *Personality and Social Psychology Bulletin, 44*(6), 823–837. https://doi.org/10.1177/0146167217752117.

Lyle, J. (2002). *Sport coaching concepts: A framework for coaches behavior.* Routledge.

McAdams, D. P., & Pals, J. L. (2006). A new Big Five: Fundamental principles for an integrative science of personality. *American Psychologist, 61*(3), 204–217. https://doi.org/10.1037/0003-066x.61.3.204.

Miller, D. T., & Turnbull, W. (1986). Expectancies and interpersonal processes. *Annual Review of Psychology, 37*, 233–256. https://doi.org/10.1146/annurev.ps.37.020186.001313.

Morgan, D. L. (2014). Pragmatism as a paradigm for social research. *Qualitative Inquiry, 20*(8), 1045–1053. https://doi.org/10.1177/1077800413513733

Morris, C. W. (1956). *Varieties of human value.* University of Chicago Press.

O'Sullivan, M., Bespomoshchnov, V. A., & Mallett, C. J. (2021). Pavel Datsyuk: Learning, development, and becoming the "Magic man". *Case Studies in Sport and Exercise Psychology*, 5(1), 173–183. https://doi.org/10.1123/cssep.2021-0022.

Rasmussen, L. J., & Sieck, W. R. (2015). Culture-general competence: Evidence from a cognitive field study of professionals who work in many cultures. *International Journal of Intercultural Relations*, 48, 75–90. https://doi.org/10.1016/j.ijintrel.2015.03.014.

Rokeach, M. (1973). *The nature of human values*. Free Press.

Schim, S. M., & Miller, J. E. (1999). *Cultural competence program core components*. Presentation at The Henry Ford Health System/Oakland University Center for Academic Nursing, Detroit, MI.

Schinke, R.J., McGannon, K.R., Battochio, R.C., & Wells, G.D. (2013). Acculturation in elite sport: A thematic analysis of immigrant athletes and coaches. *Journal of Sports Sciences*, 31(15), 1676–1686. https://doi.org/10.1080/02640414.2013.794949.

Schwartz, S. H. (1992). Universals in the content and structure of values: Theory and empirical tests in 20 countries. In M. Zanna (Ed.), *Advances in experimental social psychology* (Vol. 25, pp. 1–65). Academic Press. http://dx.doi.org/10.1016/S0065-2601(08)60281-6.

Schwartz, S. H. (2012). An Overview of the Schwartz Theory of Basic Values. *Online Readings in Psychology and Culture*, 2(1). https://doi.org/10.9707/2307-0919.1116.

Schwartz, S. H., & Bardi, A. (1997). Influences of adaptation to communist rule on value priorities in Eastern Europe. *Political Psychology*, 18(2), 385–410. https://doi.org/10.1111/0162-895x.00062.

Seeleman, C., Suurmond, J., & Stronks, K. (2009). Cultural competence: A conceptual framework for teaching and learning. *Medical Education*, 43(3), 229–237. https://doi.org/10.1111/j.1365-2923.2008.03269.x.

Stevens, S. T., Jussim, L., Stevens, L. A., & Anglin, S. M. (2018). Cultural Competence: A form of stereotype rationality. In C. L. Frisby & W. T. O'Donohue (Eds.), *Cultural Competence in Applied Psychology* (pp. 651–664). Springer.

Tao, Y., Rynne, S. B., & Mallett, C. J. (2019). Blending and becoming: Migrant Chinese high-performance coaches' learning journey in Australia. *Physical Education and Sport Pedagogy*, 24(6), 582–597. https://doi.org/10.1080/17408989.2019.1641191.

Tervalon, M., & Murray-García, J. (1998). Cultural humility versus cultural competence: A critical distinction in defining physician training outcomes in multicultural education. *Journal of Health Care for the Poor and Underserved*, 9(2), 117–125. https://doi.org/10.1353/hpu.2010.0233.

Uehara, L., Falcous, M., Button, C., Davids, K., Araújo, D., De Paula, A. R., & Saunders, J. (2021). The poor "Wealth" of Brazilian football: How poverty may shape skill and expertise of players. *Frontiers in Sports and Active Living*, 3. https://doi.org/10.3389/fspor.2021.635241.

Vaughan, J., Mallett, C. J., Davids, K., Potrac, P., & López-Felip, M. A. (2019). Developing creativity to enhance human potential in sport: A wicked transdisciplinary challenge. *Frontiers in Psychology*, 10, 2090. https://doi.org/10.3389/fpsyg.2019.02090.

Vaughan, J., Mallett, C. J., Potrac, P., Woods, C., O'Sullivan, M., & Davids, K. (2022). Social and cultural constraints on football player development in Stockholm: Influencing skill, learning, and wellbeing. *Frontiers in Sports and Active Living*, 4. https://doi.org/10.3389/fspor.2022.832111.

15
EVALUATING COACH EDUCATION AND DEVELOPMENT PROGRAMMES

Hans Vangrunderbeek and Liam McCarthy

Sport coaches play an increasingly key role in delivering positive outcomes through sport for individuals, groups, and societies at large (North, 2010; North et al., 2019).

As McCarthy et al. (2021a) note, their contribution is vast in both scale and scope. For example, sport coaches work with diverse populations (for example, young people, professional athletes, people with additional needs, and older adults) across a variety of contexts (for example, education, professional sport, and community sport). As increasing value is placed on sport coaching and sport coaches, the quality of participants' experiences in sport has received much attention. In turn, there has been increased focus on providing professional development for sport coaches (North et al., 2020). As large-scale coach education programmes are increasingly viewed as the primary mechanism for educating and developing sport coaches (and therefore increasing the quality of coaching practice) (Nelson et al., 2013), these programmes have been the subject of an emerging body of academic research studies, for example, inquiry into the role of coach education programmes in coaches' learning (for example, Erickson et al., 2008; Mallett et al., 2009; Williams & Bush, 2019), the impact of coach education programmes on coaching practice (for example, Griffiths et al., 2018; Stodter & Cushion, 2019), and coaches' experiences of coach education programmes (for example, Chesterfield et al., 2010; Piggott, 2012; Vella et al., 2013).

However, the published coach education literature lacks evidence of rigorous and meaningful evaluation work to understand (among other things) the efficacy of coach education programmes. For example, there is a scarcity of work that asks: What makes coach education programmes work? How are these programmes working? Who are they working for? Why is this the case? (McCarthy, 2022). Recognition of this problem is not new; there have been multiple calls

DOI: 10.4324/9781003251309-18

to increase the volume and quality of evaluation work over the last two decades (Gilbert & Trudel, 1999; Cassidy et al., 2006; Dohme et al., 2019; McCarthy, 2022). Considering the growing importance placed upon coach education and increasing amount of resource committed to it (for example, human, financial, and political) in a typically resource-starved sport coaching sector (North, 2010; North et al., 2019, 2020), a case can be made for prioritising this work for both coach education providers and researchers. In response to this, the International Council for Coaching Excellence (ICCE) formed a working group in 2021 to review programme monitoring and evaluation. Comprised of senior academics, policymakers, and programme designers and deliverers, the working group's remit is to coordinate, support, and undertake coach education programme evaluation work.

However, we suggest there are several reasons as to why this work hasn't been prioritised. First, according to Lyle (2021), there is a difficulty argument – "the challenges of impact evaluations of complex programmes are made evident by their absence" (p. 3). Since programmes (of any kind) represent complex social systems embedded within complex social systems (society), it is difficult to represent this through meaningful evaluation work (Pawson & Tilley, 1997; Pawson, 2013). Determining causation, often at the request of policymakers and their funders, is not easy in complex social systems. Many other personal, social, and cultural factors and experiences outside a coach education programme can both cause and prevent (un)intended programme outcomes. It is difficult to attribute (un)intended outcomes or outputs to a programme intervention itself. For example, coaches typically enter a programme through their own volition, which is challenging to account for in evaluation work. These sport coaches may be more motivated to develop themselves further as a coach compared to those coaches who don't attend such programmes. Personal motivation can be an individual trait that possibly affects the relationship between the programme intervention and the intended programme outcome (for example, increased coaching effectiveness).

Second, and related, there is a 'lack of bespoke methodology' argument (Lyle, 2021; McCarthy, 2022). While sharing reflections on programme evaluation work, Lyle (2021) argues "there were a number of initial challenges to overcome, including the absence of a suitable programme evaluation model" (p. 2). While there are some excellent examples of coach education, development, and support programmes subject to meaningful and sophisticated evaluation (for example, Muir et al., 2011; Duffy et al., 2013; North, et al., 2016; Dohme et al., 2019; McCarthy, 2022), too few of these programmes exist. The purpose of this chapter is to highlight and promote the importance and merit of coach education programme evaluation, while offering examples of how it might be undertaken. This responds directly to the work of Dohme and colleagues (2019) who contest that "more research is warranted that evaluates the mechanisms that foster the success or failure of large-scale CED [coach education and development] programmes" (p. 320).

Coach Education Programme Evaluation – How and Why?

While the difficulty argument persists (to varying degrees, depending on the approach, this type of work can be an immersive and long-term endeavour), guidance is available on evaluation methodology. In this section, we argue considerable effort, through a series of decisions, should be applied to how the evaluation work could be done and why it could be done in that way. For example, before coach education programmes can be studied, agreement is required on what a coach education programme includes. This was a question posed by members of the International Council for Coaching Excellence Workgroup on Monitoring and Evaluating Coach Education Programmes at the 13th International Council for Coaching Excellence Global Coaching Conference in Lisbon. If the intention of evaluation work is to generate new knowledge about a specific coach education programme, or the impact on coaches practice, then a view on knowledge (epistemology) must be explicitly adopted. To do this, it might be beneficial to consider the following question 'what is coach education like' with 'and therefore how can we come to know and understand more about it?'

Table 15.1 (McCarthy, 2022) offers a useful guide when answering these questions and making decisions about how to begin planning for, and doing,

TABLE 15.1 Approaches to coach education programme

	Experimental	*Constructivist*	*Realist*
Philosophical orientation	Seeks to 'manage-out' social complexity by adding control functions to the evaluation. Knowledge is generated through successionist regularity-based (thin) explanation	A view of the social world which places emphasis on meaning-making and social interaction; thus, knowledge is generated *within* and not external *to* social groups	There are regularities and patterns within the social world, which are brought about by 'unobservables'. Knowledge constitutes causal explanation based on generative principles
Goals	Inform programme design through rational choices based on truth	Empower and educate stakeholders	Explain how and why a programme works, for whom it works best, and under what circumstances
Views on programmes	Sets of variables which are classified as cause and effect	Loose constructions as a product of the negotiations between stakeholders involved	A series of fallible and partial theories which demonstrate intention; programmes work selectively
Evaluation approach	Pre- and post-test extensive research designs	Examining meaning and achieving consensus between stakeholders	Developing and testing theories in an ongoing adaptive manner

programme evaluation work. We present the following three worked scenarios illustrating the value in this table.

1. If coach education programmes are viewed as being uniform, predictable, stable, and with considerable structure, then understanding the programmes can be achieved through experimental research designs. Coach education programmes, their features and those who participate within them, will be treated as variables establishing cause and effect. The objective for this new understanding is to inform programme design. An experimental evaluation design should provide appropriate tools to do the job. For example, this approach has been used in the work of Ponnet et al. (2021) and Vangrunderbeek et al. (2022).
2. If coach education programmes are viewed as being complex, unpredictable, dynamic, and with elevated levels of participant agency, then knowledge about the programmes will be socially generated and contested. Perception, beliefs, and meaning-making will constitute much of what coach education programmes entails; to evaluate a programme might be to accept stakeholder narratives. A constructivist evaluation design should provide appropriate tools to do the job. For example, this approach has been used in the work of Driska (2018), Santos et al. (2019), and Stirling et al. (2012).
3. If coach education programmes are viewed from an 'and/both' perspective (North, 2016; 2017), meaning they are characterised by both complexity *and* stability, unpredictability *and* predictability, agency *and* structure, then an approach that reconciles both would be appropriate. A realistic approach to evaluation would seek to establish causality (what makes what happen?) in the social world (accounting for the context). For example, this approach has been adopted by Dohme et al. (2019), Duffy et al. (2013), McCarthy (2022), Muir et al. (2011), North (2016; 2017), and Redgate et al. (2020).

We posit there is no universal *best* approach to coach education programme evaluation. Decisions on how to evaluate the programmes should be made based on a (philosophical) view of what is being evaluated, alongside stakeholder goals, resources, and required outcomes. As such, we include Table 15.1 (McCarthy, 2022) to offer some structure and guidance in an underserved area of coach education research and practice. In the following sections, we provide two case studies of coach education evaluation methodology in action. In each study, a different evaluation approach is used to satisfy different ambitions, in different (sociocultural and institutional/organisational) contexts. First, a regional sport partnership organisation in Flanders (Belgium) using an experimental approach to undertake large-scale evaluation work across a wide variety of sports is shared. In this case, the evaluator was an internal member (employee) of the organisation, the work was extensive, and publicly funded. Second, a contrasting account of how an English Football Association (FA) coach education programme (the FA Level 3/UEFA B in coaching football programme) was subject to evaluation, using an underpinning critical realist research philosophy. In this instance, the evaluator was an external (to the FA) PhD student at a UK university.

CASE STUDY 1 – THE FLEMISH SCHOOL FOR COACH EDUCATION (BELGIUM)

The Vlaamse Trainersschool (VTS; Flemish School for Coach Education) is a cooperative association composed of the public government, private sport federations, and universities/schools of higher education. In 2022 it had a budget for coach education amounting to 2.7 million euro (about 1.5% of the total sports budget within the Flemish government). Each year, nearly 6,000 coaches are certified by VTS in over 50 different sports; in Flanders, VTS is the sole authority for all sport coach-related certification. The most popular coach education programmes are in soccer, tennis, gymnastics, horse riding, athletics, basketball, hockey, and swimming. The VTS defines the required competences for coaching in Flanders and monitors the professional development of coaches by granting certification to coaches who successfully complete education and continued professional development opportunities (Vangrunderbeek & Ponnet, 2020).

Within Flemish coach education legislative policy, subsidised sports federations are rewarded financially for both the quality and quantity of coach education activity (for example, number of qualified coaches active within the field). In October 2019, the Flemish Interactive Coaching Monitoring System (FICOMS) was established within VTS to advance the monitoring and evaluation of its large-scale coach education and development programmes. FICOMS connects different sources of information, including pre-existing standalone databases, into a single data warehouse. Using FICOMS, relationships between data on coach education and development programmes (data from 2010 to present), coach qualifications (1960–present), characteristics of active coaches within club-organised sports (2014–present) and sports clubs, sports participants, and sports infrastructure can be established and understood. One strength of FICOMS is translating complex information into hundreds of interactive dashboards with useful insights and statistics on coaching in Flanders for different stakeholders. All data and visualisations are presented in layers to the many different users.

The first layer is publicly available and shows information to interested citizens, policymakers, and researchers seeking a general overview. The second level is a secure, private layer, accessible for policymakers at the municipality or sports federation level, but is also available for in-depth policy and programme evaluation (for example, Sport Vlaanderen, Minister for Sport, Parliament). The data for all layers are anonymised, in compliance with General Data Protection Regulations. It is worth noting all dashboards are interactive; for example, when one page on the dashboard represents the number of active coaches on a yearly basis between 2017 and 2022, data filters are added to that page allowing a user to filter for gender, age category, qualified versus non-qualified, region, sport, sports federation, and

FICOMS

INPUT Coaches entering coach education programmes	THROUGHPUT Coaches obtaining a qualification through coach education	OUTPUT Active coaches in the sports clubs

Coaches starting a coach education programme:
• Background
  • Sport
  • Sports club
  • Sports federation
  • Age
  • Gender
  • Residence
  • Previous qualifications
  • PE-background (or not)
• Which pathways for coach education (Vangrunderbeek & Ponnet, 2020)
  • Regular course
  • Recognition of Prior Learning
  • During university studies
  • Assimilation of foreign qualification
  • (Former) elite athlete
	• Characteristics of coach education programmes
	  • Modules, items, hours
	  • Benchmarking with other sports, with other countries
	  • Success ratios of coach education programmes
	• Characteristics of coach developers
	  • Holistic Quality Control (HQC)
	  • Courses
	  • Coach developers
	  • Exams
	• Obtained qualifications
	  • How many?
	  • Trends/Differences in age, gender, regions, sports
	  • Trends over time
	  • Trends in pathways
		• Characteristics
		  • How many? Is there a lack?
		  • Qualified vs. non-qualified
		  • Trends/Differences in age, gender, regions, sports, sports federations
		  • PE-qualifications of coaches
		• Trends over time
		  • Trend in number of qualified coaches (+ qualification %)
		  • Trend in number of sports clubs with > 1 qualified coach
		  • Trend in new coaches (after obtaining qualification)
		  • Trend in drop-out of active coaches
		• Correlation studies
		  • Drop-out coaches vs. qualification level
		  • Drop-out coaches vs. size of sports club/sports federation
		  • Drop-out coaches vs. drop-out of sports participants

FIGURE 15.1 Monitoring and evaluating input, throughput and output through FICOMS.

each combination. As a result, with one page on a dashboard, a user can view dozens of graphs with specific and tailored information. For more information on how FICOMS was made possible, see Ponnet et al. (2021).

FICOMS has been developed to monitor the input, throughput, and output of coaching in Flanders, so stakeholders can intervene when performance indicators change (see Figure 15.1). Regarding the input, the background of coaches (that is, age, gender, residence, sport, sports club, sports federation, and PE background) starting a coach education programme and the different pathways coaches follow in their coach education is monitored permanently. Evaluation work deals, for example, with questioning participation rates of specific coach education programmes and the extent to which desired target groups are reached.

Regarding the throughput, the characteristics of coach education programmes (that is, modules, items, hours, and success ratios), and coach developers (that is, age, gender, residence, courses, and theory vs. practice hours), any differences between sports are monitored and coach education programmes can be benchmarked with other countries (for more benchmarking work, see also North, 2016). It enables programme evaluators to undertake immediate action when outliers are detected (for example, high course hours and low success rates). An important performance indicator for sport policy in Flanders is how many coaches obtain a new qualification every year, with trends over time, pathways, or differences in gender, age, sports, and regions.

As part of FICOMS, a holistic quality control system is also integrated to follow up on the quality of the programmes, coach developers, assessment, and perceived workload. Coaches are empowered as important stakeholders, and their voice is taken into consideration before, during, and after their programme participation. Coach narratives are used as part of the programme enhancement process, particularly where it is felt the coaches' needs are not being met or where the coaches have difficulty in responding to the demands of the programme. In one example, this included using insight from FICOMS to design an intervention study intended to understand ways in which the critical reflection capabilities of coaches might be further improved (Vangrunderbeek et al., in review). That said, the most notable feature of FICOMS relates to monitoring and evaluating coach education programme output. This includes a better understanding of the characteristics of active coaches within Flanders' sports clubs. For example, the number of (qualified and nonqualified) active coaches, the number of sports clubs with or without a qualified coach, and notable differences between sports, sports federations, regions, gender, and age. An example of a dashboard (in English) illustrating the possibilities of FICOMS can be found here:

https://www.sport.vlaanderen/kennisplatform/thema-trainers/db-coaches-active-in-flanders-belgium/

The monitoring offered by FICOMS has proved to be invaluable for identifying problems at a high 'macroscopic'/extensive level and is also an important first step for further 'microscopic'/intensive evaluation work. FICOMS is a mechanism for problem setting (that is, describing 'what' is happening in the broader landscape), which provides a point of entry for further evaluation (that is, explaining the 'how' and 'why'). To illustrate this, we will elaborate on a recent evaluation study focused on coach dropout. To understand why coaches in Flanders leave coaching, it is essential to first identify the characteristics of your coaching workforce. Analysis of data from FICOMS revealed there has been a steady increase in the number of active coaches over the past five years in organised sports in Flanders. However, 21% (N = 14,277) of coaches (N = 67,878 in 2018) in 50 organised sports dropped out and did not coach in 2019. A similar dropout rate (average: 22%) was also found in subsequent years. More specifically, between 2014 and 2021 the dropout rate of non-qualified coaches is significantly higher than qualified coaches (that is, 2019: 26.3% vs. 13.9%). Results also revealed significant differences in dropout rate between coaches of different sports, the size of the sports club, age and gender of the coaches (Vangrunderbeek & Ponnet, 2021). FICOMS data clearly demonstrate the magnitude and complexity of the problem sports federations face in retaining their coaches. This is a first step in providing evidence that encourages further research to inform policy.

Based on this large-scale helicopter point of view by FICOMS, a qualitative, constructivist evaluation study was set up in a next phase to seek further understanding and meaning regarding the complex phenomenon of coach dropout. Using on FICOMS data, ten Flemish sports federations were selected by the evaluation team, based on a range from high to low dropout rates of coaches within their affiliated clubs. Each of these sports federations was sent an invitation by e-mail, including the general factsheet on dropout of coaches, to the general manager, sports technical director, and head of coach education. This included a request to co-construct knowledge on dropout of coaches by using semi-structured interview (one interview per sports federation). Each sports federation could propose one or more experts from within the sports federation (for example, professional staff members, volunteering board members) to take part in the interview. The following selection criteria were used:

1. Clear affiliation with the sports federation
2. Ability to speak on behalf of the sports federation
3. Affinity and/or expertise with sports federation's policy for sports coaches
4. Awareness of earlier fact sheet on coach dropout
5. Acceptance of the semi-structured interview questions beforehand (for preparation)

As the main goal of the interviews is to co-construct knowledge, no limitations were placed on the number of participants who took part in each interview. By engaging these stakeholders in a constructivist approach, the goal is to understand coach dropout in Flemish organised sports, so specific policy measures can be defined and put in place.

CASE STUDY 2 – THE FOOTBALL ASSOCIATION (ENGLAND)[1]

The FA is the national governing body for football, in England. As the sole not-for-profit lead agency for the sport, they bear several significant responsibilities. These include: the administration (leagues and laws) and resourcing (working with public and private partners for capital investment to sustain and grow the game) of the game, educate stakeholders (match officials, medical professionals, and coaches), recruit and retain participants (that is, through broad and inclusive participation initiatives), and prepare national teams for international competitions, such as the UEFA European Championship and the FIFA World Cup (McCarthy, 2022). However, of most relevance to this chapter is the work they undertake with coaches. According to Dempsey (2020), the FA contribute to the professional development of more than 30,000 coaches each year through large-scale coach education programmes.

Over recent decades, the FA have adopted a variety of approaches to the design and delivery of coach education programmes (Chapman et al., 2020) Broadly mapping against wider educational trends, learning opportunities for football coaches have shifted from behaviourist oriented to more socially oriented in nature (McCarthy et al., 2021b). This is not unusual, and similar examples occur in different federations across other countries (for example, Paquette & Trudel, 2018; Ciampolini et al., 2019). In 2016, consistent with this general trajectory, the FA redeveloped their existing portfolio of programmes, basing them on the principles of social constructivism; for example, learner-centredness, situated learning, and authentic assessment (McCarthy, 2022). Implications for one such programme, the FA Level 3 (UEFA B) in coaching football programme (the focus of this case study), are outlined clearly in Table 15.2. Changes to how coaches were assessed (that is, deemed competent and subsequently certified) represented the most significant shift in practice for the FA, which, regardless of underpinning approaches, assessed coaches in a simulated, end point, practical performance. Now, however, coaches would be assessed in a more ongoing and embedded, learning oriented, and meaningful manner through the completion of a practice-focused season-long coaching project. The project brief required coaches to demonstrate, over

TABLE 15.2 A summary of the changes made to the FA Level 3 (UEFA B) in coaching football project, which is the subject of evaluation in this case study

2016 and before	*2017 and after*	*Implications*
Centralised delivery at one location	Localised delivery at multiple locations	Delivery is scaled up significantly; from a handful of programmes per year, to near 50 nationwide
For coaches working in the professional game	For coaches working in the professional game *and* grassroots game	Once relatively homogenous cohorts, programmes are now comprised of coaches with radically different prior experiences, motivations, and goals
Coach educators work with coaches only at the programme venue	Coach educators work with coaches at the programme venue *and also* in their workplace (e.g., club)	Increased resource is required to enable coach educators to visit each coach three times. This is more geographically challenging in certain parts of the country
To complete the programme coaches should perform successfully, in a simulated, end point, practical assessment	To complete the programme coaches should complete an ongoing season-long applied coaching project, concerned with their club, their players, and themselves as a coach	Focus is now placed on assessment *as* learning, rather than assessment *of* learning. Navigating the project-based assessment opportunity requires different knowledge, skills, attitudes, and behaviours from both coaches and coach educators

> at least 18 linked training sessions and games, how they meet each of the 19 competencies that are categorised into five areas of importance (who we are, how we play, the future player, how we coach, and how we support) (The Football Association, n.d.).

The shift in approach to supporting the professional development of football coaches was prompted and driven by three primary causes and conditions. First, in 2014 a series of reports by the FA Chairman's Commission posed questions such as, "are coach awards and coach development processes strong and thriving in club academies?" (The Football Association, 2014, p. 36). In doing this, there was a clear inference the standard of football coaching in England was a fundamental cause in the failure of national teams in international competitions. Second, during and prior to the period of change, the FA introduced an organisational restructuring in which many people left and new people joined (McCarthy, 2022). As FA Education became the department responsible for supporting coaches through programmes, located at St George's Park (which became the FA's 'home' in 2012), there appeared to be a deliberate strategy to recruit from the wider field of educational professionals (that is, personnel joined from further education, higher education, and public policy and qualification settings) (McCarthy, 2022). Finally, during this period of organisational change, there was, according to McCarthy (2022), "an external coach education and assessment research narrative that was making the case for social constructivism as a theory of learning to guide the design and delivery of coach education programmes" (p. 127). Like any other organisation, there is no doubt the FA, and individuals within it, were susceptible to influence from these ideas.

From several pilot programmes, the FA sensed the programme was working, they wanted to further understand how and why it was working, and for whom/which coaches in particular. Due to the nature of the question, it was determined a 'critical realist informed' approach to evaluation would be used (see Table 15.1). Due to the scale of the evaluation opportunity, one feature of the programme would be the focus (see Table 15.2). Therefore, the question driving the evaluation was: What is it about project-based assessment (as a feature of the FA Level 3 [UEFA B] in coaching football programme) that works, in what context, for whom, how, and why? The intended outcome was a series of middle-range (Merton, 1968; Layder, 1998) ideas describing and explaining in which circumstances, and for which coaches, project-based assessment worked.

The evaluation was undertaken in two phases:

1. **Theory generating:** The aim of phase one of the research was to generate theories that described and explained how and why project-based assessment was intended to work, according to those responsible/programme architects. To do this, grey literature was examined (for example, The FA Learning

Strategy, The FA Level 3/UEFA B in Coaching Football Learner Journal, and FA Coach Competency Framework), those who were connected to the programme (for example, programme authors and people whose ideas had been influential in programme development) were interviewed, and relevant academic literature reviewed. This phase concluded with a list of 'programme theories' (Pawson & Tilley, 1997) that best reflected how project-based assessment should work and why. According to McCarthy (2022), "the purpose of this work is to identify underlying causal mechanisms which help to explain how and why project-based assessment is intended to bring about desirable outcomes for programme participants" (p. 108). Within this work, consideration was given to goals, higher-level, perspectives, strategies, and resources, using a language introduced by North (2017) in the embedded, relational, and emergent conception of sport coaching.

2. **Theory exploration:** The aim of phase two of the research was to explore these programme theories in three coach education programmes/contexts in England, to better understand how coaches and coach educators were reasoning with and responding to project-based assessment as it was intended. More than 90 hours, over nine months, was spent exploring these programme theories with key individuals in each delivery site. The outcome was a set of refined and revised middle-range theories that could *best* respond to the question driving the evaluation.

Guiding both phases of the research, adaptive theory (Layder, 1998) was a key feature of the research methodology and underpinned the research approach (see Figure 15.2). In an evaluation strategy that starts and ends with theory, adaptive cycles (Layder, 1998) enabled the evaluator to move from rudimentary, to advanced, refined, and sophisticated models of understanding (McCarthy, 2022). Acknowledging that, "we never enter research with a mind clear of theoretical ideas and assumptions" (Layder, 1998, p. 51), adaptive theory promotes the explicit use of theory to drive evaluation (phase one) with the intention of

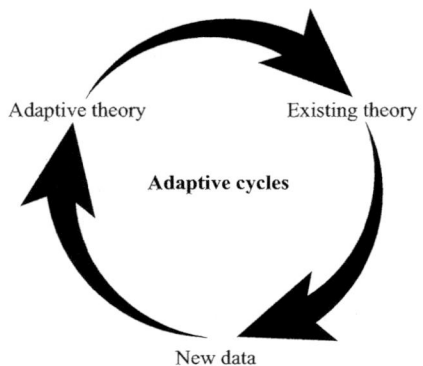

FIGURE 15.2 Adaptive theory (see Layder, 1998).

drawing on new data, existing, and the evaluator's deliberations and reflections, to develop ideas in which we have greater confidence (phase two).

From this critical realist informed evaluation project, three findings were reported to the FA to inform future coach education programme development work.

1. Project-based assessment, as a relatively open-ended activity with lots of autonomy, worked well for coaches who had a clear and shared understanding (with the coach educator) of what was required and what a good project looked like.
2. Project-based assessment, as a relatively sophisticated activity requiring the careful identification and curation of relevant information, worked well for coaches who arrived at the programme with experience and expertise in this type of activity.
3. Project-based assessment, as an approach to assessment underpinned by social learning theory, worked well for coaches who had a network of support and/or worked in a well-resourced and supportive coaching environment.

Conclusion

The purpose of this chapter is to promote the important, but sometimes overlooked, issue of coach education programme evaluation. Our argument starts with the widely accepted position that sport coaches are important and undertake societally meaningful work. To meet and maintain high standards of professional practice, coaches are supported through professional development programmes. However, in some cases, little is known about the efficacy of these programmes despite the increasing amount of value placed upon them (that is, by employers, deployers, and coaches themselves) and resources they can attract. It is reasonable that calls to undertake coach education programme evaluation work have increased over the last two decades; our aim is to amplify those calls to action with our own, while providing examples of how this work might be done. We hope this adds to the small number of excellent examples that already exist (see Muir et al., 2011; Duffy et al., 2013; North, 2016; Dohme et al., 2019; McCarthy, 2022).

Central to our case is the evaluation methodology of choice (tools to do the job) depends on both the goal of the evaluation (the job) and the view taken on coach education programmes (what is being evaluated). Table 15.1 offers some guidance on possible choices and implications. Further, we posit programme evaluation processes might be (where possible) built into the design of coach education programmes and enacted from the outset. This challenges the conception of evaluation as an after-thought, conducted in retrospect, and focused on findings for use later rather than now. Considering evaluation at the design and implementation stages of a programme has the potential to benefit and empower affected stakeholders.

Both case studies also made clear that evaluation work can both be conducted by internal or external evaluators and with a high level of stakeholder (participant) engagement. The evaluation of coach education programmes can be empowering and lead to learning and development for people working inside an organisation. As such, coach education organisations can establish an evaluation culture through commitment to self-examination, learning from and through experience, and the use of data-driven policy and practice decisions (Leahy, 2009). One advantage of an internally led evaluation exercise is the fact that the programme, organisation, and wider context is familiar. One could of course argue that external evaluators might be more objective (free of tacit organisational pre-conceptions). In some cases, internal evaluators are less costly and can promote the use of findings more effectively. To the contrary, in some cases internal members have little expertise of evaluation methodology and practice and are (unfortunately) usually too busy to spend much time and energy on evaluation work. This final point returns us to the purpose of this chapter, which is to platform, promote, and encourage the coach education community to prioritise this work.

Note

1 This case study represents a summary of a much larger and more sophisticated study by McCarthy (2022). While rudimentary processes and principles are outlined below, interested readers are encouraged to visit the original study for additional detail and guidance.

References

Cassidy, T., Potrac, P., & McKenzie, A. (2006). Evaluating and reflecting upon a coach education initiative: The CoDe of rugby. *The Sport Psychologist*, 20(2), 145–161. https://doi.org/10.1123/tsp.20.2.145.

Chapman, R., Richardson, D., Cope, E., & Cronin, C. (2020). Learning from the past: A Freirean analysis of FA coach education since 1967. *Sport, Education and Society*, 25(6), 681–697. https://doi.org/10.1080/13573322.2019.1654989.

Chesterfield, G., Potrac, P., & Jones, R. (2010). 'Studentship' and 'impression management' in an advanced soccer coach education award. *Sport, Education and Society*, 15(3), 299–314. https://doi.org/10.1080/13573322.2010.493311.

Ciampolini, V., Milistetd, M., Rynne, S. B., Brasil, V. Z., & Nascimento, J. V. (2019). Research review on coaches' perceptions regarding the teaching strategies experienced in coach education programs. *International Journal of Sports Science & Coaching*, 14(2), 216–228. https://doi.org/10.1177/1747954119833597.

Dempsey, N. M., Richardson, D. J., Cope E., & Cronin, C. J. (2020). Creating and disseminating coach education policy: A case of formal coach education in grassroots football. *Sport, Education and Society*, 26(8), 917–930.

Dohme, L. C., Rankin-Wright, A. J., & Lara-Bercial, S. (2019). Beyond knowledge transfer: The role of coach developers as motivators for lifelong learning. *International Sport Coaching Journal*, 6(3), 317–328. https://doi.org/10.1123/iscj.2019-0034.

Driska, A. P. (2018). A formative, utilization-focused evaluation of USA swimming's nationwide online coach education program. *International Sport Coaching Journal*, 5(3), 261–272. https://doi.org/10.1123/iscj.2017-0096.

Duffy, P., North, J., & Muir, B. (2013). Understanding the impact of sport coaching on legacy. *International Journal of Sport Policy and Politics*, 5(2), 165–182. https://doi.org/10.1080/19406940.2012.665380.

Erickson, K., Bruner, W. M., MacDonald, J. D., & Cote, J. (2008). Gaining insight into actual and preferred sources of coaching knowledge. *International Journal of Sports Science and Coaching*, 3(4), 527–538.

The Football Association (2014). *The FA Chairman's England Commission Report*. https://www.thefa.com/~/media/files/pdf/england/the-fa-chairmans-england-commission-report.ashx.

The Football Association (n.d.). *The playing and coaching philosophy of England teams*. Retrieved June 25, 2021, from http://www.thefa.com/learning/england-dna.

Gilbert, W., & Trudel, P. (1999). An evaluation strategy for coach education programs. *Journal of Sport Behavior*, 22(2), 234–250.

Griffiths, M. A., Armour, K. M., & Cushion, C. J. (2018). 'Trying to get our message across': Successes and challenges in an evidence-based professional development programme for sport coaches. *Sport, Education and Society*, 23(3), 283–295. https://doi.org/10.1080/13573322.2016.1182014.

International Council for Coaching Excellence Workgroup on Monitoring and Evaluating Coach Education Programs (2021, November 21). *Program Evaluation in Coach Education*. Presentation at the 13th International Council for Coaching Excellence Global Coach Conference, Lisbon, Portugal.

Layder, D. (1998). *Sociological practice: Linking theory and social research*. Sage.

Leahy, M. J., Thielsen, V., Millington, M. J., Austin, B., & Fleming, A. (2009). Quality assurance and program evaluation: Terms, models and applications in rehabilitation Administration. *Journal of Rehabilitation Administration*, 33(2), 69–82.

Lyle, J. (2021). Lessons learned from programme evaluations of Coach Development Programmes in the UK. *Canadian Journal for the Study of Adult Education*, 33(1), 35–49.

Mallett, J. C., Trudel, P., Lyle., & J. Rynne, B. S. (2009). Formal vs informal coach education. *International Journal of Sports Science and Coaching*, 4(3), 325–335.

McCarthy, L. (2022). *Coach education and assessment in football: A critical realist informed evaluation (Doctoral dissertation)*. Leeds Beckett University, Leeds, UK. https://figshare.leedsbeckett.ac.uk/articles/thesis/Coach_Education_and_Assessment_in_Football_A_Critical_Realist_Informed_Evaluation/20079551/1.

McCarthy, L., Allanson, A., & Stoszkowski, J. (2021a). Moving toward authentic, learning-oriented assessment in coach education. *International Sport Coaching Journal*, 8(3), 400–404. https://doi.org/10.1123/iscj.2020-0050.

McCarthy, L., Vangrunderbeek, H., & Piggott, D. (2021b). Principles of good assessment practice in coach education: An initial proposal. *International Sport Coaching Journal*, 1(aop), 1–11. https://doi.org/10.1123/iscj.2021-0009.

Merton, R. K. (1968). *Social theory and social structure*. Free Press.

Muir, R., Richards., Duffy, P., & North., J. (2011, November 7–13). *An evaluation of the International Community Coaching Education Systems – A review of the methodological approach and preliminary findings* [conference presentation]. Promoting Global Partnerships in Sport for Development Conference, Trinidad.

Nelson, L., Cushion, C., & Potrac, P. (2013). Enhancing the provision of coach education: The recommendations of UK coaching practitioners. *Physical Education and Sport Pedagogy*, 18(2), 204–218. https://doi.org/10.1080/17408989.2011.649725.

North, J. (2010). Using 'coach developers' to facilitate coach learning and development: Qualitative evidence from the UK. *International Journal of Sports Science & Coaching*, 5(2), 239–256. https://doi.org/10.1260/1747-9541.5.2.239.

North, J. (2016). Benchmarking sport coach education and development. In W. Allison, A. Abraham, & A. Cale (Eds.), *Advances in coach education and development: From research to practice* (1st ed.) (pp. 17–29). Routledge.

North, J. (2017). *Sport coaching research and practice: Ontology, interdisciplinarity and critical realism*. Routledge.
North, J., Piggot, D., Lyle, J., Lara-Bercial, S., Muir, B., Petrovic, L., Normal, L., Abraham, A., & Shaw, W. (2016). *Research study on the UEFA coaching convention*. Leeds Metropolitan University.
North, J., Piggott, D., Lara-Bercial, S., Abraham, A., & Muir, B. (2019). The professionalization of sport coaching. In R. Thelwell, & M. Dicks (Eds.), *Professional advances in sports coaching: Research and practice* (pp. 3–21). Routledge. https://doi.org/10.4324/9781351210980.
North, J., Piggott, D., Rankin-Wright, A., & Ashford, M. (2020). An empirical examination of UK coaches' issues and problems, and their support and advice networks. *International Sport Coaching Journal*, 7(3), 283–294. https://doi.org/10.1123/iscj.2019-0049.
Paquette, K., & Trudel, P. (2018a). The evolution and learner-centered status of a coach education program. *International Sport Coaching Journal*, 5(1), 24–36. https://doi.org/10.1123/iscj.2017-0038.
Pawson, R. (2013). *The Science of Evaluation: A realist manifesto*. Sage, LA and London.
Pawson, R., & Tilley, N. (1997). *Realistic evaluation*. Sage.
Piggott, D. (2012). Coaches' experiences of formal coach education: A critical sociological investigation. *Sport, Education and Society*, 17(4), 535–554. https://doi.org/10.1080/13573322.2011.608949.
Ponnet, H., Vangrunderbeek, H., & McCarthy, L. (2021). The Flemish Interactive Coaching Monitoring System. *International Sport Coaching Journal*, 8(2), 253–262. https://doi.org/10.1123/iscj.2020-0093.
Redgate, S., Porrac, P., Boocock, E., & Dalkin, S. (2020). Realist evaluation of the Football Association's post graduate diploma (PG Dip) in coach development. *Sport, Education and Society*, 27(3), 361–376. https://doi.org/10.1080/13573322.2020.1847066.
Santos, F., Camiré, M., MacDonald, D. J., Campos, H., Conceição, M., & Silva, A. (2019). Process and outcome evaluation of a positive youth development-focused online coach education course. *International Sport Coaching Journal*, 6(1), 1–12. https://doi.org/10.1123/iscj.2017-0101.
Stirling, A., Kerr, G., & Cruz, L. (2012). An evaluation of Canada's National Coaching Certification Program's Make Ethical Decisions coach education module. *International Journal of Coaching Science*, 6(2), 45–60.
Stodter, A., & Cushion, C. J. (2019). Evidencing the impact of coaches' learning: Changes in coaching knowledge and practice over time. *Journal of Sports Sciences*, 37(18), 2086–2093. https://doi.org/10.1080/02640414.2019.1621045.
Vangrunderbeek, H., De Backer, M., McCarthy, L., Buelens, E., & Ponnet, H. (2022). Developing critical reflection skills in a formal coach education programme. *International Sport Coaching Journal*. Online Advance Publication. https://doi.org/10.1123/iscj.2021-0068.
Vangrunderbeek, H., & Ponnet, H. (2020). The history of coach education in Flanders. *International Sport Coaching Journal*, 7(3), 380–389. https://doi.org/10.1123/iscj.2020-0049.
Vangrunderbeek, H., & Ponnet, H. (2021). Dropout of coaches in organised sports in Flanders (Belgium). *International Sport Coaching Journal*, 8(Supplement 1), S65.
Vella, S. A., Crowe, T. P., & Oades, L. G. (2013). Increasing the effectiveness of formal coach education: Evidence of a parallel process. *International Journal of Sports Science & Coaching*, 8(2), 417–430. https://doi.org/10.1260/1747-9541.8.2.417.
Williams, S. P., & Bush, A. J. (2019). Connecting knowledge(s) to practice: A Bernsteinian theorisation of a collaborative coach learning community project. *Sport, Education and Society*, 24(4), 375–389.

SECTION IV
Where Next for Coach Development?

Coaching has evolved considerably, and coach developers are critical links in this continuous development process. However, coach development is also an iterative process, so the role of coach developer will change as will the skills required. The actuality of supporting coaches will be different for every individual coach dependent on experience, knowledge, background motivation, and engagement.

We contend that coach developers need to be at the forefront of these developments, advocating for change, leading new initiatives and implementing programmes. Each of the chapter authors have their own views on coach development, and we have encouraged these throughout this book to present a range of views, contributing to the ongoing debate and discussion around coach development.

16
COACH DEVELOPERS AS AGENTS OF CHANGE

Christine Nash

There are numerous examples of top athletes using their success within the media to highlight numerous social issues, acting as agents of change. Who has not seen the images of John Carlos and Tommie Smith on the podium at the 1968 Olympics? Tennis stars Arthur Ashe and Billie Jean King were known for their political activism as well as their many titles and Muhammed Ali risked his career in boxing to protest against the Vietnam war. More recently, Colin Kaepernick, a starting quarterback for the San Francisco 49ers in the American National Football League, has become better known for 'taking the knee' than his passing skills. Since 2016 Colin has been a 'free agent' unable to find a team despite his undoubted talent, which has been widely attributed to his political activism and stance against perceived police brutality in the United States.

Sport is a political arena, and everyone involved from grass roots to elite level should be aware of this and understand how this shapes the experiences of many. Not everyone has the following to inculcate the types of change described here, especially at this stage, coach developers. From an organisational and professional perspective, it is clear a highly skilled coaching workforce is necessary and can be achieved by change, in the deployment of coach developers. However, change within any sporting context should not be approached lightly given the political and cultural tensions that exist at every level of sport (Stenling & Sam, 2019).

The concept of change agents originated in business, individuals who promote and support a new way of doing something within the company, also known as champions. This could be a new approach, suggesting a different business model, reorganisation or realignment of structures or transformational thinking. These advancements, based on evolving customer needs, new technologies and competitor analysis, influence business dynamics across industries. In business,

DOI: 10.4324/9781003251309-20

change is constant, so a key component of an effective business is a change management strategy.

Change agents do not necessarily need to belong to an organisation, although some establishments do expect managers, or their equivalent, to act as such as part of their remit. Change agents can emerge any part of an organisation, holding any job, but crucially with the right mix of skills and personality to advocate for the change process. Many businesses also hire external change agents, especially if the level of change required is extensive. Whether internal or external, these agents for change must be well respected by their peers and have an understanding of the organisation and project under review to facilitate a smoother transformation.

In Germany, Wolbring and colleagues (2021) considered the role of change agents within the physical activity arena. They identified four main drivers, each exerting a different influence such as policy decision-making:

- **Interpersonal:** For example, a teacher working with a class
- **Organisational:** For example, sports clubs
- **Community:** For example, urban planners
- **Societal:** For example, politicians

This list highlights a hierarchical sphere of influence; each of the examples shown has a growing magnitude of potential impact. It is reminiscent of the approach of Bronfenbrenner (1974) or Vygotsky (1978) where the emphasis is on social interactions at each level.

Much of the change research in the sporting contexts focusses on discrimination (Nogueira, Molinero, Salguero del Valle, Lucidi & Márquez, 2018), disability (Adeyanju, Sulieman & Yesufu, 2010) or behavioural issues (Spruit, van der Put, van Vugt & Stams, 2018). To date there is little information as to how this change is achieved within sport coaching.

Change Agents in Coaching

A number of chapters in this book have highlighted the need for coaches need to increase their knowledge base and keep learning. However, nowadays knowledge, and the possession of it, does not have the same power as previously. Information is easily available – new ideas and approaches become outdated quickly as they are accessible and easily shared. How can coaches and coach developers keep evolving their practice under these circumstances? Chapter 5 discussed how coach developers are considered 'the most important link in the chain' of coach education and development (Eade & Reid, 2015, p. 350). If this is the case, coach developers need to be agents of change. Laura Stack (2010, p. 6) highlighted the approach of 'Placing yourself in a new frame of mind requires stepping back, soul-searching, rethinking priorities, possibly defeating old personal roadblocks, and developing entirely new thought processes you can apply in all sorts of situations'. How many coach developers adopt this strategy?

What Is the Function of a Change Agent?

There are many roles a change agent can undertake, for example, a role model, a decision maker or a knowledge translator (Babey, Wolstein & Diamant, 2016; Straus, Tetroe & Graham, 2009; Butterfoss, Kegler & Francisco, 2008). Regardless of what the job title says there are some key functions considered vital to the change agent:

- How is the change going to benefit the organisation and those individuals affected?
- Identifying and clarifying the key steps involved in the change.
- Being a source of support during the change process.
- Evaluating the result to ensure the new process and procedures are working as expected and most importantly, ensuring change is delivering the anticipated returns.

The change agent essentially is the conduit between the organisation requesting the change and those impacted by the change. Regardless of what the job title says there are some key functions that need to be considered as vital to the change agent:

- **Well-developed interpersonal skills:** Coach developers would use these skills in their everyday remit of supporting coaches in their practice.
- **Good communication skills:** Again, coach developers would have honed these skills in a variety of challenging contexts while working with coaches on an individual basis or as a group. Coach developers are expected to connect and communicate both up and down within organisations.
- **Establish relationships:** Within every working environment, establishing relationships helps the coach developer better understand the motivations of individuals. Appreciating personal circumstances also demonstrates the coach developer is concerned about the whole person rather than just the coach. These relationships improve morale and encourage two-way communication.
- **Ability to prioritise:** The capacity to see the bigger picture and identify the key factors that will provide the biggest change.

None of the skills mentioned here would be beyond the scope of a coach developer so why is there not more advocacy for change within the system? Certainly, many change agents would also be required to have vision and confidence in their skills and abilities. However persuading organisations that coach developers could be uniquely placed to have considerable impact and transform elements of an organisation may take time.

Scenario	Questions
1 James is a coach developer who is self-employed and has been working with Hill Town Wanderers, a professional rugby club for the last two seasons. His remit covers all the coaches in the club, from minis to academy to first team. He has generally been working with all the coaches as a group but feels this is not effective. He wants to provide a more individualised approach but realises this will mean he needs to spend more time with the club. From his position this new approach has many benefits and no perceivable downside from James' perspective.	What is the best approach to advocate for change? What are the potential benefits and drawbacks of the proposed change? Why is the change necessary? Who will be affected?
2 Jane has recently started working with a regional swimming organisation as a coach developer. A new board has just been appointed and she is the first coach developer to be hired. She has the support of the board but feels that the established coaches within the organisation do not value or respect her input. There has been considerable change within this organisation recently, including the new board who want to change the direction of travel. Jane feels that this new vision has not been communicated well to the organisation and this may affect her ability to work with the coaches and make a difference.	Where/who will be the difficult to persuade individuals? How will these difficult to persuade individuals be convinced? How will the information be disseminated? How will feedback, concerns, ideas and questions be fed up and down? How will this change be evaluated?
3 Kit has been working within a youth soccer club for several years. One of the roles that s/he has embraced is coach development, although it is called certification and training at the club. Kit wants to achieve the Quality Mark offered by the national soccer association and has a plan ready to be implemented at the club. The problem seems to be the club response is 'This is the way we always do things' and shows no inclination to change.	

I doubt most coach developers have any experience of answering these questions. That may not be the fault of the coach developer but could be connected to the recruitment processes, policies and job remit employed by organisations. Many of the recent adverts and job specifications for coach developers concentrate on the sport rather than the learning and development expertise typically included in the role. A typical exemplar is provided below:

- Provide individualised support to identified coaches and coach developers to improve their coaching practice and behaviours.
- Provide bespoke/tailored coaching support to identified partners in 'sport'.
- Generate coaching content to support and evolve the 'sport' Coaching Offer.
- Oversee, develop and implement identified courses and workshops.

These four tasks reflect the UK coach development environment and perhaps other countries produce more nuanced information surrounding the expectations of the role.

If organisations were wanting to attract coach developers capable of implementing change, I would expect to see:

- **Knowledge base:** How diverse is this knowledge base? We need to attract individuals with novel ways of thinking, of approaching issues, not just with playing and/or coaching experience within one sport. I would advocate for an interdisciplinary knowledge base and a willingness to collaborate across cultures.
- **Extensive network:** Being part of a network is essential in many areas and coach development is no exception. However, linking to the previous point, I would suggest a network consisting of several disparate individuals, not just sport, as this provides a variety of opinions.
- **Adaptability:** This would include elements of flexibility, creativity and an openness to new ideas, highly desirable qualities in potential employees who can transform an organisation or culture.
- **Questioning:** In my view this means asking the tough questions and this can be especially hard if you do not know the answer and are relying on someone within the organisation to help.
- **Being brave:** I never really appreciated the importance of this until recently. A colleague of mine, Pelle Kvalsund, counts this as one of the key aspects he looks for in coach developers. He enjoys having courageous conversations and says it leads to clear decisions with no ambiguity.
- **Ambiguity:** Anything connected with sport is complex and coach developers must deal with uncertainty – they need to learn to fly by the seat of their pants! By this I mean a knowledge-based approach encompassing several possibilities, but this cannot be planned and prepared per se.

Incorporating some of these suggestions should shake things up a little and diversify the pool of coach developers. Job descriptions or remits could be carefully considered to incorporate more non-sport-related content plus interview questions or tasks could be refined to investigate some of these elements.

Why Is Change Important?

A change agent serves a distinct role within a change initiative as a proponent of the change, as well as a conduit between leadership and the rest of the organisation. In the current sporting landscape, the coach's role within the delivery of a sporting organisation's strategy is vital to its success (Rynne, Crudgington, Dickinson & Mallett, 2017). Associated with this is the importance of the coach developer within this process although there is little research in this area, particularly in the realm of high-performance sport (Gibson & Groom, 2019). Cruickshank and Collins (2012) agree with this and conclude the lack of research and understanding of organisational change is a matter of concern, particularly as it relates the support offered to the coach during the process of change. Achieving change will only succeed if the coaches are involved in and buy into the process, so working with coach developers with and through the coaches is critical. Many business environments undertaking change have limited support services available to those employees affected, with the general response branded as 'cheerleading'. This approach is easier to implement than mentoring, peer support programmes or well-being courses that have been shown to work (Smollan, 2017).

In my experience there is a level of interconnectedness between coaches, coach education and coach development systems – why reinvent the wheel? Change does not always mean a complete reinvention. I am a dog owner and have certain walks my dog and I go on regularly. Sometimes to shake things up we change direction and reverse the loop; I am constantly amazed by the different things I notice just by changing direction. Most people are drivers and have also been passengers in cars. When you are a driver, you must concentrate on traffic lights, other road users, pedestrians, dogs and where you are headed. With all this going on, there is little opportunity to look at other things. As a passenger you have the luxury of being able to look at the scenery, houses, shops or countryside. Although both driver and passenger are travelling the same route, both have different perspectives. What does this have to do with coach development? The examples here, reversing the route of a dog walk and being a driver or a passenger in a car, can have implications for the coach developer and how they can change their approach or delivery. If it is not possible to make wholesale changes to content, modifying an approach by changing the order of the content, 'reversing the loop', should prove beneficial for the coach developer and the coach/es concerned. The driver of the car dictates the direction so can we allow the passengers, in this case the coach/es to set the agenda and provide a changed perspective for the coach and coach developer. We must also bear in mind much coach development can now take place in a number of different formats – online, face-to-face and blended. This again alters the perceptions of coaches and perhaps challenges them to think differently. This is an area Chapter 2 suggested needs further investigation.

There are, of course, organisations and cultures that require wholesale change, and previous experience with coach education and development programmes has shown this to be badly received. Although some of that resistance could be down to the communication of the message rather than the content, in practice many people fear change for a variety of reasons (Allen, Schepker & Chadwick, 2022). New Zealand Sport commissioned a review of seven sports that had experienced change due to political, internal or financial issues. Lessons learned from the review process informed other sports (Gryphon Governance Consultants, n.d.). Similarly, a study of University Sport across Canada concluded the effectiveness of an organisation can be impacted by change to varying degrees dependent on the approach adopted (Thompson & Parent, 2021). The United Kingdom attempted to enforce change to the coaching structure with the introduction of the United Kingdom Coaching Certificate. This did not succeed as anticipated due to lack of buy-in from certain sports plus a confused four countries approach.

Webb, Collins and Cruickshank (2016) recognise the implementation of coherent coaching programmes will necessitate a 'step change' in the coach development offerings in many sports and organisations. They advocate 'the use of change agents to increase the volume and quality of coach engagement' (p. 1805). I believe we should examine that statement carefully – why should coaches not be engaged with their own development? Many of the current methods said to engage individuals require a significant participation and commitment in their own learning processes.

Mentoring

Mentoring has long been championed in many areas of work as a development tool that can change the culture of an organisation. However, many mentoring programmes advocated by workplaces are little more than buddy systems where a perception exists that the exposure to an individual with more experience (or time served) is both willing and able to structure the growth of another. There is no doubt that properly planned and administered mentoring programmes can be a useful tool for coach development but there would be certain caveats to this (McQuade, Davis & Nash, 2015).

In my experience there must be clear criteria around expectations from both mentor and mentee or else the whole process and subsequent development tends to drift. Olsson, Cruickshank and Collins (2017, p. 52) consider 'mentoring is often portrayed as a process of listening, questioning, and facilitating, as distinct from telling, restricting, and directing' but continue by suggesting coach developers may need to revisit their own conceptions of knowledge as 'cognitive excellence is impossible without excellent knowledge on how it is best acquired!' (p. 53).

The medical profession has a history of formal mentoring programmes rather than informal as they feel there is potential for exclusion of certain individuals and groups with the organic approach (Croke, Tosoni & Ringash, 2021). General surgery doctors work long hours, suffer burnout and have a high dropout rate, so the success of a formal mentoring programme addressing these concerns, particularly among female residents, is encouraging (Bingmer, Wojnarski, Brady, Stein, Ho & Steinhagen, 2019). The key elements of formal mentoring programmes include:

- What are the learning objectives?
- What is the timeframe?
- What are the rules of engagement?
- What training/support is offered?

Developing a formal mentoring programme while considering these questions will enable those tasked with implementing the programme to view mentoring through a critical lens. Setting up a mentoring programme does not ensure coaches will develop so what are the criteria for success within the programme.

Much of this depends on who the programme is designed for – novice coach, expert coaches or coaches somewhere else on the spectrum.

Professional Conversation

Professional conversations essentially are any conversations between two professionals talking about their work rather than daily events or sporting results. The definition of professional is also important. As other chapters have discussed, coach and coach developers have a wide range of sources of information, so the 'professionals' do not need to be from the same or even similar domains. We would expect coaches and coach developers to speak with each other, with support staff, such as psychologists, performance analysts and dieticians. However, similarities exist in many professions and often different solutions can be transferred from one domain to another through professional conversations. We learn socially, from one another, so these professional conversations are important to initiate the development of new knowledge and the making sense of this new information by contextualising and applying into practice (see Chapter 9).

Professional conversation is a term used in education and teaching as a method for effecting positive change. Professional conversations are more successful when evidence informed rather than a vague notion about any issues (Timperley, 2008). Segal, Lefstein and Vedder-Weiss (2018) define effective professional conversations as:

- Focussed on problems of practice
- Involving evidence, for example video or reflections
- Capturing varying perspectives
- Necessitating reasoning, interpretation and justification
- Challenging by weighing critique and support

These conversations can either be informal or formal; there is merit in each as well as being a useful tool for the coach developer. However, these types of conversations are critical to the development of adaptive expertise (see Chapter 10).

Pragmatism

There are a growing number of coach developers and researchers in coach development who advocate pragmatism. This can be a useful perspective for coaching and the coach developer, especially from an applied viewpoint. Pragmatism is a philosophical movement based in the notion that a position or approach is true if it works satisfactorily in practice and achieves results.

According to Cruickshank and Collins (2017), there has been a rise in pragmatic coaches due to the scientific-practitioner approach encouraged by involvement in higher education. This has caused many coaches to question, tweak and adapt their routines in a constant endeavour to better their practice. This forms the basis of pragmatism with the contribution of reflective practice to guide operational decisions based on 'what will work best' in finding answers for the many questions of practice that arise. At the heart of this is an expertise approach to coach development allowing pragmatic coaches to conduct research in innovative and dynamic ways to find solutions to problems of practice.

Co-creation

Knowledge has become easily accessible recently, causing many organisations and businesses to question their methods. This has resulted in change to many traditional business practices and an emphasis on innovation. Within the context of coach development there are many exciting opportunities presented by co-creating knowledge in conjunction with the coach learners. Consider the benefits of coaches working in partnership with coach developers to create meaningful learning experiences based upon unique problems of practice. There is potential for coaches to accelerate their learning (see Chapter 10) by harnessing the resources readily available in all mediums; virtual networks, online communities, expert mentors and existing partners.

There are some key features typifying co-creation; these include knowledge that is:

- Constructed collaboratively
- Interdisciplinary
- Encouraging creative thinking
- Enhances engagement
- Personalised to each learner
- Providing open access to resources
- Easily disseminated to others

Mehrpouya, Maxwell and Zamora (2013) identified four areas requiring further investigation before co-creation achieves full potential. These include:

- **Openness and clear responsibilities:** Individuals do not work in the same manner or even at the same times. Coaches collaborating from different time zones, for example, need to appreciate that not everyone follows the same working patterns. However, if responsibilities are clarified and agreed then all involved can contribute at times that suit them.
- **Participative leadership:** This model of leadership is often defined as a flat structure with no hierarchy and everyone sharing collective decision-making. In reality this collaborative style is hard to achieve, especially if coach developers are involved in the process as they can be viewed as leaders or sitting at the top of the hierarchy.
- **Sense of shared ownership:** Shared ownership is a difficult concept in business but generally easier within the context of sport coaching. However,

it is difficult to gauge the impact of the emotional and intellectual ownership invested in a project.
- **Efficient use of skillsets:** Given the collaborative nature of these co-created projects there are opportunities for everyone involved to contribute according to their strengths. This is an effective use of available resources.

Within sport coaching, Horne and colleagues found there was limited understanding between youth sport coaches and parents when it came to co-creation and suggest 'youth sport providers implement strategies designed to increase parent-coach interaction as a means to enhance alignment and co-creation' (2022, p. 16). Milistetd, Peniza, Trudel and Paquette (2018, p. 10) consider 'coaching expertise involves a process of becoming without a clear learning path' but do acknowledge the importance of influential individuals in developing coaches' knowledge.

In Summary

According to Schulenkorf (2010) change agents hold several key roles and responsibilities in the development process. Coach developers are ideally placed to lead change; they are influencers, influencing coaches who in turn influence participants and players and parents, sometimes a whole community! Coach developers will develop resources, build trust, network and lead change. Sport is changing and coaching is evolving, so it is critical for coaches and coach developers to stay relevant. There has been a noticeable shift from the traditional concepts of coach education to coach learning and development. As mentioned before in this chapter change, particularly substantial change, is never easy or straightforward.

This chapter has demonstrated the change process and putting coaches and coach developers at the centre of this process. It has examined (and re-examined) some of the ways in which coach developers can effect change. One of the key takeaways would be not being afraid to try something new. This could be a risk and could lead to failure but what if it works? Being an agent of change and for change is about trying new ideas and practices so failing is always a possibility.

Schmidt and Stoneham (2020, p. 294) present their view of sport post 2030 saying 'The gear, training, coaching, playing, watching, and betting on sports will all be "smarter" and will further sophisticate the competition between people, between machines, between cyborgs, or as a mixed form'. This short-term vision will necessitate considerable change to the practice of all involved in sport, coaches and coach developers included.

References

Adeyanju, F.B., Sulieman, M.A. & Yesufu, A. (2010). The role of sport as a change agent in the lives of women with disabilities: The Nigerian experience. *British Journal of Sports Medicine, 44*(Suppl 1), i79–i79.

Allen, W. D., Schepker, D.J. & Chadwick, C. (2022) Firms' responses to changes in frictions in related human capital factor markets. *Strategic Management Journal*, 43(7), 1347–1373.

Babey, S.H., Wolstein, J. & Diamant, A.L. (2016). Adolescent physical activity: role of school support, role models, and social participation in racial and income disparities. *Environmental Behavior*, 48(1), 172–191.

Bingmer, K., Wojnarski, C.M., Brady, J.T., Stein, S.L., Ho, V.P. & Steinhagen, E. (2019). A model for a formal mentorship program in surgical residency. *The Journal of Surgical Research*, 243, 64–70.

Bronfenbrenner, U. (1974). Developmental research, public policy, and the ecology of childhood. *Child Development*, 45(1), 1–5.

Butterfoss, F.D., Kegler, M.C. & Francisco, V.T. (2008). Mobilizing organizations for health promotion: theories of organizational change. In K. Glanz, B.K. Rimer & K. Viswanath (eds.) *Health behavior and health education: Theory, research, and practice*. 4th ed. San Francisco, CA: Jossey-Bass. pp. 335–361.

Croke, J., Tosoni, S. & Ringash, J. (2021). 'It's Good for the Soul:' Perceptions of a Formal Junior Faculty Mentorship Program at a Large Academic Cancer Centre. *Radiotherapy and Oncology*, 162, 119–123.

Cruickshank, A. & Collins, D. (2012). Change management: The case of the elite sport performance team. *Journal of Change Management*, 12(2), 209–229. DOI: 10.1080/14697017.2011.632379

Cruickshank, A. & Collins, D. (2017). Beyond "crude pragmatism" in sports coaching: Insights from C.S. Peirce, William James, and John Dewey: A commentary. *International Journal of Sports Science & Coaching*, 12(1), 70–72.

Eade, A. & Reid, B. (2015). The role of the coach developer in supporting and guiding coach learning: A commentary. *International Sport Coaching Journal*, 2(3), 350–351.

Gibson, L. & Groom, R. (2019). The micro-politics of organisational change in professional youth football: Towards an understanding of "actions, strategies and professional interests." *International Journal of Sports Science & Coaching*, 14(1), 3–14.

Gryphon Governance Consultants (n.d.). *Organisational change in seven selected sports: What can be learned and applied?* Prepared for SPARC, Sport and Recreation New Zealand. https://sportnz.org.nz/media/1827/organisational-change-in-seven-selected-sports.pdf. Accessed 31st August, 2022.

Horne, E., Lower-Hoppe, L. & Green, B.C. (2022). Co-creation in youth sport development: Examining (mis)alignment between coaches and parents. *Sport Management Review* (ahead-of-print), 1–22. DOI: 10.1080/14413523.2022.2050107

McQuade, S., Davis, L. & Nash, C. (2015). Positioning mentoring as a coach development tool: recommendations for future practice and research. *Quest*, 67(3), 317–329.

Mehrpouya, H., Maxwell, D. & Zamora, D. (2013). Reflections on co-creation: An open source approach to co-creation. *Participations: Journal of Audience & Reception Studies*, 10(2), 172–182.

Milistetd, M., Peniza, L., Trudel, P. & Paquette, K. (2018). Nurturing high-performance sport coaches' learning and development using a narrative-collaborative coaching approach. *LASE Journal of Sport Science*, 9(1), 6–38.

Nogueira, A., Molinero, O., Salguero del Valle, A., Lucidi, F. & Márquez, S. (2018). Identification of gender discrimination in sports: Training of agents of change. *Revista de Psicología Del Deporte*, 27(3), 43.

Olsson, C., Cruickshank, A. & Collins, D. (2017) Making mentoring work: The Need for rewiring epistemology. *Quest (National Association for Kinesiology in Higher Education)*, 69(1), 50–64.

Rynne, S., Crudgington, R., Dickinson, R.K. & Mallett, C.J. (2017). On the (potential) value of coaching. In J. Baker, S. Cobley, J. Schorer & Nick Wattie (eds.) *Routledge handbook of talent identification and development in sport*. Abingdon: Routledge. pp. 285–300.

Schmidt, S.L. & Stoneham, K. (2020). Beyond 2030: What sports will look like for the athletes, consumers, and managers. In S.L. Schmidt (ed.) *21st Century sports. Future of business and finance*. Cham: Springer.

Schulenkorf, N. (2010). The roles and responsibilities of a change agent in sport event development projects. *Sport Management Review*, 13(2), 118–128.

Segal, A., Lefstein, A. & Vedder-Weiss, D. (2018). Appropriating protocols for the regulation of teacher professional conversations. *Teaching and Teacher Education*, 70, 215–226.

Smollan, R.K. (2017). Supporting staff through stressful organizational change. *Human Resource Development International*, 20(4), 1–23.

Spruit, A., van der Put, C., van Vugt, E. & Stams, G. (2018). Predictors of intervention success in a sports-based program for adolescents at risk of juvenile delinquency. *International Journal of Offender Therapy and Comparative Criminology*, 62(6), 1535–1555.

Stack, L. (2010). *SuperCompetent: The six keys to perform at your productive best*. Hoboken, NJ: John Wiley & Son, Inc.

Stenling, C. & Sam, M.P. (2019) From 'passive custodian' to 'active advocate': Tracing the emergence and sport-internal transformative effects of sport policy advocacy. *International Journal of Sport Policy and Politics*, 11(3), 447–463.

Straus, S.E., Tetroe, J. & Graham, I. (2009) Defining knowledge translation. *Canadian Medical Association Journal*, 181(3–4), 165–168.

Thompson, A. & Parent, M.M. (2021). Understanding the impact of radical change on the effectiveness of national-level sport organizations: A multi-stakeholder perspective. *Sport Management Review*, 24:1, 1–23.

Timperley, H. (2008) Evidence-informed conversations making a difference to student achievement. In *Professional learning conversations: Challenges in using evidence for improvement*. [Online]. Dordrecht: Springer Netherlands. pp. 69–79.

Vygotsky, L.S. (1978). *Mind in society: The development of higher psychological processes*. Cambridge, MA: Harvard University Press.

Webb, V., Collins, D. & Cruickshank, A. (2016). Aligning the talent pathway: exploring the role and mechanisms of coherence in development. *Journal of Sports Sciences*, 34(19), 1799–1807.

Wolbring, L., Reimers, A.K., Niessner, C., Demetriou, Y., Schmidt, S.C.E., Woll, A. & Waesche, H. (2021). How to disseminate national recommendations for physical activity: A qualitative analysis of critical change agents in Germany. *Health Research Policy and Systems*, 19(1), 78–78.

INDEX

Note: Page numbers with *italics* indicate the figure and **bold** for table and page numbers with "n" for notes.

Abbe, A. 218–219, 221–222, 224, 232
abductive approaches to sensemaking 137–138; *see also* sensemaking
ability to prioritise 255
Aboriginal coaches 200
Aboriginal people 200
Aboriginal Sports Coaches, Communities, and Culture (Marlin) 200–201
Aboriginal voices 200
Abraham, A. 93
Accelerated Expertise (Hoffman, Ward, Feltovich, DiBello, Fiore and Andrews) 151
accurate social perceiver 218
adaptive expertise 162–163
adaptive theory 246, *246*
Adler, A. B. 157
adult learning theory 72, 73; *see also* learning
Aeschylus 223
African Union Sport Council Region 5 44
After Action Review (AAR) 157
Alder, J. P. 184, 187, 192
Ali, M. 253
Alizadeh, S. 217, 219
Allan, V. 203, 205
Andrews, D. H. 151
antecedent variables 222
appreciative inquiry (AI) 94

apprenticeship 104–116; characteristics, specificities, and models 107–109; contributions of andragogy 105–107; learning organizations 109–111; overview 104–105; promotion of learning organizations 112–115; theoretical foundation 105–112
Aristotle 185
Asanović, A. 45
Ashe, A. 253
Ashmore, R. D. 217
Austin, R. B. 152
Australian Sports Commission 19, 23

Bailey, C. 128
Bailin, S. 120
Bales, J. D. 70, 78
Barkell, J. 154
Bartone, P. T. 157
Becker, A. J. 127
BIPOC: coach developer 207; coaches 201; women 202
Black Canadian Coaches Association (BCCA) 202
Black Female Coach Mentorship Programme (BFCMP) 198, 202, 203
Bodilly, S. 160
Brasil, V. Z. 78
Brazil: coach development in 39–42; coach education in *40*; coaching as

profession in 42; continuous training 41–42; initial training 40–41; internships 40–41; Physical Education programs in 40–41; sport governing bodies 78
Brazilian Olympic Committee (BOC) 40, 41, 42
Brazilian Rugby Confederation 42
Bronfenbrenner, U. 254
Brown, S. J. 160
building progressive learning paths 163

Cale, L. 92
Callary, B. 79
Campbell, S. M. 77
capacity for navigating cultures 163
capitonym 55
career development: of elite coach developers 19–34; idiosyncratic pathway 20; *see also* coach developers (CDs)
caring relationships 70
Carlos, J. 253
Carson, F. 74
case study: De Highden, M. 20–23; expertise 161–162; Football Association (England) 243–245; International Tennis Federation (ITF) academy 91–92, 97–99; Lithuanian Tennis Union (LTU) 95–96; Olympic sport national governing body 186–187; Pickleball 169–181; sensemaking 144; supporting coach's development in multi-sport context 191–192; Taylor, J. 24–26; Vlaamse Trainers school 240–243; Woodburn, A. 27–29
Cassidy, T. 108
change agents: adaptability 257; ambiguity 257; being brave 257; coach developers (CDs) as 253–262; in coaching 254–255; co-creation 261–262; concept of 253; extensive network 257; function of 255–257; importance of 257–259; knowledge base 257; mentoring 259–260; overview 253–254; pragmatism 260–261; professional conversations 260; questioning 257
Charlton, J. I. 206
chartered coach developer 15–16; *see also* coach developers (CDs)
Chartered Institute for Management of Sport and Physical Activity (CIMSPA) 19
Chavan, M. 217, 219
Chiu, C. 224
Ciampolini, V. 78

Cichy, R. M. 159
cisgender 197, 206, 210n1
Club Philosophy 110
Cnann 176
coach(es): Aboriginal 200; challenge for 121, 201; as critical consumers 120–121; curious 127–128; dispositions 122–128; good 3; of high-performance athletes 3; knowledge and skillset 142; knowledge areas *54*; knowledge auditing for 87–101; knowledge transfer 6; learner 6; learning 151, 192–193; lesbian 201; perceptions of coach developers 31–33; practical application for 141; practical applications for 222–233; primary functions of 56; self-awareness 4; support on-the-job 7; values and beliefs 123–124; voluntary 3; women/female 199, 202
Coach Analysis and Interventions System (CAIS) 142
coach-centred approach 11–12
coach-centred design criteria **12**
coach-centred facilitation 6
coach developer role: contextual 71; defined 69–70, *70*, 71; within sport system 70–72
coach developers (CDs): affective factors 159–160; analysis and selection 9–10; assessment and evaluation 76; attributes of **10**; career development of 19–34; as change agents 253–262; chartered 15–16; CIMSPA about 19; coach-centred approach 11; coach education leadership 14; coaches perceptions of 31–33; coach support in field 13; continuous treadmill 33; described/defined 3, 15; development of 29–31, 68–79; educational design 72–73; effective 4, 9; essential knowledge 72–74; essential skills 74–76; as expert support practitioners 133; global reach of 16–17; group facilitation 13; high-performance sport system for 183; implications 78–79; independent/self-employed 26; individual journeys 76–78; learning and behavioural change 13; mentoring 76; missing links 76–78; outcome 11; overview 3–4; pathway 14–16, *16*; personal and professional skill and development 14; practical applications for 141–142, 222–233; professional practice *14*; programme monitoring and evaluation 13; role of *5*, 19, 133; selected and trained

8; senior 15; sensemaking for 133–145; system approach 76–78; system builder 183–194; trainers of 16; training 8, 10–12; workforce 4
coach development 5; in Brazil 39–42; coach education and 53–63; De Highden, M. 21, 22; diversification of 197–209; evolution of systems 49–50; flexible structure 47; in high-performing sport system 190–191; implications for 129; individualized 48; international perspectives on 36–50; in Japan 36–39; learning environments 47–48; minority groups, experiences of 201; ongoing 49; opportunities 90; organisational goals 23; pathway 47–49; Taylor, J. 24–25; transitions into 68–79; trends in 9; in the US 42–43; USCCE about 19; vignettes **158**; Woodburn, A. 27, 28; in Zambia 43–47
coach education 5; in Brazil *40*; changes in 7; coach development and 53–63; contextual learning 61–62; De Highden, M. 22; emerging profession 59–60; evidence-informed coaching 62–63; formal learning 6; informal learning 6; leadership 14; learning 6, 54–55; overview 53–54; professional development 60; programmes 8; science to override empiricism 56–59; standards of professionalism 60; trends override science 55–56; universal learning 60–61; unmediated learning 6; Woodburn, A. 28; workshop 7; *see also* coach education programmes (CEPs)
coach education programme evaluation 236–248; approaches to **238**; case study 240–245; methodology 238–247; worked scenarios 239
coach education programs (CEPs) 104; *see also* coach education
coaching: as an isolating environment for women 199; De Highden, M. 21; effective 152; evidence-informed 62–63, 121–122; experience 126; overview 3–4; sport 154; stereotypes 63; Taylor, J. 24; universal learning within 60–61; Woodburn, A. 27
Coaching Association of Canada (CAC) 202, 208
coaching effectiveness 29, 216, 218, 223, 231
cognitive flexibility 162
collective decision-making 261
Collins, A. 108, 160

Collins, D. 124, 134, 190, 257, 259, 260
Collins, K. 226
Collins, L. 124
Collins D. 160
Colombian Tennis Federation (FCT) 97
communication skills 255; *see also* skills
Community of Practice (CoP) 128
competition/real-life arena 155
complexity in high-performance sport 185–186
contextual learning 61–62; *see also* learning
Continuous Coach Development (CCD) 23
conversations: change agents 260; critical thinking 128; professional 260
Conway, G. E. 162
Cope, E. 119
Côté, J. 56, 61, 74, 218, 223
Crenshaw, K. 197–198
Crespo, M. 49
critical coach: challenge for 121
criticality, defined 120
critical race theory 198, 200
critical thinking: characterization 120; coaches as critical consumers 120–121; in coaching 119–129; coach's values and beliefs 123–124; conversations 128; development 129; evidence-informed coaching 121–122; potential sources of knowledge 124–126
Cropley, B. 29
Cruickshank, A. 257, 259, 260
cultural competence 215, 216–218; behavioural indicator 228; conceptual frameworks for 219–222, *221*; defined 217; in health care 217; language and 222; in social work practice 217; stereotype rationality 217
cultural self-awareness 223
culture, defined 215
Culver, D. M. 49, 119
Cunningham, G. B. 200
curious coach 127–128
curricular extension projects (CEP) 41
curricular pedagogical practices (CPP) 40–41
Cushion, C. J. 92, 119, 142
Cynefin framework 136

Dagenais, C. 124
Daly, P. 92
Data Frame (DF) model 137, 138, *139*
De Bosscher, V. 185
decision-making skills 74, 106; capability 134; collective 261; policy 254;

professionals' 109; scenarios in life-or-death situations 186; sensemaking 143; unconscious bias in 200
De Highden, M. 20–23
de la Garza, J. M 152
Del Boca, F. K. 217
Dempsey, N. M. 243
Denison, J. 55
Dervin, B. 136
Dewey, J. 120
DiBello, L. 151, 152
disability 201–202
Disney, R. 225
Disney, W. 225
diversification of coach development 197–209; approaches to learning and development 206–208; language 203–206; overview 197–198; recruitment 198–203; view of coach developer 208–209
diversifying approaches: to learning and development 206–208
diversifying language 203–206; transgender language reform 205–206; vignette 206
diversifying recruitment 198–203; Black Female Coach Mentorship Programme (BFCMP) 202; disability 201–202; gender 199–200; practice 202–203; race 200–201; sexuality 201
Dixon, M. 29
Dohme, L. C. 75, 237
Dowling, M. 173, 176
Dray, K. 75
driven benevolence 225
Duarte, T. 49, 111
Dubois, C. 200

Eaton, S. E. 125
effective coaching 152; *see also* coaching
efficient use of skillsets 262; *see also* skills
elite athletes 20
Ennis, R. H. 120
enquiring mind 127–128
epistemology 123, 134–135
Evidence-Informed Coaching (EIC) 62–63; components and importance of **122**; defined 121–122; evidence-based practice 122; fundamental aspect of 126
expectation management 125–126
experiential learning 178; *see also* learning
expertise: accelerated 151–164; adaptive 162–163; case study 161–162; debrief as feedback 157; feedback 156; knowledge in coaching 152–153; learning to optimise 153–154; practice environments 154–155; principles for 151–164; retention 160; transferability 158–160

FA Level 3 (UEFA B) **244**, 244–246
Federation Internationale de Gymnastique (FIG) 174
feedback 156; challenge of 157; debriefing 157
Feltovich, P. J. 151
Ferrero Camoletto, R. 178
Finnish sport organisations 23
Fiore, S. M. 151
Flemish Interactive Coaching Monitoring System (FICOMS) 240–243, *241*
Football Association (England) 243–247
formalisation 173
formal learning 4, 6–7, 13, 32, 44, 47–49, 55, 75; *see also* learning
Forshaw, T. 162
Fuller, A. 107

Gallegos, J. S. 217
Garvin, D. A. 109, 110, 112
Gearity, B. 79
gender 199–200
General Framework for Cross-Cultural Competence (Abbe) 219
Gilbert, W. 56, 61, 74, 218, 223
Gonzalez, E. 162
good coaches 3
Gore, J. 162
governance 173–174
Griffith, C. 59
Griffiths, P. J. 29
Grotzer, T. A. 162, 163
group facilitation 13
Guile, D. 107
gymnastics 21

Hall, E. T. 216
Hammett, G. 157
Hattie, J. 122, 127
Hedlund, D. P. 133
hedonism 226, 227
Higgins, S. 156
Higher Education Institutions (HEIs) 8
high-performing (HP) 184
high-performing sport system 183–194; building 183; case study 186–187, 191–192; coach development in 190–191; coaching and 185; complexity 185–186; definition of 183–184; evolution of 183–184; investment in coach

learning 192–193; models of 188–190; US *190*
Hill, J. G. 186
Hoffman, R. R. 151, 162
Hofstede, G. 219–220, 222, 224
Hofstede's model 218–219
Holum, A. 160
homologous reproduction theory (HRT) 199
Horgan, P. 92
Horne, E. 262
Howells, K. 75
Huang, K. 221
Hutton, R. 162

independent/self-employed coach developers 26; *see also* coach developers (CDs)
individualized coach development 48; *see also* coach development
infopollution 89
informal learning 4, 6, 48, 55, 56, 104; *see also* formal learning; learning
informal mentoring relationships 4; *see also* relationships
infoxication 89
Ingold, T. 136
institutional work 176
intercultural effectiveness 218–219; conceptual frameworks for 219–222
International Coach Developer Framework (ICDF) 3–4, 13, 15, 16, 48
International Council for Coaching Excellence (ICCE) 6–7, 8, 15, 17, 28, 36, 44, 53, 72, 92, 237
International Sport Coaching Degree Standards 8
International Sport Coaching Framework (ISCF) 53, 56, *57*
International Tennis Federation (ITF) academy 91–92, 97–99
internships 40–41, 48
interpersonal knowledge 37, 38
interpersonal skills 255; *see also* skills
intrapersonal knowledge 37
Ito, M. 38–39
Ivan Drago 184

Jackson, P. 59
Jacobs, A. M. 159
Japan: coach development in 36–39; Coaching Consortium in 38; school education in 38
Japan Amateur Athletic Association 36
Japan Basketball Association 37, 39
Japan Sports Association (JSPO) 36–37, 38

Japan Sports Association Official Sports Coaching System 37
Jenkin, C. R. 172
Jones, E. 59

Kaepernick, C. 253
Kaiser, D. 159
Key performance indicators (KPIs) 94
Kikulis, L. M. 173
kinesiology 72, 73, 74
King, B. J. 253
Klein, G. 140
Klinsmann, J. 59
Kluckhohn, C. 219, 221, 230
knowledge: change agents 257; coach(es) 142; in coaching 152–153; essential 72–74; interpersonal 37, 38; intrapersonal 37; potential sources of 124–126; sensemaking 134–135; transfer 6
knowledge auditing (KA) 87–101; accountability 92–94; case study 91–92, 95–96, 97–99; for coach developers 88–89; leadership from within 94; overview 87–88; self-awareness 89–92; strategies coach developers **100**; team dynamics 97
knowledge management (KM) 88
Koch, A. 133

lack of bespoke methodology 237
Lara-Bercial, S. 47, 78
Larkin, P. 154
LaVoi, N. M. 199
Lawrence, T. B. 176
leadership 94; coach education 14; from within knowledge auditing (KA) 94; participative 261; reinforces learning 110
learner coach 6
learners perspective 127
learning: activities 114; assessment 114; and behavioural change 13; coach 151, 192–193; coach education 54–55; environment 112–113; experiential 178; facilitation of 75–76; formal 4, 6–7, 13, 32, 44, 47–49, 55, 75; informal 4, 6, 48, 55, 56, 104; mediated 6; non-formal 6; peer 178; practices 114–115; reflective 61; supportive environment 109; universal 60–61
learning organizations 105; apprenticeship 109–111; coach developers role in 111–112; dimensions of **110**; promotion in sports settings 112–115
Leeder, T. M. 76

Lefstein, A. 260
lesbian coaches 201
Long Term Athlete Development (LTAD) work 185
long-term coach development (LTCD) pathway 14
Lu, C. 223
Lusaka Declarations 44, 46
Lyle, J. 169, 178, 237
Lynch, M. 185

MacPherson, A. C. 160
Madsberg 136
male-female gender binary 204
Mallett, C. J. 47, 185, 191
Mallett, S. 207
Mandela, N. 229
Martinovic, D. 48
mastering team dynamics 97
Maxwell, D. 261
Maxwell, J. C. 227
McAdams, D. P. 219–220
McCarthy, L. 236, 239, 245–246
McCullick, B. A. 106
McMahon, J. 55
McQuade, S. 26
mediated learning 6; see also learning
Mees, A. 124, 125
Mehrpouya, H. 261
mentoring 259–260
mentorships 203
metacognitive self-regulation 162
microaggressions 199
Milistetd, M. 41, 112, 262
Miller, D. T. 217
Model Core Curriculum for Coach Development 38
Moon, J. A. 6, 207
Morgan, D. L. 216
Mowles, C. 185
Murray, H. A. 219, 221, 230

Nash, C. 26, 126, 134, 135, 156, 160, 192
National Coaching Certification Program (NCCP) 27
national federations (NFs) 37
National Governing Body (NGB) 43, 124, 169–170
National Olympic Committee of Zambia (NOCZ) 45–46
National Sport Organisations (NSOs) 169
National Standards for Sport Coaches 42
Nelson, L. J. 124
Neurolinguistic Programming (NLP) 121
Nichols, G. 174, 176

Nippon Coach Developer Academy (NCDA) 38–39, 77
Nippon Sport Science University (NSSU) 38–39, 77
Nippon Sport Science University Coach Developer Academy (NSSU CDA) 17, 36
Nolan Committee 174
non-formal learning 6; see also learning
NSSU Coach Developer Academy 38

observe, orient, decide, act (OODA loop) 141
Occam's Razor 185–186
O'Connor, D. 154
Offiah, G. 160
Olsson, C. 259
ongoing coach development 49
openness and clear responsibilities 261
organizations: as an end process 109; as facilitator 109; learning 109–111; as learning unit 109; promotion of learning 112–115; see also learning organizations
Örtenblad, A. 109
Osei, L. A. 208–209

Pals, J. L. 219–220
Paquette, K. 12, 262
participative leadership 261
Passmore, J. 121
Patterson, K. D. 174
peer learning 178; see also learning
Peniza, L. 262
Perry Jr, W. G. 123
personal and professional skill and development 14
person-first language 204
Pickleball: as an inclusive sport 172; ball 171; case study 169–181; and coaching 178–180; court 171; fundamentals of 170–172; paddle 170; staff 177
Pishdad-Bozorgi, P. 152
Plato 223
Ponnet, H. 239, 241
potential sources of knowledge 124–126
practical application for coach 141
practical application for coach developer 141–142
practice 202–203
pragmatism 260–261
Predictive Processing (PP) 137
professional conversations 260
professionalisation 173
professionalism 60

Professional Judgment and Decision Making (PJDM) 134, 143
programme monitoring and evaluation 13
Psychology of Coaching (Griffith) 59

race 200–201
racism 197, 200–201
Rasmussen, L. J. 228
Raubal, M. 136
reflection skills 74
reflective learning 61; *see also* learning
relationships 255; building 56–57, 111; caring 70; establishing 255; informal mentoring 4; interpersonal 76; sports organizations and federations 74; workplace 92
retention 160
Rocky Balboa 184
Rodrigue, F. 75
Rossi, T. 108
Rowson, T. S. 121
Ryba, T. V. 79
Rynne, S. B. 55, 191

Saks, A. M. 159
Schempp, P. G. 61, 73
Schinke, R. J. 230
Schmidt, S. L. 262
Schommer, M. 123
Schön, D. A. 138
Schulenkorf, N. 262
Schwartz, S. H. 219–221, 226, 227
sciences in sport coaching 58
Scottish Football Association (SFA) 23
SECI spiral model 128
seeking future-oriented feedback 162–163
Segal, A. 260
self-awareness 4, 89–92, 223
Self-Determination Theory 77
senior coach developer 15
sensemaking: abductive approaches 137–138; application 134–135; case study 144; for CDs and coaches 133–145; Cynefin framework 136; Dervin, B. 136; described 135; frames 140–141; knowledge 134–135; Madsberg 136; models of 135; overview 133–134; practical application for coach 141; practical application for coach developer 141–142; surprise 138–140; tools in use 142–144; wayfinding 136–137; Weick, K. 136
sense of shared ownership 261–262
sexuality 201
shared ownership, sense of 261–262

Sieck, W. R. 228
skills: coach developers (CDs) 74–76; communication 255; decision-making 74; efficient use of skillsets 262; interpersonal 255; personal and professional 14; reflection 74
Smith, J. 176
Smith, T. 253
Snowden, D. 136
social-relational model 205
Socrates 223
sophisticated epistemology 135
Sotiriadou, P. 185
Special Olympics 39
sport and exercise psychology 73–74
sport background: De Highden, M. 20; Taylor, J. 24; Woodburn, A. 27
The Sport Coach as Educator: Reconceptualizing Sport Coaching (Jones) 59
sport coaching 75, 154
sport development 169, 173–178; achieving recognition as sport 174–175; coaching 177–178; formalisation 173; governance 173–174; institutional work 176; Pickleball, work of 177; professionalisation 173; role of people in 176–178; volunteers 176–177
Sport Education and Accreditation System (SEAS) 44
Sport New Zealand Coach Developer Training Program 77
sport organisations 20, 23; coach development opportunities 90; development of 169; external coach development 26; Finnish 23; national governing 70; in North America 200
sport science 73
sportscotland 174
Sports For Tomorrow (SFT) 38
sport-specific formal coach education 191–192
Sports Policy factors Leading to International Sporting Success (SPLISS) 188, *189*
sport system 74
Stack, L. 254
standards 13–14
Stanovich, K. E. 120
Stanovich, P. J. 120
Sterchele, D. 178
stereotypes 62; coaching 63; defined 217; gender 205; rationality 217; reasonable and rational use of 218; sport-related and racial 200
Sternberg, R. J. 122, 158

Stevens, S. T. 217, 218, 232
Stewart, F. 133
Stoneham, K. 262
Suddaby, R. 176
Summit, P. 59
supportive learning environment 109

Tacon, R. 174
Tao, Y. 230
Taylor, J. 24–26
teacher preparation models 73
Ted Lasso 224
Temple of Apollo at Delphi 223
theoretical model of relations *220*
theory exploration 246
theory generating 245–246
Theory of Basic Values (Schwartz) 219–220, 226
Thompson, A. 174
Top Gun approach 154–155
Tozetto, A. V. B. 110
trainers of coach developers 16
transferability 158–160
transgender language reform 205–206
transgender non-conforming (TNGC) 204, 205
transitions into coach development 68–79
Tripartite Framework of Personal Identity 219
Trudel, P. 12, 29, 207, 262
Tugend, A. 203
Turnbull, W. 217
Turner, D. 48

Union of European Football Associations (UEFA) 60
uniqueness in human mental programming *218*
United Kingdom Coaching Certificate 258
United Kingdom Coaching Certificate (UKCC) 26
United States Center for Coaching Excellence (USCCE) 23, 43
United States Olympic & Paralympic Committee (USOPC) 43
universal learning 60–61; *see also* learning
University of Zambia 47
unmediated learning 6; *see also* learning
user's manual 163
US Navy 154–155

values 221
Vangrunderbeek, H. 90
Vedder-Weiss, D. 260
vignettes: coach development **158**; diversifying language 206
virtual/online environment 155
Vlaamse Trainers school (VTS) 240–243
voluntary coaches 3, 121
voluntary organisation 170
volunteer-led sport (and coach) development 169–181; emerging sport development 173–175; overview 169; Pickleball 169–172; role of people in sport development 176–178
volunteers 176–177
Vygotsky, L. S. 254

Walker, L. F. 104
Waller, S. 77
Walsh, J. 74
Walters, G. 174
Wan, C. 223
Ward, P. 151, 162
Wareham, Y. 202
Washington, M. 174
Watts, D. W. 78, 92
wayfinding 136–137
Webb, V. 259
Weick, K. 136
Wenger-Trayner, B. 111
Wenger-Trayner, E. 111
Wiman, M. L. 192
Wolbring, L. 254
women/female coaches 199, 202
Women in Sport Leadership (WSLA) programme 26, 95
Woodburn, A. 27–29
Wooden, J. 59
workplace relationships 92
Wright, H. K. 79

Young, M. 107

Zambia: coach development in 43–47; coaches in 44; national coaching framework 45–46; National Football team 45; National Olympic Committee of 45–46; Police and Armed Forces 44; policies and direction 44–45; University of Zambia 47; ZamCoach360 46
ZamCoach360 46
Zamora, D. 261
Zone of Uncomfortable Debate (ZOUD) 128